Western Myths: Stone, Elixir Tales

Chelsea Burston

ABSTRACT

Classical, scientific, and Abrahamic origin stories of knowledge establish grounds. Upon excavating these grounds, this dissertation has found repeated and entangled emphases on isolation related to a materially grounded cosmology. The core evidence for this position comes from their comparable displays of the psyche/mind/soul/spirit's entry into and/or imprisonment within body, the symbolic restraint of Classical and Abrahamic progenitors with stone, and the initiation of philosophy—according to Aristotle—with a theory of materialism. Symbolic interpretations of the religious myths are supported by commentary from within the respective traditions.

Following a consideration of the existential implications of a material ground and (fundamentally) isolated self-image, the work considers mythic liberations of progenitors from stone and Einstein's liberation of scientific traditions from material reductionism. As Einstein's labors included an integration of wave dynamics into the way matter is seen, Herakles' and Christ's liberations of Prometheus and Adam are actuated by symbolic fluids. Later, their transcendence and atonement(s) are actuated by fluid. As is shown, Classical, Christian, and scientific knowledge narratives all contain reactions to a material ground of being contingent with the integration/imbibing of waves/fluids. The primary examples for this include the hydra-blood that freed Prometheus from stone and Herakles from life, the nectar of immortality he drank upon his death, the wine-blood of Christ that freed Adam from stone and his followers from mortality, and the form of waves and fields Einstein added to the theoretical particle.

This dissertation argues that the reason fluids have played such integral roles in the historical and symbolic transcendence of material/embodied isolation and Classical atoms (isolated matter) is because—unlike material particulates—fluids and waves are capable of union and harmony. My read of particle-wave duality is as a new foundation that challenges atomized cosmologies and worldviews leading many towards a vision of self as estranged from other. My final argument is that each of these prominent Western knowledge traditions present stories that follow a meta-narrative arc defined by an initial commitment to a materially grounded cosmology that is later enhanced—if not healed—by theoretical waves and symbolic elixirs.

Keywords: Mythology, Philosophy, Science, Religion, Wave

TABLE OF CONTENTS

Chapter 1: Introduction 3

Western Myths of Knowledge *4*

Method 6

Epistemological Limitations 6

Writing on the West in the Context of Globalization 8

Responding to Western Philosophical Dilemmas 8

Metaphorical Abstraction 9

Implicit Logic vs. Explicit Belief 11

Psyche, Soul, Spirit, Mind 13

"Cosmology" and "Matter" 14

Review of Literature 17

Greek and Roman Myth 17

Abrahamic Sources 19

Classical Philosophy and Science 21

Organization of the Study 26

Chapter 2: Prometheus Bound *37*

Prometheus the Progenitor 40

Prometheus the Freedom Fighter 44

Prometheus and the Sacrifice 48

Pandora 69

Prometheus Bound 81

Reflections of Prometheus 95

Chapter 3: Birth of Theoretical Materialism *103*

Philosophical and Scientific Origin Stories of Knowledge: *103*

From Myth to Philosophy 106

Milesian Materialists: The First Philosophers 114

The Pythagoreans: Ascetic Beauty and Cosmological Harmonics 123

Heraclitus: Logos 132

Parmenides Static: Monism 137

Empedocles and Anaxagoras: Pluralism 140

Atomistic Materialism: Leucippus & Democritus 144

Pre-Socratic Philosophy and the Emergence of Atomism 155

After Democritus 156

Chapter Conclusion 176

Chapter 4: Abrahamic Origin Stories of Knowledge: Adam in Mater *182*

The Garden: Trees, Mountains and Center 184

The Garden: Fruit 193

The Garden: Serpent 196

First Couple: Adam 200

First Couple: Eve 205

Satan: Fall, War, Exile, Escape 211

Fall & Exile 222

Post Exilic Reality: Exiting the Garden and Entering the Body, Senses, and Tomb. 237

Post-Edenic Reflection 254

Part I Reflection: Adam, Prometheus, and the Pre-Socratics *269*

Chapter 5 – Heracles, Christ and Einstein – A Sip Beyond Material Limitation *269*

Introduction: Herakles & Christ 269

Introduction: Einstein 283

Heracles and Christ – Hero Saviors of the Classical and Abrahamic Progenitors 296

Christ Frees Adam, Dies, and is resurrected from the cave 315

Heracles Dies and Becomes Immortal 344

The Micro-Narratives of Hero-Saviors and their Macro-Narratives with the Progenitors 357

Review of the Evidence: Liberation of Progenitors from Material Restraint 359

Review of the Evidence: Role of Elixirs 361

Einstein: Steins of Energy 366

Chapter 6: Conclusion *385*

Core Conclusion: 385

Entry into Matter 386

Material Prisons and Atomic Isolation: Existential Estrangement and Moral
Egoism 389

The Holy Grail and a Theory of Unified Fields 392

Epistemological Positions 395

Extended Frame: Further Study 400

Reflection on Comparative Myth – Diffusion and Collective Unconscious 406

Conclusory   407

If *a* is to *b* as *c* is to *x*, then:

(a) "Stein" means "stone," (b) but having become a shorthand expression of "steinkrug," the word has come to represent, for living Germans, a vessel and its portion of elixir. (c) The atom was once seen to behave like an indivisible stone, (x) but now the atom is seen as a vessel of energy and the energy in that vessel, which sometimes behaves like stones, and sometimes like waves. This transformational interpretation was triggered by Einstein, who is not only credited for having proven the existence of atoms, but also their ultimate reduction to energy—not matter—and the relationship of waves with their particulate form. The integration of wave dynamics into the standard foundations of contemporary physics reflects the unchaining of scientific history from the atomistic-stones of reductive materialism.

To imagine the behavior of waves in contrast to that of atoms, consider the difference between the musical instruments of a symphony orchestra and the notes they play. The matter of one instrument will never be able to unify with the matter of another, they will never participate in the same space. On the other hand, every note—each wave—can share space, which is why a single microphone can record all the sounds of a guitar, piano, singer and tambourine as a single wave that can then be recreated by a single-coned speaker and received by a single ear drum. This thought experiment presents the severe behavioral differences of material things and waves: where material things are limited to their boundaries, waves can unify and mutually participate with one another in a shared space.

When reduced to particulates, matter is incapable of sharing space or harmonizing at a distance. From a materially grounded persepective, there are no comprehensible behaviors of reality through which we can imagine ourselves (or atoms) to harmonize, resonate, or unify. The waveform, unlike that of an atom, is capable of union, resonance, superposition and harmony. In contrast with the form of a Classical atom, waves and fields find no hard walls between subject and object. Thus, where belief systems built around the form of Classical (or Newtonian) atoms depend on a perspective in which material things are fundamentally isolated—in which one is estranged from nature, lover, divinity and cosmos—a belief system that includes the wave-form is capable of supporting a worldview in which union and participation are foundational.

Chapter 1: Introduction

Western Myths of Knowledge

Origin stories of knowledge, perhaps more overtly than any other stories, communicate knowledge. There are three religious/mythological/philosophical/scientific traditions that have each taken their turn as the dominant source of knowledge in the "Western" world. These are the Classical, Judeo-Christian and scientific traditions. Each of them present an essential knowledge-narrative. The Pre-Socratic birth of Western philosophy with Thales' theory of a foundational substance (historically) continues beyond Einstein's establishment of wave-particle energy as a new foundation for understanding matter. Similarly, the Classical myth of Prometheus and his fire-bringing (mythically) continues beyond his rescue by Herakles' and hydra blood, just as the Abrahamic story of the Fall continues beyond Adam's rescue with the blood of Christ.

Through our survey of these three origin stories of knowledge we will discover a shared emphasis on matter upon which this dissertation will establish its foundations. From here we will consider the estranged despair of Prometheus and Adam in the context of existential isolation and egoism while contemplating the relationship of such isolated despair with materially grounded worldviews. This dissertation climaxes in Einstein, Herakles and Christ. Herakles freed Prometheus—his progenitor—from stone and ascended to Olympus. Christ freed Adam—his progenitor—from stone then ascended to Heaven. And Einstein transformed our fundamental understanding of materiality. What the following survey of these stories shows is that their respective continuations of individual knowledge narratives relate to the overcoming of various material(istic) limitations. Upon deeper analysis, it will also be shown that—symbolic and theoretical—

fluids and waves play instrumental roles in their respective liberations from material limitation(s), which, in the Classical and Christian myths, accords with atonement.

Each in their own ways, the three prominent Western knowledge narratives begin with and/or describe theoretical entries into matter. The essential examples of this we will consider are the entry of breath/fire into a previously unanimated clay body; the entry into a life within and driven by the material body (which includes eating and defecation, sexuality and death); the burial and/or chaining of mythological progenitors in stone; the birth of Western philosophy with a theory grounded by matter; the pre-Socratic focus on the psyche's imprisonment within the body; and the Milesian birth of atomism.

With atomism divisible material objects become clearly understood as made up of indivisible material particulates that are fundamentally divided. Such foundational isolation are also found in our survey of Classical and Abrahamic knowledge narratives. When Adam and Prometheus' humans become limited to a material and mortal existence the transformation is symbolized by distinct symbols like fruit and stones that trigger states of bondage and isolation to which the progenitors react. In the discussion of philosophical materialism and atomism, it will be found that many philosophers experience a form of existential anxiety over a state of isolation and estrangement that Pascal likens in form to that of an atom (Lemay 363).

After showing how the three origin stories of knowledge support a perspective of material limitation that can translate into a sense of estrangement, we will continue to follow the knowledge-narratives with Herakles, Christ and Einstein. As we will see, just as the suffering progenitors were liberated from their material limitations by Christ and Heracles, Einstein liberated the scientific community from its own form of reductive materialism. In surveying the reactions of these hero-saviors and scientists to their progenitors and forefathers, we will find that each present a way of seeing that is not limited to materiality and reductive materialism. Not only do these ways of seeing not result in a sense of estrangement, the religious and mythological narratives even link the transcendence of material limitation with the experience of divine union. Where we will find elixirs to be central to the material transcendence of the two progenitors, the integration of wave dynamics into particle theory was at the center of Einstein's transformation of science.

Fluids are the only visibly perceptible carriers of the waveform, and they appear as symbolic catalysts for the liberation of both Adam and Prometheus from material constraint. As we will see, fluids are also actuators in the divine reunion of Christ, Heracles and their followers. I believe this is because the waveform—unlike that of the atom or particulate—is capable of superposition, union, resonance and harmony. As previously abstracted, in contrast with the form of a Classical or Newtonian atom, the waveform finds no hard walls between subject and object: Where belief systems built around the form of (Classical or Newtonian) atoms necessitate the fundamental isolation of material things, a belief system that has integrated the waveform is capable of supporting a worldview in which union and participation is foundational. My argument is that the paradigmatic shifts between Adam and Christ, Prometheus and Heracles, scientific materialism and Einstein are in fact congruent representatives of a meta-narrative in which the waveform is an elixir to the isolative estrangement of worldviews grounded by matter.

The origin stories of Prometheus' fire, the fruit of Eden, and the early history of science represent the Classical, Abrahamic and philosophical establishments of first knowledge—all of which are concurrent with either a mythological or theoretical engagement with materiality. When the essays of Einstein's miracle year undermined the paradigm of materialism, they simultaneously challenged its reductive form, the particulate, which forever more became entwined with the waveform. When Christ's blood baptized Adam—progenitor and receiver of knowledge—he was freed from his stone tomb. The wine-blood was then presented as the central actuator of material liberation and divine union in both the New Testament and Grail romances. Similarly, Heracles used blood to free the stone-bound Prometheus—progenitor and bringer of knowledge—and reunited with the Gods by drinking divine nectar (after the same blood actuated his own death). In this dissertation the narratives of Western knowledge-stories are carried through to these un-doings when, in each case, the waveform is presented as a central actuator in the liberation of knowledge from limitation to the forms of materialism.

Method

Epistemological Limitations

It should be stated that though I am working with stories that have been used to make claims about objective truth, the epistemological limit of this work is fundamentally contextual. My interest is not in parlaying the resonances I recognize into support for arguments concerning some ultimate truth. Only coherence gives value to the foundations of this dissertation (that are not already assumed by the reader). The influence of Christianity and Classical Religion on contemporary consciousness is why I give such foundational interest to the traditions—not because I personally see them as foundational representations of objective Truth. My immediate interest is in the epistemological opportunity of recognizing how persistently the Greco-Roman, Christian and scientific worldviews have conditioned Western culture and its citizens with a consistent meta-narrative. As the ruling civilizations of Western history have championed at least one of these three perspectives at all times, it can be said that what they share in common has been commonly learned by citizens of the Western world. Thus the limit (and anchor) of the epistemological position underlying this dissertation depends on the contextual relationship of these stories with Western civilization—not their objective relationship to truth.

Readers may recognize one or more of these three traditions as expressions of transcendent or objective truth, and it may be the case that this is so. But as Diotima points out, there is no human-rational way of knowing if what one believes is consistent with absolute truth; and as Kant points out, reason must halt before making divine, objective or transcendental conclusions—before even concluding that the transcendental or absolute can be said to exist. This is not to say such truth does not exist, and as Kant found supra-rational support for his belief in the transcendental divine, it is certainly the right of the reader to possess such faith. On the other hand, I am absolutely obliged to clarify and construct a position that accepts the epistemological limitations of a rational human discourse with a species-wide set of barriers between the position I develop and the realm of objective certainty. Again, the strength of this dissertation depends on the inter-contextual value of the three traditions, and the epistemological significance— assigned by each reader—of their mutual concordances.

Writing on the West in the Context of Globalization

I am writing in a time that holds tension between the simultaneous desires for cultural diversity and globalization. One of the dangers that will always persist in this situation is that, when looking into the waters of another culture, an eye that cannot recognize its own reflection on the water-surface cannot distinguish itself from the image below. If we are to appreciate others, we must see ourselves clearly enough to minimize the distorting projections of our unknown selves. From this perspective I have come to feel that, to support the complementary aims of globalization and diversity, we must, paradoxically, give immediate focus to the understanding of ourselves—to our ways of thinking and being that are so natural and implicit to our worldviews that we hardly notice their pervasive presence (like what we digest from knowledge origin stories). Thus in a time when talking about *the West* seems almost antiquated, I believe in the timeliness of contemporary explorations into the Western heritage.

Responding to Western Philosophical Dilemmas

The most immediate benefits to studying the confluent answers of dominant Western paradigms is in the context of their shared questions. As I will demonstrate, materialism presented philosophical problems for Classical religion, Christianity, and science alike. In fact, a majority of the dissertation will be dedicated to the enumeration of consistent dilemmas for each of these traditions. More specifically, I will show that the problem we have come to know as the subject-object distinction has alternated as an implicit and explicit challenge to the belief and participation in union. By patterning our mind after our perception of material-patterns we have limited our metaphors to a set that excludes the possibility of union. Again, the confluences of the three traditions I am specifically interested in are their concordant responses to this problem.

Metaphorical Abstraction

To entertain a conversation in multiple languages, a meta-language is required. To this end I am looking at meta-narratives and metaphors beneath the myths and their symbols as well as history and its objects. The way I abstract metaphors and meta-narratives is through the reduction of their specifics to their abstract forms. For example, fluids, sounds and electromagnetic signals all follow the form of a wave; while stones, Classical, and Enlightenment atoms all take a form that can be abstractly described as solid, self-contained matter. Such forms as *solid* and *self-contained* can also be abstracted from their adjectival use within a narrative; for example, an author may describe a *hard* heart or a heart of *stone* in one scenario and a *melted* heart in another. This points to the notion that behavior can also be patterned after a form. *Resonance, concordance, harmony* and *superposition* are behaviors of waves—not stones or classical atoms. Where two waves can be in one place, two atoms cannot. When a character or human being is said—historically or mythically—to have been in a state of harmony or union with God or nature, the atomistic paradigm has no metaphorical foundation through which it can accept such a statement. Harmony and union, however, are native forms to waves, thus we might expect fluids (music or light) in symbolic constellation with scenes of union. This is because the abstractable metaphors between the state of union and behavior of waves—the form of fluids—are congruent.

Forms can become complex, and I will take time to explore some of the more nuanced forms of various symbols and scenarios; however, the strength of this dissertation largely relies on its avoidance of positions that depend on complex interpretations. Rather, the forms at the center of my thesis and heart of my argument are extremely basic, and with clear examples. As has been discussed, the primary sets of forms with which I am interested are those that derive from Classical/Enlightenment atoms and waves, but I should take the time to introduce a list of those symbolic objects that I take to be consistent with the Classical atomic form.

Grains of sand, specs of dust, boulders, stone or metal objects, building blocks, firm-fruit, firm-bodies, and walled cities or gardens—all of these possess solid rigid boundaries that spatially isolate that which is within. Grains of sand and specks of dust present an emphasis on smallness and manyness. Stone and metal especially convey hardness. Building blocks emphasize the ability to build with matter. Human bodies represent the isolated materiality of human existence, which is expressed on a more collective level by walls around gardens and cities. Considerable overlap will be appreciated; for example, the building of walls with blocks of stone, or the description of body as atoms and dust.

Fruit is an especially interesting example, as it appears—topically—in the form of solid matter. The image of an apple striking Newton's head became a famous myth for the paradigm of Newtonian physics. However, the fruit is also a vessel of juice, as is emphasized by the grape as a symbol. Similarly, the drinking-vessel is a solid object with rigid boundaries that is in fact full of fluid waves. We might also consider the examples as Moses drawing water from stone or Wolfram's "stein"—the Holy Grail described as a stone that drew forth water-flow. In these cases the context is essential: there is no discussion of juice or fluid when Adam and Eve eat the fruit, and Milton goes out of his way to say that the snake does not show his wave form. But in the context of Christ their savior, the fruit of interest is the grape, and its form of interest is as wine. Even the olive grove in which the Romans captured him was called, in Aramaic, the "oil press" or "vat."

There are many carriers of waves. When we talk about science, we will be talking about sound, electric, magnetic, electromagnetic and matter (AKA de Broglie) waves as exemplars of the form. In the context of myth, fluids are of primary interest—water, blood, wine, nectar, potion, poison, golden rain—however, music will also be considered. Unfortunately the exploration of sound waves in myth has been relegated to the periphery of this dissertation, but when we get to Pythagoras, Plato, and the musical education of Heracles, I will take the opportunity to describe the Orphic interest in harmony as known through music, the Pythagorean-Orphic recognition of sound as waves, and eventually Plato as a champion of form and Pythagorean harmony. Stepping deeper into the sacred stories of the Orphics we will find ancient conflations of the light, sound, and fluid waveforms in the context of secret wisdom; for example, sun-beam plectrums and songs of flowing honey—the Dionysian elixir before wine.

Implicit Logic vs. Explicit Belief

Examining the logic of a myth may reveal more than is consciously recognized by its religious adherents, but if a symbolic interpretation does not resonate with the tone of the religious interpretation surrounding it, reconsideration is in order. For example, if I were to find a way of symbolically interpreting the snake of Eden as God's superior, it would immediately feel unlikely, because this is inconsistent with how Jews, Christians and Muslims interpret Satan. In the same way, when I present arguments for the Christian myth as a symbolic demonstration of human transcendence from the limitations of materialism, it is of central importance that we discuss reasons for believing common and historical Christians connected with a resonant interpretation—even if my primary mode of interpretation is mythological. Similarly, the demonstration of a belief in material limitation within Greek mystery traditions will be imperative to the support of a symbolic interpretation of Heracles as a representative of mortal-material transcendence. Again, the symbolic interpretation of Einstein's contributions as the turning point by which the reductive paradigm of materialism came to an end will require the support of physicists who have interpreted his contributions in this way. The essential symbolic interpretations, in this dissertation, demand and will receive comparison with the interpretations of their native religions and the scientific community.

Psyche, Soul, Spirit, Mind

The dissertation is concerned with psyche, soul, spirit, and mind, which can lead to some confusion concerning the terms. While I am mostly working in the territory of their similarities, there are some nuanced differences to which I attend. I will be brief here to avoid opening up too many complications. The word "psyche" helps me to keep things simple because it is more overtly inclusive of the qualities that are typically divided into "mind" and "soul." Because distinctions between the two are not very important to my conversation, if I say "mind" or "soul" it is typically because the word is related to the historical conversations with which I am working. To some extent, I also use "mind" and "psyche" where it seems appropriate to remain in more secular territory.

I have mostly avoided the word "spirit" because conversations about its contrast with "soul" would add to the complexity of my position in a way that would not benefit my thesis. Here, however, I will note: If I were to actively engage the theoretical differences between "spirit" and "soul," I would enter into the conversation about "spirit" as fiery, energetic, upwardly moving, divisive, masculine, and dry in contrasts with a complimentary discussion of "soul" as fluid, moiste, downward moving, wave-like, and as a solvent. Were I to continue down this path, I would engage a hypothesis that questioned the alignment of the meta-narrative engaged by this dissertation with that of a progression from emphasis on the qualities of "spirit" to the harmonious integration of "soul." As I lament in the final chapter, I would like to work with the cosmological pillars of masculine and femininity, wet and dryness, fire and water, sun and moon, winter and summer; however, it has been my strict intention to focus more directly on the metaforms of particulates and waves as foundational to the formation of worldviews. The cosmological implications of seasonality could be especially helpful to my meta-narrative based thesis. In this text, however, the words "soul" and "spirit" are to be seen in the typically flattened form that does not distinguish between them—a form partially patterned after the Cartesian dualistic model of mind and body. Contextual cues should diffuse potential confusion concerning these terms, especially considering how inconsequential I consider my use of their differences to be in the formulation of my position.

"Cosmology" and "Matter"

At all times, this work struggles against the limitations of language, and "matter" presents the greatest challenge. Terminology expands the opportunity to communicate while complicating it with endless nuances that carry unintended thoughts into conversation. For the last few years, the orienting terms of this growing text have shifted many times. I tried for too long to use the phrase "metaphysical ground," but it was limiting in that I also describe matter as an inspiration for projection onto epistemological, ideological, and existential structures (to name a few) that can consequently be integrated into a coherent worldview. This was missing the bigger picture. It was also not a satisfactory phrase for the crucial bridge I am building between religious myths and the history of science. What I have since found is that the categorical conflict between mythic descriptions of psyche's imprisonment in matter and the historical entry into materialistic philosophies—the point in this dissertation's hourglass—is most efficiently synthesized through the combined use of "cosmology" and "ground." To present the abstract structure: my focus is on a microcosmic ground upon which individuals build their cosmologies.

By "cosmology" I mean something like an observer's "worldview." I mean no reference to objective conversations about reality when I use the term. There are two reasons I prefer "cosmology" to "worldview," the first is that the term "worldview" does not imply cohesion or structure so much as it suggests the sum of an individual's perspective, no matter how coherent. The word "paradigm" is useful because it implies the consistency of coherent thought structures across an infinite range of territories; for example, an atomistically anchored paradigm includes social, physical, and psychological theories that are consistent with one another through their shared use of atomistic concepts. The reason I prefer the term "cosmology" over "paradigm" is because, while a "cosmology" might be shared with a group or era, an individual can also have a "cosmology." An individual cannot have a "paradigm," in which an individual or theory might participate. The word has picked up the overtones of "zeitgeist." To be sure, "paradigm" will still be a useful word throughout the conversation, but what I really needed was a way of saying "paradigmic worldview" without "zeitgeist" overtones. I also want to accentuate the notion that observers orient themselves in relation with their worldviews, which is conveyed by the personal quality of "cosmology." Insofar as individuals develop cosmological perspectives they situate and evaluate themselves through the lens they create—to me this seems built into the term. (It might also be said that humans collectively situate ourselves within shared paradigm(s).

The other crucial reason I have come to prefer the term is that a "cosmology" can be formed through rational and symbolic modes of intelligence. This is important because the mode I use to interpret the origin stories of knowledge is symbolic first, whereas, the philosophical development of materialistm primarily follows rational arguments. What "Part I" of this dissertation shows is that the history of scientific reason, as well as the Classical and Abrahamic origin stories of knowledge, both convey establishing commitments to cosmologies grounded by matter. Where the religious mythologies are especially communicative through their symbolic expressions, the history of scientific reason has centered on rational thought; both, however, demonstrate cosmologies that are grounded by matter.

Two notes needs to be made about what I mean by "matter" when I say "materialistically grounded cosmology." The first meaning of matter I am concerned with is its most reductive version, by which I mean solid and unchanging, as conceptualized by the ancient atomists and Enlightenment Newtonians. These natural philosophers envisioned the universe as composed of solid particulated objects called "atoms," not to be confused with "atoms" as they are understood today. When I am talking about atoms as contemporarily understood, it will be obvious—and late in the dissertation—otherwise assume I mean Democritean atoms. As understood today, atoms are not consistent with Classical atoms or the reductively materialistic worldview I am describing. The first reason for this is because matter is now understood to be transmutable into energy (though matter is now understood to be made up of energy it is not said that energy is made of matter). The second reason atoms, as understood today, are inconsistent with my use of the phrase, "reductive atomism," is because qualities like wave-particle duality and superposition (not to mention entanglement) are inconsistent with the forms and behaviors of matter as comprehended by atomists for thousands of years. The sections on atomism in the third chapter engage significantly more detail about the fundamentally solid and particulated objects which anchored the reductively materialistic philosophies of Classical and Enlightenment atomists.

The second note I need to make about what I mean by "matter" has to do with the conflation of the world's material composition and the association of "mother" with cycles that anchor life as we know it—in this world composed of matter. In the chapter on Prometheus and Pandora, as well as the chapter on Adam and Eve, I show how Pandora and Eve have come to personify both the material from which humans are made and the natural mortal cycle into which all men are born. While there are various suggestions of this conflation in the history of philosophy, it does not become central to our conversation. However, in the context of the Classical and Abrahamic religious narratives, we will see that the entry into mortal and maternal cycles are contingent with the entry into a body and world composed of matter. As explained in the second chapter, "maternal" and "material" both start with "mater" because, in Latin, the word means both "matter" and "mother" (in the section on Pandora I go to great lengths to disentangle some of the gender oriented complications that arise with such a conversation). The symbolic narratives involving Eve and Pandora convey this dual entry: while on one level their stories represent a commitment to wife and motherhood, on another they convey various commitments to a material world and body. Though these commitments are made with ample awareness of a divine reality, the stories both convey a human initiation into the experience of a materially grounded reality. And to say it here as clearly as possible: what I mean by a materialistically grounded cosmology is a paradigm or worldview grounded by matter and the meta-forms upon which an observer's understanding of matter relies.

Review of Literature

Greek and Roman Myth

My study begins with the works of Homer and Hesiod—the acknowledged literary foundations of Classical mythology—most notably the *Homeric Hymns, Theogony, Works and Days, The Iliad* and *The Odyssey.* I have also looked into archeological digs at the sites of mystery cults—such as Eleusis and Samothrace—in combination with research into the ancient sources concerning their secrets. *Greek Mysteries: The Archeology and Ritual of Ancient Greek Secret Cults*, edited by Michael Cosmopoulos, has been my primary path into the archeology and ritual of the Greek mystery traditions. *Theoi,* an online tool that has collected and organized citations from nearly the entire canon of classical texts, was of invaluable assistance to my exploration into Greek, Roman and early Christian commentary on the mysteries. Karl Kerenyi's *Prometheus, Heroes of the Greeks,* and *Gods of the Greeks* has also helped me build on the sparse information we have into the beginning of what understanding is available. As he points out, the stage-plays of Aeschylus and the other great Athenian playwrights can afford deeper entry into Greek myths and rituals. *Prometheus Bound*, for example, extends and details the story of Prometheus, and perhaps with details and nuance resulting from Aeschylus' knowledge of Kabeiroi secrets—if he was an initiate. Herodotus' *The Histories* and Pausanius' *Description of Greece* are also valuable sources to my research into the myths and those sites or temples with which they were associated.

At no point will my argument be forced into using Roman or European retellings of the Prometheus or Hercules stories as primary sources to describe their myths; however, these retellings can offer their own contextual value. For example, mentioning that Ovid's *Metamorphosis* touches on the Prometheus myth is one of the most direct ways of communicating the presence of the Greek Titan in Roman literature. Similarly, his *Fasti* and *The Aeneid* by Virgil develop the story of Hercules and Cacus, one of the purely Roman myths of the hero. I am also interested in Prometheus' return to attention in the context of the Scientific, Industrial, French and American Revolutions, which were on the minds of Percy Bysshe Shelley and Mary Wollstonecraft Shelley when they wrote, respectively, *Prometheus Unbound* and *Frankenstein: The Modern Day Prometheus*.

In addition to those sources that can provide the varied, contextual, and less remembered details of the Prometheus and Hercules myths, I am also interested in those common summations and compendia that have actively communicated the Greek myths throughout the ages. Such works range from Pseudo-Apollodorus' *Bibliotheca* to *The Greek Myths* by Robert Graves, or *Mythology* by Edith Hamilton. I have already mentioned the works of Karl Kerenyi, which read as stories while providing scholarship. Joseph Campbell, in his book *Occidental Mythology*, is similarly able to blend scholarship into the stories of Prometheus and Heracles.

As Kerenyi has become my most relied upon post-Classical source, I should mention that he was one of the greatest scholars of Greek Mythology in his day, and that he published with Jung on the development of a scientific approach that recognized the congruity between psychological and mythological patterns. To complement my reliance on his work, I have also used Jaan Puhvel's book entitled, *Comparative Mythology*, which takes diffusion as the primary justification for mythological comparison. The text is also useful as a guide to the "Indo-European," "Indo-Iranian," and Vedic myths that might have had a direct influence on the Prometheus and Heracles stories.

Abrahamic Sources

Because the Abrahamic myths primarily explored by this dissertation are those of Adam & Eve then Christ, my primary sources are *Genesis* and the *New Testament*. I also turn to long-standing Jewish legends about Adam that can be found in the *Midrash & Talmud* as well as the most ancient Christian stories of the couple found in the 4th century AD works, *The Book of Adam and Eve* and *The Cave of Treasures*. I also use canonical Christian epics like Dante's *Commedia* and Milton's *Paradise Lost*, to demonstrate the enduring qualities in the myth. Similarly, as the gifts of Christ become central to the lore of Christianity, I turn to such grail literature as *Parzival* by Wolfram von Eschenbach, *Perceval, the Story of the Grail*, by Chrétien de Troyes, *Joseph d'Arimathie*, by Robert de Boron, *Le Morte de Arthur* by Sir Thomas Mallory, and *Parsifal* by Richard Wagner to demonstrate that the blood and vessel on which I focus when discussing Christ became, in fact, of utmost interest to the historical Christian imagination—from the still-enduring New Testament to still-enduring Grail legends.

In addition to the textual sources, I am very interested in the geographical and architectural expressions of the story. The Church of the Holy Sepulcher, in Jerusalem, is said to house the spot where Christ was crucified, the rock below from which Adam was freed, and the cave from which Christ was liberated. Catholics and Orthodox churches of all kinds have fought over the church, and, as officiated by Muslims, they now share its space. The other caves in which Christ is said to have been conceived, born, nursed, raised and buried are of relevance, as is the Eastern European icon of Christ's birth in a cave. Hebron, the cave where many Jews believe Adam has been buried will be discussed, as will the cave where Muhammad first received God's word. Also of interest is the mouth of the river Jordan, bursting forth from a cave in a mountain, where Christ told Peter he would build his church on "this" rock. "This rock" has been interpreted as *Peter*, as his spontaneous knowledge that Jesus is Christ, and the very rock on which they stood (from which rushed forth water). In amplification, this will also introduce the ZamZam and Chalice springs, respectively associated with the Holy Grail and the golden vessel of knowledge that Gabriel poured into Muhammad's breast.

For assistance analyzing and amplifying the story of Adam and Christ I look to both field-specific scholars and those whose work will recur throughout the dissertation. As with each chapter, I will draw from Campbell's *Occidental Mythology* and Eliade's *Essential Sacred Writings from Around the World*. Artistic representations are used at every opportunity, from the image of Adam and Eve in the Sistine Chapel to Gustave Doré's illustrations of virtually every scene I am working with. But because I am mostly using artworks as illustrations as opposed to centers of analysis, I am not entering into a discussion of the images in this section.

Classical Philosophy and Science

For support with the development of the bigger pictures going on in the historical development of Western philosophy, I turn to, *A History of Western Philosophy* by Bertrand Russell and *The Passion of the Western Mind* by Richard Tarnas. For additional support on the discussion of Greek philosophers and the development of atomism I utilize *Greek Philosophy* by Reginald E. Allen, *Classical Thought* by Terence Irwin, and *Myth and Philosophy* by Lawrence J. Hatab. Allen's book also contains a store of pre-Socratic fragments. In addition to the work of these contemporary philosophers I look to Aristotle's *Metaphysics*, in which he gave his version of philosophical history—one that has become foundational to historians of philosophy and science.

For support in the development of the bigger pictures in the historical development of Western physics I first look to the textbook, *Modern Physics*, by John R. Taylor, Chris D. Zafiratos and Michael A Dubson. I also engage the more mainstream works by Brian Greene, namely *The Elegant Universe* and *Fabric of the Cosmos*. I am interested in using the textbook because it represents the way this material has reached students of science all over the world. Similarly, I am interested in the work of Brian Greene because, as *New York Times* bestsellers (and PBS TV series), they represent the migration of this discussion into popular consideration. For more direct support on the development of atomism from a scientific point of view, I turn to G.E.R. Lloyd's *Early Greek Science: Thales to Aristotle.*

To look at the contributors to Atomism from different eras I start with the discussion of Pre-Socratic atomism, first with the fragments of Thales and the examination of his early form of materialism. I then look at the fragments of Heraclitus, and his contribution of *logos*. The discussion then adds the emphasis on geometrical form introduced by Pythagoras and the Pythagoreans. From here I look at the emergence of atomism itself, as theorized by Leucippus and Democritus. I have drawn these fragments from various histories of philosophy, encyclopedic texts, and specific translations.

To describe Plato's disdain for Democritus I turn to the fragments of Aristoxenus. To examine Aristotle's embrace of the theory, I rely heavily on his lecture notes that later became called *Metaphysics*. Aristotle's logic is also patterned after the materialistic atom, which I explore in his *Organon*, six books he wrote on logic. The conflicts between the Platonic and atomistic paradigm are thoroughly examined in the context of Plato's *Parmenides*, in which Aristotle (a character name in the dialogue) provides materialistic challenges to a theory of the forms presented by a "young" Socrates. For context, other works of Plato and Aristotle are referenced in *Plato: Complete Works* edited by John M. Cooper, and *The Complete Works of Aristotle,* Revised Oxford Translation.

The spread of materialism into Hellenic Greece and the Roman Empire can be tracked in Stoicism and Epicureanism—both of which started in Greece and were popular in Rome until the rise of Christianity. The first stoic was Zeno. None of his writings survive save for fragments, which I draw from Allen's book. To look at how thoroughly stoicism spread into Rome we turn to *Meditations*, by Marcus Aurelius. To look at Epicureanism and its involvement with the spread and development of atomism we start with the writings of Epicurus himself. For this I rely again on *Greek and Roman Philosophy after Aristotle*. From here I examine the spread of Epicureanism into Rome through the poetry of Lucretius, especially *De rerum natura*, and *Lucretius on the Nature of the Universe*.

The last major philosopher we examine before the arrival of Newton is Descartes, who is credited for having solidified the Subject-Object distinction and epistemological Foundationalism. For more on Descartes than can be found in his *Meditations*—including his embrace of an atomistic perspective—I use *The Philosophical Writings of Descartes*, put together by John Cottingham, Robert Stoothoff, and Dugald Murdoch.

The behavior of the atom was mostly philosophical until Newton discovered the mathematics capable of describing the movement of things, on the ground and in the sky. His enlightened mathematical principles were capable of explaining the movements of planets and cannonballs. In the Enlightenment, the motion of all empirical things became mathematically comprehensible. The classic ideal that everything should be explainable by empiricism and math was fulfilled by Newton in his *Principia Mathematica*. The work of Newton kicked the Enlightenment into full swing, which spread to America. One of the central conversations of the day was about Deism, which pushed atomism into a state of materialistic determinism. To get into the deistic understanding of an atomistic clock-work universe, we look at *De Veritate* by Lord Herbert Cherbury, the "Father of Deism." We also look at Benjamin Franklin's essay, *On the Providence of God in the Government of the World,* in which he aligns himself with deism and expresses the general sentiment that God acts outside the mechanical laws of nature. Ultimately, the general acceptance of this paradigm at the time of the American Revolutionary War will be seen as powerfully responsible for its momentum in the United States.

Many non-scientific theories have since been inspired by the atomic model. In his book, *The Selfish Gene,* Richard Dawkins theorized that all thoughts could be reduced to atom-like constituents he calls *memes*. Wittgenstein also modeled a theory of thought after atomism in, *The Philosophy of Logical Atomism*. Similarly, Russell, upon whose history of philosophy this dissertation largely relies, was known for a theory of logical atomism, which can be found in his book *Logic and Knowledge*. In the field of mythology, Lévi-Strauss wrote an essay entitled, *The Structural Study of Myth*, in which he defines mythemes as the smallest unit of a myth and compares them with atoms. The book unnerved Roman Jakobson by projecting atomism onto his linguistic theory of phonemes. On one level we recognize the extended pervasiveness of atomism; on the next we dutifully examine how congruent these theories really are with atomism; and on the next we realize that, if the theories are explained and understood in atomistic terms, all atomistic qualities will inevitably be projected on these theories whether intended or not—consciously and perhaps unconsciously.

When a theorist uses the term, "atom," though they may consciously steer their reader through a very particular path, the word is still a que that the reader's active mind connects with the (many) neural network(s) entangled through their thoughts on atoms and atomism. This is why symbolism. Intentionally used, these connections enable a multi-layerd and hyper-rich form of communication. In the context of "atom" as an idea for export, the—perhaps unintentional—consequences are that no matter how particular one is about what they mean with their use of the term, additional associations will be made by the reader's brain. My point is not to criticize the import of atomism into social theories, it is to highlight the importance of making sure common sense atomism is updated to resonate with scientists born in the 19th century. As this dissertation will show, common sense acceptance of Classical and Newtonian atomism—and the projection of this theory into social models—can be extremely damaging, especially to human psyches.

Despite the widespread popularity of atomic theory, for the majority of its history there has been little to no empirical evidence of their existence until an essay entitled, *On the Motion of Small Particles Suspended in a Stationary Liquid, as Required by the Molecular Kinetic Theory of Heat,* which was written by none other than Albert Einstein. This was the first of his *Annus Mirabilis* papers—the four breakthrough essays he wrote in 1905. The second was entitled, *On a Heuristic Viewpoint Concerning the Production and Transformation of Light,* which describes the Photo-Electric Effect and theorizes the photon. The photon represents the new smallest unit of matter, and the revolutionary yet simple description this paper offers depended on frequency equations. This introduced wave behavior to the particle in a way that absolutely reformed the persepective of scientists. The third essay was entitled, *On the Electrodynamics of Moving Bodies*; it described Special Relativity, and explained away the misconception of an objective universe. The fourth essay was entitled, *Does the Inertia of a Body Depend Upon Its Energy Content?* which made way for the development of General Relativity and introduced his equation, $E = mc^2$. This breakthrough undermined the materiality of matter, and ultimately led to an understanding of all matter as reducible to energy. The study of energy in the form of waves, emerging from his elucidation of the photon, became a central effort for the global community of physicists. To more thoroughly explore the life and contributions of Einstein, I will use his magnificent biography, *Einstein: His Life and Universe*, by Walter Isaacson.

To examine the most current understanding of the atom and its implications to spirituality and religion, I look to the stable of Templeton Prize winners. This is the largest monetary prize given to an academic in the world, and having been a philosophy major on the mountain where John Templeton was born and built his personal library, I have become very interested in the books and speeches of its prizewinners. For example, John D. Barrow's *Artful Universe* explores the relationship between artistic creations and historical patterns of human life. And for more direct consideration of the current interpretations of the atom, I rely on Bernard d'Espagnat's *Veiled Reality, An Analysis of Present-Day Quantum Mechanical Concepts.* Ultimately, nothing I will say about modern physics will be beyond the most foundational knowledge that students would learn in their first examination.

Organization of the Study

Part One of two will concentrate, one at a time, on the three most prevalent Western origin stories of human knowledge: Prometheus & Pandora (chapter 2), Materialistic Science (chapter 3), and Adam & Eve (chapter 4). The order in which the stories will be considered is that of their entry into common Western consideration: thus, Classical Myth→Classical Science→Judeo-Christianity. In each chapter, after a general introduction, I will offer a detailed telling of the story I am engaging. I will then examine each story's most pronounced features on its own terms with the help of secondary sources. With each of the first three stories, their most pronounced features demonstrate their commitment to a materialistic paradigm. In some way, each of them theoretically engages or symbolically represents *materialism*. Each of them entertains the notion of fate or *fatalism*, which in the context of materialistic physics can be seen as causalism (which adherents such as Epicurus took into a fatalistic context). They all also present some form of *revolution* from a former state that leads to materialistic interests. They all deal with the issue of *estrangement,* which is consistently recognized in the context of materialism. *Bondage* is also a recurring theme, and all three are set in the context of *knowledge* or *reason*. These themes and considerations are expressed in the most central features of each story; thus, instead of using them to repetitively organize each chapter, they will organically enter into each conversation by way of the more direct consideration of each story on its own terms. For example, in analyzing the Prometheus story I would rather have a section on fire theft than knowledge, or getting chained to stone than materialism, because these are the self-presented dynamics as opposed to an imposed organization.

Chapter 2 features Prometheus. After introducing and contextualizing the great Classical progenitor, I will work through his story by way of its sequential focal points. The first topic of consideration will be his role as progenitor and creator of humans from clay. This will lead into a conversation about his role as a rebel and freedom fighter, as he demonstrated by fighting with Zeus against the Titans, then siding with humans against Zeus. From here we will discuss the Promethean sacrifices. The next section will be on the fire-theft itself, and the next on his consequent bondage. Finally we will address Pandora's creation from clay. Throughout these sections, beneath their surfaces, key themes will be considered: materialism, fate, rebellion, estrangement, bondage, and knowledge, which simultaneously emerge from the story and speak to the emergence of materialism as the paradigm of first knowledge. Ultimately the conclusion of chapter two will be angled towards a summated exposition of the story's elements and their communication of an entry into materialism.

Chapter 3 begins where the history of Western philosophy always begins, with Thales in Miletus. I will follow the development of his premise—materialism—through to the decline of Classical philosophy and science. I will then examine the recurring emphasis on *matter* as primary, then the fundamentality of causation, the revolution of an empirical epistemology, the recognition of estrangement as a consequence of materialism, philosophical interpretations of matter as shackles or bonds, and ultimately the paradigm of knowledge these motifs constellate. In chapter two I avoided the direct patterning of the chapter after these motifs because I wanted to approach the story on its own terms; however, in the case of philosophical and scientific materialism, these motifs represent the core features of their conversation.

While I stop the story of materialism with Classical history, I involve European scientists in the exploration of their motifs, whose abbreviated story is appended for those with interest. There is chronological reason to tell the story of Enlightenment science after the introduction of Judeo-Christianity, but I have decided against two chapters on science, and to stay focused on origin stories in Part One. That said, European science built on and elaborated the Classical model of materialism. And it will be of central importance to communicate the consistency between their vision of materialism as the joined forces against which Einstein and others would later react. The consistency can be recognized through the growth of the first into the next. For example, while certain Classical philosophers recognized the notion of estrangement as a consequence to material existence, the clarification of this point—as we recognize it now—came from Descartes' description of the "subject-object" divide. Bacon developed their empirical interests into the scientific method; and though the first atomists gave theories about mechanistic causality, Newton developed a mathematical model to describe such interactions. The complication is that, while I am not telling stories about Perseus or

Moses that exist in the middle of the narrative developments engaged by this dissertation, Enlightenment science is not just a story in the middle. In many ways, the Scientific Revolution is its own origin story that restarts science, almost, at the beginning. However, though it may seem like the origin of the materialistic paradigm as we know it, they were reading and referencing the contributions of the Classics who initiated their knowledge. Again, for these reasons I am compromising by involving European science in the consideration of those motifs Classical philosophers understood to be central features of a materialistic science.

Chapter 4 features Adam and Eve in Eden. After introducing the symbols and figures of the garden and offering a detailed telling of their story, I will enter into analysis in much the same way as in chapter two. By my reading, the story demands the organization of its analysis into a consideration of the garden, tree, snake, first couple, satan's fall, the first couple's fall, post-exilic life, and death. y engaging the religious myth on its own terms, the conversations of materiality, fate, rebellion, estrangement, bondage and knowledge emerge organically. Ultimately, as in chapter two and three, the conclusion will be a summary of how the story communicates an un-separated entry of human beings into the paradigm of materialism and/as first knowledge.

The Conclusion of Part One will consider chapters 2, 3 and 4 in each other's contexts. In this short reflection on the conversation through chapter four, the consistency of these origin stories and their communication of an entry into worldviews grounded by matter will be the central point. In this segment I will also entertain some of the implications and nuances of the scenario, and unlock the door "Part Two" seeks to open.

Part Two articulates three responses to materialism as presented by Heracles, Christ, and Einstein: release from materialism, participatory union, and the actuation of these transformations by way of an elixir or waves. Once the conclusion of part one brings the three traditions into a concordant expression of materiality, I do not want to re-divide the conversation into each mythological tradition—especially when my effort is to demonstrate their similarities. Also, there is an impulse to step back and tell the stories of Christ, Heracles, and modern physics in their relative entirety, but beyond impractical, it would take us away from their specific responses to the questions and problems presented by their progenitorial origins. All of Heracles' labors are available to our conversation, but the only stories that are a priority to tell are those relating to Prometheus and the consequences of his actions. The entire life of Christ is available for consideration, but the stories that will necessarily appear in the dissertation are those involving Adam and the consequences of his actions. Similarly, while an exploration of quantum mechanics and string theory would be an adventure (especially considering the limitation of my knowledge about them), this is not required by the argument. In Part II, I am seeking to isolate the moments in those narratives started by Prometheus, Adam, and Thales when reductive materialism is transcended and participatory union is actuated, by elixirs.

Chapter 5 starts with a consideration of material negation, liberation from the material world or flesh, and the theoretical pivot from reductive materialism. This will include symbolic interpretations of Adam's liberation from Golgotha's stone—as presented by the Church of the Holy Sepulcher—Christ's liberation from both his cave and material-mortality, Prometheus' liberation from the stone, Heracles' liberation of material-mortality, and physics' liberation from reductive materialism. The essential conclusion from this content is that the Classical, Judeo-Christian and Scientific traditions present moments of pivotal release from materialism, and that they are actuated by the great hero, savior, and theorist: Heracles, Christ and Einstein.

The next part of Chapter five looks specifically at the achievement of union and the possibility thereof: the return of Adam and Christ to divine union, and the extension of this promise to their followers; the reconciliation of Prometheus with Zeus and the return of Heracles to Olympus; and some of the first/key ways that scientists have come to acknowledge and utilize participatory union. This will involve both a symbolic interpretation of the story as well as a look at participatory rituals, common beliefs, and interpretations pertaining to the traditions.

The last portion of chapter five considers the symbolic elixirs or theoretical waves in each story as the catalysts or actuators of both material liberation and union: the hydra-blood that killed Prometheus' eagle (which was procured with the fire-brand as a weapon) and allowed Heracles to set him free, the same blood which triggered Heracles return to Olympus by way of death, the divine nectar that was given him by, Hebe, the cupbearer of the gods, and the milk he drank from Hera's breast. Further vessel and elixir symbolism surrounding Heracles will be considered: the golden chalice Zeus gives Alcmene when Heracles was conceived, the cornucopia he won with a wife from a fight, the Sun's golden cup-boat he used to cross the ocean, the use of wine and cup to retrieve the golden apples that are also found on the wreath of Dionysus, the waters with which he cleaned the stables, the golden rain by which his grandfather (Perseus) was conceived, and so on. In the context of Christ's story we will start with his interaction with Adam, when the blood and water poured from his wound on the cross and baptized the progenitor, freeing him from the stone below and restoring him to union with God. The same blood and water filled the legendary Holy Grail, from which he last drank wine. With these events in mind, I will consider the milk grotto where he was nursed, baptism, the rock at the mouth of the Jordan on which he built his church, his walking on water, his healing with water, the turning of water to wine, and other stories.

Before moving into a discussion of wave dynamics in physics I want, in this single section, to amplify freely into Classical and Abrahamic examples of waves as actuators of material liberation and/or union with the divine, nature or lover. For example, I will look at the wine and blood of the Christ story as found in Grail romances across Europe: the blood of the spear, the wine of the cup, the blood of the decapitated head, and the water Merlin's knights drink in the *Vita Merlini* to undo that madness they entered by eating poison apples. Water of the ZamZam well and the story of Gabriel using a golden vessel to pour its knowledge into Muhammad's breast will be considered, as will Rumi's use of water droplets to describe one in many and many in one. The hemlock that returned Socrates to a state of undisrupted wisdom will be considered, as will the wine of Dionysus, the music of Orpheus, the waters of Lethe, Mnemosyne, and the waters withheld and by Demeter when Persephone is in the underworld that she restores upon her return. A note on the grail legends' influence on J.R.R. Tolkien will be considered in the context of Bilbo's retrieval of the silver cup in juxtaposition with Thorin's search for a stone *heart of the mountain*, as will T.S. Eliot's emphasis on water as that which redeems wastelands.

Thales, Pythagoras and Plato's theories on water and harmony will also have to be reconsidered in this context, which will introduce a perspective by which their paradigmatic counter position to materialism will be anchored to the rational-mechanics of wave dynamics. This reconsideration of harmony in the context of waves will lead us to the reconsideration of waves in the context of harmony. When engaging the introduction of wave mathematics to the materialistic history of physics, I will be focused on the demonstration of how this implies a revolution in Western intellectual thought that allows for participatory union to play a role in world-view formation. This conversation will start with the photoelectric effect, but extend into a deeper consideration of electromagnetic waves, gravity waves, and De Broglie or *matter waves*. It will also be supported by more accessible examples of wave dynamics, from mechanical waves on a string to kinematic experiments (in which matter participates in sound).

The Conclusion of Chapter 5 will organize and summarize the consistent and repetitive presentation of waves as actuators of freedom from the limitations of matter and the achievement of union and/or its conceptual possibility.

Chapter 6: The Conclusion starts with a re-examination of the details I have extracted from the stories of Prometheus and Heracles, Adam and Christ, and the theoretical paradigm of materialism that emerged from philosophy and science. From here I attempt to build my Irish wall. From the web-like negative of its cracks, I deduce its implied statement: Paradigm A leads to a wasteland which is redeemed by paradigm B. Paradigm A is generally recognized as reductive materialism, but what it really depends on is the metaphor system beneath, which we project on ourselves and grow into wounding worldviews. Paradigm B is especially recognizable by its integration of the metaphors implicit in wave dynamics—the behaviors of fluid—and the potential for union implicit therein. This sets up the statement that the relationship between these two paradigms can be understood through reason—as preferred by science—or symbolic narratives—on which a connection with religious mythology most greatly depends.

Where billiard ball atoms, particles and material things are fundamentally isolated by their rigid boundaries, one microphone can record the simultaneous sounds of an entire orchestra as a single wave. From a paradigm of strict atomistic materialism, fragmentary isolation is fundamental. On the other hand, resonance and union with nature, lover and God(s) become philosophically conceivable when metaphors abstracted from the behavior of waves are integrated into the foundations of one's belief system. This occurred within physics when Einstein combined wave dynamics with particle physics to describe the photoelectric effect, and in Western religious mythology when Heracles and Christ imbibed the apotheotic elixirs of nectar and blood-wine. In the context of their traditions, Einstein freed the philosophical mind from the reductive materialism by which it was born (according to Aristotle). Similarly, Heracles and Christ freed Prometheus and Adam, who, after giving knowledge and suffering to humanity, were chained to or buried under stone.

This will lead us to conclude: If the restriction of Western mythical progenitors (Prometheus and Adam) to stone can be seen as paradigmatically congruent with the founding of Western thought on material grounds (as stated by Aristotle), and if the imbibing of apotheotic elixirs by their saviors (Heracles and Christ) can be seen as paradigmatically congruent with the integration of wave dynamics by Einstein and later physicists, then the solution to reductive materialism by Western myth and science should be seen as mimetically dependent on the form of waves and their behavior—fluid, EM, or any other.

After I have tightened my dissertation into the essential statements, I want to demonstrate how a congruent turn in narrative can be seen in recent history. Among other examples I will address, the dematerialization of money and entertainment combined with the explosive embrace of wireless wave technology point to our collective transition towards new "common sense" foundations that resonate with those I have shown to free us from the paradigm of reductive materialism. Technology is dematerializing our lives and bringing them into closer participation with one another by utilizing waves. Perhaps the Apple iphone is the most familiar example: unlike an axe, fruit or lever, the iPhone has zero value in the material world or to the material body save maybe as a paperweight. However, the Apple iPhone is the Swiss Army Knife of our day, and one of the most useful tools in modern life. Floating in a sea of electromagnetic waves, it connects with such immaterial realities as a typing interface, the internet, video and game worlds, photo albums, online banks, and so on. Its touch screen furthers the dematerialization of human interfaces that we saw in the first computer screen, which many of us have come to spend more waking ours looking through than moving through materiality.

While widespread technological (and thus behavioral) dematerialization is readily noticed by the astute citizen of the modern world, so too is the sense that we are inundated by radio, TV, cell phone, Wi-Fi and satellite waves, which enable the union of an object with its prioritized source—despite its physical isolation there from. Examples of dematerialization and the utilization of a wave's capabilities of participatory union are becoming so ubiquitous, so second nature, that the evolution of common human intelligence beyond the dated paradigm of materialism seems virtually unavoidable. The interest of my dissertation is to draw specifics of this paradigmatic shift into distinct consciousness by contextualizing what I see to be going on with the most pervasive traditions in Western memory: The paradigmatic shift through which we are going mimes those paradigmatic shifts between Prometheus and Heracles, Adam and Christ, and the tradition of materialistic physics overturned by Einstein and modern physicists. Beyond their congruent negations of the materialistic paradigm, they present symbolic or theoretical waves—capable of union and harmony—as the appropriate response.

Chapter 2: Prometheus Bound

Prometheus, as I will show, created humans and ignited the psyche. He counseled Zeus in his war against the Titans, and created a "black hole" to imprison the former rulers (Aeschylus, *Prometheus Bound* 326-328). But once the Olympian monarch established his rule of order, Prometheus rebelled against the first decree: a flood that would kill all humans and wipe the slate clean for Zeus. By advising his progeny to "fashion an ark" (Pseudo-Apollodorus 1. 45), he saved the young race; until, at a feast, a rift was roused between gods and men. To resolve the issue and establish a bridge between disputing parties he invented the burnt offering. Though this gesture became a ritual standard, for attempting to trick Zeus into receiving unwanted waste as a generous gift, humans were deprived of fire. In an act of necessary rebellion the progenitor stole back the fire in a hollow fennel stalk, with which he delivered knowledge beyond instinct—how to work clay, wood, metal, numbers, and words to make art, food, and tools. This defiance of Zeus brought punishment upon Prometheus and his people. To humans he gave Pandora—not a woman like Prometheus' wife or his ally Athena—a misleading fiend, a plague on humanity, a contorting influence on the human psyche. Once married to Epimetheus, Prometheus' brother, she opened the jar—mistranslated centuries ago as a 'box'—and introduced suffering to human life. By this time the human benefactor could do nothing, as he had been exiled to "a rock at the edge of the world" (Aeschylus, *Prometheus Bound* 176-7)—to the place of the sunrise. Chained to a stone, furious at Zeus, he declared his foresight of the tyrant's downfall. And for refusing to reveal the prophecy, a ravaging eagle was loosed on his regenerative liver. Still, true to his foresight, Zeus' own son later freed him from bondage.

This chapter will expand on the story of Prometheus summarized above through a somewhat sequentially ordered examination of its key motifs, after which we will consider crucial details that seem to symbolically convey the establishment of material limitation and the psyche's imprisonment. Until the second portion, the chapter will read as survey and introduction to the Classical progenitor and the origin story of knowledge. The discussion of Pandora's Box and Prometheus' binding will be reserved for our transition from survey to reflections concerning material entry and limitation. However, we will not be prepared to use the refined language of materialism and the isolative structures of atomism until after our next chapter on Greek philosophy.

Aeschylus describes Prometheus as the "patron of the whole human race" (*Prometheus Bound* 903). Kerenyi describes him as "the immortal prototype of man" (*Prometheus* 17). And Tarnas tells us that, "in the ancient mysteries, man had been symbolized as the great mythic figure" (*Passion of Western Mind* 215). Like Adam, Herakles and Christ—the main characters in this dissertation—Prometheus is a deity with which to identify. With this foundational frame in mind, we should dive deeper into the details of his story with an eye open to its commentary on the condition of human life and its mortal narrative. As we become increasingly immersed in his myth we will find the Classical benefactor of humanity to be more than a personification of human life. We will find that he has long served as a beacon for human spirit—such spirit as is required for creating art, fighting for freedom, pursuing new ideas, and stomaching the consequences of conscientious acts.

He fought for Olympian order, then against Zeus' tyranny. When Aeschylus wrote *Prometheus Bound*, it was to Athenians who remembered the overthrow of their last tyrant, the establishment of democracy, and two freedom wars against Persian tyranny. When Lord Byron, Percy Shelley and Mary Shelley were writing around the figure of Prometheus, it was to an audience that remembered the revolution of science from religious repression as well as the French and American democratic revolutions against power-abusing monarchs. The spirit Prometheus awakens is that rebellious insistence on the right to personal freedom—the desire to not be beneath or limited by the will of another. Fundamentally, this is the right to live, but it is also the right to create, to learn, and—in Percy Shelley's *Prometheus Unbound*—to love.

As we will see, Prometheus is the man at the sunrise, the bringer of the fire, the spark, the exuberant creative force, that which brings inner light to outer expression, and the unwavering defender of our human right to this nature. We will find that, as a titan, he is more raw than the Olympians, but as his raw qualities include intelligence and ingenuity, his abilities to improve and refine are limitless. He is the opposite of static, in fact, as Tarnas describes it, *progress* is a Promethean enterprise. When Zeus chains him to stone, it is not only to punish his disobedience, but also to neutralize him. Beyond his rebellious nature and insistence on freedom, innovation and the innovative spirit pose great threats to regimes that rule over the status quo. When Prometheus appears, so too does change—from outside the system or states in which Promethean stories and attitudes surface. Change can require defiance and become rebellion, which many governments have, historically, avoided with violence and exile. When Zeus chains Prometheus to the mountainside, we might see Karl Marx being exiled, the Nazis driving artists from their borders, or the Soviet party banning *We,* a (Prometheus Award winning) novel by Yevgeny Zamyatin. With *A Brave New World* and *1984,* these dystopian realities provide perfect examples of ultimate Promethean nightmares in which creativity, love, individuality, freedom, invention, and knowledge are completely denied by tyrannical leadership. As we continue into a survey of his myth, the qualities of his character will continue to break through the surface.

Prometheus the Progenitor

In that he is sometimes presented as the creator of humans and sometimes as their first father, Prometheus is consistently presented as the human progenitor. Sappho, Aesop, Plato and Ovid offer stories of Prometheus as the creator of first humans. For example, in one of Aesop's fables we read that, "Following Zeus' orders, Prometheus fashioned humans and animals," and that "the clay which Prometheus used when he fashioned man was not mixed with water but with tears" (Aesop 515). In the version of the story told by Protagoras, the first Sophist, and recounted by Plato, "the gods molded [humans] of earth and fire. [And,] when they were ready to bring them to light, the gods put Prometheus and Epimetheus in charge" (320).[1] Ovid writes, in *Metamorphosis*, "the creator of the universe, originator of a better world, fashioned him from divine seed or earth ... and was mixed with rain water by Prometheus, the son of Iapetus, and fashioned by him into the likeness of the gods who control all" (I. 76-88).[2]

Though his role as human creator is a common quality of his character, his creation of humans is not referenced in Aeschylus' *Prometheus Bound* (though it may have been included in one of his other missing plays on the benefactor of humanity). The detail is also absent from Hesiod's *Theogony* and *Works and Days*. However, in a later text attributed to Hesiod, the author "states in the first *Catalogue* ... 'that Helen was the son of Deucalion and Pyrrha,' the survivors of the flood, and 'that Deucalion was the son of Prometheus and Pronoea'" (Scholiast *III.1086)*. Insofar as he is a grandfather of all

flood survivors, he is presented as the father of all living-humans. This is not unlike

Adam, whose story of creation and first knowledge is—in *Genesis*—followed by an age-

ending flood.[3]

His status as father of the first human beings was recognized by the Kabeiroi—a

name used to signify the primal humans as well as initiates into a mystery cult we will

encounter repeatedly in this chapter. It is impossible to determine whether or not

Aeschylus was an initiate of the Kabeiroi mysteries, but the fact that he wrote an entire

play about the Kabeiroi suggests he was highly familiar with their beliefs and practices.

As Deucalion was sometimes seen as Prometheus' child, so too were the Kabeiroi. As

Karl Kerenyi explains, "the Kabeiroi … were primordial beings ... the original men"

(*Prometheus* 61). And "Prometheus … proves to have been the most venerable of the

Kabeiroi, their father and ancestor" (58).[4]

Creator, father, teacher, benefactor—these are all true expressions of the

Promethean essence that blend with one another and appear on their own. The connection

between progenitor and creator is essential to the understanding of Prometheus. As we

will see, Prometheus is, in many ways, an expression of the father's creative potency,

which can be taken as the literal power of human creation. At the same time, his creative

power exceeds his progenitorial potency, as his gifts of knowledge and craft initiate

humans into the creative abilities that separate humans from animals. In fact, if he may

say so, "All human culture comes from Prometheus" (Aeschylus, *Prometheus Bound*

738). "Prometheus himself is the prototype of the culture god or hero ultimately

responsible for all the arts and sciences" (Morford 49). "More than any other, his portrait offers the towering image of the Titan, the bringer of fire, the vehement and weariless champion against oppression, the mighty symbol for art, literature, and music of all time" (49). "Fundamental to the depictions of both Hesiod and Aeschylus is the conception of … Prometheus as mankind's benefactor" (49).

His role as benefactor extends into his role as mentor—to Zeus, Hephaestus, Athena, (and later Herakles), who similarly carry the creative capacity he represents. For example, the chieftain of the gods—himself a mentor and personification of divine reason—was only able to establish the order of Olympus with Prometheus as his counselor. The Titan boasts, "Thanks to the strategy I devised, the black hole of Tartaros holds and hides archaic Kronos" (Aeschylus, *Prometheus Bound* 326-328). As mentor to Zeus in the defeat of Titanism, Prometheus parallels his role as counselor to humans. His help in establishing the Zeusian order of Olympus mimes his bringing of conscious reason to humanity in that both represent the emergence of intellect from an (inner and/or outer) reality governed by rawer and more ancient instincts.[5]

Like Zeus, his other divine protégés, Hephaestus and Athena, represent something more refined than the Titan. As teachers of knowledge and craft, Hephaestus and Athena carry on the mentoring and creative roles of their exiled elder. Where Prometheus brings spark as the first craftsman, Hephaestus and Athena are next-generation-masters of his introduced crafts. But more than craftsmen, the two are creators. Much as Prometheus made men from clay, Hephaestus formed Pandora on the potter's wheel; and as the gestures of Prometheus tend to establish new norms, the gift formed by Hephaestus and clothed by Athena brought mortality to the human race. The two were also foundational in the establishment of Athens. Not only did Hephaestus give birth to Athena from Zeus's head, he also impregnated the soil with Athens' first king, Ericthonius, when lusting after

Athena. Further demonstrating the overlap of Prometheus and Hephaestus, in a "variant

on the Athenian myth of the birth of Erichthonius … it was Prometheus (not Hephaestus)

who lusted after Athena" (ctd. by Dougherty 50; Duris); and in Euripides' *Ion*, it was

Prometheus (not Hephaestus) who cut Zeus' head open to deliver Athena. In both cases,

Prometheus and Hephaestus are—with a goddess of wisdom—in roles of the father,

creator, bringer of civilization, and the cranial midwife.[6]

Returning to the figure of Metis, her name represents what Christine Downing

describes as a *watery wisdom* (Downing 117). And the freeing of Metis' daughter from

Zeus' head is mimetic with the loosing of wisdom from the mind, which is essential to

the function of Prometheus, whose "name contains the root 'metis'" (Dougherty 49). The

birth of the first Athenian from spilled semen expresses both the father's creative

potency, and the ability of the progenitor to create life with earth (as he does with clay).

In this image of Ericthonius' birth—founder of Athens—is the synchronization of

paternal potency with the potency to build civilization. Though his creative powers are

clearly connected to those of the father, on a deeper level, "Prometheus expresses, the

divine creative power inherent in human beings" (95). As we will continue to see, this

power translates into far more than the progeny of children.

As the creator of humans and father of Erichthonius, the Kabeiroi, and/or first

humans; as the mentor of Hephaestus, Athena, and Zeus; as the bringer of knowledge,

inciter of technology, and deliverer of civilization; Prometheus is the Classical benefactor

and progenitor of humanity, the arts, sciences, technology and civilization. Having

established this frame in which the foundational roles of Prometheus are recognized, we next turn to his roles as freedom fighter, sacrifice(r), and fire-thief, followed by the stories of Pandora's "box" and Prometheus' bonds.

Prometheus the Freedom Fighter

Prometheus foresaw both the beginning and end of the Olympian rein. After helping Zeus to create the Olympian order from a Titanic age, the monarch of the gods began to undermine human freedom—starting with the flood and their right to live. "Fundamental to the depictions of both Hesiod and Aeschylus is the conception of Zeus as the oppressor of mankind and Prometheus as mankind's benefactor" (Morford 49). By defying Zeus in myth, Prometheus became a symbol for those in history who fought tyrants of Athens, Persia, France, England, Russia, and the Catholic Church. He became "a symbol of protest against traditional religion and morality, against any limitation to human endeavor, against prejudice and the abuses of political power" (Mayerson 46). Campbell even associated him with the Nietzchean proclamation of God's death.[7]

In Goethe's free verse poem, *Prometheus*, translated by Herbert Nehrlich, the fire bringer scathes the way of Zeus in the favor of human presence and creation. When Goethe's Prometheus insists, "my earth is mine," he speaks as a rebel and creator at once. The earth is his land and his clay, his space and his working material. As Kerenyi points out, "In Goethe's mythologem Prometheus' work of creation is indeed limited exclusively to what he can create on the earth" (*Prometheus* 8). He fights for the human right to be, and from the progenitor's point of view, to be human is to be a creator, is to work earth on earth.

Of course, even in peace there is something inherently rebellious about creation and change. As will become increasingly clear, Prometheus represents the spirit in humans that seeks to change the world from how it is to how humans want it to be. "His gifts to men rests upon the belief in progressive stages from savagery to civilization … a penetrating account of man's evolution that in many of its details is astoundingly modern" (Morford 44). He is the ageless spirit of progress and the unending will to change. In this section we will look more closely at the stories of his rebellion, but as we engage his rebellious nature we will find it to be an outgrowth of his essence as a creative progenitor. The plot points in Prometheus' myth are acts of both rebellion and creation— his defiance of the Titan rule creates the Olympian order, his salvation of humans from Zeus' flood protects his creators, his creation of the sacrificial bridge between gods and humans was in the form of a defiant trick, his gift of fire—the power of creation—was a direct act of defiance, and his rebellious refusal to reveal Zeus' downfall was for the sake of a new age's creation. All of these creative and rebellious acts were on behalf of his ultimate creative rebellion from the status quo—his creation of creators. It is for these creators that he serves as a benefactor, as a teacher, as a defender, and when the circumstances require—as a freedom fighter.

Like Goethe, Lord Byron "looked to Prometheus as a symbol of heroic individualism at odds with tyrannical powers both human and divine" (Dougherty 97). His Prometheus "was written in the revolutionary spirit of the early nineteenth century" (Mayerson 46). And as Dougherty points out, he was working "in the footsteps of Aeschylus, celebrating Prometheus' tireless endurance of all that the tyrannical forces of Zeus can dish out'" (Dougherty 98). Tarnas expands on Prometheus' historical presence in those revolutions that inspired such (pre)-Romantics as Goethe, Byron, Mary, and Percy Shelley:

… in the extraordinary era that brought forth the American and French Revolutions, the Industrial Revolution, and the beginning of Romanticism. In all these coinciding historical phenomena, the figure of Prometheus is of course readily evident as well: the championing of human freedom and individual self-determination, the challenge to traditional beliefs and customs, the fervent revolt against royalty and aristocracy, established religion, social privilege, and political oppression: the Declaration of Independence and the Declaration of the Rights of Man, *liberté* and *egalité* the beginnings of feminism, the widespread interest in radical ideas, the rapidity of change, the embrace of novelty, the celebration of human progress, the many inventions and technological advances, the revolutions in art and literature, the exaltation of the free human imagination and creative will, the plethora of geniuses and cultural heroes. Here too were the Romantic poets with their great paeans to Prometheus himself.

(*Cosmos* 95)

We find the Promethean drama played out time and again—when tyranny needs to topple. And we find that both artists and philosophers have consistently recognized his presence, power, and importance—not only to the revolutions in which they see his efforts, but also to their own work.

The romantic utopia described by Percy Shelley in his *Prometheus Unbound* is not wholly unlike the utopian dreams of Karl Marx. Percy wrote of a reality in which "thrones were kingless, and men walked / One with the other even as spirits do / —none fawned, none trampled" (III.IV 131-133). As Prometheus' potency was carried from the

Romantic period into the communist spirit, new rebellions were mounted against religious, state, and economic tyrannies. Leszek Kolawski, a Marxist theorist, said "Marx was certain that the proletariat as the collective Prometheus would, in the universal revolution, sweep away the age long contradiction between the interest of the individual and that of the species'" (Kolakowski 1.312-13). When such hope was put into practice against Russian Czars, John Lehman, an English poet and magazine editor, wrote:

> *Prometheus and the Bolsheviks*, a 1937 book on the Caucasus … [that] invoked Prometheus as a powerful symbol of the Bolshevik cause to deliver man from tyranny and barbarism by seizing material power. … Lehman recounts a dream of Prometheus that he had while sleeping aboard a Soviet steamer crossing the Black Sea. In this dream the Titan says to him: 'I find myself passionately on the side of the Bolsheviks when I hear accounts of the Civil War struggles. It reminds me of my own struggles with Jove over the fire business.' (Dougherty 132)

By recalling great rebellions in human history and recognizing the acknowledged projection of Prometheus into their situations, we get a sense of what he stood for and why—and when—humans have continued to seek him out.

Perhaps there is no better antithesis to the Promethean will than the statement of Power in *Prometheus Bound*. He says, "every job's a pain, except for the God at the top, only Zeus is free" (Aeschylus 88-90), to which the Promethean will responds, "no one dared stand up against this … but me! I alone had the courage. I saved humanity from going down, smashed to bits, into the cave of death" (339-355). Prometheus is that one, who, when all else yields to the might of a tyrant, refuses to kneel. And when no courage can be found in the hearts of the living, his spirit is loosed to waken the brave. He is the fearless leader, the wise advisor, he who will sacrifice for humanity's greater good, and he who takes responsibility for the establishment of freedom—freedom not to be created anew, but defended as something natural.[8]

Prometheus and the Sacrifice

It would seem there is no limit to the sacrifices Prometheus is willing to make for creative freedom—no suffering he cannot handle. No torture will break his integrity. This is a character he could not be if he was unwilling to make sacrifices—to be ostracized by Zeus, exiled, put in bonds, wedged into stone, disemboweled, and to continue his defiance in the face of further threat. Less attention is given to his establishment of the sacrifice than the sacrifices he made, in this section; the great acts will be considered in the contexts of one another.

Before proceeding with the premise of their entanglement, I should explain that the emphasis on the liver of our prophesying Titan is what makes his link with the sacrificial animal so apparent. As Kerenyi explains, the ancient Greeks often "practiced the form of soothsaying known as hepatoscopy" (*Prometheus* 39) which means the reading of prophetic messages from a sacrificial liver. And in his *Astronomica,* Hyginus wrote that after Heracles "killed the eagle … men began, when victims were sacrificed, to offer their livers on the altars of the gods to satisfy them in place of the liver of Prometheus" (2.15). Like a sacrificial animal, Prometheus was bound and placed on a rock. Where the animal was cut and burned to sustain daily life with food and favor, the ignition of the new day brought a slicing beak to eat from the deity's liver. And as soothsayers read divine messages from sacrificial livers, the titan of the tormented liver became a herald of prophecy.

The scene of the first sacrifice is particularly detailed in Hesiod's *Theogony*, in which we read that the humans and gods had entered into a dispute, and as the specific dispute is not given, the emphasis conveyed to the reader is simply that this first-mentioned dispute has arisen. To settle the dissention, Prometheus cut "up a great ox and set portions before them trying to befool the mind of Zeus. Before the rest he set flesh and inner parts thick with fat upon the hides, covering them with an ox paunch; but for Zeus he put the white bones dressed up with cunning art and covered with shining fat" (20-21).[9] When he "tried to deceive Zeus by concealing the best meat in entrails" (Freeman 195) while giving him "thigh bones wrapped in fat" (Aeschylus 724-731), the themes of concealing and giving enter the story" (*Pandora* 277).[10] In response, "Zeus became a god of wrath, and to such an absurd degree that he withheld from mankind the precious gift of fire" (Campbell, *Primitive* 280).

Upon reflection, Kerenyi explains, "This story is based on the assumption that gods and men had not yet been separated by the 'sundered power,' as Pindar calls it. This … came about when in Mekone gods and men disputed (ἐ κρίνοντο) in the sense of 'separating' and 'differentiating'" (*Prometheus* 42).[11] As any dispute implies a polarity between those in disagreement, the ontological separation between humans and gods was a contingent consequence of their dispute (or visa versa). To put it into context, Kerenyi points out:

> The invention and first offering of the characteristic sacrifice of a religion
>
> may well be regarded as an act of world creation or at least as an act

establishing the prevailing world order ... [Concordantly,] Hesiod characterizes the sacrifice as an act of establishment, as the foundation of our world, by stressing the difference in the division and explaining it on the basis of a contest. After the division, the world came into being—a world in which gods and men were absolutely different. *(43-44)*

To relate the scene to a more familiar example he recalls the Christian mass, "by which the Christian world order was established. Once Christ's action at the Last Supper took on the significance of a prototypical ritual act, it became a foundational sacrifice, the great sacrifice by which the world of salvation was established" (43-44). The key difference, however, is that Christ's sacrifice was the ultimate sacrifice that ushered in an age of divine and mortal reconciliation; whereas Prometheus' sacrifice was the first, the beginning, and the establishment of a human-divine distinction (such as will be resolved by Christ and Heracles).

From a deeper viewpoint, the division that arose with Prometheus' sacrifice was not absolute, as "every division presupposes a whole to be divided and a common bond between those who do the dividing" (43-44). In this way, "the idea of the Greek sacrifice takes in both the distinction and the common bond between gods and men" (43-44). Though the distinction is apparent, the whole is implied, and in the Greek tradition, it was divine-flame that bridged between humans and gods. Doughterty explains in her book on Prometheus that "fire functions as the key medium for communication between the divine and human worlds. ... Fire transfers men's gifts to the gods ... [and] rituals involving fire, especially sacrifice, enable a two way communication between gods and men even as they reinforce their separate worlds" (49). From this light we can see the human deprivation of divine fire as a loss of connection with the divine, like a colony with no path to home (or E.T. without a phone).[12]

Some scholars have argued that Prometheus' fire theft suggests his inherent lack of flame, but whether or not he is capable of starting his own fires, to do so would not fulfill his intention of bridging humans with the divine. The start of the human flame in the Olympian domain is consistent with fire-bringing rituals in which the holy fires of Delphi, Delos, and other religious centers were used to ignite Greek hearths across their world.[13] Similarly, "a lighted torch accompanied a young bride bringing fire from her father's hearth to light that of her new husband … [And] on a much larger scale, a flame from the civic centre of the mother-city accompanied those settlers embarking on a colonial expedition" (Dougherty 48). In stealing fire from Zeus, Prometheus made human life a province of the divine and gave them recourse to the Gods on high.[14]

As the burnt offering was a sacrifice, the creation of the offering and the theft of flame was a severe sacrifice for the foresighted Prometheus. As is often the case in myth and ritual, to open the bridge between mortals and the divine requires an opening of the bridge between life and death. To practice hepatoscopy, the liver must be between both realms to bridge them. In that all animal sacrifices are killed, the immortality of Prometheus—who teeters between human and divine—undermines his continuity with the mortal sacrifice at Mekone until the centaur Chiron—who bridges the divide between human and animal—died in his place. Heracles, who made this arrangement, arrived in Olympus through an earthly pyre. In the next section we will continue our examination of the fire motif, but in the context of the first sacrifice (at Mekone), and his sacrifice (on the stone), it is essential to understand that these acts were required to establish a link between humans and gods.[15]

The setting of Prometheus' sacrifice further develops the reality-bridging motif. For one, he is in the location of the rising of the solar fire, which, in that moment, is emerging from a mysterious and other worldly place. Prometheus is also on a mountain, where earth reaches into the heavens. Throughout the world's religions and mythologies, the motif of a bridge between human and divine realms is common, and within the occurrences of the motif, it is common to find its association with a tree or mountain that visually demonstrates an extension between earth and the heavens. These locations are centers for major mythological events, like the enlightenment of the Buddha, the crucifixion of Christ, the sacrifice of Odin, and perhaps the suffering of Prometheus. In his book, *Tree of Life Archetype*, Haynes explores the axis mundi motif, and argues that key details from Prometheus' myth are commonly constellated with those found in the context of an axis mundi. He writes,

> As with his brother Atlas, the axis mundi characteristics of Prometheus are numerous. Although Apollodorus says that Zeus chained him to a pillar, we hear from Hesiod that the pillar (or shaft) was actually driven through his middle ... In typical fashion [of characters associated with the axis mundi], Prometheus suffers from a wound to the side; it is inflicted by an eagle that eats at his liver each day ... Blood relatives of Atlas often share associations with the axis mundi. Four of his daughters, the Hesperides, guard the Tree of Life. Another daughter, Calypso, lives on an island at the navel of the sea. Both Prometheus and Atlas are linked to pillars ...

[The] image of a plant, bush, or tree that glows with fire occurs frequently in axis mundi mythology. Mount Meru is said to be covered with magic plants that shine in the darkness, and Moses encounters a divine bush on Mount Horeb (also called Sinai) that burns but is never consumed by the fire. In Greek myth, Prometheus is the creator of human beings, having fashioned them from clay. In this function he joins the ranks of creator gods—or father-gods—who are themselves hung on the axis mundi in world mythology. Odin, called All-father, hung on Yggdrasill. The infant Zeus—called the father of gods and men—hung in his cradle on a tree at Mount Ida. Prajapati, the Hindu creator god was sacrificed at the world pillar: 'He is the progenitor, the only Lord, and upholds with his arms the falling heaven and earth ... [And] Christ, the Christian creator of the world, is sacrificed on the cross at Golgotha ... Prometheus assumes the role of the deity conferring blessings and prosperity, commonly associated with the axis mundi...Gods formerly worshiped as embodiments of the galaxy, and who are later displaced by Zeus in that capacity, are traditionally hung, pierced, or fixed to pillars at the axis mundi ... In addition to Prometheus, Atlas, Hera, and Ixion share this fate. (205-7)

The multi-valence of Haynes's argument is hard to pull into pieces, but his demonstration of Prometheus' consistency with other characters and images of world-centers is clear—his wound, his role as a benefactor, his conjunction with the pillar, his location on the mountain, and the fiery plant thereon.[16]

Though Haynes only mentioned the fire bringing qualities of the man on the mountain, beneath him were flowers associated with his fire. In the *Argonautica*, Apollonius of Rhodes describes "the charm of Prometheus … [which] sprang from the blood-like ichor of Prometheus in his torment (3. 844):

> If a man should anoint his body therewithal, having first appeased the Maiden, the only-begotten, with sacrifice by night, surely that man could not be wounded by the stroke of bronze nor would he flinch from blazing fire; but for that day he would prove superior both in prowess and in might. [The flower] shot up first-born when the ravening eagle on the rugged flanks of Caucasus let drip to the earth the blood-like ichor of tortured Prometheus. And its flower appeared a cubit above ground in colour like the Corycian crocus, rising on twin stalks; but in the earth the root was like newly-cut flesh. The dark juice of it, like the sap of a mountain-oak, she had gathered in a Caspian shell to make the charm withal, when she had first bathed in seven ever-flowing streams, and had called seven times on Brimo, nurse of youth … the dark earth shook and bellowed when the Titanian root was cut; and the son of Iapetus himself groaned, his soul distraught with pain. And she brought the charm forth and placed it in the fragrant band which engirdled her, just beneath her bosom, divinely fair. (63)

The association of his sacrifice with the elixir of invulnerability will become increasingly interesting to us as we proceed into the later chapters of the dissertation—especially in the context of mythical world centers.[17][18] For now we need only acknowledge the cutting

of the root as an additional emanation of Prometheus as living sacrifice.[19]

The most familiar version of the fire theft comes from Hesiod's *Theogony*, in which

Prometheus "outwitted [Zeus] and stole the far-seen gleam of unwearying fire in a hollow

fennel stalk" (21). And *Works and Days*, in which the chieftain of the gods "hid fire:

[before] the noble son of Iapetus stole again for men from Zeus the counselor in a hollow

fennel-stalk, so that Zeus who delights in thunder did not see it" (42).[20] As in Hesiod's

stories, Zeus takes it personally in each telling. In differing variants the fire is more

directly stolen from the holy hearth of Hestia, the forge of Hephaestus, the solar chariot,

and sometimes with the help of Athena. Plato writes, in Socrates voice, "a gift of gods to

men, as I believe, was tossed down from some divine source through the agency of a

Prometheus together with a gleaming fire" (*Philebus* 16b).[21]

In *Prometheus Bound*, the "flower fire" was stolen from Hephaestus, and was

seen as "the power of all works of hands" (Aeschylus 1-24).[22] The image of the flower

will be revisited throughout the dissertation, but most immediately we should consider its

flowering gesture in the context of a volcanic blossom. Along with Aetna, with which

Hephaestus was associated, his immediate home, "the island of Lemnos … possesses a

kind of volcano: the fiery crater of Mosychlos on the north side of the island where

Hephaistos had his sanctuary and his city of Hephaistias" (Kerenyi, *Prometheus* 81).

With this in mind, we may imagine that if Prometheus … [had] stolen the fire from

Hephaistos' smithy" (81), the "flower fire" he stole may have been volcanic.[23] This is

consistent with Prometheus' association with Mt. Elbruz, a dormant volcano and the tallest mountain in Europe.[24] Following this imagery, the restraint of the fire-bringer to Mt. Elbruz is mimetic with the restriction of the great volcano.

We will return to this imagery when we discuss the flowers growing on the peak around Prometheus, but for now we should focus on the fire shared by Prometheus and Hephaestus as a way into studying their relationships. The theft of the craftsman's fire from the mythical forge reinforced the common notion, as expressed by Servius,' that "both gods, [Hephaistos and Prometheus] are associated with fire, metalwork, and crafts" (Dougherty 50).[25] Plato even presented the idea that Prometheus stole "wisdom in the practical arts together with fire [because] without [it] this kind of wisdom is effectively useless)" (*Protagoras* 320).[26]

In this story recounted by Plato, the wisdom was stolen from both Hephaestus and Athena, who shared a temple and hearth overlooking the Athenian agora. In other Classical variants, Athena was accentuated as the giver of fire to Prometheus. For example, in a common version of the story she "helped [Prometheus] get the fire that would animate minds, [by] scaling the heights of Olympus to light the torch from the wheels of Helios' chariot" (Servius, 6.42; Dougherty 50).[27] Like Hephaestus, she was also worshiped and admired as a teacher of craft. As Athens grew into a "kind of industrial center of the Aegean world, so did Athena's prominence as a patroness of arts and crafts. She was not only concerned with spinning and weaving … her influence extended to all kinds of trades and she was worshiped or regarded as a teacher of such artisans as potters and goldsmiths" (Mayerson 172).

The fire-giving quality of Athena can also be found in the story by which she became the benefactor of Athens. When Poseidon and Athena were vying to represent the city, Poseidon "demonstrated his power by striking a rock on the Acropolis with his trident and causing a spring of sea water to gush forth. As her gift to the city, Athena planted an olive tree which much impressed the gods who sat in judgment" (100). Where the salt-water spring provided no material value, the olive gave them food, wood, and oil, from which the Athenians made fire. They named their city Athens and chose her olive gifts, by way of which it can be said that the goddess of knowledge gave fire to Athens.

As a vessel of knowledge, the symbol of fruit offers its own set of nuances. For example, the life cycle to which the fruit brings fruition is a cogent expression of mortal truth. Not only is the fruit capable of sustaining human life by way of the digestive process; but, as in the life of a human, the narrative cycle of a plant's growth begins with the parting of the mother or earth, the planting of the seed, gestation in the womb/earth, birth, growing up (erect), the achievement of sexual maturity, mating, and finally the growth of offspring who are cut free—when ripe—by stem or umbilical cord. The knowledge of these cycles and their congruity is a profound and initiatory achievements of mortal intelligence and abstract thought.

As a specific fruit, the olive is not just capable of sustaining the digestive burn; but by providing fuel for literal fire it resonates with the metaphorical description of mortal life as a fire that ignites at birth and burns out upon death. The metaphor can be found in the story of Meleager, who was prophesied to live until his firebrand burned out.[28] When considered in the context of one another, the firebrand and olive—gifts from Prometheus and Athena respectively—both convey the concept of mortality. To run out of energy is to die, which, for as far back as memory extends, has been communicated by the poetic images of a flame dying out, day becoming night, summer becoming winter, and other such images of fading light.

On the scale of human civilization, the loss of Promethean flame was equated with the loss of that knowledge that kept civilization alive. In *Works and Days,* Hesiod wrote, "the gods keep hidden from men the means of life. Else you would easily do work enough in a day to supply you for a full year even without working … But Zeus in the anger of his heart hid it, because Prometheus the crafty deceived him … He hid fire" (42). Without fire humans did not possess the means to sustain human life, for which Prometheus takes full credit:

> … what wretched lives people used to lead, how babyish they were—until I gave them intelligence, I made them masters of their own thought. I tell this not against humankind, but only to show how loving my gifts were … Men and women looking saw nothing, they listened and did not hear, but like shapes in a dream dragged out their long lives bewildered they made hodgepodge of everything, they knew nothing of making brick-knitted houses the sun warms, nor how to work in woof. They swarmed like bitty ants in dugouts in sunless caves. They hadn't any sure signs of winter, nor spring flowering, nor late summer when the crops come in. All their work was without thought until I taught them to see what had been hard to see: where and when the stars rise and set. … What's more, for them I invented NUMBER: wisdom above all other. And the painstaking, putting together of LETTERS: to be their memory of everything, to be their Muses' mother, their handmaid! And I was the first to put brute beasts under the

yoke, fit them out with packsaddles, so they could take the heaviest burdens off the backs of human beings. Horses I broke and harnessed to the chariot shaft … I alone invented the sea wandering linen winged chariots for sailors. All these devices, I invented for human beings… Without drugs people wasted away, until I showed them how to mix soothing herbs to ward off every sort of disease. … All human culture comes from Prometheus (Aeschylus, *Prometheus Bound* 630-738).

Father, creator, giver of all arts, Prometheus is not just the progenitor of human life; he is the progenitor of the human way. He is that spark and starting place. As Tarnas puts it, "The symbol of Prometheus's fire conveys at once a rich cluster of meanings—the creative spark, the catalyst of the new, cultural and technological breakthrough, brilliance and innovation, the enhancement of human autonomy, sudden inspiration …the solar fire and light … sudden enlightenment, intellectual and spiritual awakening" (*Cosmos* 94). Where Hephaestus is the master craftsman, Prometheus is the sparking insight. He represents the lit fuse or the light bulb moment; in fact, he represents all light bulb moments and the resulting technological landscape of human life. "He is a true culture hero" (Mayerson 43). "Without fire mankind would have perished" (Kerenyi 79). But, thanks to Prometheus, fire "shines forth: a teacher showing all mankind the way to all the arts there are" (Aeschylus *Prometheus Bound* 165-169).[29] Prometheus gave humans the means to make.

It is hard to be sure where Prometheus originated, for one we look to the Caucasus. We also look to the Phoenicians, who were historically responsible for teaching the Greeks many things that would enable civilization. We will later discuss

Melqart in the context of Herakles, for now we turn to the Phoenician "Promathe." For the Phoenicians, "*The gods*, as … seen in the *Sanconiathon*, were the discoveries made by the Phoenicians in science" (Bethram, *Eturia* 160-2). They each represented "discoveries made in science by their learned men" (Mooney 41). Such a religious tradition is consistent with the attitude of Prometheus (and later scientists), who championed human innovation over submission to divine authority. Most specifically, the Phoenician *Promathe* has been seen as an "allegory which they built up on their discovery of the South Seas … A certain voyage to the south, made by Promathe, the constellation of Gemini, in the heavens, was fully developed. … He is represented as climbing up to heaven, and from thence bringing down fire" (Mooney 41). "This discovery was not made until Phoenician mariners were able to sail both by night and day on the ocean. … Prometheus is represented as climbing up to heaven, and from thence bringing down fire, which meant nothing more than sailing to the south, by which new stars and constellations, and a warm climate were discovered" (Betham, *Eturia* 160-2).[30] From this interpretation the fire he brought down from the heavens was the knowledge of how to read heavily fire—the stars—for the purposes of navigation. Like Prometheus, Promethe "ridiculed the gods, that is, he made light of their discoveries. [And] he taught men many useful arts" (Mooney 41). In this way he was seen as "the *very good god,* or *great discovery*" (Betham, *Eturia* 160-2), an understanding of Promethe that exports smoothly into a vision of Prometheus, who similarly personified human discovery as a benefactor and "good god" to mortal humans.

To build civilization on a Promethean scale, the titanic forces of nature and psyche had to first be limited. As previously mentioned, the participation of Prometheus in the Titan Wars (Titanomachia) extends his role of mentor and knowledge bringer into his relationship with Zeus, making him more than a mere bringer of knowledge from gods to humans. By helping to establish the rule of Zeus he helps to establish an entire order of reality governed by such order as represented by Olympus.[31] As he claims in *Prometheus Bound*, it is only because of his guidance that "the black hole of Tartarus holds and hides archaic Kronos" (Aeschylus 326-328). That being said, Prometheus is himself a titan, who, for the sake of Olympian order, Zeus restrained. Though his arts built cities, he is perhaps too raw to participate as a citizen.

In Plato's *Protagoras,* humans without more than Promethean knowledge still "wronged each other, because they did not possess the art of politics" (320-321). For which reason Zeus "sent Hermes to bring justice and a sense of shame to humans, so that there would be order within cities and bonds of friendship to unite them" (320-321).[32] Where Prometheus is stubborn and uncompromising, Hermes is a smooth talker. Hermes communes with all of the gods, and Prometheus is mostly abandoned. In Prometheus there is raw brilliance, blinding talent, infinite creativity, power of mind, intense lucidity and ready leadership; but for those of us who know people like that, they can often be overwhelming, shamelessly full of themselves, and when at their worst, solipsistically isolated in their own self-obsession. A good example might be Joseph (of the coat with many colors), who had no idea that telling his older brothers they would all bow to him could be taken as offense. He exuded a profound radiance, but was abandoned in a pit and sent far from home. The shameless display of talent and potency still makes others insecure, and the implicit self-obsession that is not sensitive to that draws ire, and, as the dialogue suggests, is curbed by the feeling of shame. The fire bringer carries a raw and radiant creative shine, but this productive strength is inherently without a sense of reflection, restraint, hesitation, or as Plato wrote, *shame*.[33] As such shamelessness resulted in the abandonment of Joseph, Prometheus was also trapped in exile.

Despite the differences between Prometheus and Hermes, their similarities are numerous and informative. As is commonly known, "the herald of the gods was Hermes. His was the function and character of one traveling eternally back and forth, connecting antithetical realms, Olympus and Hades" (Kerenyi *Prometheus* 51). Similarly, according to Herychios, the Greek lexicographer, "the word 'Ithas' meant the 'Herald of the Titans, Prometheus, whom others call [or refer to as] Ithax" (50). Both bridged worlds as communicators and personifications of knowledge, for which reason a number of their stories overlap. For example, though in one of Aesop's fables Prometheus stole fire, in another Zeus fashioned humans and "ordered Hermes to give them intelligence" (520). Similarly, where Homer described Hermes as "the mighty runner (*eriounes*)" (*Odyssey* 8.323), the great fire races of ancient Greece were inspired by Prometheus' theft.

Between Hermes and Prometheus, the two brought the constituents of civil society: the knowledge required to build cities and the social aptitude required for humans to live together.[34] Runner, torch, and the initiation of civil society converged in the fire-runs of ancient Athens, which were not to be understood as "a repetition of Prometheus' act, but as a sacred action, which he inaugurated" (Kerenyi *Prometheus* 70). According to Pseudo-Hyginus, it was "a practice for the runners to run, shaking torches after the manner of Prometheus" (*Astronomica* 2. 15). And according to Pausanius, "if all the torches go out, no one is left to be the winner" (1.30).[35] "The competitors in the torch race were members of the Ephebeia, a political institution designed to structure the transition of young Athenian males into political life … [which] emphasizes the many aspects of the torch race that link it to key Athenian political institutions" (Dougherty 55). According to Aristotle, the man in charge of the torch race, "The Archon Basileus, [was] the one who administered all sacrifices instituted by ancestors and those ritual acts that guaranteed the harmonious functioning of society" (Dougherty 55). Offering further description of the relationship between the races and civic life, Carol Dougherty explains:

> Torch races were common to the cult activity of the three gods associated with fire and its technology: Prometheus, Hephaestus, and Athena. Each god had a shrine in the Academy from which the torch race proceeded through the Kerameikos into the city. … Taking their start from the altar of Prometheus at the Academy, torch races as part of the celebration of Hephaestus and Athena … trace a direct link between Prometheus and other major figures of Athenian religious civic life as well as between the Academy and other significant sites in Athens' topography. (56)

In the vision she describes, we can imagine the fire of Prometheus spreading its wisdom from the academic center of learning through the entirety of the ancient city. This is not unlike the rituals discussed in the last section of fire spreading from the divine hearth to humanity, from the hearths of Delos or Delphi through Greece, or from a mother city to its colonies.

The spreading of light throughout the world is a motif that finds its most consistent expression in the journey of the sun across the sky.[36] Taking us back to the stories in which fire was stolen from the sun, I want to consider what is perhaps the most obvious interpretation of fire bringing—the arrival of the sun each morning. In

Aeschylus' trilogy, Hephaistos told Prometheus, "When the bloom on your cheek is burnt black by the sun you'll be glad when night with her veils of star cloud covers up the glare, And again glad when at dawn, the sun scatters the hoarfrost" (34-47).[37] Here, before the eagle even appears, he is said to endure his punishment between sunrise and sunset. As alluded to by Hephaistos, the "suffering [is] day itself," even before "the eagle of Zeus … appears with the day" as "little more than a metaphor for the sun" (Kerenyi, *Prometheus* 39).[38] Upon imagining the fire bringer at "the end of the world" (Aeschylus line 1) in "the land of the rising sun" (Kerenyi, *Prometheus* 56), the association between sunrise and fire theft becomes unavoidably apparent.

After further examination, his association with the sunrise extends into his family relationships, with his brother and sometimes his wife. According to Carol Dougherty, "some traditions name Asia, instead of Klymene, as Prometheus' mother; others claim Asia was his wife" (5). Kerenyi adds,

> Asia would assuredly not have become the name for the Orient if it had not originally signified 'the Eastern' or the 'Morninglike' or been related in some other way to what, from the Greek point of view, was the land of the rising sun' … Herodotus has it that the wife of Prometheus bore this name and at the same time tells us that the eastern continent had taken its name from none other than her. (*Prometheus* 56)

We can see then that, according to the telling of Herodotus, he was bound by marriage to the land of the eastern sunrise.

Complimenting his marriage to the land of the sunrise, his brother Atlas stands in the land of the sunset. As seen in many ancient vases, Prometheus is often juxtaposed with his brother Atlas,[39] "who stands where evening is, pressing his shoulder to the unbearable pillar that holds the sky from the earth!" (Aeschylus 507-513).[40] As Kerenyi writes, "His situation—charge and punishment in one—at the western edge of the Greek world—corresponds exactly to that of the punished Prometheus at the eastern edge" (38).[41] The Chorus of *Prometheus Bound* tells him, "One other Titan god before this I have seen in distress, enthralled in torment by adamantine bonds—Atlas, pre-eminent in mighty strength, who moans as he supports the vault of heaven on his back. The waves of the sea utter a cry as they fall, the deep laments, the black abyss of Hades rumbles in response, and the streams of pure-flowing rivers lament your piteous pain" (Aeschylus 425).[42] If we consider the lighting up and going out of the sun each day in the context of an ignited and extinguished flame, we are reminded of the ritual association of fire with the mortal cycle. As the sun goes under each night and returns each morning, consciousness sleeps and awakes, is born and dies.[43]

If we consider the Golden Apples of the sunset in the context of Prometheus' fire-flower and sunrise sentence—or the flowers there that grow from his blood—we see that just as the sun travels from Prometheus to Atlas, the plant grows from flower to fruit. The word for apple in Greek, *melon*, actually means fruit. The same sequential pattern can also be recognized in an overarching narrative between Prometheus and Heracles. Not only is fire given before the Golden Apples are achieved, but the story in which Heracles obtains the apples of gold was immediately preceded by his conference with the teacher of humankind at the eastern edge of the world.[44] In teasing out key relationships between sunrise, fire-flower, and the knowledge bringer with sunset and its golden fruit, we are reminded that the fruit of one's labor is sparked by creative insight and the learning of knowhow. This returns us to the anchoring characteristic of Prometheus as the giver of human knowhow, the starting place of technological achievement, and the inciting spark of artistic creation.

Perhaps the most quintessential Promethean sunrise in contemporary artistic memory can be found in the opening sequence of Stanley Kubrick's film, *2001: A Space Odyssey*, in which—in front of the rising sun—apes catch a divine (or alien) spark that triggers their discovery of knowledge and progression into human beings. Referring to this scene, Dr. Tarnas wrote that "the entire Promethean trajectory, the alpha and the omega of the Promethean quest [is] to liberate the human being from the bonds of nature through human intelligence and will, to ascend and transcend, to gain control over the larger matrix from which the human being was attempting to emerge" (*Cosmos* 20). In a deep way, the story of Prometheus reflects the abstract or even synesthetic association between the ascertaining of knowledge and a light coming on. Beyond the indescribable yet visceral sense of waking up with illumination, fire played memorable roles in the birth of humanity. Not only did it enable humans to light up the dark, it was sometimes even the literal boundary between the life of a torchbearer and an aggressive animal—in both circumstances, which predate even homo-sapiens, fire was a perceived difference between humans and non-humans.

In addition to lightening up the night, fire warms the cold and allowed early humans to adapt to new places. The power of fire became the power to cook, to harden wood, to fire clay, work metal, and separate molecules. When the power of fire progressed into the power of electric lightning (resulting in the division of new molecules), the alchemical arts became the science of chemistry. Concurrent with this progression was the scientific revolution against the religiously motivated repression of scientific discovery. On the one hand, the insistence on creative and scientific freedom can be interpreted as a paradise, as is written about in Percy Shelley's *Prometheus Unbound*, but it can also be taken to a shadowy extreme, as can be found in Mary Shelley's *Frankenstein: A Modern Day Prometheus*. Close reads of these works convey reverence for both the positive and negative Promethean qualities, which are each essential to our understanding in an age of technological Titanism. In his book on *The New Prometheans*, Robert De Ropp suggests, "Pioneers in the field of atomic energy may be regarded as 'the most Promethean of the Prometheans' … in a very short period of time they transported humankind from one age into another: 'By releasing the power latent in the nucleus of the atom they made the theft of the original Prometheus seems like a very minor piece of effrontery.' (Dougherty 122). This passage is ominously reminiscent of a prophetic statement delivered by Prometheus in Aeschylus' play, "what an unbeatable wonder it is, this giant who'll discover fire hotter than lightning, explosion" (1415-18). The stakes are obviously higher now than when fire was the most advanced technology, or swords. Humanity now has the technological means to destroy itself and/or sculpt our flesh—not just with nuclear bombs, but with chemical weapons, genetic mutations, cloning, bionic upgrades, and every other sci-fi dream or nightmare that we are (un)-intelligently designing.

Whether one wants to see the Industrial Revolution as the unbinding of Prometheus, the escape from the atmosphere as the unchaining of science from the rock, the development of quantum computers as a liberation from technologies that are limited to causal chains, the manipulation of DNA as the breaking of those chains that limit our human form, or even the invention of wireless technology as an expression of his unbound freedom; we can see that, in countless ways, the Promethean enterprise is increasingly unrestrained. The question is, if science continues to shamelessly progress and create—if it forgets the gifts of Hermes from the *Protagoras*—will it eventually undermine the existence of civilization? Might the Promethean enterprise bring an end to the civilization it began?

In the myth, when Zeus agreed to let the Titan free, he "bade him bind his finger with … stone and with iron. Following this practice men have rings fashioned of stone and iron, that they may seem to be appeasing Prometheus" (Pseudo-Hyginus 2.15). The iron ring represented the chinks of his chain, and the stone was to remind him of their anchor. In theory, the ring was worn to remind those who worshiped Prometheus the purpose of restraint in those situations where restriction is not forced. In *The Universe in a Single Atom*, the Dalai Lama calls for exactly this—a memory of restraint in a time of unbinding and the ethical considerations of our scientific endeavors. As he puts it, "There have been too many tragedies related either directly or indirectly to science and technology for the trust in science to remain unconditional … my plea is that we bring our spirituality, the full richness and simple wholesomeness of our basic human values, to bear upon the course of science and the direction of technology in human society" (208). The concern is that, if humans are not attentive and considerate, we will open a box of Pandora's and create a Frankenstein that could threaten or even destroy human life.[45] Some of these boxes may even be open already, and Frankensteins could be among us, but the opportunities of this conversation will be richer later on, after conversations about Western science and Eve.

Having started this section with the first literary appearances of the Promethean fire theft, we have come to see overlap between the titan's skills and those of both Hephaestus and Athena, to whom he served as mentor (or father) and midwife. In looking at the fire flower from Hephaestus' forge and the fire-giving fruit from Athena's olive tree, we have explored some of the real and symbolic relationships between mortality, craft, and fire. In looking to the similarities and differences between Prometheus and Hermes, we have had a chance to consider the titan's unsocial qualities in the context of the city's paradoxical need for his fire, which was ritually spread throughout Athens from his hearth in the Academy. The progress of the Promethean flame through the phases of its scientific kindling was also brought into our conversation, especially in the context of those threats posed by the release of Prometheus, which is very much underway in our technologically driven society.

Pandora

For the theft of fire Prometheus and his human creations were punished. The benefactor was chained to a stone at the precipice where the sun rises, and Zeus sent humans a jar with Pandora. These punishments represent, among other things, the initiation of human life into mortal suffering: birth, labor, sickness, and death. As Morford writes, "in the person of Pandora the existence of evil and pain in the world is accounted for" (49). She "like Eve, for example, is created after man and she is responsible for his troubles" (49). The reason for this is "complex, but inevitably it must lay bare the prejudices and mores inherent in the social structure" (49). It also, perhaps on a deeper level, presents "the woman and her jar as symbols of the drive and lure of procreation, the womb and birth and life, [and thereby] the source of all our woes" (49).

Pandora was the first human wife and mother to bear a human child, and in this role she was associated with the prototypical Greek wife and mother responsible for managing the home and its stores. In addition to the association of the woman's womb with vessels of goods, it was also "inextricably associated with … the enclosed chamber. … Not only did the word *muchos* identify both a woman's body and the interior of a house, but the same word, *eschara,* referred to both the central hearth of a house and a woman's sexual organs*" (Women as Containers* 197).[46]

Beyond the association of the women with the domicile, the womb of the mother was also seen to be in alignment "with the earth, which was considered the quintessential womb" (197). This common Greek understanding of the womb and field as vessels of gestation found expression in the relationship between Gaia and Pandora, who "rises up out of the soil in the manner in which Gaia is consistently represented" (*Pandora* 278). As Downing writes in her book, *Goddess,* Pandora "is Gaia in human form" (153-4). Thus, as I will continue to demonstrate, what Hesiod presents as the curses of Pandora are simultaneously the gifts of Gaia—the same gifts in which all mothers participate as fertile vessels capable of generating life from their own matter.

The association of Pandora and the human wife/mother with earth, womb, field, home, and vessel carry meaning, weight, and insight. At the same time, the reduction of women to these roles (and the resistance to projecting them into men) has proven detrimental to the social, psychological and even physical wellbeing of women on a repeated historical basis. As we move through the next section there will be friction between contemporary ideals about women, ideals of contemporary women, and the ideals of Ancient Greece beneath the symbolic potency of Pandora and her "box."

Consider this a disclaimer: Pandora should not be reduced as a representative of women, and her relationship with matter should especially be recognized. No statement about Pandora as a symbol of matter or anything else is meant—coming from this author—as a reduction of women to that which she may have symbolized. Though it may read as a digression from the chapter on Prometheus, our discussion of Pandora will lead into our consideration of the stone to which the progenitor is chained. By the end of this section, what I will attempt to argue is that both Hesiod's Pandora (with her jar) and Prometheus' stone symbolically depict the marriage of the human mind to a paradigm in which substance is seen as the foundation of reality, life therein, knowledge, and *elpis*, "a word various translated as 'hope' and 'wishful thinking' (*Pandora* 277).[47]

With Pandora comes the birth of children, labors of life, sickness, deception, and death. Like "the bones [Prometheus] wrapped in glistening fat, like the fire hidden in the fennel stalk, Pandora was literally and figuratively the epitome of irresistible packaging. Beneath her sparkling exterior of gold jewelry and fine garments, there was only earth and water, as well as a thieving temperament and the overpowering weapon of language" (278). Despite her "beautiful exterior [she had] a worthless interior. Like the portion offered to men, concealed in the paunch of the ox, she is a hungry belly, insatiable of food … a fire that consumes man by her appetite for both food and sex" (Zeitlin 50).

She was made by Hephaestus, who was ordered by Zeus to "mix earth with water and to put in it the voice and strength of human kind, and fashion a sweet, lovely maiden shape, like to the immortal goddesses in face" (Hesiod *Works* 42). Athena was tasked with teaching "her needlework and the weaving of the various web" (42). Golden Aphrodite was commanded to "shed grace upon her head and cruel longing and cares that weary the limbs" (42). And Hermes was charged with giving "her a shameless mind and a deceitful nature" (42), not unlike his own. "So he ordered. And they obeyed the lord Zeus" (42). Hesiod writes, in *Works and Days*:

> Forthwith the famous Lame God molded clay in the likeness of a modest maid, as the son of Cronos purposed. And the goddess bright eyed Athene girded and clothed her, and the divine Graces and queenly Persuasion put necklaces of gold upon her, and the rich haired Hours crowned her head with spring flowers. And Pallas Athene bedecked her form with all manners of finery. Also the Guide, the Slayer of Argus, contrived within her lies and crafty words and a deceitful nature at the will of loud thundering Zeus, and the Herald of the gods put speech in her. And he called this woman Pandora, because all they who dwelt on Olympus gave each a gift, a plague to men who eat bread. (43)

This scene is mimed in Hesiod's *Theogony*:

> Forthwith he made an evil thing for men as the price of fire; for the very famous Limping God formed of earth the likeness of a shy maiden as the son of Cronos willed. And the goddess bright-eyed Athene girded and clothed her with silvery raiment, and down from her head she spread with her hands a broidered veil, a wonder to see; and she, Pallas Athene, put about her head lovely garlands, flowers of new grown herbs. Also she put upon her head a crown of gold which the vary famous Limping God … worked with his own hands as a favor to Zeus his father. On it was much curious work, wonderful to see; for of the many creatures which the land

and sea rear up, he put most upon it, wonderful things, like living beings with voices: and great beauty shone from it. But when he had made the beautiful evil to be the price for the blessing, he brought her out, delighting in the finery which the bright-eyed daughter of a mighty father had given her, to the place where the other gods and men were. And wonder took hold of the deathless gods and mortal men when they saw that which was sheer guile, not to be withstood by men. (22-23)

Considering the importance of image to the character of Pandora, it seemed necessary to provide the literary descriptions of her creation in full. The emphasis of Hesiod on the appearance and adornment of Pandora is consistent with the image of the Greek wife, "who was carefully adorned, even hidden behind, a profusion of finery and presented to a husband as unfamiliar to her as she was to him. She was also expected to be passive to the point of objectification, as we see in vase-paintings where the bridegroom lifts his new wife on a chariot to take her to her new home" (*Pandora* 278). The objectification of women in Greek culture is alarming, but clarifying the matter allows us to recognize the image of Pandora as, perhaps, the first objectified woman.

"Pandora was manufactured by a craftsman, who labors in his workshop as if he were producing one of the clay vases or clay statuettes with which Hesiod was familiar" (*Pandora* 278). To the potter her "clay essence, [which] associates her with Gaia," (278) is the substance of his work. She is the object of his art to be crafted and fired. The conflation of the mother with passive clay in the potter's hands is expressed by the Latin word, *mater*, which means both matter and mother and is predated by the Greek word *meter*, as in *Demeter*, who—like Gaia—is a motherhood goddess of women and the field.

The alignment of mother and matter will be further explored when we address the Stoic belief in matter's passivity in the next chapter. As Zeno of Citium is cited to have said, "the principles for the universe are God and matter. The former is the active, the latter the passive," (Achilles Tatius SVF I, 85c). Or as expressed by Stroebaeus, "matter is arranged by the universal reason, which some call fate, and which is similar to the seed in the womb" (SVF I, 87a).[48] As we can see, the same metaphorical structure applies to both situations—as with Pandora, passive matter is molded by divine reason, which is described inherently distinct from the matter itself. Here we see the duality of Promethean fire (reason) and earthen clay (mater) in the form of a fundamental and dualistic understanding of the cosmos. In compliment, Stroebaeus has given us the image of the mother as the passive matter into which the male seed enters to order the creation of a human child. As can be seen, this structure presents the literal objectification of mater—wife, mother, and matter. Pandora is made by a male craftsman, like the living statue of Pygmalion. Taken to its extreme, such objectification can be seen in the form of contemporary sexual fetishes in which women are presented as material goods.[49]

Opposite the image of male seed organizing the passive matter of a woman's womb is the notion of womb as fundamentally generative and nourishing of life in every way. "Pandora and Gaia do, indeed, have much in common, because Gaia is the womb that originates and nourishes all life. On her part, Pandora is made from earth and water, and the clay pithos that she opens initiates the cycle of life and death among mankind" (*Pandora* 286). This relationship between Pandora and Gaia is also suggested by "her very name, 'rich in gifts,' 'all-giving,' a name also of earth itself" (Downing 153-4).

"Above all, as wife and mother, woman is herself also a giver of gifts, because she produces children from her belly and gives them nurture" (Zeitlin 50).

A link between the woman's "own fertility [and] the renewal of the earth's vegetation" (*Women* 198) was recognized in the rituals of the Thesmophoria:

> In its most distinctive feature, women retrieved from underground chambers, or Megara, the remains of piglets that had been thrown in there some months before. Pigs were intimately linked with fertility, and in Greek slang a woman's genitals were referred to by terms relating to pigs. We are told by ancient commentators that the women threw back into the pit images made from dough that represented male genitals. (198)

With this example the pits of earth are associated with the womb of the woman, which completes the constellation between Gaia as the womb of nature and Pandora as the womb of humankind.

As previously mentioned, the conceptualization of the womb was extended to that of the vessel. "From earliest times we find that the Greeks were fascinated by the image of a pregnant woman containing an unseen baby inside of her. … The logical comparison of a woman's body to a container is well documented in Greek thought" (*Women as Containers* 195). "Hippocrates likened the womb to a cupping jar, and the same word, *amnion*, is used both for the membrane that surrounds the fetus and a vessel for collecting the blood of a sacrificial animal. … Aristotle speaks of the womb as an oven, and elsewhere we find the female body correlated with a treasure chamber'" (195). "Perhaps the most compelling mythical example of a vessel as a metaphor for a woman's body is the pithos (storage jar) that Pandora brings with her to Epimetheus. As Froma Zeitlin demonstrates ... the pithos is an image for Pandora's own body" (Women as Containers 196). She explains, "'the act of opening the pithos signifies the opening up of Pandora's body through sexual intercourse and childbearing" (*Pandora 277*).

Not only did "the motif of the container traditionally carry connotations of a woman's body ... mythical children are constantly associated with containers, as indeed in real life even into Classical times children were buried in vessels" (*Pandora* 277).[50] "So closely, in fact, were deceased babies associated with vessels that the slang expression for the exposure of unwanted babies was 'to put [it] in a pot'" (*Women as Containers* 196). But before proceeding from our examination of Pandora as a jar into an analysis of the jar in the myth, the story should be recounted. As Hesiod tells the story, before "the woman took off the great lid of the jar with her hands ... and her thought caused sorrow and mischief to men" (*Works* 44) they "lived on earth remote and free from ills and hard toil and heavy sickness" (44). But once the jar was opened:

> Only hope remained there in an unbreakable hime within, under the rim of the great jar ... by the will of Aegis-holding Zeus who gathers the clouds. But the rest, countless plagues, wander amongst men; for earth is full of evils and the sea is full. Of themselves diseases come upon men continually by day and by night, bringing mischief to mortals silently. (44)

With Pandora's "box" comes the reality of mortality, which is presented by Hesiod as laborious and filled with suffering—a scenario we will also find in the myths of Adam and Eve. "What is hope doing in the jar along with countless evils?" one might ask (Morford, *Classical Mythology* 49). "Is Hope, in the last analysis, the one thing that enables man to survive the terrors of this life and inspires him with lofty ambition, Yes, is it also by its very character delusive and blind, luring him on to prolong his misery? …

The hope bestowed is called blind" (49). This is a paradox that is, perhaps, never meant

to be reconciled.

The fertile wombs of Gaia and Pandora simultaneously bring the gifts of life they

presented and their promises of death, both of which were associated with "containers in

myth, ritual, and everyday life, [and were] often connected not merely with femaleness

and female fertility, but also with the human life cycle" (*Women* 195). As Sheila

Murnaghan has shown, the "woman's gift of life was always simultaneously viewed as a

gift of mortality" (*Women* 195). "Intrinsic to the birth of a child is recognition of that

child's mortality, as a life cycle begins that will inevitably end in death" (*Pandora* 277).

In the Greek tradition, "it was women who ushered the deceased out of the world through

a funerary ritual marked by anguished cries analogous to those that accompanied

childbirth" (*Women* 195). And reflective of this relationship, "In Greek myth it is the role

of the mother to tell her child that he will die; so does Hecuba remind Hector of his

mortality, and so does Thetis inform Achilles" (195).

While Aeschylus seems to present mortality as something to engage with

Promethean art and science, Hesiod's interpretation reads more like that of Silenus, the

mythic teacher to Dionysus who said that "it is best not to be born at all; and next to that,

it is better to die than to live" (ctd. by Plutarch, *Moralia;* Aristotle, *Consolatio ad*

Apollonium, sec. xxvii). According to Hesiod, mortality is a curse brought by women.

After describing the creation of Pandora in the *Theogony*, he writes:

> From her is the race of women and female kind: of her is the deadly race
>
> and tribe of women who live amongst mortal men to their great trouble. …

>And he gave them a second evil to be the price for the good they had: whoever avoids marriage and the sorrows that women cause, and will not wed, reaches deadly old age without anyone to tend his years, and though he at least has no lack of livelihood while he lives, yet, when he is dead, his kinsfolk divide his possessions amongst them. And as for the man who chooses the lot of marriage and takes a good wide suited for his mind, evil continually contends with good; for whoever happens to have mischievous children, lives always with unceasing grief in his spirit and heart within him and this evil cannot be healed. (*Theogony* 22-23)

If one does not believe in a preceding reality of immortal human life without struggle or death, Hesiod's disdain for Pandora is consistent with a general distaste for the mortal experience of human life. As previously mentioned, the angst aimed towards Pandora is reinforced by displaced anger at Gaia for the creation of life and its plane of existence.

The simultaneous release of both hope and despair from the inside of the jar given to Pandora is resonant with both the birth of a child and life's promise to an uncertain future. According to Aeschylus, "humans used to foresee their own deaths" (*Prometheus 374*), but Prometheus "ended that" (*374*), and "sent blind hopes to settle [human] hearts" (*Prometheus* 376). From this point of view, uncertainty of one's own death and hope for a desirable future are gifts to be received with the certainty of eventual death and inescapable despair.

According to a fantasy in which humans once existed in an idyllic and immortal state, the mythic action by which they were initiated into mortality is understood as the cause for a figurative *fall*. Accordingly, after the telling of Pandora's story, Hesiod recounts the fall of humanity from a golden age in which humans were free of death and toil (*Works* 169c). This notion of a "fall" will be repeatedly explored in the following chapters on philosophical materialism and the Garden of Eden, for which reason the deepest analysis of the theme will wait for the conclusion of the dissertation's first half. But the primary motifs we are going to explore can all be found in the story at hand, namely the entry into mortality and the initiation of knowledge in the context of first mater (as both mother and matter).

The most challenging task ahead is to differentiate the fall into mortality and into materiality that both trigger their own forms of existential despair. This is the challenge of splitting mater into matter and mother—perhaps as difficult as splitting a water molecule—but it must be done if we are to redeem motherhood as a gift by revealing material limitation at the foundation of Zeus' curse. The entry into mortality is obvious and has been discussed. What I have yet to emphasize is the association between the creation of humans from matter and the entry of into matter by the divine soul. What will ultimately be seen is that the fall of human life into mortality is contingent with the entry of the soul into matter; While many Greeks imagined the soul to be immortal, the material body is absolutely mortal.

The idea is captured particularly well by an Orphic tale that has been consistently associated with a story in which two Kabeiroi brothers decapitated a third, whose blood gave growth to vegetation. In the Orphic story it was said that two Titans ate Dionysus, were turned to ash by lightning, and that this ash was moistened into the clay from which humans were first formed. [51] This story is taken to express the imprisonment and entry of soul into matter—my sense is that the Promethean creation of humans from dust similarly conveys the imprisonment of psyche in matter. As we will discuss in later chapters, soul-matter duality is consistent with the way Plato (and Socrates) spoke of a divine intellect in the corporeal body as well as the way scientists came to use the description, "the ghost in the machine." The story of Eden has been similarly understood as a symbolic expression of the soul's mortal entry into material flesh.[52]

As the mind-matter (and mind-body) problem has been consistently entangled with the distinction between subject and object, so too have these aforementioned falls. Not only does the woman's act of childbirth represent mortal entry into material life. The woman herself—in both Greek civic life and the myths of Pandora—was especially objectified in the context of marriage. Though the purpose of the wedding is presumably a union, the woman was "hidden behind, a profusion of finery and presented to a husband as unfamiliar to her as she was to him" (*Pandora* 278). And, as "in the *Theogony* … man and woman remain distinct and disjoined entities" (Zeitlin 51). This expression of the impenetrability between lovers, between subject and object, matter and soul—mortal and divine—is reinforced throughout Greek (and Western) thought.

Comparatively, in Hinduism and Buddhism there are similar notions of the soul's entry into mortal flesh, and—as in the stories of Pandora and Eve—the personification of mortal and material life is a maternal figure, Maya, who appears as the Buddha's personal mother by the name of Mahamaya (Great Maya). The key difference between Maya and Mater is that while Eve is deceived into taking the fruit and Pandora the deceiver opens the box, the deception Maya personifies is that of human perception.[53] Implicit to her character is the notion that the mortal and material world that we experience as reality is in fact a misleading illusion. If there is truth in this perspective, to assume that matter is fundamentally real is to be deceived. For the husband to associate the reception of his wife with the potter's acquisition of his clay is for him to reduce the woman to matter, to which nothing should be reduced. For the husband to accept his wife as an object, as a potter accepts clay, is to fall for Zeus's trick. The mind that objectifies, as we will see throughout this dissertation, is a curse that triggers a sense of one's own estrangement and emerges in concert with matter-inspired-reason.

To pubish the god of human knowledge, the misdirection of human wisdom was a targeted punishment that could have only been delivered by Hermes. "Every negative quality Pandora possesses is a gift from Hermes … foremost among which is deceitfulness, one of Hermes' own more prominent traits" (*Pandora* 285). Considering the damage that has been done by the conceptual association of women with matter and their subsequent objectification, it should seem natural to consider this premise as the essential deception intended by Zeus. If this is true, the objectification of women and the contingent paradigm of materialistic reductionism was exactly what Zeus tricked humans into accepting, engaging and wedding.

Prometheus Bound

Long before Prometheus made men or triggered their mortality he and his family were already associated with conception and death. Hesiod wrote, "Iapetus took to wife the … maid Clymene, daughter of Ocean, and went up with her into one bed. And she bore him a stout hearted son, Atlas … very glorious Monoetius, clever Prometheus, full of various wiles, and scatter-brained Epimetheus, who from the first was a mischief to men who eat bread" (*Thegony* 19).[54] In introducing this set of brothers, Hesiod chose to draw attention to their sexual conception, which both resonates with the mortal overtones that the four of them carry and precedes the emphasis on death they introduce.

By some accounts, "Prometheus and his brother, Epimetheus, were the first mortal men" (Wolverton, 9). And Epimetheus' daughter, with Pandora, "was said to be the first mortal born" (Kerenyi, *Prometheus* 61). Similarly distinct qualities of mortality can be found in Atlas, the titan general, and Menoitios. Menoitios means "'he whom *oitos*, mortal doom awaits' … [he] may have been the 'first mortal'" (37). His death was certainly on display when "Zeus struck him with a lurid thunderbolt and sent him down to Erebus because of his mad presumption and exceeding pride" (Hesiod, *Theogony* 19). Similarly, Atlas maintained the western station where that which was above becomes that which is below, where the light goes out, and where, in so many religious mythologies, the soul goes when the body dies. Completing a hologlyphic image of mortality, Prometheus was bound as a counterpoint to his brother, at the place of the sunrise, where that which was once below becomes that which is now above, illuminated, and known.

The image of Prometheus bound to the precipice is the most pronounced in the entire story. To bind him is to restrain creativity, knowledge, craft, and rebelliousness. For the ultimate defender of freedom to be restrained is to suffer. And as with the other prominent motifs in the story, Pandora's emphasis on the mortal entry into material limitation is represented by the image of Prometheus bound to stone. But before returning to the symbolic congruity of his tether with that of the father/husband to wife and child, I would like to look more directly at Aeschylus' descriptions of Prometheus' bound and the recurring motif of the stone itself.

Aeschylus' tragedy, *Prometheus Bound,* opens with the lines of Power, a subordinate of Zeus, who has traveled with Prometheus to oversee his binding:

> And so we've come to the end of the world. / To Scythia: this howling waste/ no one passes through. / Hephaistos, now it's up to you. / What the Father wants done/ you've got to do. / On these overhanging cliffs/ with your own shatter-proof irons/ you're commanded: / Clamp this troublemaking bastard to the rock. / After all, Hephaistos, it was your glowing flower / FIRE / —the power behind all/works of hands— / he stole it, he gave it away/ to *human beings*. / That's his crime, and the Gods demand / he pay for it. / He must submit / to the tyranny of Zeus / and like it, too. / He'll learn. / He's got to give up / feeling for humanity. (1-24).

The location is a land of barren waste, the act is submission by force, the crime was the disobedient theft of fire/knowledge/ability, and the anchor of his restraint is the very rock of the mountain.[55] The kinetic activities of his rebelliousness are stifled, he is silenced as a creator, ostracized as a citizen, made impotent as a human benefactor, and in solitude— bound to rock—he suffers as feast to "a long-winged eagle, [that ate] his immortal liver … the whole day" (Hesiod, *Theogony* 20).

In the section on sacrifice we discussed the relationship between the liver of Prometheus and that of the sacrificial animal. And in the section on fire, we discussed the eagle as a symbolic representative of both Zeus and the sun. My interest in this section is more specifically on the binding of Prometheus than his sacrifice, which calls for the consideration of the stone and its recurrent appearances in the story. For example, in Pausanius' *Description of Greece,* he wrote:

> At Panopeus [in Phokis] . . . [in a] ravine there lie two stones, each of
> which is big enough to fill a cart. They have the colour of clay, not earthly
> clay, but such as would be found in a ravine or sandy torrent, and they
> smell very like the skin of a man. They say that these are remains of the
> clay out of which the whole race of man was fashioned by Prometheus.
> (10. 4. 4)

Prometheus was "worshipped as a potter in Athens" (Servius, Dougherty 50), and was identified in one of *Aesop's Fables* as "that potter who gave shape to our new generation" (Plato 530). As a potter he put the clay "statues in the kiln" to harden them to stone by way of fire (530).

Prometheus' first men and Hephaestus' Pandora were made of stone from clay. And in a complimentary story Apollodorus describes the recreation of humanity from stone. After he was saved from the flood by Prometheus and received instructions from Themis—who takes on the role of Gaia—Deucalion "picked up stones and threw them over his head; and the stones that Deucalion threw became men, and those that Pyrrha threw became women. That was how people came to be called *laoi*, by metaphor from the word *laas*, a stone" (2.2). The description of these stones as the earth's bones suggests a similarity between this story and the growth of men from (bone) teeth sown by Cadmus and Jason, both of whom were mythically initiated into the Kabeiroi cult.

The stones of Deucalion and Pyrrha, the bodies of laoi, and the hardened clay in Boeotia all reinforce the association of the human body with stone. Similarly, the reduction of humans to Pandora's clay and the reduction of all life to "Gaia, the goddess of Earth, who is described by Aristotle as the ultimate mother" (*Pandora* 286) both represent the foundational image of human life as earth and stone—as matter. Similarly, as mentioned when discussing the relationship between Gaia and Pandora, the two are both commonly presented—on ancient vases—as emerging from the earth. For example, on a vase in the Oxford museum, Pandora is accompanied by hammer wielding satyrs who appear to be working earth into her form. Presumably associated, Sophokles wrote a satyr play "between about 470 and 460 ... entitled *Pandora* or *The Hammerers* ... the few surviving fragments ... indicate that the creation of Pandora was parodied by a chorus of hammer-wielding Satyrs who participated in beating the clay that formed Pandora's image" (*Pandora* 286).[56] If we recognize Prometheus as a representative of humans, the association of the human body with stone combines with the image of Prometheus' restraint to stone to hint at the image of human bondage to body as stone.

Though the suffering of Prometheus was clearly associated with that of humanity, as the personification of a creator his bondage to stone can also be seen in the context of an artist's dependence on material. Kerenyi points out, "In Goethe's mythologem Prometheus' work of creation is indeed limited exclusively to what he can create on the earth" (8). As potters, clay is the matter of their art. As metallurgists (or Alchemists), the analogy translates into the material from which they make their work.[57] The same could be true of any material for any art; and though we have been discussing the relationship between humans and their material bodies, the limitation of the creator to material substance limits human creativity and intelligence to the boundaries of matter. From this angle we can see that the chaining of Prometheus to stone as expressive of the limitation of a creator to their material resources.

The power of Promethean creation is depicted as chained to the earthly domain, and the creation of humans is consistently from earthly matter, the embodiment of which is Pandora, mother of all humans. We should note, as Pandora was associated with Gaia, Gaia has been associated with Cybele, *Magna Mater*, the Phrygian mother goddess who was known in antiquity as "Mountain Mother" (Haspels, I. 293).[58] With this in mind, we might see Prometheus' bondage to the mountain as mimetic with human marriage to Pandora. In this way, insofar as the woman was associated with her stores and the mountain its resources, we again recognize the motif of the father/craftsman's restraint to resource. Having considered the material limitations of humans and creators, we should more fully consider the typically oversimplified interpretation of Prometheus' tether as a symbolic representation of the husband/father bound to wife & child.

In the context of mortality, "hope" concerns future life, which distills to its purist form in the image of a baby. Not only does new life bring hope, but as hope clings to the jar while the plagues rush free, the baby remains bound to the mother when the water and bloody afterbirth are expelled by a screaming (or dead) woman. With this image we recognize the umbilical flesh as a bond between the new human and mother—who personifies the fertile earth. This image of the baby bound to mater (mother) is not unlike the image of Prometheus chained to mater (stone), where new day opens from the earth. The parallel continues into the resonance of hope with both Prometheus and the child, as they both represent new life and spark. If we follow this alignment, then we see an image of hope stuck to the rim of the jar as resonant with both the image of Prometheus chained to the rim of earth,[59] and a baby bound by its umbilical cord to the opening of a maternal vessel. Prometheus and the baby embody hope, and similarly, the clay mother from the potter's wheel is both mater and vessel—the stone and the jar.[60] If we continue following these connections then we have to consider the binding of hope to the mother, and the binding of Prometheus (as man) and child to the same mother, which together present the structure of a nuclear family.

The association of marriage with Prometheus' shackles is reinforced by his marriage to Asia, whose name is associated with the land of the rising sun and his bondage to stone at the place of the sunrise. A link between the ring and marriage was known to antiquity through a version of the wedding between Peleus and Thetis in which Prometheus was said to bear "'the faded scars of the ancient penalty,' that is, the ring" (Kerenyi, *Prometheus* 124).[61] This ring was given to him by Zeus as a replacement for his bondage after "warning [Zeus] not to marry Thetis," which led to the scene of her marriage with Peleus (123). Rings are worn today as an expression of marriages, in Spanish the word for "wife" is literally "handcuffs" (*esposa*), and we still hear wives (tastelessly) referred to as a "ball and chain." The association of marriage with bondage and the ring with that binding is as understood now as it was in ancient Greece—as is the difference between points of view that see bonds as shackles or links. But whether we want to live with a life-affirming or life-negating point of view—such as Aeschylus' or Hesiod's respectively—to be married and to have a child is to be bound, for which there is ready symbolism in the umbilical cord and shackle.

Blame has been heaped on the first mortal woman and her "box;" but this sounds like a husband blaming a wife for being married, having children, and the reality of life entailed thereby. Where one man will blame his wife and child for his work to feed them, or the stress they load into his life, another man (or the same man on another occasion) will describe his lover and child as a source of joy. The man's perspective is as relevant to interpreting the situation as the innate character of his wife.[62] This is why it is crucial to remember the positive relationship between Prometheus and Athena as evidence that, as a whole, the myth of Prometheus does not communicate a message that women are all evil—no matter how Pandora is understood.

In the context of a wife, there is no avoiding the fact that a personification of freedom is going to feel constrained by such ulterior responsibilities as a wife and child. On the other hand, Prometheus is resolutely paternal, and whether we are talking about an individual child or the entirety of humanity, parenting is the quintessential form of human creation. It should also be noted that there is no mention of tension between Prometheus and his wife; in fact, in Percy Shelley's *Prometheus Unbound*, the Titan remembers "drinking life from her loved eyes" (I.I 123) and laments over the loss of his life with Asia, "who, when [his] being overflowed, Wert like a golden chalice to bright wine, / Which else had sunk into the thirsty dust" (I.I 809-11).

If we are to see beyond the domestic interpretation of Prometheus bound while continuing to recognize that his bondage is expressive of the reality Pandora brings, we will have to continue our contemplation of the riddle into the less-human figure of Gaia and her world of material mortality. If we recognize the relationships between the material world and mortal life represented by Gaia and Pandora, then the stone to which Prometheus is bound becomes illuminated as a symbol of this world itself. Thus we see the progenitor as restrained to both the Earthly and the Earth, the worldly and the world, a life with a wife on the planes of her earth.

If the stone can be seen as representative of Gaia and her matter, its location at the sunrise should be associated with her cycles. In addition to emerging from the mother's matter, her cycles give rise to humans. In a previous section we discussed the fruit given by Athena as a symbol of mortal knowledge that conveys a mimetic relationship between the sexuality of mothers and earth: Both must be parted for impregnation, and penetrated. A seed must be planted, which will gestate and grow until born through her surface. After cutting the umbilical cord or plucking the fruit, the increasingly independent offspring grows erect. Upon maturation the process repeats, whether we are talking about the lifespan of a human or nature's annual seasons, which, like the body of a woman, changes in cycles.[63] Just as the birth of the new sun is associated with the birth of a child,[64] so too is the opening of Pandora's vessel, or rather, the vessel that is Pandora.

Once individuals come to recognize that they are made of substance and from a cycle it is only a matter of time before some come to imagine themselves as limited to their substance and trapped within their cycle. As it is from the mother's matter and cycles that an individual is born, it seems obvious—if not infantile—to blame ones mother for being born, and thus for the entry of the soul into the fallen earth of suffering and limitation. As in many traditions, prominent strains of the Greek religion present life in the flesh and in the cycle of mortality as an imprisonment within a fallen reality. We have already discussed the Orphic myth in which divine essence becomes trapped in human flesh by way of the Titans.

The Pythagoreans, who advanced the Orphic tradition, perpetuated this point of view, as did Plato, a student of the Pythagorean tradition who, through the story of Socrates' death, taught a comparable view of immortal souls in corporeal bodies. These philosophers all recommended an ascetic transcendence of the body and its cravings, which were treated as both prisons of the mind and as agents of polluted thought. Though the negative attitude towards matter was withdrawn by Classical and European scientists, the variously imagined "ghost in the machine," mimes the same pattern as that presented by Plato, Pythagoras, the Orphics, and the stories of Prometheus in which matter and psyche are seen to be craft and captain.

From this paradigm, to choose to enter into the reality of material mortality requires a seduction, which is exactly what Pandora represents. Gorgeous and garlanded, she represents the soul's fundamental attractions that commit it to this world. Expressive of the sexuality in her seductive allure was Aphrodite's gift to her, "*pothos*, a word that means sensuous longing" (*Pandora* 277). As decreed by Zeus, the "sheer, hopeless snare" (Hesiod, *Works* 43) made humans "glad of heart while they embrace[d] their own destruction" (42). Though Pandora's first snare was her material beauty, perhaps nothing more fully commits an individual to life in this world than the creation of a bond with spouse and child. From this line of thinking, the seduction of Pandora's material body is into the reality of mortality, which—like the bones in glistening fat—was seen as the deceit of a misguiding appearance. As the world herself, "she was, Hesiod tells us, a kalon kakon, a beautiful evil" (*Pandora* 277). As mentioned in the last section, comparisons with these notions can be found in the Hindu and Buddhist figure of Maya—a female personification of the seductive reality to which humans are limited— and in Abrahamic interpretations of Eve. Common to all of these stories is the seduction of divine essence or soul by (and into) matter as personified by a mother.

It is essential to distinguish a difference between a reaction to the fall of one's soul into material existence, and an individual's commitment to parenting and marriage. We talked about interpretations of bondage that are based on family life, and why these interpretations seem shallow and inconsistent with the deeper nature of Prometheus—an archetypal father figure. Still, there is a reason for this entanglement. Implicit to the world-negating ascetic belief systems—as were common in Greece—is the notion that, if one's psyche or soul is not attached to this world, it will be able to transcend to a purer existence. There is no deeper source of attachment to this world than a child and spouse.

In Hindu traditions, the liberation from one's attachment to this world is called *moksha*. But from this perspective the fall is not into Mater, it is into Maya—not into the substance of reality, but into its web of entangled delusion. More specifically, what keeps one trapped in this fallen or less free reality is specifically the delusion of one's own mind. From this paradigm, if we believe the fall is into matter, it is because we perceive Maya as matter without recognizing that matter reduces to Maya. This seems to be exactly what is going on in the story, if not in the history of Western materialism—the delusional reduction of reality to matter when the experience of matter is in fact misleading our knowledge.

As the body of Prometheus was restrained—by matter to matter—Pandora participated in the psyche's imprisonment of itself in the materialistic paradigm. My interpretation is that this is what Zeus gave "men as the price for fire" (Hesiod, *Works* 42). Fire is the knowledge of how to work matter, to which Zeus responded by tricking humans into gladly imprisoning themselves within matter, or rather, in the system of *thought* that finds its foundations in matter. The immediate consequence of the philosophical misstep is the reduction of mother to material and the objectification of women, which limits the psyche's potential for knowledge. What could be more traumatic to Prometheus than this: The corruption of human wisdom by way of corrupting the human understanding of matter and mother in such way that leads to an enmity between the sexes, objectification, and the limitation of creativity?

The wisest of humans have dedicated their undivided efforts in various attempts to show us the difference(s) between reality and reality-as-we-know-it through perceptions, thoughts, and misunderstandings. In the Hindu and Buddhist traditions, liberation from Maya is sometimes understood as a transcendence from the world, but the interpretations I most connect with—and that I consider most relevant in this context— suggest that moksha is a liberation from the suffering and limitations produced by misunderstandings of reality. The liberation is not from reality, or from nature, it is from the self-generated illusion of reality that results from miss-interpretations. If the understanding is that the liberation is from earth, then nature and mater are demonized; but if the liberation is from a state that results from misunderstanding nature and mater, then such demonization is clearly misplaced. This makes all of the difference. This is the distinction that must be made if we are to simultaneously appreciate the lessons of Pandora and Eve without falling into the trap of demonizing mater.

In our final analysis before concluding the chapter, we should return to the most iconic image of the Promethean mythologem in which he is chained to stone. This is the culminating image of our conversation about the creation of humans from stone and the limitation of the human mind to the materialistic paradigm. The stone to which he is chained is not unlike the hardened clay that can still be found in Boeotia or the stones thrown by Deucalion and Pyrrha. On one hand Prometheus' binding to stone is representative of his commitment to humans—the laoi—like a father to his child; and on the other hand, it presents stone as that which limits the humans he represents.[65]

To be bound is to have boundaries. If matter sets the boundaries of all humans, then humans are bound to the matter out of which they are made. Reinforcing this parallel, Prometheus is not just chained to stone, he was "wedged … into [the] ravine," (Aeschylus, *Prometheus Bound* 910). This is more consistent with his Georgian counterpart, Amirani, who was buried under chains in a cave within the Caucasus mountains for teaching humans the art of metallurgy (Colavito 6). Similarly, a local account from the days of Alexander the Great describes "Prometheus' cave, where he had been chained" (Arrian, 1983, p. 5.3.2). So while humans are limited to their bodies, to their stone(s), Prometheus' body is described as bound both to and within stone. Another parallel can be found in the Nart version of Pkharmat, who stole fire to save humans (freezing) in a cave for which he was punished with shackles at the top of (the Caucasian) Mt. Kazbek.[66]

The image of being enclosed by restraints is reiterated when Power tells Hephaestus to "slap those iron bands around his ribs" (Aeschylus, *Prometheus Bound* 112-113)." And again when a link in his chain became a "ring to bear" (Kerenyi, *Prometheus* 124). It can also be found in the image of the wreath he was given as a "reminder of his captivity" (124). While amplifying on the image of circular enclosure, it should be noted that one of his few allies in the plays of Aeschylus was Oceanus, the world encircling serpent/ocean. Though the god is benevolent in this story, in the

Egyptian and Norse traditions the world-encircling snake is a limiting if not imprisoning force that must be defeated to end a day/age and establish a new dawn.[67]

These images of enclosure and the Promethean personification of humans as restrained to stone are both consistent with the religious understanding, as exampled in the Orphic story, of the human spirit becoming tethered to the human body—to the stone. This might be seen as the birth of the divine into the human body—the role first committed by Pandora. In the stories within the Promethean mythologem, the body is repeatedly associated with clay and stone as the raw matter from which humans are formed—and to which humans are bound. Meanwhile, the power of animation, consciousness and intelligence are presented as non-native to matter. Like the later European vision of ghost-like consciousness within a material machine, the Promethean myth presents fire (perhaps in the form of a metaphor) as that which brings body to life.

The interlinked stories of Pandora and the punishment of Prometheus both convey the entry of humanity into material and mortal lives. Hope is all that remained once humans became mortal, married and material. Hesiod's stories are laden with animosity for the mother and wife, but the inconsistencies of this animosity with the character of Prometheus triggered our deeper investigation into the other qualities of Pandora— namely her material form. What we found is that, when seen in association with (Gaia) earth and bodily birth, the negative interpretation of Pandora constellates with the negative interpretation of body and the imprisonment of human essence by later Greek philosophers and mystery traditions like the Orphics, Pythagoreans and Platonists (to be discussed in coming chapters).

Reflections of Prometheus

In the last two sections we introduced details of the myth that communicate a symbolic entry of knowledge/reason/consciousness—fire—into mothers/bodies/ stone/clay/civilization to which such living and theoretical intelligence as represented by fire become limited/restrained—bound. Before we amplify our focus into these examples and what they mean, I want to offer a more general reflection on the details of the myth this chapter has explored. We have worked through the central scenes in which Prometheus creates humans, opposes Zeus for human freedom, invents the sacrifice, steals knowledge, and is bound. What I will now attempt to reveal is that the essential qualities of each major scene emanate throughout the entire myth. For example, we have the scene of Prometheus creating humans, but his creative essence is not bound to the act. We have seen his first ritual sacrifice, but we have also explored sacrificial expressions throughout the myth. This section will listen to the echoes of Promethean creativity, the fight for freedom, sacrifice, fire/knowledge delivery, bondage (and connectivity) that reverberate throughout the narrative.

Stretching back to the beginning of the myth, we see his creative qualities in every step: He advises Zeus on how to defeat the titans and create the Olympian order; he created humans and ensured their existence beyond the flood; he created a simultaneous bridge and rift between the gods and humans; he stole and shared the fiery knowledge required to create, for which Zeus mandated his protégé, Hephaestus, to craft a reality in which the progenitor is bound and first mother wed (by making the wife and shackles). This makes the act of Prometheus responsible for the creation of human life as we know it—with birth and death as mothers and fathers who are yoked for their family's food and wellbeing in the face of countless threats and inevitable suffering. In times of human suppression and creative repression Prometheus is a rebel and creator of freedom. In his unbound and free state, he is a husband, teacher, and craftsmen-artist.

It is not just as creator that he acts in each story, the major motifs of his actions can be found in every turn. As a rebel he rebelled against the Titans with Zeus, the Olympians with humans, the Persians with Athens, European tyrannies, Catholic tyrannies, and so on. Creation itself is a rebellion against the status quo, in its very nature it is change. This is the rebelliousness of his station, the sunrise, which brings a brand new day with each rising. Creating humans and mentoring them into creators is an exponentially larger reiteration of the same rebelliousness. His salvation of humans from the flood was outside Zeus' orders, at Mekone his trick on Zeus was a jeer at his authority, and once fire was withheld and he stole it back he became a full-fledged rebel in exile.

His most directly rebellious acts are heavy with sacrifice—fighting against his beloved brother Atlas to support the Olympians, the sacrifice itself at Mekone, and the sacrifice of himself for the retrieval of fire. The burnt offering is in response for human creation and their survival of the flood, and is meant to sustain the existence of humans by way of divine favor. And while Prometheus sacrifices himself to deliver fire to humans, humankind pays the penance of life after Pandora. Chiron later self-sacrificed to take Prometheus' place, and the ritual sacrifice of animal livers continued in his stead.

Prometheus' shared knowledge with Zeus on how to defeat the titans, and with the knowledge of a craftsman made humans, whom he animated with the fire of consciousness and knowledge. He gave foresight to Deucalion and Pyrrha to save them from the flood. And he invented the burnt offering, which angered Zeus and triggered his rebellious theft of fire, without which the wisdom he has shared—according to Plato's *Protagoras*—is effectively useless. For his theft he was chained to the Caucasus Mountains, where the solar fire rises; and was tortured by an eagle, which is a simultaneous representation of Zeus and the sun. Fire and/or knowledge appear in every turn of the myth—except the making of Pandora and the opening of her jar. These are not the results of using fire, they are the consequences of its implicit rebelliousness.

Every consequence carries the qualities of bondage. Beyond the restraint of Prometheus to stone by tyrannical forces and the restraint of the Titans in Tartarus, the appearance of Pandora spells the beginning of marital, parental, natural, and corporeal bonds. As the mater of human kind, she has been used to represent the matter into which the human psyche has entered (to be born) and the resulting limitation of life to material flesh—described as clay and stone. Her story represents the original bonding of *mother* and *matter* into the image of *mater*. This conflation has participated in the binding of human minds to a mater-born self-image. This myth also reinforces the reductive (and obstructive) view of women as object—not just as matter, but as the male subject's object to be molded. Beyond the wife/mother, matter itself is presented as the craftsman's object to mold. Reflecting on the original creation of humans from clay, where life is interpreted as bondage, bondage is the creation of humans—by Prometheus or Pandora.

But a bond is also a bridge. The foundation of the burnt offering not only bound mortals to gods by sacrifice, it also established a bond and bridge to divinity. This is the function of Prometheus at the sunrise, to bridge the world below to the world above—the darkness to the light—in the form of prophecy, as midwife to Athena, and as the spark of knowledge we all know and seek. This is the function of the parent, whose bond with the child brings them from the unknown world they came from—with what essence they brought with them—into this world as parent and guide. It might also be suggested that lovers can do this for one another, that their bond allows them to elucidate and draw forth qualities from depths that would otherwise go unstirred. The two-sided nature of the bond is at play in the mythologem of Prometheus as much and as consistently as the fire motif, sacrifice, rebelliousness, and creation.

When we look at the stories of Prometheus in light of one another, on one level the chronology is essential, and on another, it completely dissolves. Of course creation comes before survival, which comes before a relationship with the divine can be established, which comes before a rift can occur, which comes before punishment, which explains why there is death, necessary birth, the need to eat, and the unavoidable work required to obtain food and sustain a family's livelihood. There are valuable insights to be gained from a chronological analysis, but the a-temporal overlay of the myth's core motifs has shown that their essences can be found in every major scene. What this suggests is that each of these elements are core to the myth's essence and meaning.

No over-complication is needed to say that these are Classical stories on the origins of our human conditions. Our bodies are made of material—clay or stone in the myth(s). We have intelligence that we can experientially distinguish from the material plane of our body's existence, presented by Prometheus as the gift of fire. At a level to which no animal can compare, we use conscious knowledge to change reality from how it is to how we want it to be, which often means creating clever tools and methods to procure food, make wares, and construct shelter. We suffer and will all know mortality, but if we follow Prometheus, the human way to engage our lives is through the creative arts, sciences, and the pursuit of knowledge.

Having further explored the inner-net of the mythic narrative between the creation of humans and the establishment of the human condition. I want to pull out the core elements and details that convey an entry into and/or imprisonment within substance. The most obvious images of human entry into and restraint to matter are those in which, 1, Prometheus brings the spark of consciousness to the men he makes from clay, and 2, his own bondage to rock. Not only does the remainder of the clay harden into stone, but so were humans known as stone, laoi, after Prometheus' offspring, Deucalion, repopulated the earth with stone-born humans. He also told Deucalion and his wife to enter into an ark to hide from the flood, which mimes the entry of psyche into a bodily vessel. Prometheus participated in the imprisoning of titans within the earth—including his father. His brother is similarly in bondage as the carrier of the earth (and sometimes cosmos). As Prometheus and Deucalion populated the planet with clay and stone, Pandora and all subsequent mothers have birthed the population from their material bodies, which, as we have seen, were highly associated with matter itself (most specifically earth). In this way the figures of Pandora and Gaia, as mothers of all, personify material primacy. The congruence of the umbilical cord and chain (to mother and mountain) further express such bondage to mater. Even Pandora and Gaia themselves were presented as emerging from earthen ground. In these examples, they are often surrounded by craftsmen to be associated with Prometheus or Hephaestus, who, like the master and protégé, used substance to craft. Like all creators of material things, the limitation is material resource. Insofar as the mountain symbolizes those resources, the restriction of the creator to the mountain conveys his dependence on resource. Insofar as his restraint keeps him on earth as opposed to Olympus, we see his bondage as expressive of the human captivity in the world below heaven. According to the myth, the post-golden age humans are mortal and they labor for food in a world filled with such strife as was freed by Pandora.

We have reflected on the bondage motif already, and so we should naturally recognize its resonance with such entries into matter and/or restraint thereby. What we can see is that the entry into bondage and enclosure, while constellated with an entry into matter, is the more overt theme. In the next chapter we will explore why this constellation is so important. For now I want to extend the images of bondage and material entry into those of enclosure, isolation, and the separation of humans from gods.

The schism between mortals and humans was notably established at Mekone, experienced as the mortalization of humans, and symbolized by the benefactor's exile. The association of separation with material restraint—to the body or the stone—is a key motif for our dissertation, one to which we will return after our chapter on Adam. Unfortunately, we do not know the secrets of the Kabeiroi cult, which must have involved a profound interpretation of human clay, fire, Prometheus' restraint, the imprisoned Titans, and their iron rings. But we do know that the Greek philosophical and Orphic mystery traditions later permeated the Mediterranean with a shared view of the soul as that which animates body—not unlike the fire of Prometheus. We also know that Orpheus was mythically initiated into the mysteries of the Kabeiroi as an Argonaut, with Herakles, and that the labor of the great hero that followed his encounter with Prometheus and Atlas included an initiation into the Eleusinian mysteries, which, like the

Orphic mysteries, were concerned with immortality. We might recall that, at least in myth, Prometheus and Hephaestus, as Kabeiroi, accepted the mysteries of Demeter and Persephone. Though there is too much mystery to assert with any certainty, it seems that the geographical and mythical entwining of the Kabeiroi mysteries with those of Eleusis and Orpheus suggest a continuity of concern for the human soul. The prevalence of such concern in Greek philosophy further suggests that the interest in an immortal soul within a mortal body was a major part of the religious and intellectual atmosphere surrounding the Kabeiroi mysteries.

Beyond such contextual evidence for the interpretation of the myth as expressive of psyche's imprisonment within matter, I have attempted to demonstrate how it symbolically communicates this perspective rather clearly. The creation of humans with clay and their animation with spark followed by the restraint of the knowledge-bringer to stone seem to especially convey such an understanding. If the myth is to be interpreted this way, Prometheus' restraint to stone would be a precursor and parallel to the Orphic/Pythagorean/Socratic/Platonic view of the soul as imprisoned within the body (which has been associated with stone throughout the myth of Prometheus). In the next chapter we will look more closely at these later developments in Greek religious thought and reflect on the legacy of Prometheus' myth. Perhaps the variant image of Prometheus imprisoned within a cave (as mimed in the images of Amirani and Chiron) best conveys the notion of the fiery soul imprisoned within the material body. As we will see, this image mimes that of Adam in his cave.

Mixed into this story of the establishment of human life is a foundational curse or inciting misstep—perhaps even a delusion—that leads to all that is evil in this world.

When Prometheus created humans and Pandora gave birth to the human race, the step being taken was the entry of the human psyche into the paradigm of corporeal matter. This is synchronic with the binding of Prometheus to stone, which is the same matter as that fire-hardened clay he animated with knowledge. Unlike the story of the flood, sacrifice, or fire theft, Prometheus was restrained and unable to help when Pandora appeared. For each good step in human creation he was free, but the negative and restrictive qualities of human life could only be established with Prometheus bound. The question of just how negative this is and the overlay of a world-negating paradigm will be of our continued consideration.

By no means has enough been said in this chapter, and after further conversations around matter and Eve, whether or not to affirm life in this world—what Camus considers the most pressing question of the human condition—will remain a challenging center to our discussion. It would have been a distraction from this chapter to spend enough time on Pandora and the mother, Greek religion, and Greek philosophy; but all of these subjects will be more deeply addressed as we proceed into the next chapters on the Greek rise of philosophical and scientific materialism followed by a more religious exploration into the expulsion of Adam and Eve. As the mythological approach I have taken in this chapter grows to include the philosophical conversations of the next, we will follow the growth of Promethean knowledge into Greek intellectual thought—fire—to track its recurrent reduction of nature to matter and the ushering in of the philosophical, scientific, and eventually common sense paradigm of materialism.

Chapter 3: Birth of Theoretical Materialism

Philosophical and Scientific Origin Stories of Knowledge

The focus of this chapter is on the intellectual origin story of Western philosophy and science remembered as the "Pre-Socratic" period. We will begin in Miletus, the Eden of Western thought where the often retold stories of philosophy, science, materialism, and the atom begin. With Thales, Anaximenes, Anaximander and Leucippus—all Milesians—we will witness the first philosophers present the foundational premises of materialism and atomism.

In the following wave of Pre-Socratics, from Pythagoras and Heraclitus to the Monists (Parmenides and Zeno) and Pluralists (Empedocles and Anaxagoras), the clear notions of flux (logos), geometric form, singular *monad(s)*, and the plurality of sensate-experience were added. Returning to Miletus, Leucippus and his student Democritus synthesized all of these contributions into their theory of atomism, which reduces the cosmos to a plurality of monadic matter whose interactions result from the mechanical interaction of geometric mass in motion. As many scholars from our conversation will attest, the theory of atomism remained influential throughout the Alexandrian and Roman eras before influencing European philosophers and scientists like Descartes and Newton, whose scientific theories became uniquely responsible for the atomistically anchored Scientific Revolution and Enlightenment.

What working through this history will show us, I believe, is first that materialism (and atomism) are essential to the Pre-Socratic origin story of Western philosophy and science, and second, that these foundations continued to serve foundational roles throughout the historical development of the traditions—especially through the

Enlightenment. Insofar as the philosophical convictions behind the Scientific Revolution and *Declaration of Independence* were deeply rooted in Enlightenment philosophies—many of which were inherited from Greek predecessors—such Elightenment anchors as materialism and atomism played integral roles in the paradigm of an era that witnessed the breakthrough liberation of Western individuals from religious and governmental tyrants. An echo can be heard from the previous chapter, in which an entry into a materialistic cosmology is contingent with rebelliousness against God and state.

While the topical tension between the history of atomic theory and the attention modern physicists give to wave dynamics is central to the dissertation, the reason I find it so important is because I believe we can and do project the meta-structures of atoms onto human beings (citizens) and material goods (things). This is where the conversation at hand carries ideological implications. The projection of atomistic metaphors into economics and politics (as well as moral theory) is natural when one is considering these fields of study from within a paradigm that assumes a foundation of causal interactions between material atoms. As we will see, even the first atomists were interested in the moral implications that derive from the theory. That having been said, later chapters will discuss the evolving understanding of atoms and how the social, moral, psychological, and cosmological theories they inspire might correspondingly evolve. As we will see, the Enlightenment tendency to reduce bodies, things (and more) to billiard-ball building-block atoms continues today despite radical transformations within atomic theory. And as we will find, when (Classical) atomic projections are withdrawn from citizens and products, we also withdraw patterns of isolation and internally inert matter from objects.

*   *   *

From the Promethean origin story of human knowledge to the origin story of Western philosophy, we turn from an analysis of myth to a recounting of history. The communication of Western thought as a story has been a tradition since at least the time of Aristotle, whose lecture notes present the premise of materialism as philosophy's first move. Even today, Thales is dutifully presented as the first philosopher, and his belief that everything is made up of water is consistently interpreted as a reduction of all things to one type of thing—*matter*. By the end of the dissertation it will seem necessary to re-examine this interpretation in the contexts of, one, his parallel description of matter as ensouled, and two, his emphasis on water—the substance that most clearly demonstrates (non-particulated) wave behavior; however, the following chapter is primarily dedicated to the story of Western thought as it has been remembered and retold. As compared with the story of Prometheus, in which the relevance of materialistic concepts were, perhaps, symbolically overt, the following chapter will demonstrate the explicit centrality of theoretical materialism to the storied birth of philosophy.

As a mythologist retelling this history, I have to step back and make a certain point. The start of the story with Thales and the focus on the historical developments of theoretical materialism is becoming a less interesting narrative as a result of global intellectual movements that simultaneously recognize the limitations of materialism and the development of science outside Classical and European spheres. If the story towards materialistic theory is no longer a narrative of how we came to Truth, it is a story of how we came to the – extremely fruitful – paradigm of materialism. As we tell it now, the story continues into the breakthroughs of Einstein, who, as one of the essential heroes in the history of science, showed matter to not be foundational ($E = \mathrm{mc}^{2}$), and that particles are more than mere stones (Nobel Prize: Photoelectric Effect). For this reason, when we retell the mythic narrative of philosophical history, previously ignored historic details are now essential plot-points in the narrative as it unfolds towards our contemporary scientific perspective. For the purposes of this dissertation, the narrative to which this chapter tends carries both agendas: to walk through the history of materialistic theory *and* to recognize non-materialist plot-points in history that demonstrate philosophical interest in wave dynamics. Above these agendas, as in the last chapter on Prometheus, I will do my best to include oft told details of the story whether or not they relate to the dissertation's themes.

In retelling the narrative I also mean to emphasize the influence of religion and mythology on the psyches of canonical Greek philosophers. This means that—in addition to further examining the usual recognition of Orphic tendencies in Pythagoras and Plato, or Homeric justice in philosophical theories of balance—I want to look at the environment of mythic beliefs from which Milesian philosophy was born. Naturally, our most immediate curiosity concerns the potential influence of Prometheus. Following the last chapter it might be theorized that a religious relationship with the Titan of knowledge and the Kabeiroi could lead to an idealized pursuit of human knowledge on what could become a philosophical level. Whether or not this historically occurred is difficult to discern, but the storied first philosophers certainly came from a city where the Kabeiroi were worshipped. Such connections will be the threads through the following section.

From Myth to Philosophy

Before starting into a secular history of Greek thought, to enter the mindset of the first philosophers and their peers, "we must," according to Guthrie, "realize how completely identified were the state and its religion" (82). "The gods were worshipped at festivals which were state occasions, and participation in them was part of the ordinary duties and activities of a citizen as such" (82). All of the philosophical figures we will be investigating would have been intimate—as citizens—with the festivals, rites, and stories at the heart of their cities. With this in mind, we should be sensitive to the echoing of religious beliefs through early philosophical history.

While Hesiod wrote from Boeotia, in mainland Greece, Homer is said to have lived in Smyrna—just north of Miletus and south of Troy—on the Ionian coast of modern-day Turkey. His epics were well known throughout Ionia, and were certainly represented in Miletus, which boasted the largest agora in the Mediterranean during the first philosopher's lifetime. Terrence Irwin writes—foreshadowing the philosophical study of order—as "Homer conceives the gods, they are not mechanisms ... not random ... [they have] steady purposes and intentions" (14). He points out, "Zeus and the fates ... suggest two different types of order" (17). "The many gods and natural forces suggest that the world is only partly predictable, and only partly under intelligent control. The role of the fates suggests total determination, but perhaps without intelligent control" (19). While the fates suggest an impersonal amoral order independent of human or divine choice, Homer also presents the idea that "Zeus's will is in control...[and] concerned with justice in human societies" (17). In the context of philosophical history, though Homer "presents his views (or the views expressed in his poems) in narrative verse, not in philosophical argument; [they] are neither primitive nor unreasonable" (7). Irwin even goes as far as to say that, in "looking for regularity, laws, and order in natural processes, Homer begins a search that dominates Greek ... philosophical thinking" (14).

The themes of human justice and anthropomorphic order foreshadowed the self-referential world-views of Protagoras and the Sophists.[68] Similarly, the theme of an impersonal and unconscious order can be found in the earlier Egyptian notion of Ma'at, for example, and later, in the philosophical development of the Heraclitean Logos. This kind of impersonal order might also be compared to the Chinese *Tao* or Japanese *Wa*. Even the scientific vision of calculus and mechanical causality was seen by Newton himself as organically related with the divine.[69] Similarly, both Einstein and Hawking follow the tendency of describing our universe as "the mind of God."[70] Though the birth-story of science is usually described as an ascent towards secularism—a central theme in our ongoing conversation—we should recognize the religious roots and continued relevance of divinity in visions of cosmic order.

In addition to the influence of Homer and Hesiod, magic was common in Ancient Greece before, during, and after the rise of philosophical thought. Guthrie writes, "Fundamental was the law of sympathy, which posited a natural connection between certain things which to us seem to have no such connection at all. … This sort of connection exists between a man and his image or portrait … between things or people and their names" (Guthrie 12-13). He gives the example, "even to write the name of an enemy on a lead plate, transfix it and bury it (thus consigning it to the powers of the underworld), could injure or kill him" (12-13). The laws of sympathetic magic and symbolism are virtually mimetic; in fact, it might be said that both depend on the power of mimesis itself. Mimesis, symbolism, and sympathetic magic are based on the recognition of a valued potency in the resonant or congruent sameness of color, sound, shape, gesture, cycle, narrative, or any form of form.

Synesthesia and abstract thought play crucial roles to this mode of intellectual development. Where synesthesia supports the recognition of key likenesses across different sensory and emotional experiences—the 'sharpness' of cheese for example, or the 'melting' of a heart—abstract thought seeks a comprehension of sameness beyond substance, for example, the elucidation of 'circle' from separate experiences of sun, moon, fruit, and eye. This sort of thinking naturally nourishes the philosophical development of geometric forms and unchanging abstract ideas. Among the first philosophers, Guthrie writes, "the Pythagoreans, being a religious brotherhood as well as a philosophical school, show many traces of [sympathetic thought]. The earlier of them maintained that 'things were numbers'. To demonstrate it they said: 'Look! 1 is a point (·), 2 a line (—), 3 a surface (Δ), and 4 a solid (■). Thus you have solid bodies generated from numbers'" (14). From their line of reasoning, as we will see, number, shape, and pitch were seen as interrelated forms that establish and transcend human sensate reality.

The most direct religious influence on Pythagoreans came from the Orphics, who we introduced in the last chapter. Campbell writes,

> In the earlier Orphic system a negative attitude had been assumed toward the world. According to the great Orphic myth, man was represented as a compound of the ashes of Dionysus and the Titans. The soul (Dionysus factor) was divine, but the body (Titan factor) held it in bondage. The watchword, therefore, was *soma sema*, 'the body, a tomb.' And a system both of thought and of practice, exactly paralleling that of Indian asceticism, was communicated by initiated masters to little circles of devotees. The soul, it was declared, returned repeatedly to life, bound to

the wheel of rebirth (compare the Sanskrit samsara). Through asceticism (Sanskrit, tapas) however, the body could be purged of its Titan dross (Sanskrit, nirjara, 'shedding') and the soul released (Sanskrit, moksha, 'release')" (*Occidental* 183).

This notion of the soul's liberation from the body conveys an implicit vision of the body and mind as divisible. Socrates and Plato perpetuated this perspective of the Pythagoreans and Orphics. As the story goes, when faced with the requirement of his own suicide, Socrates anticipated the liberation of his psyche and the wisdom that would follow its freedom from body.

In the last chapter we looked at several Orphic references of Prometheus and the Kabeiroi. We also considered the potential that its myth conveys the psyche's constriction to substance—a belief shared by the Orphics, Pythagoreans, and Plato. If we look for the potential presence of the Kabeiroi somewhere near the roots of philosophical history, we find them in Miletus – the storied birthplace of philosophy. Sandra Blakely recounts the story:

> The king of Assessos was murdered by his brother, and his children, fearing for their lives, fled to neighboring Miletos. Their murderous uncle pursued, with the army of Assessos, and laid siege to the town. The people prayed for relief, and were told that help would come from Phrygia. This help appeared the next day in the form of two young men, Tottes and Onnes, who appeared out of Phrygia, bearing a *kiste*, a basket, between them that they carried with two poles; inside were the sacra of the Kabeiroi. They promised to save the town from its aggressors, if the

people would establish the rites of the gods. The city council accepted the cult, and the next day the two youths led the army out to battle behind the sacred *kiste*. The sight of the sacred container struck the attacking army with fear and panic, and they fled, eventually to join the Milesians in celebration of these gods. Pausanias (I.4) and Aristides (*Panegyrikos* 2.469) note the Kabeiroi were the most ancient gods of Pergamon, another coastal Asia Minor city. Their ethnicity remains fluid: they may be Phrygians, and share their names with the Kabeuric mountains of Phrygia; Philo of Byblos makes them the sons of Phoenician Sydyk, part of a large family of culture heroes who invent writing, magic, prophecy, and metals, celebrated alongside Poseidon in Beiruit. (17)

The Phoenicians and Phrygians both spread the Kabeiric cult, and by sea and land they sandwiched Miletus. The first philosopher was "Phoenician by ultimate descent" (Herodotus, *Histories* I.170) and a resident in a city that had adopted the Kabeiroi cult.[71] Whether or not the "first philosopher" identified with the mysteries, it seems likely that, as a Phoenician and Milesian, he was familiar with what the Kabeiroi were about.[72]

While direct similarities between Kabeiric beliefs and early philosophical concepts are intriguing, the resonance between the attitude and tone of Prometheus—especially his championing of humanity and knowledge over divine will—is most relevant. The famous intellectual and scientific zeal that emanates through Western memories of Greek culture is what defines the Promethean essence. Exemplifying this perspective, Blakely writes, "Antigone's praise of thinking man, the technological revelations of Aeschylus' Prometheus, and Isocrates' pride in Athens as the bringer of technology, culture, and law are familiar examples of the evolutionary model of history that dominated for over a thousand years" (30-31).

The Phoenician heritage of Thales is especially relevant to the always-told story about his prediction of an eclipse. It is known that the Phoenician sailors were quite familiar with the stars, and their priests are believed to have been capable of predicting days on which an eclipse was likely.[73] As the Phoenicians dominated Mediterranean trade, Miletus was one of the great trade centers in the Mediterranean world. It can thus be readily seen that ideas and entertainment—like goods and wares—found Miletus from across the ocean. The reason this is important is because of how similar Thales' theory was to a number of religious myths.

Though Thales' belief that water is the essential substance to which all reality reduces is presented as the demarcated beginning to philosophical history, it was not without precedent. As Campbell points out, he seems "to be saying little more than the myths had been saying for centuries, which is that all things are full of gods and emerged from the watery abyss" (*Occidental* 181). For example, in the traditions of Egypt, from which he "introduced geometry into Greece" (Curd), everything is said to have emerged from the primal waters of Nu.[74] This is not the story of *Genesis,* in which God stirs the waters with breath. The belief in water as origin was not the breakthrough development, "the novelty [was] a new attitude: not faith or passive acceptance of a received doctrine, but active, reasoning inquiry" (181).

As we now proceed into the canonical story of philosophy we will recognize that, while certain concepts and ideas appear familiar, the tone—as Campbell and others have suggested—had changed. The reliance on divine authority or state law was not requisite for their bold proclamation of rationally discovered thought. As Terrance Irwin describes,

"Between the age of Homer (mid-eighth century) and the age of Socrates (late fifth

century), the Greeks began systematic rational study of the natural order and the moral

order" (Irwin 20). "Ultimate, universal questions were being asked, and answers were

being sought out from a new quarter—the human mind's critical analysis of material

phenomena" (Tarnas, *Passion* 20). Tarnas even suggests that the Greeks may have been

the first to see the world "as a question to be answered," and that out of "that quest came

the birth of the Western mind" (69).

Part of what enabled "these prototypical scientists" to start down this path was the

"remarkable assumption that an underlying rational unity and order existed within the

flux and variety of the world" (20). In Guthrie's words, "the basis of physical science in

Greece was the search for permanence or stability, and for an underlying unity, in a

universe superficially mutable and unstable, and consisting only of a most confusing

plurality" (65). With this search the first philosophers "began to complement their

traditional mythological understanding with more impersonal and conceptual

explanations based on their observations of natural phenomena" (20). In searching "for

something permanent" that persists "through the chaos of apparent change" they asked,

"'what is the world made of?'" (Guthrie 23). And, "in answering the eternal question, the

Ionian thinkers and later the atomists gave their reply in terms of matter, the

Pythagoreans, Socrates, Plato and Aristotle in terms of form" (21). Thus in all likelihood,

when Aristotle described Gaia as the ultimate mother (*Pandora* 286), he was using the

mythic language of his peers to convey a belief in material primacy while referring to the

corroborative religious tradition that presented the personification of matter as primary.

Following the materialists, "the primitive universe ruled by anthropomorphic deities began to give way to a world whose source and substance was a primary natural element such as water, air, or fire" (Tarnas, *Passion* 20). Eventually, "these primary substances would cease to be endowed with divinity or intelligence, and would instead be understood as purely material entities mechanically moved by chance or blind necessity" (20). Despite the religious and mythological influences on early (and later) philosophers, the trajectory—especially as we tell the story—was decidedly towards secular thought. The vision of nature had begun its long transition from a wholly divine order to an entirely material and mechanical cosmos, which was continued during the scientific revolution, Enlightenment, and still today.

Milesian Materialists: The First Philosophers

"Philosophy begins with Thales" (Russell 1). "Philosophy begins in Miletus" (Allen 1). "Many have followed Aristotle in taking the naturalists to be the first philosophers and scientists" (Irwin 20). And "according to Aristotle, Thales was the first of the 'natural philosophers' who sought to explain the world by reducing its various aspects to a common natural element" (Hatab 162). His student and fellow Milesian, Anaximander, termed this element, *Arche,* a word Homer used to express "the mythical meaning of 'beginning'" to which he added "the philosophical sense of 'origin' or 'principle'" (194).

As the story is commonly told, the belief in an arche—and the belief that it was material—was the first premise and starting point of philosophical history. "The evidence of unbiased common sense suggested that the world was constituted by visible matter" (Tarnas 29). And, "in accord with their newly naturalistic outlook, early Greek philosophers such as the Ionians and the atomists began regarding the heavens as composed of various material substances whose movements were mechanically determined" (50). As Allen writes, "The revolution Thales' pupils carried forward … may be measured by its fruit" (Allen 5). One might say that the fruit it bears is the kind of recognition that each time we weigh fruit, by way of its form, mass, and movement of the scale, it reinforces our belief in the affective qualities of substance itself—a system of study ignited by the Milesians.

Miletus was "an Ionian city on the Mediterranean shore of what is now Turkey. A great port with a large carrying trade, Miletus served not only Greece, but also Egypt and Babylonia, then at the height of their culture. The thought of the Milesian philosophers, Thales, Anaximander, and Anaximines, shows traces of this influence" (Allen 1). Stories about Thales present him as a virtually mythic figure. He fell into a well when looking at the sky (Crichley, "What is a Philosopher?"). [75] And when a merchant called philosophy worthless, he used his knowledge to become wealthy: he predicted an early olive harvest, leased the presses for cheap, then charged monopoly prices when the fruit ripened early that year (Aristotle, *Politics* 1259a9-18).[76] He also split an un-forgeable river into two streams his king's army could cross (Herodotus I.75).[77] The seven sages of ancient Greece were each associated with a saying. His has been variously reported as either, "Water is Best" (Glasgow 20),[78] which is consistent with his foundational beginning of philosophical thought, or "Know Thyself," which has served as its own starting place of philosophical development, especially for Socrates, his fellow "Father of Philosophy" (Plato, *Protagoras* 343).

The standard citation for the materialistic interpretation of the Milesians is Aristotle's *Metaphysics* (938b6). "In Aristotle's view, the naturalists … want to find the nature of things by finding their basic matter" (Irwin 22). "Aristotle claims that the naturalists identify the nature with the 'matter' (hule) or 'basic subject' (hupokeimenon) of things" (21).

> Most of the first philosophers thought that principles in the form of matter were the only principles of all things: for the original source of all existing things, that from which a first comes-into-being and into which it is finally destroyed, the substance persisting but changing its qualities, this they declare is the element and first principle of existing things, and for this reason they consider that there is no absolute coming to-be or passing away, on the ground that such a nature is always preserved … for there must be some natural substance, either one or more than one, from which the other things come-into-being, while it is preserved. Over the number, however, the form of this kind of principle they do not all agree; but Thales, the founder of this type of philosophy, says its water" (Aristotle, *Metaphysics,* 938b 6-17; Allen 29).

> Most of the first philosophers thought the origins of everything were material. For, they say, there is some <subject> that all beings come from, the first thing they come to be from and the last thing they perish into, the substance remaining throughout and changing in its attributes; and this is the elementary basis and the origin of beings. And for this reason they think nothing either comes to be or perishes, since they assume that in

> every change this nature [i.e. the subject] persists. For just as we say
> Socrates does not come to be unqualifiedly whenever he becomes good or
> musical, and does not perish unqualifiedly whenever he loses these states,
> since the subject, Socrates himself, remains, so also, they say, nothing else
> either comes to be or perishes unqualifiedly since there must be some
> nature, either one or more than one, that persists while the other things
> come to be from it. (Aristotle, *Metaphysics*, 983b 6-17; Irwin 21)

From Aristotle's telling, it is as though materialism should be seen as the starting point of Western rational thought, as the Big Bang of philosophical development. However, as Le Grice points out, Thales' original emphasis could have been on neutral monism as opposed to the materialistic premise (personal correspondence); for which reason, I consider it important to include multiple uses of Aristotle's quotation in currently circulated histories of Western thought. While the premise of materialism—via the understanding of everything as emergent from substance—certainly appears in the contributions of Thales, it seems that Aristotle is at least partially responsible for the strong emphasis on the birth of materialism at the beginning of Greek philosophy. And more importantly than when and why this emphasis became part of the narrative, it is essential to note that Aristotle's interpretation remains in common circulation.

Specifically, for Thales, the *arche* was imagined as *water*. Aristotle wrote that "the most ancient account we have received, which they say was given by Thales the Milesian" is that "the earth rests on water ... floating like a log" (Aristotle, *De Caelo* 2941 28). Seneca wrote, "For [Thales] the world is held up by water and rides like a ship, and when it is said to 'quake', it is actually rocking because of the water's movement"

(Seneca, *Qu. nat.* III, 14). "Thales chose water as his primordial stuff, for water is an ancient symbol of life. Thales, no doubt, thought that it is life, thought that, in the living liquid, there was no distinction between its life and its liquidity" (Allen 2).[79] This returns us to Campbell's comments about the consistency of Thales' beliefs with a common religious belief among Egyptians and Semites.

"At this pivotal stage," Tarnas writes, "there was a distinct overlap of the mythic and scientific modes, visible in the principal statement attributed to Thales in which he affirmed both a single unifying primary substance and a divine omnipresence. 'All is water, and the world is full of gods'" (19). To Thales "the soul was something kinetic … he said that the [Magnesian] stone possesses soul because it moves iron" (Aristotle, *de anima* 405a 19). According to Aetius, "Thales said that the mind of the world is God, and that the sum of things is besouled, and full of daimons [spirits]; right through the elemental moisture there penetrates a divine power that moves it" (1, 7, 11). Aristotle recorded that "some say [soul] is intermingled in the universe, for which reason, perhaps, Thales also thought that all things are full of gods" (*de anima* 411a 7).

While Aristotle and subsequent historians of philosophy like to see Thales as the first materialist, it is essential to keep the animistic qualities of his perspective in mind. When someone calls themselves a reductive materialist today, it is most likely that they envision matter to be dead, soulless, and internally inert. This is not how Thales saw the world. According to the "first philosopher," the cosmos simultaneously reduced to *water*, which was pure matter and pure soul. The paradox is not dissimilar from the Christian recognition of Christ as one hundred percent god and one hundred percent matter.[80]

Thales' student, Anaximander, offered the first known philosophical refutation. He disagreed with his mentor, arguing, "If one element were unbounded, variety would have ceased" (Aristotle, *Physics* 204b 24). If water was the unbounded element, air, fire and earth would have been overpowered from existence. "Anaximander had presented a question to Thales: How is the qualitative diversity of the world to be reconciled with the primordial unity of its source?" (Allen 3).

His own solution was that the known elements operate "like a pendulum, [maintaining] equilibrium through the alternation of … extremes" (3). What he theorized was that these elements all derive from another more fundamental and "unbounded" substance he named *apeiron*. Simplicius attests that, for Anaximander, "it is neither water nor any other of the so-called elements, but some other indefinite nature, from which came into being all the heavens and the worlds in them" (13). According to Aristotle, "the opposites are separated out from the One, being present in it" (Aristotle, *Physics* 1871 12). "The source of coming-to-be for existing things is that into which destruction, too, happens 'according to necessity' for they pay penalty and retribution to each other for their injustice according to the assessment of Time'" (Simplicius 13). As Irwin describes, "the Unbounded maintains the order of the opposites … [and] maintains the stability of the present world order" (Irwin 23).

While on the one hand we can see a clear development of a reason based cosmological order, on the other, Anaximander's thought is still clearly influenced by moral notions of justice. Allen writes, "The principles by which Anaximander interprets the universe are closely linked to that psychology of the tragic passions by which Aeschylus interprets human life. The order of nature is essentially a dramatic order: the agonists are the warring opposites, alternately triumphing in the cycle of days and seasons" (Allen 4).[81]

As a founder of scientific thought, it should also be noted that he planted clear seeds for the theory of evolution. He believed "all land-animals, including man … evolved ultimately from a sort of fish" (Guthrie 28). He also made a number of other scientific and technological contributions. According to Suda, "Anaximander … kinsman, pupil and successor of Thales … first discovered the equinox and solstices and hour-indicators, and that the earth lies in the center. He introduced the gnomon and in general made known an outline of geometry (Suda, s.v.). He was also "the first to draw the inhabited world on a tablet" (Horowitz, Muller 2.471).

This "first map" was "a stone disk with ocean around its edge and Delphi in its center" (2.471). This was how "the ancients drew the inhabited world … round, and Greece lay in the middle, and Delphi (lay) in the middle of it for it is the umbilicus of the earth" (2.471). Around the Earth, "swift flowing Oceanus completed a circle" (2.471). But this image of the world, or *imago mundi*, did not start with Thales. According to Hesiod's description, "around the rim Ocean was flowing, with a full stream … [that] enclosed all the cunning work of Heracles shield" (*Shield of Heracles* ll. 316). Similarly, "the shield of Achilles illustrates the oceans as the boundaries for the land" (Slattery 351). "On [Achilles] shield, Hephaestus depicted Ocean, the mighty river, flowing all around the outer edge" (Homer, *Iliad* 18.525).[82] In the middle of all three images—each encircled by a serpentine ocean—Greek people fill the center.[83] This self-centric world image would later develop into the self-centric cosmic image of Aristotle and Ptolemy with the Earth in the center of our (spherical) universe. Dante and the medieval church would later perpetuate this cosmic vision. Structurally, from macro to microcosm, the same self-centric thought process was consistent with Greek anthropomorphism and the Sophistic belief that 'man is the measure of all things.' All of these points of view constellate to support the development of the Greek "ego" and the strong favor for individuality in the West; they also demonstrate the tendency towards cosmological persepectives anchored by centers and humans. One thinks of Atlas, a personified god and foundation of the earth and heavens.

As Anaximander to Thales, Anaximenes to Anaximander. He was his pupil. Both of them lived in Miletus. Anaximenes was known for his "simple and unsuperfluous Ionic speech" (Doigenes Laertius II, 3). His belief was that "the material principle [arche] was air and the infinite; and that the stars move, not under earth, but round it" (II, 3). He agreed with his teacher that "the underlying nature is one and infinite, but not undefined as Anaximander said but by rarity and density. Being made finer it becomes fire, being made thicker it becomes wind, then cloud, then (when thickened still more) water, then earth, then stones" (Theophrastus *ap.* Simplicium, *Phys.* 24, 26). [84]

With this description he had left the divine mind and human justice behind for a purely natural explanation of how the universe interacts with itself. However, though his argument was rational, and the first to be considered empirical, its reference was still within his own headspace: "Breath blown through compressed lips is cold, but with the mouth open, it is warm" (Allen 4). Thus, he thought, "matter which is compressed and condensed is cold, while that which is fine and 'relaxed' … is hot" (Plutarch, *de prim. Frig.* 7 947f).

Though, in many ways, his thought follows a secular trend in philosophy, he also "says that the air is God" (Aetius I, 7, 13) and engages the relationship between soul and air expressed in their shared word, *pneuma.* "Our soul, he says, being air, holds us together and controls us, so does wind and air enclose the whole world" (I, 3, 4). Guthrie writes that:

> [For] Anaximenes a small portion of this soul-stuff, which properly belongs by its nature to the outermost reaches of the Universe beyond the adulterated atmosphere which we breathe, is imprisoned in the body of each animal or human being, and forms its soul. …One of his followers [said] … man's soul is 'a small part of the god', the god being the Universe, which we thus learn is still thought of by these men as being alive (30).[85]

With this in mind we recognize that Anaximenes, of Miletus, shared this common Greek belief with the Orphics, Pythagoras, Socrates, and Plato that divine soul is imprisoned in the material of the body. We should also recognize the consistency of this belief with Thales' world of en-souled substance. "As Cornford put it, 'If we would understand the sixth-century philosophers, we must disabuse our minds of the atomistic conception of dead matter in mechanical motion and of the . . . dualism of matter and mind' (Guthrie 31). "From recent science we have inherited the notion of matter as in itself something dead or , which needs to be called into motion by an outside force" (31). But, "the earlier Greek … idea that the world as a whole was a living creature" (31), and the belief in the animation of matter, had a heavy influence on early philosophers.

Despite the lingering influences of religion and animism, "'Anaximenes' fundamental conception will be kept: the notion that the world consists in matter and its arrangement, that the ultimate explanation of it must be quantitative and mechanical" (Allen 5). From this position "Anaximenes stands in a direct line with Democritus … who foreshadowed most clearly the scientific world view which has dominated thought from the time of Newton to the present" (5). Like Thales and Democritus, "Anaximenes answered the riddle of the *arche* by suggesting, "very simply … that the primordial unity is to be treated as a stuff, a matter out of which things are made. The diverse elements of the world are to be attributed to changes in this primitive matter, changes that are quantitative" (4). And from his line of reasoning, the "qualitative differences … are to be accounted for by the thickening and thinning, condensation and rarefaction, of a primordial stuff" (4).

The Pythagoreans: Ascetic Beauty and Cosmological Harmonics

From the first philosophers of Miletus the story travels to the nearby island (Samos) and coastal city (Ephesus) of Pythagoras and Heraclitus respectively. However, though Pythagoras was "an Eastern Greek by birth [he] … migrated to South Italy around about 530 B.C." (Guthrie 33). Mimetic with his geographical distancing from the Ionian tradition, the line of thought he developed was diametrically oppositional. As the story is told, "the two main streams of tradition in early Greek thought were spoken of in later antiquity as the Ionian and the Italian. The latter begins with Pythagoras" (33).

Elaborating on the Pythagorean tradition, Tarnas writes, "while the main current of Greek thought was breaking away from the mythological and religious ground of archaic Greek culture, Pythagoras and his followers conducted philosophy and science in a framework permeated by the beliefs of the mystery religions, especially Orphism"

(*Passion* 23). In sync with this philosophical schism between those moving towards and

away from religion and myth was a parallel movement away from and towards religion

and spiritual philosophy. "Broadly speaking, the Ionian tradition was materialistic …

Pythagoreans, on the contrary, sought explanation in terms of structure or form" (Allen

6). As mentioned in the section, *From Myth to Philosophy*, this line of thinking was

foreshadowed by the abstract thought and synesthesia of sympathetic magic and religious

symbolism. Nurtured by the Pythagoreans, Greek abstract thought grew towards the

study of geometry, mathematical reason, and harmony. Plato—heavily influenced by this

tradition—pushed abstract thought to a theory of pure *ideas,* or *forms,* and *Harmony*.[86]

Before exploring the philosophical contributions of Pythagoras and the

Pythagoreans, we should recognize certain complications that come with studying their

work. Guthrie writes, "Among the Pythagoreans, the motive for philosophy was not what

it had been for the Ionians, simple scientific curiosity. They were a religious brotherhood,

and this had certain consequences" (34). Some such consequences make it as difficult to

study the Pythagoreans as it is to research the mysteries of Eleusis or the Kabeiroi.

Emerging from a background of religious communities and mystery rites, "a rule of strict

secrecy was maintained by his school, and an aura of legend surrounded it from its

beginnings" (Tarnas 23). And because "the founder himself was canonized, or regarded

as semi-divine ... it is difficult to disentangle the life and teaching of the historical

Pythagoras" (Guthrie 34). Fortunately, his influence and remembered content is far more

important to this dissertation's interests than fragmented history or forgotten secrets.

Regardless of what has been lost, his influence is canonical. Allen writes, "The ideals of the science he founded—ideals of simplicity, economy, and rigor—were to influence every facet of Greek art and thought" (8). Such influence was especially catalyzed by their legendary persecution and exile led by Cylon of Croton—a story with Promethean overtones that will later reverberate in the trial of Socrates (Fideler 116). "By the fifth century, scattered Pythagorean communities were to be found in various parts of Greece" (Guthrie 34). And with this Mediterranean diaspora of the Pythagoreans their mathematical, geometrical, and harmonic breakthroughs fertilized the old world's art, architecture, and music while updating and enriching its Orphic tradition. In the study of philosophical history, it is easy to miss that, beyond the influence of the Pythagoreans on specific philosophers, their religious ideas made a strong impact on the entire Greek world. Jung dialogues with Nietzshce, ""these teachings cannot be dismissed as the mystical humbug of 'backwoods' philosophers, as Nietzsche claimed, or as so much sectarian cant, for already in the sixth century B.C. Pythagoreanism was something like a state religion throughout Graecia Magna" (*Essential* 136). This image is in contrast to the more common consideration of the spreading Ionian emphasis on substance and the transition from myth, religion, and magic to philosophy and secular science.

In this early phase of materialistic philosophy the Ionians did not yet believe that matter was dead or inert. The Pythagoreans "agreed with the Ionians'" in this belief that "the Universe as a whole was a living creature" (Guthrie 35). And, like the Ionians, instead of merely relying on the authority of religion or state in the pursuit of understanding the animated universe, they employed their own faculties. What set their paths apart were the paths of reason they traveled. While the Ionians engaged an intellectual paradigm of materiality in a way that grew to isolate itself from a relationship with the divine, the Pythagoreans and Platonists engaged an intellectual and spiritual paradigm based on harmony that emerged from an earlier Orphic worldview.

Instead of assuming a fundamental materiality to the universe, the Pythagoreans studied the numeric relationships between phenomena in an attempt to comprehend something more eternal than the particular stuff of experience that clearly decays. "By seeking its first principles in a higher realm of reality," writes Proclus, "Pythagoras turned geometrical philosophy into a form of liberal education" (*Eucl.* 65). Aristotle (famously) wrote:

> The Pythagoreans, as they are called, devoted themselves to mathematics; they were the first to advance this study, and having been brought up in it they thought its principles were the principles of all things. ... Of these principles numbers are by nature the first, and in numbers they seemed to see many resemblances to the things that exist and come into being—more than in fire and earth and water. ... They say that the attributes and rations of the musical scales were expressible in numbers. ... All other things seemed in their whole nature to be modeled after numbers, and numbers seemed to be the first things in the world of nature. They supposed the elements of numbers to be the elements of all things, and the whole heaven to be a musical scale and number. And all the properties of numbers and scales, which they could show to agree with the attributes and parts and the whole arrangement of the heavens, they collected and fitted into their scheme ... these thinkers also consider that number is the

principle both as matter for things and as forming their modifications and their permanent states. (*Metaphysics* 985b 23)

Aristotle's description shows Pythagorean philosophy to be based on the mathematically numerical synergy between form, sound, and the sensory world. Similarly, the likening of the cosmos to a musical scale finds reverberations in the description of the universe as a *cosmic symphony* by string theorist Brian Greene (*Elegant Universe, Part III: The Cosmic Symphony*). The recognition that all things can be reduced to numbers might also be recognized in the creation of modern video-games and CGI enhanced movies that rely on the convincing recreation of reality with mathematics and code. The difference is that—though both are interested in number as capable of constructing sensate reality— the Pythagoreans focus on the qualitative symbolic significance of the transcendental forms. It might be said that game designers and writers both express Pythagorean interests—the former through the work with number as arche and the latter through the use of form as a medium-transcending language.

In the terms of the Ionians, it might be said that the Pythagoreans believed *number* to be *arche*. In Aristotle's words, "The Pythagoreans, because they saw many attributes of numbers belonging to sensible bodies, supposed real things to be numbers— not separable numbers, however, but numbers of which real things consist" (*Metaphysics* 1090a 20). For example, they believed that the "four elements, fire, air, water, earth, emanated from the first four numbers, 1, 11, 111, 1111" (Mordell 65).[87] The problem with reducing their *arche* to numbers, however, is that the statement sets up a modern reader to miss the consolidation of counting numbers, shapes and sounds into their understanding of what numbers are. Through shape and sound, numbers actualize into our sensory reality. The Pythagorean thus recognizes the presence of the transcendent in the presence of numerical form.

The school's philosophical interest in sound is exemplified by their work on the octave. If the group's most famous discovery was the "Pythagorean Theorem," their next most-remembered contribution was their recognition of structured relationships between number, spatial-form, and pitch. Pythagoras discovered the octave and scale when "he found out that those intervals of the musical scale … can be expressed arithmetically as ratios between the numbers 1, 2, 3 and 4" (Guthrie 38). By recognizing ratio in sound, despite its immediate invisibility, he ignited the mathematical study of waves.[88]

The school offers a concentrated symbol—a microcosmic vision—of their cosmos. "In the teachings of Pythagoras, the philosophic quest for the ἀρχή [*arche*], the first cause and principle of all things, was carried to a consideration of the problem of the magic of the Orphic lyre itself, by which the hearts of men are quelled, purified, and restored to their part in God" (Campbell, *Occidental* 185). Instead of recognizing the substance of the lyre as the cosmic arche, the Pythagoreans emphasized the numerical synergy between its form, ratio, and sound.[89]

On a macrocosmic level they viewed the cosmos as a "Harmony of the Spheres." Allen writes, "They assumed that the world is a *harmonia*, an orderly and proportionate adjustment of parts within a complex whole: they assumed that the book of nature … is written in the language of mathematics" (Allen 6). In Aristotle's words, "the movement of the stars produces a harmony, i.e., that the sounds they make are concordant. … Starting from this argument and the observation that their speeds, as measured by their distances, are in the same ratios in musical concordances, they assert that the sound given forth by the circular movement of the stars is in a harmony" (Aristotle, *de caelo* 290b 12). For the long period in scientific history driven by mechanistic materialism, this was believed to be impossible. However, understanding planetary interactions by way of gravitational and electromagnetic waves has since become standard scientific theory, and the sound of celestial objects has become a general astronomical interest (Diaz "Scientists Reveal the Sound of the Comet 67P/Churyumov-Gerasimenko").

It is said that Pythagoras was the first to give the name *kosmos* to the universe, "an untranslatable word which combined the notions of order, fitness, and beauty" (Guthrie 37). In compliment with this notion, he "believed that each one of us is a kosmos in miniature" (37). According to Pythagoras, "the breath or life of man and the breath or life of the infinite and divine Universe were essentially the same" (35). The goal of the philosopher was to recognize this, and to remove dissonant interferences between the harmony of the human and cosmic soul. From the Pythagorean angle:

> The Universe was one, eternal and divine. Men were many and divided, and were mortal. But the essential part of man, his soul, was not mortal, and owed its immortality to this fact, that it was a fragment or spark of the divine soul, cut off and imprisoned in a mortal body. Man had thus an aim in life, to shake off the taint of the body and, becoming pure spirit, rejoin the universal spirit to which he essentially belonged. (35)

The relationship of the individual with the universe was thus seen as one of microcosm and macrocosm. From their point of view, macro and micro—the universal One and individual— are separated by body.

Because of this line of reasoning, an emphasis on an ascetic relationship with the body on its path towards soul is a hallmark feature of the Pythagoreans, Socrates and Plato. For the Pythagoreans, "Philosophy, or inquiry into the nature of things, was understood as a way of life whose aim was salvation—the purification of the soul and its release from the prison of the body" (Allen 6). Such purity had been hitherto "sought by ritual, and the observance of mechanical taboos such as the avoidance of corpses. Pythagoras retained much of this, but added a way of his own, the way of the philosopher" (Guthrie 36). This was the way of thought, the ascetic purification of the body, its influences on thought, the rigorous pursuit of incorruptible truths, and the raising of the soul to the eternal realm by way of philosophical contemplation. "In life the slavish men go hunting for fame or gain, the philosophers for the truth" (Diogenes Laertius VIII, 8).[90] As Campbell writes, with this shift "knowledge, not rapture, became the way to realization" (*Occidental* 185). "To comprehend scientifically the order of the natural universe was the Pythagroean *via regia* to spiritual illumination … education that culminated in the human soul's assimilation to the world soul" (Tarnas 23). As the body represented a challenge to the soul's pursuit of oneness, the body's influence on mind was believed to imprison the mind with materialistic ideas.

The association of sound and soul was more than theoretical for "the Pythagoreans, [who] according to Aristoxenus, practiced the purification of the body by medicine … the soul by music" (Cramer, *as. Par*. I 172; Allen 36).[91] Though music was not used to heal the body directly, its metaphors were extended into the medical arts. The "dogma of the importance of maintaining— or restoring in the case of sickness— the right quantitative relationships between opposite qualities became the corner-stone of

Greek medicine, which started in a Pythagorean atmosphere with the work of Alcmaeon of Croton" (Guthrie 31).

Before concluding this section on Pythagoras and the Pythagorean interpretation of matter and soul, a note should be made about their interest in reincarnation. The Pythagoreans did not believe in the mere binary ascent and descent between the human and divine soul. They believed in the reincarnation of an immortal soul "and its progress through a series of incarnations not only as man but also in the bodies of other creatures" (34). This Pythagorean vision of the transmigration of souls is not unlike the better known Hindu model, in which the reincarnating human soul is believed to have experienced past lives in the animal kingdom. As the Pythagoreans understood the afterlife, "until the soul could purify itself completely, it must continue to undergo a series of transmigrations, exchanging one body for another. This meant the retention of individuality so long as the allotted cycle of births was incomplete, but there can be little doubt that the ultimate aim was the annihilation of self in reunion with the divine" (35).[92]

As we will see, while perpetuators of the Pythagorean school will continue to pursue the foundations of form beneath our sensory experience the school of philosophy that sees matter as essence will continue down a path that associates the sensory world with materiality. For the Pythagoreans, the reduction of the sensory world to materiality is a misstep. Between the relationships of sound and numerical form the belief in matter was not seen to be required. "Each separate thing was what it was not because of its material elements" (40). Following their development of the Orphic belief in the soul's imprisonment within matter, the mind was seen to be deceived by the influences of the body. The solution was the "discovery [of] the existence of an inherent order, a numerical organization within the nature of sound itself" (39).

Heraclitus: Logos

Though on one hand, it feels more natural to progress immediately from the Milesians to Heraclitus, whose focus on fire reads to some as elemental, "his position in the history of philosophy is fixed well enough by the fact that he criticized Pythagoras by name and is himself fairly obviously alluded to by Parmenides" (Guthrie 43). "The riddling gnomic character of [Heraclitus'] writings won him the name of 'the dark one' in later antiquity" (Allen 9). "His method of communication is like that of the Delphic oracle, which, he says, 'neither utters nor hides its meaning, but shows it by a sign'" (Guthrie 43).[93] Philosophically, despite the seductive simplicity of associating his theory of fire with the Milesian theories of water and air, he is distinctly *not* a materialist. He believed, despite our experience of seemingly solid things and static objects, that the foundation of reality is flux—*logos*.

Like the philosophers before him—whose foundations of water, air, *apeiron* and form did not exclude the foundational role of soul—he associated *arche* with mind. He wrote, "You would not find out the boundaries of soul, even by traveling along every path: so deep a measure does it have" (Fr. 45). "A later commentator says that according to Heraclitus 'we draw in the divine logos by breathing', i.e. the divine mind that steers the universe is … identical with the mind in us, as with the Pythagoreans" (46). And perhaps reminiscent of Prometheus' myth, "According to another ancient expositor of Heraclitus, [he believed] 'fire is intelligent, and is the cause of the arrangement of the whole'" (46).

The reason we are unaware of the Logos and spirit beneath material experience is because, according to Heraclitus, "The real constitution of things is accustomed to hide itself" (Fr. 123). He says, "Evil witnesses are eyes and ears for men, if they have souls that do not understand their language" (Fr. 107l). "'The learning of many things does not teach understanding … otherwise it would have taught Hesiod and Pythagoras.' … Such learning is got through the senses. … The senses show a different world to each man" (Guthrie 43-44). However, though "human disposition does not have true judgment … divine disposition does" (Fr. 78). And for Heraclitus, the divine disposition was not sought through human interactions with human priests, instead, the pursuit was to "look within yourself— i.e. to your own mind—[to] discover the logos which is the truth … common to all things" (Guthrie 43-44). "For Heraclitus, 'the hidden order is stronger than the apparent' and it can be revealed through the recognition that "the whole process is regular and orderly, with no gaps" (Irwin 26). As Aristotle describes, "all things are in motion all the time, but … this escapes our perception" (*Physics* 253b 9).

If one pursues this line of thought they recognize that "the stable features of the universe … are not the rocks, trees, and other ordinary objects that appear to common sense … but the processes of change that these ordinary objects undergo" (Irwin 26). Heraclitus "could no longer accept the simple Ionian cosmogonies, nor find it easy and natural to confine life and thought in the straitjacket of material substance" (Guthrie 46). As he saw the world, "ceaseless changes may seem to imply instability in the universe; but in fact they are stable because … [these] changes conform to regular and stable laws of nature" (Irwin 26). Thus, as with the Pythagoreans, there was no room for substance at the foundation of his worldview. "Herakleitus dissolves things into processes" (25), and into process all substance dissolves.

As Allen dutifully recounts, "Both Plato and Aristotle ascribed to Heraclitus the doctrine of perpetual flux" (Allen 10). Heraclitus' "view of the universe turns on his concept of logos—an untranslatable word which in fact means 'word,' but which has connotations of proportion, measure, and perhaps even here pattern. The logos is the first principle of knowledge … [And] also the first principle of existence" (9). As Guthrie writes, "the logos is true for ever, all things come to pass in accordance with it, it is common to all, and 'one must follow what is common'" (45). "This unity lies beneath the surface, for it is a unity of diverse and conflicting opposites, in whose strife the logos maintains a continuing balance: the world, in being drawn asunder, is drawn together—a back stretched connection, as in the bow and the lyre" (Allen 9). With this image of the lyre and metaphor of opposites in tension we can sense the influence of Pythagorean thought, but where Pythagoras' described forms and ratios as the foundation of existence, Heraclitus gave this role to flux. Where Pythagoras would describe the seemingly static lyre as a harmonic balance, Heraclitus sees it as "a continuous tug-of-war" (Guthrie 44).

This introduces Heraclitus emphasis on strife and union. He wrote, "out of all things there comes a unity, and out of a unity all things" (Fr. 10). But "the Pythagorean ideal of a peaceful and harmonious world he rejected as an ideal of death. 'War is the father of all', he said, and 'Strife is justice'" (Guthrie 44). The word translated here as strife is in fact, ἔ ρις, which is also translated as "Eris," the name of the goddess who delivers the golden apple of discord that leads to the fall of Troy. This, of course, cannot fail to remind us of the fruit in Eden—often remembered as a (golden) apple—which inspires a similarly epic fall. "Everything depends on a ceaseless struggle between opposites" (Irwin 25).[94] Reminiscent of the back and forth between Zeus and the fire-bringer, he says the "thunderbolt steers all things" (Fr. 64). "'Homer was wrong,' wrote Heracleitus of Epiphesus, 'Homer was wrong in saying: 'Would that strife might perish from among gods and men!' He did not see that he was praying for the destruction of the universe; for his prayer was heard, all things would pass away" (Huxley, *Brave New World*, Forward). Aristotle continues, "there would be no musical scale unless high and low existed, nor living creatures without female and male, which are opposites" (*Eudemian Ethics* 123a 25). According to Heraclitus' point of view, "The basis of equilibrium is struggle, which is therefore good in itself, since it is the source of life" (Guthrie 44-5). He states, "'Good and evil are one'" (46).

In one of his more famous dictums he proclaimed, "The road up … and the road down … are one and the same'" (Irwin 25). Irwin explains, "his ability to recognize the 'unity of opposites' is contingent with his 'rejection of a continuing subject" (25). "Listening not to me but to the Logos it is wise to agree that all things are one" (Fr. 50), which might be taken to mean something like, 'from the point of view that all things reduce to process—i.e. there is no continuing subject—all seems unified.'

Where Anaximenes described the unification of elements by way of condensation and rarification in the falling order of fire→air→water→earth, Heraclitus wrote that "for souls it is death to become water, for water it is death to become earth; from earth water comes-to-be, and from water, soul" (Fr. 36). He also wrote, continuing the use of *death* as his metaphor of transformation, "'Fire lives the death of air, and air of fire; water lives the death of earth, earth that of water" (Guthrie 44). The way up and the way down are presented as the same: transformations can take place in both directions. We will later see these kind of progressions through the elements in the descriptions of the Stoics, who, like Heraclitus, saw fire as both intelligent and of central significance. European alchemists also developed an association of elements with substances involved in their metallurgical aims toward the philosopher's stone. In comparable Indian traditions, the progression through an ascending sequence of elements was associated with the Kundalini climb of the chakras towards transcendent states of mind.

Though Heraclitus, like Thales, envisioned a relationship between soul and water, he also wrote that "those who drink to excess make their souls wet, and accordingly harm them (B117), for a healthy soul is dry (B118)" (Graham, "Heraclitus"). Fire, for him, was of utmost importance. It was his primary poetic expression of the logos. He wrote, "All things are an equal exchange for fire and fire for all things, as goods are for gold and gold for goods" (Fr. 64). But, we would be misguided to read him "like the Ionians, [as though he] believed in a primordial stuff out of which the world had evolved … fire provides rather a kind of symbol of its nature" (Guthrie 45). Perhaps he is most famous for saying that "this world-order did none of gods or men make, but it always was and is and shall be: an everlasting fire, kindling in measures and going out in measures" (Fr. 30). In this statement he not only offers a strong *logos* image, he also states, resolutely, that the order of the cosmos was not established by gods, which supported the secularization of his idea as it became critical to later atomists and natural philosophers.

His other dictum concerning flux may be more famous than the philosopher himself. Plato recounts his words in his *Cratylus*, "you would not step twice into the same river" (402a). The idea is again that "all things are in process and nothing stays still" (402a). Another key point to make about this reference is that he uses *water* to describe the Logos in this passage—not fire—which returns us to his key point that the Logos is not elemental, it is the word for flux itself. This distinction is the very boundary between the duals of his worldview: the ignorant embrace of human knowledge through the senses vs. the ability of mind to see the hidden Logos.

Parmenides Static: Monism

Forsaking the sensory experience of plurality and change, the Eleatics were absolutely monistic in their hyper-logical interpretation of being. "Their claim for priority of reason over the senses and their radical skepticism of common sense sharply altered the course of future philosophy … The most prominent members of the school were Parmenides, its founder, and Zeno, his pupil" (Allen 10), who reappear in Plato's highly enigmatic text, *Parmenides*. The founder of the school "was born about 515 B.C. in Elea, a Greek city on the coast of Italy" (10). In a continuation of the Italian school, "he was associated in his youth with the Pythagoreans, against whom he later reacted" (10). "Zeno was born in approximately 490 BC and became a pupil of Parmenides while still a young man. His philosophical activity was primarily negative, devoted to refutation rather than construction; his pattern of argument, the *reductio ad absurdum*, he borrowed from the geometers" (12).

According to philosophical tradition, "most significant was Parmenides's declaration of the autonomy and superiority of the human reason as judge of reality. For what was real was intelligible—an object of intellectual apprehension, not of sense perception" (Tarnas 21). "All that men imagine about the Universe, he said, all that they think they see and hear and feel, is pure illusion" (Guthrie 49). Allen writes, "The primary object of Parmenides' poem is to demonstrate that the common-sense belief in the reality of the physical world, a world of plurality and change, is mistaken, and to set in its place a One Being, unchanging, ungenerated, indestructible" (Allen 11). His "distinction between appearance and reality and between opinion and knowledge laid the foundation for [Plato's] ... objections to change and plurality" (11). They also continued the long-developing tradition of recognizing the sensory world as the deceiver from truth.

Parmenides' position on sensory experience and pure reason is one of the most characteristic examples of an *either-or* position in Western history. His poem, "The *Way of Truth,* is the first philosophical demonstration in history" and its "demonstration rests upon a disjunction which, reduced to its lowest terms, is simply, 'it is, or it is not'" (10). He writes:

> Nor will the force of true belief allow that, beside what is, there could also arise anything from what is not; wherefore Justice looseth not her fetters to allow it to come into being or perish, but holdeth it fast; and the decision on these matters rests here; it is or it is not ... it is all full of what is. So it is all continuous; for what is clings close to what is. But motionless within the limits of mighty bonds, it is without beginning or end, since coming into being and perishing have been driven far away, cast but by true belief. Abiding the same in the same place it rests by itself, and so abides firm where it is; for strong Necessity holds it firm within the bonds of the limit that keeps it back on every side, because it is not lawful that what is should be unlimited; for it is not indeed, if it were, it would need all. But since there is a futherest limit, it is bounded on every side, like the bulk of

a well-rounded sphere, from the center equally balanced in every direction … what can be thought is only the thought that it is. For you will not find thought without what is, in relation to what is uttered; fettered is to be entire and immovable" (Fr. 8 lines 42-49 and 34-41).

His position seems to be that since one cannot think of what is not, what is not cannot be, which means the answer of the question 'is' or 'is not' must be 'is'. This logical dance is often reduced to semantic mistakes by some historians of philosophy. Guthrie writes, "Plato's *Sophist*, cleared up the point that although they used the same word 'is', Parmenides and the people against whom he was arguing meant two different things" (Guthrie 48). "To Parmenides, the first to reflect consciously on the logic of words, it seemed that to say that a thing is could and should mean only that it exists, and this thought came to him with the force of a revelation about the nature of reality" (48).[95] It has been suggested that he was influenced by his proximity to "the primitive magical stage at which a word and its object formed a single unity" (47).

Because 'is' and 'is not' cannot simultaneously be true, there can be no becoming of 'is not' from what 'is' or 'is' from what 'is not.' "The real world, then, all that is, must be a changeless, immovable mass of one kind of substance, and in eternal and changeless stillness it must always remain" (49). There can be "no such thing as empty space" (49). "He was the exact reverse of Heraclitus. For Heraclitus, movement and change were the only realities; for Parmenides, movement was impossible, and the whole of reality consisted of a single, motionless and unchanging substance" (47). To believe in flux or plurality was "the way of mortal opinion, which supposes real the world of nature, whose contents come to be and cease to be … there are two, and *only* two ways, (Fr. 2)" (Allen

11). But though his thought structure was dualistic, his choice of one over the other led him to reduce "'it is and is not' … to 'it is not'" (11).

Empedocles and Anaxagoras: Pluralism

In response to Parmenides, "The pluralists—Empedocles, Anaxagoras, and the atomists, Leucippus and Democritus—all undertook to … justify the reality of motion and the existence of the sensible world" (Fr. 17). From their point of view, "'No object comes-to-be or passes away, but is mixed or separated from existing objects.'" (Allen 13). The Pluralists' systems "adhered to Parmenides' view that what was real could not ultimately come into being or pass away, but they interpreted the apparent birth and destruction of natural objects as being the consequence of a multiplicity of fundamental unchanging elements which alone were truly real" (Tarnas 21). Anaxagoras and Empedocles shared the belief that "No object comes-to-be or passes away, but is mixed or separated from existing objects" (Anaxagoras, Fr. 17). Empedocles wrote, "Coming into being from that which in no way is inconceivable, and it is impossible and unheard-of that that which is should be destroyed" (Fr. 11).

Empedocles was from Acragas in Sicily. Like a wizard or magi he claimed "that his knowledge is the key to power over the forces of nature, that by it men can arrest the winds, make rain, and even bring back the dead from Hades. [Like Pythagoras] he was a firm believer in the transmigration of souls" (Guthrie 51). And like Pythagoras, he participated in the initiation into Orphic mysteries (Campbell, *Occidental* 185). Despite what one might think of his relationship with the Orphics, his contributions to scientific thought were essential to progress.

Where Anaximander had described the emergence of the elements from the unbounded *apieron*, Empedocles' believed "the only 'realities' are the four root-substances [that] have existed from all time and always will exist" (Guthrie 53). Allen writes, "From Parmenides he takes the Sphere of Being, everywhere full. But the sphere is now full of four sensible opposites, the hot, the cold, the wet, and the dry, which change places in the sphere, combine and separate in varying proportions" (Allen 13). "The various complex substances of the world—its men and tables, horses and trees—come to be and pass away; but that is because they are mere arrangements of elements that do not" (13). Guthrie suggests that, in his written philosophy "there is no creative god, no mind adapting organisms to a purpose. Living creatures, like other natural bodies, have originated in purely chance combinations of the elements" (53).

Parmenides, "whose pupil [Empedocles] is said to have been" had permanently impacted the "Ionian notion of material substance … as a living thing" but Empedocles found this position to be "no longer tenable" and considered it "necessary to posit a separate motive cause" (52). He "posited two, which he named Love and Strife" (52). He wrote, "things never cease from continual shifting, at one time coming together, through Love, into one, at another each born apart from the others through Strife" (Fr. 17). Simplicius suggests that, though "He makes the material elements four in number, fire, air, water, and earth … his real first principles, which impart motion to these, are Love and Strife. The elements are continually subject to an alternate change, at one time mixed together by Love, at another separated by Strife" (Phys. 25, 21). To Empedocles, love relates to union, and strife to separation. His belief was that, "when Love is supreme, the elements are fused together in a mass. When Strife has the victory, they exist in separate concentric layers— for the whole is conceived as spherical— with earth at the centre and fire at the circumference" (Guthrie 52). This balance of love and strife is reminiscent of *justice*, as described by Anaxamander, and the potential fusion of human moral experience with the natural order. As we will see in the next chapter on Satan in Eden, such emphasis on strife and separation—in contrast with love and union—is comparably represented in Abrahamic texts.

A further projection of the human order on that of the cosmos can be found in his *imago mundi.* Where Anaxamander placed Delphi in the center of the earth, Empedocles—like Aristotle and Ptolemy to come—envisioned "The mass of earth is at the center" of the cosmos (Parry, Empedocles). He ended his life by jumping into a volcano (Diogenes Laërtius, viii. 69).[96]

Anaxagoras, a contemporary of Empedocles and fellow pluralist, was "from Clazomenae near Smyrna, from the cradle of rational thought, and lived in Athens, where he was a member of the enlightened and skeptical circle which gathered around Pericles and Aspasia in the middle of the fifth century" (Guthrie 54). "He played an important role in the intellectual life of the city in its golden age. He was exiled from Athens in middle life, and retired to Lamsacus, a colony of Miletus, where he founded a school" (Allen 14). Quite famously, "he was indicted for saying that the sun was not a divinity, but only a white-hot stone rather larger than the Peloponnese" (Guthrie 54), "and that the Moon was composed of an earthy substance, which received its light from the sun" (Tarnas 24).

Like his fellow pluralists, "Anaxagoras denied that things come to be and pass away. He held that generation and destruction are really mixture and separation of ingenerable and indestructible elements" (Allen 14). What makes his theory different than Empedocles' is his belief in two seemingly paradoxical principles. "The first is homeomereity: a natural substance, such as gold or bone, consists solely of parts, which are like the whole. Divide gold however fineley, and the remnants are still gold. The second principle, that there is a portion of everything in everything, appears to mean that a piece of gold, or of any other natural substance, contains portions of everything else" (14). The notions that something can be purely one thing, but that all pure things contain all things within them, is difficult to conceptualize. For Anaxagoras, "the things in the one world-order are not separated one from the other nor cut off with an axe, neither the hot from the cold nor the cold from the hot" (Fr. 8). What this means is that, despite the plurality of the elements and the things they form together, nothing exists free from mixture or in isolation.

Anaxagoras' philosophy further develops the Ionian notion of mind in matter through his postulation that "mind rules the world and has brought order into it out of confusion" (Guthrie 55). This dualistic notion of a world brought under order by reason should be reminiscent of the chapter on Prometheus—especially through the image of Pandora given form by Hephaistos. Anaxagoras' belief that "the creation of a world is always the imposition of order on an already existing chaos of matter" (55) will reappear in our study of the Stoics, and the mind-body dualism of Descartes.

For Anaxagoras, all motion starts with mind. He wrote, "When Mind initiated motion, from all that was moved separation began" (Fr. 13). Mind, he says:

> Is the finest of all things and the purest, it has all knowledge about
>
> everything and the greatest power ... the things that are mingled and
>
> separated and divided off, all are known by Mind. And all things that were

to be, all things that were but are now, all things that are now or that shall

be, Mind arranged them all, including this rotation in which are now

rotating the stars, the sun and moon, the air and the ether that are being

separated off. And this rotation caused the separating off. And the dense

separated from the rare, the hot from the cold the bright from the dark and

the dry from the moist. (Fr. 12)

In this passage he uses Anaximenes' notion of condensation and rarefication. Unlike

Anaximenes, however, he clearly differentiated mind and substance. With the

development of his philosophical perspective it was "the first time a clear distinction was

explicitly drawn between matter and mind. He boldly said, not only, like Empedocles,

that there must be a moving cause apart from the matter which was moved, but that

whatever was not matter must be mind" (Guthrie 55). While on the one hand he clearly

articulated a position on the centrality of mind, on the other hand he simultaneously

affirmed the reality of matter. This position distinctly diverges from those of Pythagoras,

Heraclitus, and Parmenides who saw the belief in substance as a misinterpretation of the

sensory world instead of assuming an intrinsic reality to substance itself.

Atomistic Materialism: Leucippus & Democritus

Returning to the birth-place of materialism in Miletus, Leucippus, the first

atomist, "seems to have flourished about 440 BC" (Russell 64). Democritus, who brought

the ideas of Leucippus to Athens, was "from Abdera in Thrace, and was born about 460

BC" (Guthrie 56-7). Between the two, a theory emerged that would remain essentially

"unchanged until the nineteenth century" (57). This fixed-stone of philosophical theory

presented an image of reality as formed by space and matter, which they imagined to be microscopically small bits of pure being whose size, shape and motion necessitate mindless and mechanical collisions and combinations theoretically capable of constituting the macroscopic world we sense. Without such alterations as those made by Lucretius or Benjamin Franklin, the strict materialism of the atom necessitates a belief in determinism, and without the recognition that particles exhibit the qualities of waves, it is impossible to conceive of in intra-penetrative union between one atom and another.[97] The universe of Democritus is made of fundamentally disparate atoms that interact in accordance with mechanical cause. Attacked and defended by Aristotle, this theory was eventually transferred through Epicurus and the Stoics through Alexandrian Greece and Roman history before eventually serving as the foundation of Enlightenment science.

Democritus must have met Leucippus when he was traveling through "southern and eastern lands in search of knowledge" (Russell 64). It should be noted that he is also believed to have traveled to Egypt and Persia before exhausting his inheritance and receiving support from his brother, Herodotus, who (enviably) toured the known world in search of wisdom.[98] Leucippus was "a shadowy figure, whose very existence was doubted by [his] great follower Epicurus and has been denied by some modern scholars" (Guthrie 56). "Democritus is a much more definite figure" (Russell 64). Though he lived in Athens and was the brother of the famed historian Herodotus, he is known to have said, "'no one knew me [in Athens]'" (65). In contrast to its later success, "for a long time his philosophy was ignored in Athens" (65). "Plato never mentions him in the Dialogues, but is said by Diogenes Laertius to have disliked him so much that he wished all his books burnt" (65). Aristotle, however, "admired him greatly, and has much to say about him" (Guthrie 56-57), "for he too was an Ionian from the North" (Russell 65).

According to Bertrand Russell, a 20th century philosopher who described his own philosophy as *logical atomism*, "Leucippus, if not Democritus, was led to atomism in the attempt to mediate between monism and pluralism, as represented by Parmenides and Empedocles respectively" (Russell 65). Inspired by monism, the atomists believed in a singular substance of pure being that was perfectly solid and internally static. Inspired by pluralism, they believed in countless quantities, varieties, and mixtures of atoms that were constantly in flux. Tarnas writes:

> In an attempt to fulfill the Ionian's search for an elementary substance constituting the material world, while also overcoming the Parmenidean argument against change and multiplicity, Leucippus and his successor Democritus constructed a complex explanation of all phenomena in purely materialistic terms: The world was composed exclusively of uncaused and immutable material atoms—a unitary changeless substance, as Parmenides required, though of infinite number. These invisibly minute and indivisible particles perpetually moved about in a boundless void and by their random collisions and varying combinations produced the phenomena of the visible world. (*Passion* 21-22)

The *arche* of the atomists might be called pure being, but non-being was seen as equally essential to cosmic motion. The key addition they made to Parmenides' and Empedocles' theories was what they called, 'the void.' Leucippus "conceded to the monists that there could be no motion without a void" (Russell 69), but his vision of the cosmos is not as a singular object, like Parmenides', he sees it as a disjointed plenum of void and atoms. He states, "what 'is' in the strict sense of the term is an absolute plenum. This plenum, however, is not one; on the contrary, it is a many. ... The many move in the void ... and by coming together they produce coming-to-be, while by separating they produce passing-away" (Aristotle *On Generation*, 325a).[99]

Democritus "calls space ... 'the void,' 'nothing,' and 'the infinite,' while each individual atom he calls ... the 'compact,' and 'being.'" (Aristotle, *On Democritus, apud Simplicius, de caelo* 295, 1). These two combine to create a whole cosmos that is itself infinite, "part of it is full and part void" (Diogenes Laertius ix, 31). In Aristotle's words, "the elements are the full and the void; they call them being and not-being respectively. Being is full and solid, not being is void and rare. Since the void exists no less than body, it follows that not-being exists no less than being. These two together are the material causes of existing things" (*Metaphysics* 985b 4).

Looking more specifically at their notion of empty space, Aristotle suggests that "one would define void as place bereft of body" (*Physics*, 208 b). Russell points out, "this view is [later] set forth with utmost explicitness by Newton, who asserts the existence of absolute space, and accordingly distinguishes absolute from relative motion" (Russell 70).[100] The presence of void in substance is recognized through weight. "Democritus distinguishes heavy and light by size ... in compound bodies the lighter is that which contains more void, the heavier that which contains less" (Theophrastus, de sensu 61). "What we feel as hard has its atoms closely packed. Soft things are made of atoms wider apart, they contain more empty space and so are capable of compression and offer less resistance to the touch" (Guthrie 58). "Each atom ... was impenetrable and indivisible because it contained no void. When you use a knife to cut an apple, the knife has to find empty places where it can penetrate; if the apple contained no void, it would be infinitely hard and therefore physically indivisible" (Russell 71).

Turning more specifically to the atomistic understanding of substance, Russell writes that "Each atom is internally unchanging, and in fact a Parmenidean One" (71). This is to say, the unchanging cosmos of Parmenides was imported into the atomistic vision of minute substances. In this way the atoms "were entirely material and possessed neither divine order nor purpose" (Tarnas 22). Democritus "infers that the atoms which constitute reality have only weight, shape, size and motion" (Irwin 58). "They believed that everything is composed of atoms, which are physically, but not geometrically, indivisible ... that atoms are indestructible ... that there are infinite number of atoms, and even of kinds of atoms, the differences being as regards shape and size" (Russell 65). "The only things that atoms do are to move and hit each other, and sometimes to combine when they happen to have shapes that are capable of interlocking" (71). By combining the Pythagorean notion of pure form with a soulless vision of pure matter the atomists created a theory of pure substance that is purely differentiated by form: "the atoms were qualitatively identical, different only in shape and size" (Tarnas 21-22). Shape was defined by the spatial extension of matter and void. [101]

These atoms were "far too small to be perceived by our senses," but their sizes, shapes, "differences in their relative positions, motions, and distances from each other, were sufficient to account for all the differences of which our senses make us aware in perceptible objects" (Guthrie 58). Democritus "agrees with Heracleitus' view that 'the hidden order is superior to the apparent', and that the senses are bad witnesses if they are not interpreted correctly" (Irwin 48). His belief is that "reason can discover the hidden order that is inaccessible to the senses. [And that] rational argument, independent of the truth of sensory appearances, shows us … reality must allow the possibility of change" (49). Again we return to the recurring motif of transcending common sense and the perceptions with reason that we encountered with Heraclitus, Parmenides, and the Pythagoreans. However, where reason led Parmenides to a static permanence, it led the atomists to accept change (through a vision of subjects and objects that do not change).

Though the mechanistic causality of material things may be foundational to one's common sense understanding of the world, the belief that this is going on at a microscopic level most certainly is not, nor was the notion that geometric qualities of the particulates could lead to non-spatial perceptions like taste or smell. So while Enlightenment philosophers might talk about atomism as common sense, Classical philosophers argue that it is in opposition to what is commonly obvious.

How secondary qualities emerged from primary qualities was a topic of direct debate. Democritus says, "'by convention [nomos] there is sweet, bitter, hot, cold, colour, but in reality atoms and void. [By this] he means: perceptibles are conventionally supposed and believed to exist, but in truth none of them, but only atoms and void exists " (Irwin 49). "Like Locke, Democritus held that such qualities as warmth, taste, and colour are not really in the object, but are due to our sense organs, while such qualities as weight, density, and hardness are really in the object" (Russell 72).[102] As Allen explains, "the characteristics of these particles are geometrical, not perceptual; the colors and sounds and tastes of the world are secondary qualities, which arise in virtue of the interaction of certain kinds of physical objects (such as eyes and ears) with others (such as tables and chairs)" (Allen 15). In "their distinction between primary and secondary qualities, and most of all, in their insistence that explanation of natural processes shall be mechanical, the atomists anticipated much in the world view of modern science" (15). As simple mechanical interactions are easily understandable with an atomic interpretation, qualities like color are less intuitively explainable with atomic theory. Where those who emphasize the common-sense qualities of atomism can refer to the everyday experience of material and mechanical interactions, the explanation of qualities like warmth and taste by way of atomic theory is hard to relate to common-sense.

Despite the strength of the atomic theory and its perpetuation throughout history, there was no empirical confirmation until well after the Enlightenment. Atomism was not science, without an empirical approach it was a philosophy of the natural world. But in ancient times "there was not very sharp distinction … between empirical observation and logical argument" (Russel 68). Despite the fact that "the atomists hit on a hypothesis for which, more than two thousand years later, some evidence was found … [but] their belief, in their day, was none the less destitute of any solid foundation" (68). "Why the Greeks, for all their brilliance of intellect, made at this time so little use of experimental methods, and no progress at all in the invention of apparatus for controlled experiment, is a complicated question" (Guthrie 57). Guthrie wonders if the "Aristocratic tradition and the presence of slaves … had something to do with it" (57).

Though it has become the narrative standard to note the absence of empirical evidence for atomism, empirical evidence that material things mechanically interact is offered in every moment of our experience—and has been for much longer than even our first whispers of atomistic theory. If there was no empirical evidence for the atoms themselves, there was certainly an empirical motivation behind the atomistic belief in causality. To the cosmos, "the atomists asked the mechanistic question, and gave a mechanistic answer" (Russell 67). "In Democritus' universe everything is the necessary consequence of the movements of atoms conforming to general laws … the movements of the atoms depend only on their nature and their previous state" (Irwin 52). "They seem to have thought that, given infinite empty space with an infinite number of microscopic bodies loose in it, the bodies would inevitably move, and move aimlessly in any direction. This would naturally lead to collisions, and these to entanglements and combinations" (Guthrie 60). "It was common in antiquity to reproach the atomists with attributing everything to chance. They were, on the contrary, strict determinists, who believed that everything happens in accordance with natural laws" (Russell 66). "Democritus explicitly denied that anything can happen by chance" (66). And according to Leucippus, "nothing occurs at random, but everything for a reason and by necessity" (Fr. 2). "Atoms have no goals or purposes, but just move because of their properties and the forces exerted on them" (Irwin 50). This emphasis on efficient causation would become as influential to the development of science as the premise of materialism, and what atomism represented was an intuitive synthesis of materialism and causation.

Where the origin of motion may seem like a philosopher's question, deterministic atomism comes at the expense of free will, which is an important question for anyone. "According to Aristotle, Democritus regarded the soul as composed of one kind of atom, in particular fire atoms" (Berryman, "Ancient Atomism"). And these atoms interacted with other atoms in the same deterministic ways as the rest. From an atomistic point of view, "Human beings and their minds are part of nature; they are composed of atoms, conforming to the same laws as other atoms" (Irwin 51). This means that, "though we often say we act because we have chosen or decided to act … these explanations belong to 'convention'. And cannot describe a reality that consists only of atoms and their interactions" (51). Accepting this argument "commits us to the rejection of our belief in mental states as one of the illusions of common sense" (132). To Democritus free will is an illusion—like color it is a topical quality. Beneath our experience, the truth of the atomists is that our lives are governed by the material causality of our body's constituents. It was for these reasons that, "in later anecdotes, Democritus was presented as the laughing philosopher, laughing at the meaninglessness and pointlessness of human lives: 'there is nothing in them to be taken seriously, but they are all vain and empty, a movement of atoms and infinity'" (51). Such interpretations of absolute determinism as conflicting with free will continues to be hotly debated to this day.

The seemingly soulless and purposeless explanation of a universe limited to the mechanistic laws of matter, motion, and form "eliminate Aeschylean cosmic justice" (Irwin 57). The Epicureans expanded on the materially grounded cosmos of the atomists to see "the world as a great machine with all its parts as material bodies acting in accordance with fixed rules set by nature" (Saunders 7). This perspective was picked up by Enlightenment philosophers and Deists who famously viewed the cosmos as a clock (Dolnick, "Clockwork Universe"). To simplify the imagery of efficient causation, the gears of the clock were sometimes envisioned through the mechanistic interactions of "Billiard Ball atoms." David Hume, for example, famously preferred the metaphor. He critiques, "We fancy, that were we brought, on a sudden, into this world, we could at first have inferred, that one Billiard-ball would communicate motion to another upon impulse; and that we needed not to have waited for the event, in order to pronounce with certainty concerning it" (18). Reflecting on "the doctrine of necessity" common to these descriptions, Peirce writes:

> Its first advocate appears to have been Democritus, the atomist, who was led to it, as we are informed, by reflecting upon the 'impenetrability, translation, and impact of matter'… having restricted his attention to a field where no influence other than mechanical constraint could possibly come before his notice, he straightaway jumped to the conclusion that throughout the universe that was the sole principle of action—a style of reasoning so usual in our day. … The proposition in question is that the state of things existing. … At any time, together with certain immutable laws, completely determine the state of things at every other time parents for a limited to future time is indefensible parents. ("The Doctrine of Necessity Examined" 88-9)

This discussion of the problems associated with the doctrine of necessity and reductively materialistic atomism will be revisited throughout the dissertation in the context of its influence on the cosmology of an individual committed to these foundations.

One of the vulnerabilities of Democritus' interpretation of atomistic causation, as Russell explains, is that "atoms were always in motion … there were impacts, and the atoms were deflected like billiard balls" (65-66). This position led to one of their primary criticisms: how atoms began moving in the first place. "Aristotle accused them of 'lazily shelving' the question of the origin of motion" (Guthrie 61). According to Irwin, "Democritus assumes an original movement of the atoms" (52), but "gave no reason why the world should originally have been as it was" (Russell 66). Such consequences lead to a number of philosophical positions with religious and moral implications. When we reach Aristotle and discuss his four types of causality, what we will find is that he particularly diverged from Democritus where purpose—*telos*—was escluded.

As the dissertation continues, especially when it reflects on the Western origin stories of knowledge and the emergence of the materialistic paradigm, the religious and psychological implications of this and other reductively materialistic worldviews will be extensively considered. Democritus himself "disbelieved in popular religion" (Russell 72), and "considered that human belief in gods was no more than an attempt to explain extraordinary events like thunderstorms or earthquakes by means of imagined supernatural forces" (Tarnas 24), an idea mythologists continue to use. For these reasons he, and other atomists, considered the structure of their worldview in the context of the social sphere. It was argued, "If hot and cold, sweet and bitter, have no existence in nature but are simply a matter of how we feel at the time, then, it was argued, must we not suppose that justice and injustice, right and wrong, have an equally subjective and unreal existence" (Guthrie 68)? We will engage this question more deeply in the "After Democritus" sections.

Democritus believed, contrary to the religious-myths we tell ourselves, "The first human beings lived a 'disorderly and bestial life'; fear, not intelligence, taught them to collect in groups. … 'In general need itself was the universal teacher for human beings'" (Irwin 52). Thus "neither free choice nor design, but inevitable reaction to circumstances, caused human beings to form their characteristic way of life" (52). As the coming sections show, he shared these prototypical survival-of-the-fittest and social contract-like interpretations of human social evolution with Thucidides, Hobbes, and Freud.

Pre-Socratic Philosophy and the Emergence of Atomism

Not all schools of Greek philosophy were dedicated to materialistic interpretations of sensory experience. The reason this dissertation is so focused on atomism is because it consolidated a number of theories in a way that "foreshadowed most clearly the scientific world view which has dominated thought from the time of Newton to the present" (Allen 5). From Thales comes the premise of materialism. From Anaximines they took "the notion that the world consists in matter and its arrangement that … must be quantitative and mechanical" (5). They adopted the Parmenidean vision of an unchanging singularity with a materialistic point of view and knowledge of Pythagorean geometry. This all worked towards a vision of solid and unchanging material things defined by their geometric forms that mechanically collide with one another in a vacuum. This is the metaphysic that the Epicurean Alexandrians and Romans would come to adopt, which would later be inherited by European and American intellectuals who fortified the cosmology with calculus and empiricism. This is the metaphysic that gave foundation to the Scientific Revolution against religion with which many individuals still identify. This is the metaphysic of Deists and Newtonian physicists. Allen writes, "In their atomism, their theory of motion, their distinction between primary and secondary qualities, and most of all, in their insistence that explanation of natural processes shall be mechanical, the atomists anticipated much in the world view of modern science, and many historians have hailed them as far in advance of their time" (15). In Russell's words, "the world of the atomists remains logically possible, and is more akin to the actual world than is the world of any other of the ancient philosophers' (71). The reason we are focused on the origin story of atomism is because it is the origin story of a paradigmatic metaphysic that

has had, and continues to have (despite the influence of Kant's *Transcendental Aesthetic*
on analytic philosophy) a major influence on Western thought.

After Democritus

The chapter has thus far shown a path to atomism. At this point, instead of
continuing the survey between Socrates and the Enlightenment, I will offer a brief
summary with essential notes on the history of this dissertation's key themes—
materialism, atomism, the isolated ego, and the imprisoned soul. This will include
conversations about cultural relativism and egoism that have been associated with
theoretical atomism, the development of a system of logic consistent with materialism,
the development of atomic theory by Epicureans (from the Hellenic period to the
Democratic revolutions that established today's world), and a consideration of
atomism's impact on existential philosophy.

Following the path towards secularization, the Sophists, famous for their dictum,
man is the measure of all things, rejected the religious authority of the state based on
their recognition that impious men wrote divine constitutions (Guthrie 70). However,
where most Sophists came to believe in cultural relativity with tones of amoral egoism,
their attacks against transcendent truth and morality were attacked by Socrates.[103]
Together, Socrates and the Sophists present foundations of doubt against which
philosophy and science have been and will continue to be tested. At the same time, they
present strong foundations for the self—both the moral individual and self-referential
ego.

In contrast with Socratic and Platonic visions of the moral self as part of a
harmonic whole,[104] the early arguments for a shamelessly self-serving ego have been

frequently associated with the philosophical developments of Democritus and the natural philosophers by way of their material, atomic, and mechanically amoral interpretation of the cosmos. Terrence Irwin perpetuates the narrative tradition when he writes, "Just as Democritus seeks to explain natural processes by the basic laws of atoms, Thucydides (c. 460.-c.400) seeks to explain social and historical processes, and especially the disturbances caused by wars and revolutions, by the basic laws of human nature" (53). He continues:

> Thucydides assumes that, since we compete for limited resources that we all want, each of us has desires that tend to conflict with the desires of other people. I therefore want to prevent interference by others; I fear others who threaten interference; and so I want power over them, to prevent their interference. Hobbes (1588-1679) develops Thucydides' point: 'So that in the first place, I put for a general inclination of all mankind, a perpetual and restless desire of power after power, that ceaseth only in death, and the cause of this is not always that a man hopes for a more intensive delight than he has already attained to, or that he cannot be content with moderate power; but because he cannot assure the power and means to live well which he has present, without the acquisition of more.' Coexistence with someone else of roughly equal power is inherently unstable, since it will always be in the interest to each of them to dominate the other; hence freedom and security for oneself seem to require rule over others. But if I am free to attack others of roughly equal power, and they are free to attack me, I will be worse off than if none of us attacks any of

the others, we must therefore constitute some authority with the power to

keep the peace and … compel us to stand by the agreement. (Irwin 53-4)

As mentioned, this is much like Democritus' alternative view in which struggle as

opposed to divine intelligence resulted in the distinction of humans from animals.

As Irwin associates the points of Thucydides with Democritus, Hobbes' competitive

theories were also influenced by atomism.[105] And like Hobbes, Thucidides, and

Democritus, the atomistically minded Freud, father of *ego psychology*, also theorized the

human sacrifice of "instinctual freedom for security" to join "social groups and ultimately

in civilization" (Le Grice, personal correspondence).

One of the things we do have to consider is the obvious potential to align

atomistic theory with egoistic isolationism—the sense of one's limited enclosure within

the *I*-speaking self. This mimes the Cartesian subjectification of self within the

objectified body from which it says *cogito*. In the first chapter we discussed the virtually

geometric congruity between an atom and ego—both are seen as enclosed, isolated, and

individual. It is thus of no surprise that theories of moral egoism emerge in

concurrence—and even overlap—with the development of atomism.[106]

Alongside the co-supportive developments of atomism and egoism, any such

morality as might challenge an egoistic attitude was eroded by materialistic challenges. If

sensations are subjective and materiality the truth, why should one assume morality is not

similarly a product of human experience? Guthrie explains:

> In the physical field Democritus had said that the sensations of sweet and
>
> bitter, hot and cold, were only conventional terms. They did not
>
> correspond to anything real. It was all a matter of the temporary

arrangement of the atoms in our bodies and their reaction to the equally temporary combination in the so-called sensible object. The transference to the field of morals was only too easy, and was first made about this time, indeed, if later tradition is to be trusted, by an Athenian named Archelaus, a pupil of Anaxagoras. If hot and cold, sweet and bitter, have no existence in nature but are simply a matter of how we feel at the time, then, it was argued, must we not suppose that justice and injustice, right and wrong, have an equally subjective and unreal existence? (67-68)

Such an association between atomic and amoral theories is a common step in the mythical narrative of western philosophy. Tarnas echoes the same point made by Irwin and Guthrie, "If the experience of hot and cold had no objective existence in nature but was merely an individual person's subjective impression created by a temporary arrangement of interacting atoms, then so too must the standards of right and wrong be equally insubstantial, conventional, and subjectively determined" (Tarnas 28).

If one sees morality as relative and the self as an isolated arrangement of atoms, what ground reinforces love for others? The view of the self as isolated (and arbitrarily created) reinforces the solipsistic potential to ignore and even de-value the inner experiences and concerns beyond one's inner space. One who accepts cultural relativism has stepped onto the slippery slope towards two notably self-serving and/or damaging positions: 1, that there is neither objective morality nor a transcendental authority enforcing an objective moral code; which 2, leads many towards such an extreme interpretation of relativism that it borders on or becomes nihilistic. Further reducing any potential sense of guilt, atomists challenged the reality of free will:

We sometimes suppose that we differ from rocks, trees, and dogs because we have free will; we choose freely and are morally responsible, open to praise or blame, for what we have freely chosen to do. We don't blame a rock for falling on us, or a bee for stinging us, because we agree they have no free choice. But if we agree with Democritus, we may easily conclude that we are no different from rocks and bees; they are just collections of atoms and so are we, since we are determined by the same laws. The atomist Leucippus (mid-fifth century) strongly asserts naturalist determinism: 'Nothing happens at random, but everything for a reason and by necessity'; and the necessity derived from the atoms seems to remove individual responsibility. In later anecdotes Democritus was presented as the laughing philosopher, laughing at the meaninglessness and pointlessness of human lives: 'there is nothing in them to be taken seriously, but they are all vain and empty, a movement of atoms and infinity.' (Irwin 51)

From this point of view, "human beings and their minds are part of nature; they are composed of atoms, conforming to the same laws as other atoms. Though we often say we act because we have chosen or decided to act, we must apparently be wrong" (51). Peirce reflects, "Whosoever holds that every act of the will as well as every idea of the mind is under the rigid governance of a necessity coordinated with that of the physical world, will logically be carried to the proposition that minds are part of the physical world in such a sense that the laws of mechanics determine everything that happens according to immutable attractions and propulsions" (89). Such a perspective "cannot logically stop short of making the whole action of the mind a part of the physical universe" (95). "Indeed, consciousness in general thus becomes a mere illusory aspect of a material system" (95)

What these passages reveal is that atomic theory possesses the ability to inspire a set of beliefs that nurture an amoral ego: belief that individuals are made of atoms in isolation; that morality is a human convention; that human nature is to seek power over other humans; and that no one is ultimately responsible for their actions. It is this dissertation's contention that these positions, through the continued prominence of atomism, continue to have a major influence on contemporary psyches in the Western world. This is not to say, on the other hand, that such reinforcement of the self-asserting ego is unmitigatedly negative. As I will continue to address, the emergence of self-authority gives rise to significant benefits. In what seems like a paradoxical schism and concert, one recognizes the self-liberating lack of responsibility suggested by determinism reinforcing the self-liberated image that the radical atom empowers.

Socrates and Plato were strongly opposed to cultural relativity, moral egoism, and the primacy of the material world. In many ways, the Sophists were their nemesis. In addition to challenging the trajectory towards moral egoism and materialism, Plato and Socrates perpetuated and expanded upon the Pythagorean and Orphic belief in the immortality of the soul and its imprisonment in the material body. Plato and his school of philosophy sought to dismiss the delusions of the senses for the sake of knowledge through the soul. On the other hand, while Aristotle agreed with their inner pursuit towards harmony with the forms, he saw substance as essential. Instead of withdrawing from the senses he engaged them as primary tools. Where Plato highly disliked atomism, Aristotle appreciated, and, perhaps more importantly, taught the theory.

Plato's Academy was a center for geometry and abstract philosophy. Aristotle's Lyceum was a center for the natural sciences. Though it may be that Plato was the more popular philosopher in antiquity, it was Aristotle's materialistic perspective and corresponding study of nature's predictability that nurtured the emerging zeal for natural philosophy in the Hellenistic, Roman, and later European worlds. Thus, despite the reaction of Plato and later Platonists against the path towards materialism, his own pupil, Aristotle, solidified its course.

His interest in matter and causation led to the categorization of four causes. "In *Physics* II 3 and *Metaphysics* V 2, Aristotle offers his general account" (Falcon, *Aristotle on Causation*):

- The material cause: "that out of which", e.g., the bronze of a statue.

- The formal cause: "the form", "the account of what-it-is-to-be", e.g., the shape of a statue.

- The efficient cause: "the primary source of the change or rest", e.g., the artisan, the art of bronze-casting the statue, the man who gives advice, the father of the child.

- The final cause: "the end, that for the sake of which a thing is done", e.g., health is the end of walking, losing weight, purging, drugs, and surgical tools. (*Aristotle on Causation*)

The first cause demonstrates Aristotle's interpretation of the cosmos as materially constituted. The second cause is presented here as relating to "shape," like "the shape of a statue." And the third cause, described as "the primary source of the change or rest," reads like Newton's law of motion pertaining to the change of an object's motion or resting state. Together, such an interpretation of the first three causes is consistent with the atomistic cosmological vision in which the mechanical interactions of material things with unique shapes account for reality as experienced through human senses and apparati. In his discussion of Aristotle's four kinds of causes, David Bohm suggests that the above interpretation presents a modern projection onto Aristotle's second and especially third types of causation, which, for our purposes, is more immediately relevant than Aristotle's original meaning.[107] The tendency is to interpret these laws through a contemporaty lens, which might also be described as weaving past work into a living myth.

Where Aristotle particularly diverges from the atomistic theory of Democritus is the fourth type of causation. As Falcon writes, "In thinking about the four causes, we have come to understand that Aristotle offers a *teleological explanation* of the production of a bronze statue; that is to say, an explanation that makes a reference to the *telos* or end of the process" (*Aristotle on Causation*). It might be said, the fourth law identifies where reductive atomism can fully break away from theistic and psychological models that see the cosmos to be in relation with free or divine will and purpose.[108] Though atomists throughout the ages would take each side of the argument between a random and purposed universe, Democritus, not unlike most of today's scientists, rejects the fourth law of causation.

In addition to championing matter as foundational and categorizing causation, Aristotle helped to establish a system of logic that reinforced the development of rational thought and scientific theory. As we will see, this system is consistent with the way the material world works. While this may have been intentional for Aristotle and appreciated by reductive materialists, for anyone who does not consider substance to be the ground of all being, his logic limits reason to the structures of materialism. It also reinforces the tendency to project the behavior of material things into such philosophical territories as ethics and political ideology. While in this section it is only essential to show the consistency between his logical system and materiality, in chapter five we will explore the discoveries of Einstein and their simultaneous challenges to Aristotelean logic along with reductive materiality.

Aristotle argues in Book 1 of his *Metaphysics* that "before embarking on this study of substance … first philosophy, the most general of the sciences, must also address the most fundamental principles—the common axioms—that are used in all reasoning" (Shields, "Aristotle"). As the mythic narrative of Western philosophy goes, "Aristotle's logical works contain the earliest formal study of logic that we have" (Smith, "Aristotle's Logic"). Perhaps what is so remarkable is that the "highly developed logical theory … was able to command immense respect for many centuries: Kant, who was ten times more distant from Aristotle than we are from him, even held that nothing significant had been added to Aristotle's views in the intervening two millennia" ("Aristotle's Logic").[109] For this reason, "Aristotelean Logic" has been highly conflated with "classical logic." He supported all of the "three Classical laws of thought."

The three essential laws are *identity, noncontradiction,* and the *excluded middle.* On the law of *identity,* Aristotle writes, "Each thing itself … and its essence are one and the same in no merely accidental way, as is evident both from the preceding arguments and because to know each thing, at least, is just to know its essence, so that even by the exhibition of instances it becomes clear that both must be one" (*Metaphysics*, VII.17). Elsewhere in the *Metaphysics* he says, "Now 'why a thing is itself' is a meaningless inquiry for—to give meaning to the question 'why'—the fact or the existence of the thing must already be evident" (VII.17). His position is "that a thing is itself is the single reason and the single cause to be given in answer to all such questions as why the man is man, or the musician musical, unless one were to answer, 'because each thing is inseparable from itself, and its being one just meant this.' This, however, is common to all things" (VII.17).[110] Mathematically simplified, this generates the logical statement, A=A, where A is understood as inseparable from itself, internally unchanging, isolated and whole. From his point of view, "if a definition is an expression signifying the essence of the thing ... the predicates contained therein ought also to be the only ones which are predicated of the thing in the category of essence" (Aristotle, *Topics* VII. 1).

The law of identity is resonant with God as met by Moses in Exodus 3:14 when he said to him, "I am who I am" (English Standard Version). As the being of God is here described as self-sustaining, A=A because of "A" with no need of "B" or any other sustainer of "A". This is not just how Aristotle understands such logical statements, this is how he sees objects—they are because they are. He does not need an explanation beneath them, they are their own foundation to the explanation of their being. St. Thomas Aquinas, who transmitted Aristotle's philosophy through several commentaries on the figure, followed a similar line of thinking.[111]

Though many logicians see the law of identity as the first of the Classical laws, Aristotle presented it as a derivative of the law of contradiction. According to his vision of the principle, "It is impossible for the same thing to belong and not belong simultaneously to the same thing in the same respect" (*Metaphysics* V: I). "This is the most secure of all principles, Aristotle tells us, because 'it is impossible to be in error about it'" (Shields, "Aristotle"). "The principle of non-contradiction (PNC) [is] the principle that 'the same attribute cannot at the same time belong and not belong to the same subject and in the same respect'" (1005b19). Thus this premise must be true for the logic built on top of it to stand. According to Aristotle, "it cannot, however, be proved, since it is employed, implicitly, in all proofs, no matter what the subject matter. It is a first principle, and hence is not derived from anything more basic" (Cohen "Aristotle's Metaphysics"). For Aristotle, this is the table on which the logical house of cards is built.

Translated into a physical example, a baseball can be heavy and white because color is a different (and thus non-contradictory) aspect of the baseball than weight. On the other hand, a baseball cannot be a baseball bat because there are several competing principles. For one, their shapes are not the same, their colors are not the same, and their weight is not the same—these dimensions of comparison show the two entities to be contradictory to one another. One of the foundations to this understanding is that for a baseball to be a baseball bat the two would have to share space as one, this is impossible for material solids. A homerun is the result of the fact that a baseball and a baseball bat cannot share the same space and become one with one another. If A is not B it is not B, if B is not A it cannot be A. Of course, those who see the identity principle as more foundational than non-contradiction want to say that this relies on the more essential statement that A=A and B=B. And indeed, he gives a version of the identity principle as a reverse proof for the principle of non-contradiction.[112] Returning to Aristotle's words, "It is impossible for the same thing to belong and not belong simultaneously to the same thing in the same respect" (*Metaphysics* V: I), we see that a baseball bat cannot be both spherical and not spherical, it cannot be brown and not brown, or not white and white.

The third essential and mythically famous Classical law of thought is the "Excluded Middle," which essentially derives from what we have discussed about the other two. "Of any one subject, one thing must be either asserted or denied" (*Metaphysics* 1011b24). "The law of non-contradiction tells us that a statement cannot be both true and false at the same time" (Horn, "Law of Non-Contradiction"). A baseball cannot "be" and "not be" any more than it can be "true" and "not true" that it is a solid sphere. It cannot be true and not true that a man has a brain. All such statements that are true about a man are true to its identity and cannot be contradicted.

As we notice, these three rules of reason are completely consistent with Aristotle's materialistic worldview. One might even postulate that they emerged from and not before his conclusions about the foundational qualities of substance. As we will see in chapter five, both this system of logic and the materialistic metaphysic with which it finds common sense congruity results in a limited vision of nature and sense of reason. Eventually we will discuss scientific and mythical examples that reveal the limitation of these synchronized modes of thinking, but our task at hand is to follow the perpetuation of these forms of thought into later Greek and Roman philosophy as well as the European and American Enlightenment.

As the student of Aristotle, "Alexander carried with him and disseminated the Greek culture and language throughout the vast world he conquered. Thus Greece fell just as it culminated, yet spread triumphantly just as it submitted" (Tarnas 73). Over the next two hundred years, the Hellenistic culture excelled "in the field of natural science"

(79). "The geometer Euclid, the geometer-astronomer Apollonius, the mathematical physicist Archimedes, the astronomer Hipparchus, the geographer Strabo, the physician Galen, and the geographer-astronomer Ptolemy all produced scientific advances and codifications that would remain paradigmatic for many centuries" (79).

In a quite opposite way than Plato, who hoped to separate the body from the study of soul, the later scientific movement engaged the separation of soul from the study of material bodies. "In the wake of Aristotle's expansion and classification of the sciences, a specialization that gradually separated science from philosophy [emerged]" (76). During this period, science "became more thoroughly rationalistic, shedding the virtually religious impetus and goal of divine comprehension formerly visible in Pythagoras, Plato, and even Aristotle" (78).

Despite the later conquest of the Romans, "Greek high culture still presided over the educated classes of the greater Mediterranean world and was rapidly absorbed by the Romans. The most significant scientists and philosophers continued to work within the Greek intellectual framework" (74). During this time, the "Romans succeeded not only in conquering the entire Mediterranean basin and a large part of Europe, but also in fulfilling their perceived mission of extending their civilization throughout the known world" (87). Throughout this period, "The Greek *paideia* flourished. Thus the earlier Hellenic achievement was scholastically consolidated, geographically extended, and vitally sustained for the remainder of the classical era" (79).

However, "While Plato and Aristotle continued to be studied and followed, the two dominant philosophical schools originating in the Hellenistic era, the Stoic and Epicurean, were of a different character" (75). Neither of these systems is particularly concerned with God—their shared emphasis is on humanity at present. Both are founded on materialism. The Epicureans were explicitly atomistic. Based on their vision of the body and soul as matter, the two dominant schools of philosophy throughout Alexandrian and Roman history were skeptical of an afterlife.

This is not to say Romans (or Alexandrians) were unconcerned with the soul; rather, the growing separation of religion and science left the "culture's emotional and religious demands [to be] met most directly by the various mystery religions—Greek, Egyptian, Oriental—which offered salvation from the imprisonment of the world, and which flourished throughout the empire with ever increasing popularity" (78). This note is essential for this dissertation in that, while we follow the trajectory of de-spiritualized matter, we also have to recognize that Western culture continued to engage the vision of soul as imprisoned in this world.

Before moving on from the Epicureans, as mentioned in this chapter's intro, Thomas Jefferson was a self-proclaimed Epicurean.[113] This was not uncommon in the Enlightenment: Gassendi's work on Epicurus had become highly influential for Isaac Newton, Robert Boyle, John Locke, and Benjamin Franklin.[114]

As the story goes, in the Roman transition to Christianity and the European transition that followed Rome's fall, Classical philosophy became all but lost in the Western World. Meanwhile, Eastern Rome continued to thrive for a long time before it was eventually conquered by an Islamic empire. The Muslims tended the traditions of Classical philosophy, and it was from their libraries that the work of the Classic philosophers was translated into European languages. Though this is the common story, recent scholars have challenged whether or not atomism was ever truly lost in the West. In the Encyclopedia of Medieval Philosophy, in an article on atomism, Robert writes:

> It has long been thought, until the end of the nineteenth century, that there were no atomist theories in medieval philosophy and that ancient atomists, such as Epicurus or Lucretius, remained unknown until the Renaissance, before Poggio Bracciolini worked on the manuscript of the *De Natura Rerum* discovered by him in 1417. This view of the history of atomism has been challenged during the last two centuries. In the nineteenth century, Kurd Lasswitz and Le´opold Mabilleau already endeavored to make room for medieval theories in their essays on atom- istic philosophy (Lasswitz 1890; Mabilleau 1895). … If we now focus on western Latin philosophy, it appears that atomism never really ceased to exist during the Middle Ages … it must be noticed, as Philippe has shown in his pioneering study (Philippe 1895,1896), that Lucretius' poem was copied and discussed throughout the Middle Ages with no interruption from the era of the Church Fathers to the twelfth century. The same is also true for Epicurus, whose works were partially known through a still longer chain of intermediate sources (Cicero, Lactantius, St. Jerome, St. Ambrose, St. Augustine). In the twelfth century, John of Salisbury dealt with Epicureanism in his Metalogicon and in his Entheticus, where he tried to refute its principal tenets. On the contrary, we find a defense of Lucretius and the Epicureans in the works of William of Conches, notably in

> his *Dragmaticon philosophiae* where he quotes passages from
>
> Lucretius' *De Natura Rerum*. (125)

He then goes on to describe examples of atomism in the 1400s, well before the influential work of Gassendi, who lived between 1592 and 1655.

Even if atomism were present in the Dark and Middle ages, it was not as popular as it was among the Epicureans and those who received Gassendi's transmission of Epicurean atomism. Though "Newton had started out with the traditional educational program that emphasized Aristotle and the Scholastic world-view … he quickly abandoned it for studies of the writings of an English follower of Gassendi, Walter Charleton" (Cook, *Epicurus*) who was one of the primary disseminators of Epicurean philosophy throughout England. "Atomism became a cornerstone of Newton's thinking, as can be seen in the early drafts for the second edition of his monumental *Principia* where Newton included ninety lines from *De Rerum Natura* in connection with his concept of inertia" (*Epicurus*). Together, Lock and Newton "were the harbingers of modern science and modern social organization" (*Epicurus*). And atomism was a clear foundation for their scientific and social paradigm(s). There is a reason school children continue to believe Democritus invented democracy, and it is not just the name—there is a clear conflation between his metaphysics and the democratic order.

In the late 19th century, Susan E. Blow (who started the first kindergarten in St. Louis), offered an eloquent articulation of just how pervasive atomism had become:

> It has often been observed that the dominant idea of an age gives form
>
> alike to its science, its politics, its philosophy, its theology, and its
>
> education. Thus the age of scientific atomism was also an age of political

atomism, reaching its climax in the French Revolution; of philosophic

atomism as illustrated in the sense theory of knowledge, and carried to its

logical consequence by Hume in the denial of causality and true self-hood;

of theological atomism, shown in the crude deism which excluded a kind

of atomic divinity from that aggregate of atoms which could only by

courtesy be called the universe; and of educational atomism, as set forth in

the *Émile* of Rousseau. (3)

As much of this dissertation has been trying to convey, atomism presents a potential

foundation and meta-structure that can be applied to systems that may or may not be

themselves material—from the microcosm of the self to the macrocosmic universe as

well as the ethical, ideological, and existential models at the center of human life.

As mentioned, American forefathers like Thomas Jefferson and Benjamin

Franklin were heavily influenced by atomism – much like the majority of Enlightenment

(and Deist) intellectuals.[115] The contemporary global community they initiated was not

just founded on the democratic revival and its revolutions against the tyrannies of kings

and popes. It was born from the entire paradigm of Enlightenment thought in which

atomism and democracy were only topically divisible: at their foundations they are both

founded on a vision of interacting subjects and objects that possess distinct individualities

(deserving of rights).[116]

While the revolutions in America, France and elsewhere liberated individuals

from the hierarchical tyrannies of kings and religious leaders, the current vision of the

individual was as isolated. On one hand this leads to will, power, and ego-centric

philosophies that value if not champion the individual; on the other hand, such thought can also lead towards the depths of existential philosophy, which is significantly inspired by the perception and experience of human individuals as estranged. Pascal directly associated the atom with his vision of himself as isolated in an existential-like state of despair. He writes, in his 17th century work, *Thoughts on Religion*:

> I know not who sent me into the World, nor what the World is, nor what I am myself. … I know not what my Body is, what my Sense, nor what my Soul is; and this very part of my self that thinks what I say, and that reflects upon it, and upon itself, knows not itself…I behold the vast distances of the Universe that contains me, and find myself confined to a Corner of this vast Body, not knowing wherefore I am placed rather in this place than another; nor why the little time allotted me to live, is assign'd me at this Point rather than any other, of that Eternity that has gone before, or shall follow after me. I see nothing but Infinities on all sides that swallow me up like an Atom, and like a Shadow that remains but a Moment and passeth away: All that I know is, that I shall shortly die; but what I know most of all is, that I do not know death itself, which I cannot avoid. (Lemay 363).

In this single passage Pascal "combined thoughts of the infinity of the universe , the vanity of man, the limitations of our knowledge, the nature of God, and a kind of existentialist angst concerning the place of human beings in nature" (363). In the description he shows how the self-image inspired by atomism translates into one of isolation and meaningless finitude. Tarnas echoes this image when he describes the contemporary cosmological tendency to objectify the world and turn "the human self into an object," which he considers "an ephemeral side effect of a random universe" that results in the image of oneself as "an isolated atom in mass society, a statistic, a commodity, passive prey to the demands of the market, prisoner of the self-constructed modern 'iron cage'" (*Cosmos* 33). He also describes how pervasive the thought of how small we are in a massive cosmos has become in our culture's media and conversations.

Other existentially oriented philosophers were similarly brought to despair by their sense of solitude.[117] For example, Kierkegaard's "knight of faith has simply and solely himself, and therein lies the frightfulness … The Knight of Faith is alone in everything … the true knight of faith is always absolute isolation" (69). In response to an atomistic like notion that the individual is void of the eternal, a common cover for *Fear and Trembling* reads, "If at the bottom of everything there were only a wild ferment, a power that twisting in dark passions produced everything great or inconsequential, if an unfathomable insatiable emptiness lay hid beneath everything, what would life be but despair?" As the sense of isolation fuels existential anxiety, the philosophical development of isolated matter—and the projection of the associated notions into the isolated self—fuels and gives foundation to this existential angst. Reflecting on this anxiety of isolation, Paul Tillich writes:

> When Kierkegaard broke away from Hegel's system of essences he … realized that the knowledge of that which concerns us infinitely is possible only in an attitude of infinite concern, in an existential attitude. At the same time he developed a doctrine of man which describes the estrangement of man from his essential nature in terms of anxiety and despair. Man in the existential situation of finitude and estrangement can

reach truth only in an existential attitude. 'Man does not sit on the throne of God,' participating in his essential knowledge of everything that is. Man has no place of pure objectivity above finitude and estrangement. His cognitive function is as existentially conditioned as his whole being. This is the connection of the two meanings of 'existential'" (125-6).

The problem Kierkegaard isolated was that a finite being can only operate with its finite knowledge, which means it is not operating with knowledge of any sort of totality—like the universe or a divine plan. This gap between how one might act if they knew what God knew and their actions as a finite being is an essential cause for existential anxiety. At the foundation of this perspective is the premise of finitude, at the foundation of which is the notion of an isolated object (and lonely subject). Tillich remarks, "doubt is based on man's separation from the whole of reality, on his lack of universal participation, on the isolation of his individual self" (49).

Tillich describes what he calls an existential point of view, which is not so articulated as fully fledged existentialism as he understands it. He believes:

> The existentialist point of view is present in most theology and in much philosophy, art, and literature. … After some isolated forerunners had appeared, existentialism as protest became a conscious movement with the second third of the 19th century, and as such has largely determine the destiny of the 20th century. Existentialism as expression is the character of the philosophy, art, and literature of the period of the world wars and all – pervading anxiety of doubt and meaninglessness. It is the expression of our own situation. (126)

He offers a few examples with which we are now familiar. He writes, "most characteristic, and at the same time most decisive for the whole development of all forms of existentialism, is Plato. Following the Orphic descriptions of the human predicament he teaches the separation of the human soul from its 'home' in the realm of pure essences" (126-7). Here Tillich begins to connect the existential sense of estrangement and isolation with the ascetic image of the body as that which is responsible for the soul's estrangement.

He also explores the examples of the classical Christian doctrine concerning the fall and salvation. He describes the structures as "analogous to the Platonic distinctions" (127). "As in Plato, the essential nature of man and his world is good. It is good in Christian thought because it is a divine creation. But man's essential or created goodness has been lost. The fall and sin corrupted not only his ethical but also his cognitive qualities. He is subjected to the conflicts of existence and his reason is not exempted from them" (127). Here Tillich draws attention to the cognitive fall of humanity and the corresponding estrangement from divinity and goodness, a focus of our conversation. In the next chapter we will consider the numerous details of the story that present such estrangement as a narrative entry of humanity into matter and isolation.

Chapter Conclusion

As we have seen, materialism, atomism, and mind/body dualism have been foundational structures in the history and development of Western philosophical thought. They have been around since the "Pre-Socratic" origin period of Western philosophy— though perhaps in less specifically articulated form—and they continue to endure. As the story is told, Western thought has been on an evolutionary path that originally emerged from a religious under-use of reason into the materialistic philosophies that gave rise to science. This narrative quite clearly starts with Thales and what Aristotle took as the root premise for materialism—'everything is substance.' Whether or not the premise of materialism is The theoretical foundation of Western science, it is undoubtedly the inciting incident in its narrative lore. If Thales represents the first step in the origin story of Western philosophical and scientific knowledge, that first step is remembered as materialistic.

The words "starting point" are as ambiguous as the word *arche*, as they could mean the first in a sequence or the first premise of a thought. If we remember from the section on Thales, the word *arche* meant a chronological starting point for Homer before it became a philosophical term for a thought's starting point. This blur is beyond language, as anyone can supply evidence for themselves that it is the want of their reason to start sequential chains of philosophical statements (mental or spoken) with the most secure premise(s) available. In this way, materialism was not just the chronological first thought, it also served as a foundational premise for Western reason and its development of science. In this way the Western philosophical origin story of knowledge began with a commitment of theory to a materialistic mode of thought.

Beyond materialism, atomism has also been fundamental to the development of science and Western reason. We have seen that it emerged from the same Edenic origin point as materialism—Miletus—and from within the same "Pre-Socratic" origin-period. The question this begs is whether or not atomism is essential to the development of philosophy in more than a historical way. Though the philosophy that did take hold remembers materialism as a chronological starting point and theoretical foundation, to attempt a statement concerning the objective (as opposed to empirical) dependence of philosophy's birth on materialism would take the dissertation beyond its stated epistemological frame.

Without my narrative-based argument, it might be posited that causation and the study thereof has been as or more foundational to Western science than the premise of materialism. Whether or not this is the case, what atomism represents is the synthesis of materialistic and causal theories that immediately became a talking point for Plato, a teaching point for Aristotle, and a foundation for Epicurean philosophy in Alexandrian Greece, Rome, Newtonian physics and Enlightenment philosophy. It should also be noted that the ideological patterns through which the contemporary world operates were established by thinkers from within this (Enlightenment) paradigm. Locke, Hobbes, Marx, Franklin and Jefferson, to name a few, revolutionized the political theory and ideologies of today's Western states.

The way atomism synthesized materialism and causation in the form of mechanics emerged as an intuitive vision of the microscopic reinforced by the material world with which we interact (things bounce off each other or combine based on their shapes and momentum). This picture became prominent with the emergence of science as the *modus operendi* of Western reason. The champions of science, in their historic challenge to religion, found strength in their confidence that the medieval Christian cosmology was wrong *because* it was inconsistent with their science, which was founded on the study of material causes like those of a machine.

As we have seen with Democritus and Epicureans, the reduction of the self and soul to its body has theoretical consequences. The meta-form of a Classical atom is as matter with distinct and impervious boundaries. Constellating this microcosmic image with the microcosmic image of self is to see the material boundaries of the body as distal limits of an isolated self. As we noted in our brief look at Pascal, Kierkegaard, and Tillich existential anxiety is significantly fueled by the feeling of isolation, which has been repeatedly poeticized in the form of a conflation between atom and self. If atomism can be seen as foundational to a paradigm of thought, if atomism reinforces an isolative self-image, and if the sense of self-isolation fuels existential anxiety; then it can be seen that where classical atomism is foundational to a cosmological system, those committed to such an intellectual paradigm are vulnerable to the existential anxiety exacerbated by isolation.

On the other hand, it might also be said that such foundations and cosmologies lead to ego-affirming philosophies that place self in the center. In fact, we have repeatedly seen the emergence of moralistic egoism and survival-of-the-fittest-based social models in the context of atomistic conversations. The question this begs—especially considering the congruent enclosures of ego and atom—is whether or not the theoretical ego and atom codependently arose through a feedback loop of essential projections upon one another. One might also ask whether or not a positive answer to this question would suggest an objective or transcendent reality of the particulated form shared by atom and ego. Again, to answer such questions would take this dissertation beyond its epistemological framework. To remain in empirical territory, what can be said is that theories of atom and ego emerged concurrently and contingently. My interests is in implications of the fact that this is the history of Western consciousness.

This sense of isolation within one's material body engages another essential current in Western thought—mind-body-dualism and the notion of the soul as imprisoned within the body. This conversation sometimes has and sometimes has not mixed with the conversation about atomism and materialism. What is important for us to recognize is that the Pre-Socratic origin story of knowledge contained recurring conversations about the imprisonment of the soul in the body and the delusion of the mind by way of its senses. The Pythagoreans were especially known for this view, and Plato after them, though Anaximenes, Heraklitus and Empedocles expressed comparable perspectives.

Descartes' later distinguished the inner mind and outer body in the context of a machine-like body that became increasingly associated with atoms over time. Meanwhile the mind of Descartes (or soul of Plato) became associated with the Christian soul and its liberation from the (atomized) flesh. To be sure, Descartes' theories were invariably influenced by his Jesuit education that introduced him to both Christian and Classical theories of the body and soul's relationship (Britanica, *Death*). Though many atomists and Enlightenment thinkers diverged entirely from the belief in miracles and soul, we can see how individuals dedicated to both threads of Western consciousness were capable of associating their religious belief in a soul with the *mind* of Descartes' more secular *mind-body* conversation. As the (typical) experience of an individual is the isolation of their psyche within a body, the atomic vision of isolated material entities only reinforces the psyche's potential awareness of isolation. We can see then that, the perspective of the psyche or soul as imprisoned within the body and the vision of bodies as made up of isolated matter reinforce one another insofar as they represent human life as an experience of isolation.

This conversation about isolation and the imprisonment of the psyche or soul within matter is becoming increasingly reminiscent of that which emerged in the chapter on Prometheus. In more abstract terms, the myth of Prometheus developed the notions of isolation and imprisonment, materiality, and the entry of intelligent animation into matter. If we were to fully engage the relationships between the Promethean myth and Western philosophy we would not be ready to include the essential involvement of Christian history and Abrahamic traditions. As we will learn in the next chapter, the religion that replaced what we now know as Classical mythology provides a story comparable with that of Prometheus and the Classical conception of soul as imprisoned within body. Once we have finished working through the last of these three stories we will consider the first half of this dissertation's thesis—that the Classical, philosophical, and Abrahamic origin stories of knowledge reinforce a shared narrative of the psyche's entry into a materialistically grounded cosmology. From here we will be able to consider potential congruities between the materialistic paradigm defined by atomism—in this chapter on natural philosophy—and the material world into which the first humans entered—in the myths of Prometheus and Adam.

Chapter 4: Abrahamic Origin Stories of Knowledge: Adam in Mater

The story of Adam and Eve in Eden has been perceived as a foundation (and propagated as inspiration) everywhere that Judaism, Christianity, and Islam have become the dominant religion for at least some period of time. This includes a majority of the Middle East, Mediterranean, Western Europe, Russia and the Caucasus,[118] the Americas, South Pacific, Australia and parts of Africa. Additionally, Christianity is growing in influence within China, Korea and Japan. In all reality, there are few corners of the world that the Abrahamic mythologies have not reached and substantially influenced.

According to Abrahamic traditions, the story is the account of first humans, first knowledge, and the inciting incident of life's labors. As such, the story of Eden has participated in the conscious and unconscious formation of thoughts, memories, and belief systems for thousands of years and billions of people. Unique versions of the story have been written by Jews, Christians, Muslims, Egyptians, Georgians, Greeks, Romans, Irish and Englishmen. Americans like Mark Twain and Joseph Smith recorded variants. Some versions are highly religious—as in *Genesis*, the *Quran*, and the Christian Books of Adam. Others are folkloric, like the *Midrash* and *Talmud*, or fairy tale-like as in Hans Christian Andersen's *Garden of Paradise*. Examples like *Canterbury Tales*, *Paradise Lost*, the *Divine Comedy*, and *Saltair Na Rann* blur the lines between epic poetry and religious myth. While a certain historic and religious weight will be given to the version found in *Genesis*, which is older than these others, this dissertation is especially interested in the unique nuances and repetitive qualities that the collection reveals.

In addition to the original story of Eden and its retellings, it will be important to consider the story's roots in Semitic mythology from Akkadian Sumer and Babylon to

Assyria and the Phoenician seas. Because of the recurring Egyptian influences on the region and on its people before, during, and after the writing of *Genesis*, it will be important to remain attentive to parallels between the core elements of the Eden story and striking comparisons from Egypt. As this study includes Classical content, this discourse will certainly be sensitive to potential Mediterranean influences through Israeli shores (and their Phoenician neighbors).

In researching this material I have come to suspect a major historical influence on the story involving the fall of the Assyrian world and Jerusalem with it, but I want to avoid engaging this historical riddle. Though historic narratives are certainly of interest when examining the many variants of the Eden myth, settling historic truths is not essential to this dissertation's focus on the myth's influence. That being said, in a deleted appendix I engage what I take to be a strong constellation of facts and details that seem to convey a relatively clear example of at least one historical environment represented by the myth.

The more direct obligation of this chapter is to show the consistency of this dissertation's essential themes with the story from *Genesis* and its retellings—namely entry into matter and isolation. To address these themes and do service to the myth we will have to introduce the many characters and elements in play as we work through the narrative. Special attention will be given to the garden, tree, fruit, snake, couple, Satan, seduction, fall and exile. As we will see, each play a role in communicating a narrative in which—as in the myth of Prometheus and Pandora—divine soul enters a human body that labors for food and childbirth after becoming mortal and material. In the first sections we will discuss the elements and characters of the Garden. In the next we will follow the story's arc from Adam's creation to his burial. Like Prometheus' creation of

humans from clay and restraint to stone, we will see Adam created from clay and buried

in rock—as isolated from Jehovah as Prometheus became from Zeus. Beyond the

metaphysical implications of materialistic isolation, Adam and Eve will offer us a chance

to witness the human emotions and psychological responses of the entry into body,

world, and the labors of life.

The Garden: Trees, Mountains and Center

In the chapter on Prometheus we discussed his residence at the Eastern point of

the sunrise, Eden, too, resides in this conceptually geographical location of temporal

origination.[119] In *Genesis*, "the Lord God planted a garden eastward in Eden" (English

Standard Version 2:8), which Milton repeats in *Paradise Lost,* "Of God the Garden was,

by him in the East, / of Eden planted" (IV. 209-10).[120] Implicit in this locational context

is the suggestion of mimetic relationships between mornings and beginnings: between

first light and lit land. As this chapter will show, this locational and temporal context

mirrors the extensive number of new beginnings and initiations—onto being, knowledge,

sexuality, self-reflective consciousness, isolation, clothing and covering. Even death, the

ultimate end, is new.

Before "The Fall," four rivers watered the garden, where the lord God made grow

"every tree that is pleasant to the sight, and good for food" (*Genesis* 2: 8-15). It is

generally believed that in the garden there was enough provision for the first humans "not

to go hungry nor to go naked, nor to suffer from thirst, nor from the sun's heat" (*Sura XX

Ta-Ha* 7:118-119). "In the happy Garden ... / [mankind reaped] immortal fruits of joy

and love, / uninterrupted joy, unrivaled love" (Milton, III. 67-68).[121] "Every tree that is planted in it is sacred" (*Book of Jubilees* 15; 3). According to Andersen's fairy tale, it is an "Isle of Bliss, where death never comes … a delightful place to be" (*Garden of Paradise* 85). In Milton's description, the fruit was actually "burnished with Golden Rind … Hesperian fables true" (67). The Garden is where humans existed before they were mortal, before they were hungry, before they labored. As the paradise of heaven follows death, the paradise of Eden preceded life's labors.[122] In this un-fallen place, the divine couple was, according to Milton, "incapable of mortal injury Imperishable, and though pierced with wound, / Soon closing, and by native vigor healed" (VI. 434-436). The situation of Eden in the east, in the context of beginnings, implies this was not to last.

In addition to the comprehension of Eden at the Eastern starting point of our world and its time, it is also conceptualized as the world's center. "The Jewish apocalypse and a Midrash state that Adam was formed in Jerusalem. Adam being buried at the very spot where he was created, i.e., at the center of the world" (Eliade, *Eternal* 16-17). In the Syrian text, *The Cave of Treasures*, which is among the earliest Christian retellings of the Eden myth, it is said that, Adam rose and "stood upright in the center of the earth, he planted his two feet on that spot whereon was set up the Cross of our Redeemer; for Adam was created in Jerusalem" (169-173). This Christian notion of Golgotha can also be found in *The First Book of Adam and Eve*, in which it is explained that "the Church of the Holy Sepulcher is believed to have been constructed on this hill" in Jerusalem (Malan, XLII. 13). Milton perpetuates this tradition with his account that, "Here Pilgrims roam … to seek/ In *Golgotha* him dead" (III: 475-8). The twelfth century Pilgrim, Therva, wrote that, at the Church of the Holy Sepulcher, in "the center of the world … on the day of the summer solstice, the light of the Sun falls perpendicularly from Heaven" (Eliade, *Sacred* 40). To this day one can still visit the church of the Holy Sepulcher to see a crack in the stone from which Adam was liberated when Christ was crucified—a story to which we will return when we shift our attention to Christ.[123]

While Jewish traditions do not confirm the Church of the Holy Sepulcher as the site of Adam's burial and center of the world, they have similar traditions that recognize both Jerusalem and Adam's burial with the world's center (Eliade, *Sacred* 41).[124] Even in Islamic tradition, it was from Jerusalem that Mohammad ascended to heaven in the story of the *Miʿrāj*.[125] Interestingly, though the Muslims associate the Kaaba with the spiritual center of the world instead of a Jerusalem site (38-9),[126] they still believe it was "Adam [who] journeyed to the holy city in Arabia, where he built the Kaaba, having through fasting and silence gained the partial forgiveness of God" (Jewish Encyclopedia, "Adam"). Though the mythic center of the world is not completely agreed upon by the various Abrahamic points of view, by the varying Abrahamic accounts, Adam was created, placed and buried in the center. He built the Kaaba in the center, and the first temple—which Adam was shown—was created in Jerusalem and similarly described as the center of the world. In their own ways, Jewish, Christian, and Muslim traditions reinforce the association of Eden and/or Adam with religious and mythic centers.[127]

Comparative mythologists look to a broad collection of "world centers" in their comparisons with the Garden of Eden—trees, mountains, gardens, temples, etc. In this tradition, Eliade and Campbell both emphasize the role of the Garden's tree of knowledge as an "axis mundi," for which I should offer their theoretical descriptions. In all instances we are talking about a center of the world's horizontal plane (x) that extends on the vertical axis (y) in the form of a tree, pillar, mountain, or something of the sort, which provides a visual image of connectivity along that axis, bridging the high with the low while sometimes gathering the broad.

Campbell refers to the "axial pole" (*Occidental* 264-5), and describes "a world-uniting and supporting Cosmic Tree, World Mountain ... or sacred sanctuary, to which both the social order and the meditations of the individual are to be directed" (Campbell *Primitive* 359).[128] In his book, *The Sacred and the Profane,* Eliade describes his understanding of center:

> (a) a sacred place [that] constitutes a break in the homogeneity of space; (b) this break is symbolized by an opening by which passage from one cosmic region to another is made possible (from heaven to earth and vice versa; from earth to the underworld); (c) communication with heaven is expressed by one or another of certain images, all of which refer to the *axis mundi*: pillar (cf. the *universalis columna*), ladder (cf. Jacob's ladder), mountain, tree, vine, etc.; (d) around this cosmic axis lies the world (=our world), hence the axis is located 'in the middle,' at the 'navel of the earth'; it is the Center of the World. Many different myths, rites, and beliefs are derived from this traditional 'system of the world'. (*Sacred* 37)

Whether we are talking about closeness to the heavens or to the center of creation, the axis mundi represents a nearness to the holy, the worlds of the god(s), spirits, heaven, death, numinosity, the divine other, and perhaps the immaterial. In Eliade's words, "the center ... is pre-eminently the zone of the sacred, the zone of absolute reality. Similarly, all the other symbols of absolute reality (trees of life and immortality, Fountain of Youth, etc.) are also situated at a center" (*Eternal* 17-18).

For the reasons described by two of history's greatest mythologists, I find mythic centers to convey substantial philosophical meaning through both the symbolic structure and narratives therein (or therefrom). Considering the dual representation of Eden as in the east and center, we see a recurrence of the conflation implicit in the Greek word *arche*, which Homer used to mean beginnings before it was repurposed by the Milesians as a term for foundations. The story of Eden represents both of these—the place of foundations and beginnings.[129]

From the point of view of the last chapter on philosophy, we are looking at the symbols, narratives, and locations of the Eden, Prometheus and Pandora myths because they seem to be situated in a way that communicates ideas about physical, metaphysical, cosmological, ethical, political, and existential foundations. From the point of view of the chapters on Eden and Prometheus it can be seen that Western scientific philosophy has offered a comparable perspective on ideas around which foundational myths have repeatedly been centered.

Before returning more directly to Eden, the symbols and notions of height and depth that constellate around *axis mundi* imagery should be considered. Philosophical and or religious interest in the notions of height have symbolically gravitated towards tall trees with vertical trunks and/or high reaching mountains. Eliade lists a number of cultures who refer to "mountains, real or mythical, situated at the center of the world" (*Sacred* 38).

> Examples are Meru in India, Haraberezaiti in Iran, the mythical 'Mount of
> the Lands' in Mesopotamia, Gerizim in Palestine—which, moreover, was
> called the 'navel of the earth.' Since the sacred mountain is an *axis mundi*

connecting earth with heaven, it in a senses touches heaven and hence marks the highest point in the world; consequently the territory that surrounds it, and that constitutes 'our world,' is held to be the highest among countries. This is stated in Hebrew tradition: Palestine, being the highest land, was not submerged by the Flood. According to Islamic tradition, the highest place on earth is the *ka'aba*. … For Christians, it is Golgotha that is on the summit of the cosmic mountain. All these beliefs express the same feeling, which is profoundly religious: 'our world' is holy ground *because it is the place nearest to heaven*, because form here, from our abode, it is possible to reach heaven; hence our world is a high place. (38)

The axis mundi is the epicenter of what is sacred, whatever the framework of sacredness may be, and at this epicenter is the connection of below with above.[130] Such transcendent heights have certainly been associated with Eden. Ezekiel and Dante both refer to the Garden as atop a mountain. As Ezekiel describes, in "Eden, the garden of God; every precious stone was [Adam's] covering" (28: 13), before he was cast down, "out of the mountain of God" (13:16).[131] And for Dante, the climbing of this mountain—in immediate contrast with the fall—is a spiritual ascent. Campbell notes, "Dante's holy mountain of Purgatory, [bears] on its summit the Earthly Paradise" (*Primitive* 148).[132]

Without this image in which the garden "was placed upon the mount of Eden, higher than every other mountain in the world" (*Book of Bees*: *Of Paradise*), "The Fall" may be imagined in relation to the falling fruit while only conceptually applied to the couple's departure from Eden. What Eliade's emphasis on height and these strong visual descriptions provide is a strong sense of the Fall's vertical quality, which translates as a distancing from God that is specifically seen as a descent from near-heavenly heights. Keeping Prometheus in mind, we recall the fall of Hephaestus, his protégé, from the cosmic mountain—when Zeus cast out the man who attracted the most beautiful of wives with his material skills. As Le Grice points out, such descents depict a "spiritual fall from identity with God into a world of existential alienation" (personal correspondence).

In constellation with the concepts surrounding *axis mundi*, the tree of knowledge is the high reaching point (on the high reaching mountain) where the heavenly comes to know the hellish, the high the low, and the divine the mortal. This is the place where divine innocence meets terrestrial sexuality and the place where such opposites become separated. In ways we will continue to consider, the tree functions as an axis between realms, modes of being, and the corresponding mythic phases of human existence. The tree is "a threshold image, uniting pairs-of-opposites in such a way as to facilitate a passage of the mind" (Campbell, *Primitive* 120-121). This passage is symbolized by an exile from the garden, the wearing of clothing, hiding from god, making babies, eating bread and dying. One of the details that will be particularly interesting to this dissertation's thesis is that the transformation was sometimes conveyed by the withering of the tree in the garden following the fall (Malan, *First Book of Adam and Eve* III: 8), but this is symbolism we will engage more closely when we discuss the 'wasteland' like qualities of the first couple's exile.

Returning more specifically to the tree. In the Garden of Eden, two trees are often described, "the tree of life. … and the tree of knowledge of good and evil" (*Genesis* 2: 8-11).[133] According to Milton, the Tree of Life was the "The middle Tree and highest [in

Eden] that grew" (IV: 195). *The Cave of Treasures* also describes the tree as "fixed in the middle of the earth" ("Symbolism of Eden"). Compared to all other trees, "it was of noblest kind for sight, smell, taste. … High eminent, blooming Ambrosial Fruit/ Of vegetable Gold; and next to Life: / Our Death the Tree of Knowledge grew fast by—/ Knowledge of good bought dear by knowing ill" (Milton IV. 217-222). Like Milton who describes the tree of life as covered in golden fruit, Andersen gives fruit of gold to the tree of knowledge, in the middle of the garden he describes there stood a "huge tree, with luxuriant, hanging branches, golden apples, big and small, hung like oranges among the green leaves. This was the Tree of Knowledge, of whose fruit Adam and Eve had partaken. From each leaf dripped a glistening red drop of dew! It was as if the tree were crying tears of blood" (Andersen 89).[134] In contrast, some "have said that the tree of life is the kingdom of heaven and the joy of the world to come; and others that the tree of life was a tree in very truth, which was set in the middle of Paradise, but no man has ever found out what its fruit or its flowers or its nature was like" (*Book of Bees*: *Of Paradise*). We will return to the question of the tree's type when we discuss the fruit itself. Before moving on, we should consider an image of the tree of life as surrounded by a shrub, on which grow the fruits of knowledge. In his work, *Legends of the Jews*, Ginsberg writes:

> In paradise stands the tree of life in the tree of knowledge, the latter forming a hedge around the former. Only he who is cleared a path for himself through the tree of knowledge can come close to the tree of life which is so huge that it would take a man five hundred years to traverse a distance equal to the diameter of the trunk, and no less fast is the space is shaded by its crown of branches. From the beneath flows fourth the water

that irrigates the whole earth, parting then into four streams, the Ganges,

the Nile, the Tigris, and Euphrates. (37)

This image of the shrub encircling the tree reinforces the image of the wall enclosing the

garden; and, as we will discuss, the skin surrounding the body or fruit, the clothes

enclosing the sexual organs, the enclosure of the womb around the child, tomb around the

corpse, and snake around the tree—all images from within the narrative.

As this dissertation has continued to follow the association of isolation with

sensory delusion, we should consider the *Zohar* and its interpretation of the tree:

The tree of the knowledge of good and evil symbolizes those whose

intellectual faculties are directed only to phenomenal objects that can be

seen and handled … and thus it will be until the times of error and

darkness pass away; then … human nature transformed and enlightened

and purified, mankind will become as a tree that, in its stately form and

beauty, is pleasant to the sight. The tree of the knowledge of Good and

Evil occasioned Israel to fall into error … and penalty of spiritual death

involving loss of union with the Divine, without which there can be no

interior enlightenment, no spiritual development. … As expressed and

typified in the words, 'And the river shall be dried up.' (Ia. xix. 5; 134)

From this point of view, the tree of knowledge is exactly the tree that leads to the

delusion of the senses by the phenomenal (visible/touchable) world, which results in

spiritual death and isolation from the divine. Returning to the images of the shrub around

the tree, skin around fruit, and walls around the garden, we see the geometric repetition of

foundational isolation in these basic images of inner and outer. As we saw in the last chapter, such foundations of inner and outer define subjects and objects in a way essential to the structures of atomism, which is dedicated to the description of phenomenal experience. Not unlike Plato's rejection of the atomists, the *Zohar* reacts against the spiritual repercussions of prioritizing the world of hands and eyes in the context of spiritual isolation.

The Garden: Fruit

It is common knowledge that the type of fruit (if there is one) was not named in *Genesis,* which suggests that the specific fruit is less important than the symbol of fruit itself. For this reason, before turning to the specific references, I want to look more directly at fruit. Its package is typically composed of seeds surrounded by the meat/flesh/fruit and skin. Though mostly fluid (juice), fruit is generally experienced as a solid from the outside. Fruits like apples become more solid towards the core. Inside the center can be found the seed(s), the most solid part of the fruit. The driest part is the outermost, the skin, which, like human or animal skin, encloses the body. Fruit rind also tends to be harder than the meat. Many fruits—including those commonly associated with Eden like the apple and fig—hang from stems along axis that parallel the verticality of both tree and human trunks. Grain, however, grows straight up. Like the fruit has skin, the seed has chaff—both are solid and carry seed. Like dust, sand, and other seeds, grain is granulated. But unlike most other fruits, grain requires a substantial amount of effort and knowledge to transform into a food supply.

Beyond the atemporal qualities of the fruit, it is also an essential symbol of cyclicality. As the ripe fruit represents an end (fruition) its seed inside will start (seed) a new cycle. We talked more about this in the chapter on Prometheus, to which I will refer.

The conversation included a vision of the tree as omphalos and the plucking of the fruit from its stem as the symbolic severing of an umbilical cord. [135] Not only does this reinforce the image of separation, it also reinforces the repetitive association of the fruit with the body of an animal. We recall the conflation of apple and mutton in the form of "the dolorous fruit of the Hesperides and the dread gold of Phrixus' fleece" (Statius, Thebaid 2. 281). We should also consider the comfortable use of "meat" as a synonym for fruit, as well as the plant and animal synonyms for "skin" and "seed". Similarly, the flower, as a sexual organ and sign of mature readiness for fertilization, precedes the adult phase of "fruitfulness." According to God's first blessing of humanity, this is its first task, to "be fruitful and multiply" (*Genesis* 1:28). Such fruitfulness, of course, would be impossible if the matter of fruit (or meat) did not sustain matter of the body. In this way, the fruit can be seen as the foundation for both plant and human life. At the same time, the eating of *fruit* implicitly conveys a commitment to substance: as we will later see, some versions of the story even describe this as the cause for such digestive organs as were previously unrequired of the not-yet-fallen couple.

In considering the cyclical qualities of fruit, we should also note the relationship of growth with the solar year and civilization feeding flood cycles. The daily cycle is mimetic with the life cycle, with its youthful rise and ripened descent. (Perhaps as long as we live on this earth, sunsets will inspire our memories of passed loved ones). The human life cycle is also mimetic with that of nature, which experiences new life in the spring and death in the winter. The overlay of all these cycles of birth and death present an abstract wisdom that seems essential to the story of Adam and Eve, Prometheus and Pandora, Jason's Fleece and Hercules Apples. Through their own sets of symbols, these stories convey the mimetic cyclicality of day, year, vegetal seasons, human life, and the knowledge of their congruities.

As we transition from fruit to seed, I want to call attention to Milton's vision of how Satan saw the garden—as his fruit to pluck. According to him, Eden dangles as a "pendant world" (II. 1052) between "Heaven and Earth. ... Hung over my realm, linked in a golden chain" (43). This conflation of Eden/Earth and fruit is echoed in the Irish *Saltair Na Rann*, in which it is said that the "the globe, [was] fashioned like a goodly apple, truly round" (4). What these images suggest is that the distilled form of the garden was that of the fruit itself.

Inside the fruit, seed is the miniscule microcosm and starting point for all trees. This is not unlike the description of "Rabbi Ben Gorion [in which] the rock of Jerusalem: '... is called the Foundation Stone of the Earth, that is, the navel of the Earth, because it is from there that the whole Earth unfolded" (Eliade, *Sacred* 44-45). A seed is like the "*shetiyyah* ["foundation stone"] from which the world was started" (Tanh. B., Lev 78). And like a seed drawing water, the "rock of the Temple of Jerusalem reached deep into the Tehom, the Hebrew equivalent of Absu ... the name for the waters of chaos before Creation" (Eliade, *Sacred* 41). Planted in the earth a seed will draw matter into itself to become what it is to become—not unlike the father's seed, which, when planted in the mother's matter (mater), will grow into a human. An example of the symbolic conflation between human and plant seeds can be seen in the stories of Cadmus and Jason, who plant dragon teeth that grow into men.

In Matthew, John the Baptist allegorizes the soul and body through the imagery of grain seed and chaff (3:12).[136] This association of soul with seed is consistent with the

Hindu description of soul, or atman, as a seed.[137] The atman is seen as a portion of divine essence in a way similar to the beliefs of the Pythagoreans, Gnostics, Cathars, and Kabbalists, who recognize humans as endowed with divine spark—a motif in the Prometheus myth. Echoing these notions, "in a teaching that resembles that of Kabbalah, fourteenth-century Christian theologian and mystic Meister Eckhart taught: 'there is something in the soul that is so akin to God that it is one with him, God's seed is within us … Here God glows and flames without ceasing, in all His abundance, and sweetness and rapture" (Prophet, Spadaro, Steinman 101). On one hand our emphasis should be on these visions of one and manyness provided by the seed and spark,[138] on the other, we should recognize seed as a symbol of progeny. And again we should recognize the arche-like qualities of the seed as a foundation stone and point of origin.[139] According to the Eden myth, Adam and Eve are the human progenitors. Combining these notions of seed they are not just parents: They are the first parents whose story explains how seed and/or spark initially entered (or fell into) material flesh.

The Garden: Serpent

The final element of the garden we should examine before moving into the narrative is that of the serpent, which we have already seen wrapped around various incarnations of axis-mundi-like centers. Stepping outside historical context for a moment, we should amplify into the implicit qualities of the serpent's form.

One of the clear and most essential qualities of the snake is its "wonderful ability … to slough its skin and so renew its youth [which] has earned for it throughout the world the character of the master of the mystery of rebirth—of which the moon, waxing and waning, sloughing its shadow and again waxing, is the celestial sign" (Campbell,

Occidental 9-10). As such a personification of life and death, the serpent tells Eve that when she eats of the fruit she "will not surely die" (*Genesis* 3:4), though it is to this act she will owe her mortality.

Considering the frequent reliance of knowledge on logic and logic on duality, the split tongue and two pointed body of the snake – combined with its ability to make a dividing line and enclosing circle – naturally represent such knowledge as relies on conceptual duals like "is"/"is not", "true"/"false", "I"/"other", "subject"/"object", and so on). The sexual imagery presented by the single snake is also dualistic, androgynous even. While its "phallic suggestion is immediate, as swallower, the female organ is also suggested" (Campbell, *Occidental* 9-10). As a consort to Eve the snake is imagined as a male, but we are not to forget the snake's feminine qualities and relationship with earth.[140]

There is a difference between side-by-side duality and that of inner and outer. Where the split tongue and two-sided nature of the snake convey a simplistic version of duality, the ability to bite its own tail—as the *ouroboros*—enables it to also convey enclosure, and with it the specific breed of duality geometrically seen as inner and outer. Biting its tail, the snake conveys enclosure in a geometrically spatial way while at the same time communicating the temporal enclosure of beginnings and ends within looping cycles, such as day, year, and mortal round.

To stick with this image of the self-enclosing snake, I feel as though there is extreme significance to the fact that the snake can form as many shapes as the imagination can provide. Straight on a snake is a point, pulled taught a line, enclosed it is a circle, triangle, square, or some other polygon. It can be wavy or spiral—flat or as a vortex. A snake—unlike any other animal besides the comparable worm, eel or oarfish—can take virtually any form, and, in this way, I would like to suggest that it implicitly symbolizes the mastery of form itself, which might also be recognized as knowledge and/or power. While the ability to slough off skin and renew its bodily form may exemplify the snake's possession of knowledge and power over life and body, it is the literal ability of the snake to transform into any shape that communicates—most directly—its mastery over form and the knowledge thereby entailed. As master of the knowledge of life and death, of duality, and of form, the serpent is a rich and layered symbol of knowledge.

The identification of the snake with the shape shifter is a consistent motif, which surfaces when Satan takes the form of a serpent in the Garden, and when, in the *Cave of Treasures,* he shifts into numerous deceptive forms. In *Paradise Lost,* when the demons fall, they are "all transformed/ alike, to serpents" (Milton IX. 519-20). Because of the snake's wide range of bodily shapes, its symbolic meaning is extremely diverse. One of the odd notes from Milton is that the snake was specifically not in the form of a wave when it confronted Eve, but as a Straight spine rising from circular coils, "enclosed/ in serpent/ … not with indented wave, / Prone on the ground, as since, but on his reare, / [a] circular base of rising folds, that towered" (VIII. 497-98).[141] As self-enclosure and the wave-form play central roles in this dissertation, this is but one example of many that will recognize the choice of the snake's form—especially as a wave or closed circle.

Despite the enmity between the people of Yahweh and the serpent, we should note the serpent staffs of Moses—first the one he turned into a serpent in front of the pharaoh and also that which he made of bronze at the behest of God. The story of the brazen serpent, "Viewed historically merely … was derived from the so called Elohim (E) text of c. 750 B.C., and was apparently the origin legend designed to account for the serpent-god of bronze that was in those days worshiped in the Temple of Jerusalem, together with certain images of his Canaanite goddess spouse, Asherah" (Campbell, *Creative* 153-54). The "approved Christian allegory is simply that as the serpent of bronze lifted up by Moses on a staff counteracted the poison of a plague of serpents, so the lifting up of Jesus on the cross countervailed the poison of the serpent of the Garden … the earlier is read as a prefigurement of the later" (153-54). Another parallel between the serpent staff and cross can be found in Moses's release of water from the desert stone, which might be recognized as mimetic with the depiction of the crucifixion as a fountain, the fluids of which promise eternal life. Further examples of the association between Christ and the serpent can be found in the writings of Saint Hippolytus and Theodosius I, 'The Great', who describe Christian Ophitic sects that venerated serpents in the place of Christ. Even today, certain Pentecostal churches use snake handling to develop their Christian relationship with God.

To travel deeper into the mysteries of serpent symbolism is an appealing project, but having introduced some basics, we should continue into the Eden narrative. Moving forward, what we should take with us is that the snake is a far older symbol than the book of Genesis. The serpent was associated with the earth on which it crawls and the fecundity of nature that emerges from therein. It is a natural symbol of rebirth and mastery over form. It is visibly masculine and feminine. The entwining of copulating snakes can be recognized in Ningizzidda, the Caduceus (most typicallty of Hermes), and the inciting incident of Tiresias' sight beyond sight.

First Couple: Adam

Having considered the key pre-existing elements of the garden, we are ready to consider the appearances of Adam and Eve, "two of Mankind, but in them, the whole included Race" (Milton VIII. 415-416). Like Prometheus, Adam is the "patriarch of mankind" (V. 507) " our great Progenitor" (V. 544) "prime of men" (V. 563). From the Abrahamic traditions, Adam is "our father," words used in the *Cave of Treasures* ("Death of Adam"), *The First Book of Adam and Eve* (Malan, 1. 8), and the *Life of Mohammad* (Ishaq 185), to name a few of the sources in which the reference appears.

In addition to uncountable word puns, the most direct etymological foundation to the name of Adam is likely "the Hebrew *'adama*, meaning "ground"/ 'soil," (Andreason 182). This direct association of the human with the soil itself is consistent with the modern day English words *human* and *humus*. "According to the oldest Semitic notions … men not only came from and returned to the earth, but actually partook of its substance" (Jewish Encyclopedia "Adam"). Adam is created "from the dust of the ground" (*Genesis* 2:4:6).[142]

This imagery is reiterated in the Jewish legend of the Golem, who was created "from clay and dust of the earth" (*Golem: How Maharal Created Golem*).[143] The vision of the Yezidi is similar.[144] As raw dust or as the synthesis of all elemental substance, Adam was crafted in the "image and likeness" of his creator (*Cave of Treasures* 169).[145] And in versions that accentuate the differences of the human body before and after the fall, everything about this first form of Adam is divine:

> When the angels saw Adam's glorious appearance they were greatly
>
> moved by the beauty thereof. For they saw the image of his face burning

> with glorious splendor like the orb of the sun. … The light of his eyes was
>
> like the light of the sun, and the image of his body was like unto the
>
> sparkling of crystal…He rose at full length and stood upright in the centre
>
> of the earth … in Jerusalem. (*Cave of Treasures: Creation of Adam*).[146]

After discussing the fall, we will return to this narrative and the others in which the body

transforms and begins to decay. This is not unlike the fruit, to which Adam is likened in

Paradise Lost, "maist thou live, till like ripe Fruit thou drop / Into thy Mothers lap, or be

with ease / gathered, not harshly plucked, for death mature: / This is old age" (Milton X.

533-37).

The *Zohar* gives specific emphasis to the vision of Adam's creation as the import

of divine light into earthly matter:

> 'And the Lord God formed man' (Gen. ii. 7), that is, Israel. Here the word
>
> vayitzer (formed) is written with two yods or I's, indicating that the Holy
>
> One formed him with two natures, the higher and lower self; the one
>
> divine, the other earthly, and impressed upon his form the divine name, I
>
> V I, expressed by the two eyes and the nose between them, thus: I. The
>
> numerical value of these letters is 26, which is also that of the divine
>
> name, Jehovah. … Man also in himself represents the union and blending
>
> together of the higher and lower Shekinas, symbolized by the repeating of
>
> the Shema, morning and evening. (Manhar; 133)

According to this take on the story, before Adam fell he had been "a recipient of divine

wisdom (hochma) and heavenly light (52a-52b) and derived his continuous existence

from the Tree of Life to which he had free access" (223). However, "as soon as he allowed himself to be seduced and deluded with the desire of occult knowledge, he lost

everything, heavenly light and life through the disjunction of his higher and lower self,

and, the loss of that harmony that should always exist between them" (223). As a result of

this disjunction, "he who implicitly and blindly follows the dictates of his lower nature or

self shall not come near the Tree of Life" (223).

Following a similar vision of disjunction and disunion, before the creation of Eve,

or what might be seen as a separation of Eve from Adam, "they had been one" (Campbell

Occidental 30), "Adam was both male and female" (Campbell, *Primitive* 104). Like the

combination of the elements, this undifferentiated wholeness of Adam's gender "clearly

indicate[s] the aspect of Adam as the Self" (E. Jung 334). Tishby describes another

example of separation in the story of Adam on which Neumann reflects in his

conversation about the development of human ego, "In the view of the Cabala, original

sin consisted essentially in this: that damage was done to the Deity. Concerning the

nature of this damage there are various views. The most widely accepted is that the First

Man, Adam Kadmon, made a division between King and Queen, and that he sundered the

Shekinah from union with her spouse, and from the whole hierarchy of the Shepiroth"

("The Doctrine of Evil and the 'Klipah' in the Lurian Cabala"). Neumann continues,

"Here we have … the old archetype of the separation of the World Parents" (120)—a

story recognized in the Egyptian separation of Geb and Nut for example—but also clearly

demonstrated in the division of Adam and Eve. What he later brings this back to, is the

"problem of the First Parents and the formation of the ego" (400).

Neumann's conversation brings the story of Adam and Eve into the context of ego

development within a child. This association of the first humans with children—and their development with that of the child—is a valuable overtone to add beneath this entire discourse. One of the simpler things it does is connect the psychological sequence of Adam and Eve with that of other (all) humans. This is something Dante and Andersen became particularly engaged with in their creative work. Dante, for example, says that he himself "had so much of Adam with me" (*Inferno* IX), in reference to his own experience of Adam's ability to be seduced. This is again expressed—in similar reference to Adam's vulnerability—by the main character in Andersen's fairy tale who believes, "it should have been [him], then it would never have happened! Never would sin have entered the world!" (Andersen 78). As is the nature of humans, he is proven wrong when he submits to temptation like the rest of us.

As Neumann and others argue, this self-assertion towards desire and the separation of opposites is essential to the development of self-awareness, if not ego. I will reflect further on this later, but I should pause to point out that, while deeper readings might reveal the positive newness associated with a fall from Eden, the surface story— from Genesis to H.C. Andersen—is that what happened is negative and carried devastating consequences. I hope it will be seen that I am addressing and doing justice to the emergence of self, ego and consciousness—I am not an ego enemy. The chapter on Prometheus was designed to emphasize its myth's more present focus on the positive emergence of human consciousness. That having been said, this dissertation was significantly inspired by insights into the story as it is told—as a Fall.

As the fulcrum or entry point of sin into the world, we should return to our consideration of the axis mundi in the context of Adam and the human being. In addition to mountains, trees, and temples, the human himself has often been imagined as an axis between heaven and earth. In fact, there can be found "a whole system of micro-macrocosmic correspondences. Such, for example, is the assimilation of the belly or the womb to a cave, of the intestines to a labyrinth … of the backbone to the *axis mundi,* and so on. … Some systems of man-universe correspondences were fully elaborated only in the higher cultures (India, China, the ancient Near East, Central America)" (Eliade, *Sacred* 169). As humans, we are the only land-walking animals with a vertical spine. While bears, rodents, and monkeys may stand for some time, this is generally not their mode of locomotion. Verticality is something the human trunk shares with trees—a distinctly unique and visual feature for those seeking to understand what makes humans distinct from the other animals. Even today, interesting questions remain to be answered about the relevance of the vertically oriented electromagnetic field of the human body and what it could mean for its environmental relationships.[147]

In *Genesis* it is said that "God took the man and put him in the Garden of Eden to work it and take care of it" (2:15). And in *The Book of Jubilees* it is said that "Adam and the woman were in the Garden of Eden for seven years cultivating it and looking after it, [while] we gave him work and we instructed him to do everything that is suitable for cultivation" (15-16). Campbell points out:

> One of the chief characteristics of Levantine mythology here represented
> is that of man created to be God's slave or servant. In a late Sumerian
> myth told in Oriental Mythology it is declared that men were created to
> relieve the gods of the onerous task of tilling their fields. Men were to do
> that work for them and provide them with food through sacrifice. Marduk,

too, created man to serve the gods. And here again we have man created to
keep a garden. (*Occidental* 103)

This scene is also not unlike that of Matthew 20, in which the Kingdom of Heaven is likened to a vineyard in which workers are employed. What is hard to discern without focused research is the difference between that work in the garden and the work that will follow. It may be that some of this complication has to do with variants of the story that predate ancient Israel.[148]

First Couple: Eve

In Genesis "The LORD God said, "It is not good for the man to be alone" (*Genesis* 2: 18). And in the *Book of Jubilees* it is similarly accounted, "the Lord said unto us: 'It is not good that the man should be alone: let us make a helpmeet for him'" (3:4). God saw that of "all the wild animals and all the birds in the sky … no suitable helper was found" for Adam (2:19-20).[149] In *Paradise Lost* he first informs the progenitor, "What next I bring shall please thee, be assured, / Thy likeness, thy fit help, thy other self, / Thy wish, exactly to thy heart's desire" (Milton X. 287-288). Chaucer writes, "God on high, having created Adam/ and seeing him all alone and destitute/, then said in his great goodness, / 'Let us now make a help unto this man/ like himself' / … man's help and comfort, / his earthly paradise and his source of pleasure" ("The Merchant's Tale" 81-88).

To create Eve, "the LORD God caused the man to fall into a deep sleep," (*Genesis* 2: 18) "and he slept" (*Book of Jubilees* 3:1). In most versions of the stories, he then proceeds to make "woman from the rib he had taken out of man" (Genesis 2: 23). This can be said of the Christian texts, *The Cave of Treasures* (51) and *Paradise Lost* (155), as well as the Jewish *Book of Jubilees* (3:4), *Talmud* (Bachot 61a), and *Midrash* (Bereshith

51). A Yezidi source frames it similarly, "Gabriel was away from Adam for a hundred years. … Adam was sad and weeping. Then God commanded Gabriel to create Eve from under the left shoulder" (Joseph, *Devil* 39).

Though the rib is most generally recognized as the source of Eve, "Rab and Samuel explained this differently. One said that [this 'rib'] was a face, the other that it was a tail" (Berachot, *Talmud* 61a). The association of Eve's creation with the face of Adam shifts into the androgynous interpretations of Adam that hinge on the statement in Genesis 5:2 that "male and female he created them. According to some, God "created [Adam] with two faces, then split him and made him two backs – a back for each side" (*Genesis* Rabbah 8:1). In *The Legends of the Jews*, Ginzberg writes, a "view is cited, according to which Adam was created as 'androgynous,' and was subsequently separated into man and woman. The … view [related] to that of Plato's *Symposium* … is [also] found among the Babylonians" (5:88). Campbell recounts, "They had been one at first, as Adam; then split in two, as Adam and Eve" (*Occidental* 30-1).[150] What should be noted before we go on; however, is that while the emphasis on their split emphasizes their isolation from one another, it also sets up the conversation of their union through physical love—the recombining of the flesh (*Genesis* 2:24). Such recombination, as in the Roman Catholic position, we think of Eve as *Mater*, then the sexual act of entry is another example of the entry into matter.

Eve was God's final creation, and she was a "beautiful" (Milton 73) finale, "angelic" (87), "fair indeed and tall" (72). "The Rabbis maintain that Eve was the most beautiful woman ever. To illustrate this, they say that all humans resemble apes (i.e., are ugly) in comparison with Sarah's beauty, while Sarah, in turn, looked like an ape in comparison with Eve (Kadari "Eve: Midrash and Aggadah"). Milton says she was "more adorned [and] more lovely than Pandora, whom the Gods Endowed with all their gifts … when the unwise Son of Japhet … stole Jove's authentic fire" (IV. 714-19). This association of Pandora and Eve dates back to "the fathers of the Christian church in the late Roman Empire (30 BCE-476 CE) who first equated Pandora with Eve." Lyons recalls, "Tertullian (c.155 or 160-after 230 CE) uses Pandora as both a positive and negative figure, while for Greek prelate Gregory of Nazianzus (c. 330-c.389 CE) she exemplifies vanity, unhealthy curiosity, and other negative traits. Christian writer and teacher Origen (c. 185-254 CE) explicitly compares the *pithos* or jar with the forbidden fruit in the Garden of Eden" (Lyons; 1082). In all cases the emphasis on the seductiveness of her beauty is present and associated with the eating of fruit or opening of the jar through which humanity will become initiated into the knowledge of such beauty and joy as only discord and suffering can show. Like Pandora and the men created by Prometheus, "in the Midrashic account, Eve was created whole (with all her limbs fully developed), as was Adam; according to one view, they were created as twenty year olds" (*Gen. Rabbah* 14:7).

According to Milton's account, she woke for the first time, "reposed/ under a shade on flowers/ … [Where] water issued from a Cave and spread/ into a liquid plain" (IV. 450-55). According to the Abrahamic story, Eve is the only virgin of her line to be born sexually mature, as fertile as a flower. Like water that firsts escapes the cave or the flower that finally opens, she conveys the blossoming of life into the world. This is not unlike the birth of Aphrodite as the scallop shell opened from the sea, the same shell that can later be found above countless shrines to Mary, the "second Eve" (Milton V. 387).

The association of the birth of these beautiful and seductive women with water will contribute to our central focus when we reach the relationships of Mary, Hebe and the Grail Maidens with Christ, Hercules and the Grail Knights.

In continued expression of Eve's resonance with water and beauty, one of her first experiences is the discovery of her reflection. As beautiful as she was, and as unaware as she was of her own image, it can be of no surprise that she was transfixed by the aquatic reflection of her own face until "a voice thus warned [her], 'What thou see … fair creature, is thy self'" (Milton IV. 467-68). The scene's similarity to the story of Narcissus and the emphasis on innocent self-love should be noted, as Milton would have clearly been familiar with its narrative. The scene also reinforces the seductiveness and seducibility of Eve as simultaneously beautiful and attracted to beauty. As Atalanta, who attracts suitors to her beauty but is only seduced by the beauty of golden apples, Adam will be seduced by the beauty of Eve after she is seduced by the beauty of the fruit. The shallowest interpretation of these stories is probably unavoidable, as it is true across numerous species that the female is attracted to sex by the prospect of the child (fruit) while the male is presumably attracted to the female directly, considering that many species of males will leave the mother to raise children alone. That interpretation being noted, the stories seem to point more directly at the female character's representation of beauty itself, as both its personification and receiver; again, not unlike Aphrodite, to whom Paris gave his golden apple.

When Adam awoke "out of his sleep" (*Book of Jubilees* 3:1-4), she was "brought … to the man" (*Genesis* 2:22), who received her as his "other half" (Milton V. 560), which he called "bone of my bone and flesh of my flesh" (Jubilees 3: 1-4). Made from the same source, the couple "must live in unity/ … [with] one will, in happiness and in sorrow" (Chaucer, *Merchant's Tale* 1290). Eve says, "Adam shall share with me in bliss or woe: / So dear I love him, that with him all deaths/ I could endure; [and] without him live no life" (Milton VIII. 831-33). She was fair and worthy of his "cherishing, honoring, and love, / not subjection" (VII. 1206-7). Adorned she indeed attracted his "love, not [his] subjection" (VII. 1147-48). And with this mutual respect and love, Adam led Eve "to the nuptial bower/ … blushing like the morn" (VII. 1147-48).

Though the better known memories of Eve are as a menace, through many eyes she was given as a gift (139). In the Midrash a matron of the Rabbi José presents Eve as the thief of Adam's rib, to which he replies, "If one were to take away from your house an ounce of silver, and give you in return a pound of gold, that would not be stealing" (*Midrash*, Genesis Rabba 52). Again, Eve is presented as "God's gift" (Chaucer, *Merchant's Tale* 1322). She is "a helper" (*Genesis* 2: 18), "his earthly paradise," his "other half" (Milton V. 560), "flesh of [his] flesh," and his "wife" (*Book of Jubilees* 3:3; *Genesis* 2: 18-25; Chaucer, *Merchant's Tale* 1335).

Campbell writes, "Eve in her pre-Hebraic incarnation was the consort of the serpent" (*Occidental* 152). However, "In Eve's scene at the tree … nothing is said to indicate that the serpent who appeared and spoke to her was a deity in his own right, who had been revered in the Levant for at least seven thousand years before the composition of the book of *Genesis*" (9). And unlike the story in Genesis, in the ancient seals of the Near East, there is not "any sign of divine wrath or danger to be found … There is no theme of guilt connected with the garden. The boon of the knowledge of life is there, in the sanctuary of the world, to be culled. And it is yielded willingly to any mortal, male or female, who reaches for it with the proper will and readiness to receive" (*Occidental* 13-14). Without a perspective of the fruit as forbidden there are no notions of guilt associated with the snake, woman or natural *mater*ial world. There is no fall, only the positive discovery of knowledge. A conflict between these two interpretations of knowledge arriving can be seen in the myth of Prometheus, whose gift of knowledge was both catastrophic and championed. We have discussed the mythic revolution in which the beneficent serpents became seen as the enemies for Yahweh, Zeus, and Indra to defeat when establishing their new (patriarchal) rule. These stories are not to be disassociated from those of Eve and Pandora, who, with the serpent, similarly represent earth and its nature. It would seem, from the point of view of both *Genesis* and the *Theogony*, that, together and independently, the tension with wife and battle with serpent symbolically convey a clashing of God and the human soul with *mater*iality, which, in the Abrahamic tradition, is a fallen world.

Having examined some of the key symbolic qualities of the garden, tree, fruit and first couple, we are now prepared to engage the narrative of the Fall. Before we do, however, we should address the absence of Eve in the *Quran*. She is not absent from the tradition, as we will discuss folklore in which she appears, but the fact that she is not named in the *Quran* leaves an opening for a number of interpretations. The obvious complication is that the character so associated with the Fall is not even named in this essential source. This is in complete contrast with the Rabbinic tradition that recognized Eve as responsible for the fall (*Gen. Rabbah 17. 8*). What this variation in the *Quran* points towards is a twist in the Islamic telling in which the primary fall of interest is that of Iblis—not Eve. As echoed in *Paradise Lost,* the *Quran* describes a story of the fallen angel who parallels the Biblical "Lucifer, son of morning" said to have "fallen from heaven" (Isaiah 14:12). For this reason, before we return to Eve and the fruit, we turn now to the first fall.

Satan: Fall, War, Exile, Escape

Like the serpent exiled from the garden, according to an array of Jewish, Christian, and Islamic narratives, a host of angels and their leader were cast down from heaven. The Christians know this figure as Lucifer, the Muslims as Iblis, and the Jews recognize the leader of the fallen angels as Semjaza (with Azazel). They also apply the story of Satan's fall to the king of Tyre, who was part of the Assyrian alliance that—upon breaking—led to the destruction of Solomon's temple and the Babylonian exile. Semjaza and Azazel were leaders of the angels who were cast out for descending to earth with the desire to procreate with human women—a clear echo of the divine call into mortal materiality by way of the woman's seductive desirability. Similarly, Lucifer/Iblis was joined by a hoard of fallen angels in a war against God's army.

Like Hades, a name for both the location and lord of the underworld, Milton's Satan claims that every "which way I fly is Hell, myself am hell" (Milton IV. 75). Before falling under earth; however, Satan was the 'morning star … the seal of perfection' (Ezekiel 28:12). And to occultists and those influenced by their wake, he was even recognized as an arch angel (Webster 115). This association of Satan with the morning star reinforces his resonance with Prometheus as the light and fire bringer—as keenly recognized by Milton, Origen, and others.

The primary scene of Satan's fall comes after the creation of Adam, after which God tells Iblis: "we have created man out of sounding clay, out of dark-slime transmuted whereas the invisible beings We had created, [long] before that, out of the fire of scorching winds" (*Al-Hijr*, 10-43). He "said unto the angels: 'Behold, I am about to create mortal man out of sounding clay, out of dark slime transmuted; and when I have formed him fully and breathed into him of My spirit, fall down before him in prostration!'" (10-43). Without dissent, "the angels prostrated themselves, all of them together save Iblis: he refused to be among those who prostrated themselves" (10-43). Iblis' refusal to bow or prostrate before Adam, a man of earth made after himself, not only necessitates a sense of self, it also carries the classic act of disobedience associated with The Fall.

In the Georgian *Book of Adam* (from the Caucasus) which is generally believed to have been a Jewish text, the Devil recounts this from the *Quran* with manipulative tears. He tells Adam he has blamed him since he "fell from [his] dwellings ... [and became] alienated from [his] throne" (12.1). According to his version of the story:

> The very day when you were created, on that day, I fell from before the face of God, because when God breathed a spirit onto your face, you had the image and likeness of the divinity. And then Michael came; he presented you and made you bend down before God. And God told Michael, "I have created Adam according to (my) image and my divinity." 14.1 Then Michael came; he summoned all the troops of angels and told them, "Bow down before the likeness and the image of the divinity." 14.2 And then, when Michael summoned them and all had bowed down to you, he summoned me also. 14.3 And I told him, "Go away from me, for I shall not bow down to him who is younger than me;

indeed, I am master prior to him and it is proper for him to bow down to me. 15.1 The six classes of other angels heard that and my speech pleased them and they did not bow down to you. 16.1 Then God became angry with us. (13.2-16.1)

The Coptic (Egyptian) versions of the story are not dissimilar.[151] In the Syrian *Cave of Treasures*, it is written that "when the prince of the lower order of angels saw what great majesty had been given unto Adam, he was jealous of him from that day, and he did not wish to worship him" (1st 1000 years).[152] This introduction of the experience of jealousy will re-appear in the dialogue of Satan when he speaks with Eve. Beyond the simple recognition of self, the beginning of covetous jealousy is the beginning of one self-desiring that which is perceived to be possessed by another, which is to implicitly prioritize *me* over someone else.

Satan believes that instead of bowing to Adam, "He should worship me, because I am fire and spirit; and not that I should worship a thing of dust" (1st 1000 years). Not only does this reflect the attitude that earth was below fire, even in a hierarchical way, but also that fire and the invisible beings were created before Adam, which the angel-to-fall saw as meriting a sense of seniority. He said, "It is meet that he should worship me, for I existed before he came into being" (*1st 1000 years*). This same notion of fire not bowing to earth is likewise expressed in the *Quran*, in which Satan is written to have said, "It is not for me to prostrate myself before mortal man whom Thou hast created out of sounding clay, out of dark slime transmuted!" (*Al-Hijr* 10-43), "I am better than him. Thou created me of fire while him Thou didst create of mud" (*Al-Araf*, 7:12). This rejection of the earthen element seems paradoxical in the context of a devil figure who will become so associated with materiality, but on a deeper level, his refusal to bow to this material being resonates with his understanding of matter as lesser or corrupt.[153]

Because of Satan's refusal to prostrate, God says to Iblis, "Go forth, then, from this [angelic state]: for, behold, thou art [henceforth] accursed, and [My] rejection shall be thy due until the Day of Judgment!" (*Al-Hijr*, 10-43). A similar story can also be found in that of Ethana and Zu from the Babylonian tradition in which "he was led by his pride to strive for the highest seat among the star-gods on the northern mountain of the gods (comp. *Ezek.* xxviii. 14; Ps. xlviii. 3 [A.V. 2]), but was hurled down by the supreme ruler of the Babylonian Olympus" ("Lucifer").

Satan tells Adam, "God became angry with us and commanded us, them and me, to be cast down from our dwellings to the earth ... I had been alienated because of you" (*Book of Adam* 15.1). And described in the *Cave of Treasures*:

> The Rebel ... would not render obedience to God, and of his own free will he asserted his independence and separated himself from God. But he was swept away out of heaven and fell, and the fall of himself and of all his company from heaven took place on the Sixth Day, at the second hour of the day. And the apparel of their glorious state was stripped off them. And his name was called "Sâṯânâ" because he turned aside [from the right way], and "Shêdâ" because he was cast out, and "Daiwâ" because he lost the apparel of his glory. And behold, from that time until the present day, he and all his hosts have been stripped of their apparel, and they go naked and have horrible faces. (*1st 1000 years* 55-6)

When this happened, Jesus "saw Satan fall like Lightning … from Heaven" (Milton IX. 184; Luke 10:18). Before getting too close to this story, we should consider its parallels in Jewish tradition.

In Hebrew lore, the fall of the angels is often associated with the giant offspring that resulted from the marriage of mortal women with angels who had descended at Mount Herman. In the Midrash text of Rabbi Eliezer it is written:

> The angels who fell from their holy place in heaven saw the daughters of the generations of Cain walking about naked, with their eyes painted like harlots, and they went astray after them, and took wives from amongst them, as it is said, "And the sons of Elohim " saw the daughters of men that they were fair; and they took them wives of all that they chose " ' (Gen. 35b, and Gen. Rab. xxiii. i. Pal. Targum to Gen., loc. cit). Rabbi Joshua said : The angels are flaming fire, as it is said, " His servants are a flaming fire " (Ps. civ. 4), and fire came with the coition of flesh and blood, but did not burn the body ; but when they fell from heaven, from their holy place, their strength and stature (became) like that of the sons of men, and their frame was (made of) clods of dust, as it is said, " My flesh is clothed with worms and clods of dust " (Job vii. 5). Rabbi Zadok said : From them were born the giants". (Rabbi Eliezer 159-160)

The story repeats the motif of earthen and dusty humans as well as those of the divine's descent and feminine seductiveness.

The Book of Enoch tells a similar story: "It came to pass when the children of men had multiplied that in those days were born unto them beautiful and comely daughters. And the angels, the children of the heaven, saw and lusted after them" (6:1-2). They all chose wives:

> And they began to go in unto them and to defile themselves with them, and they taught them charms and enchantments ... and made them acquainted with plants. And they became pregnant, and they bore great giants. ... Who consumed all the acquisitions of men. And when men could no longer sustain them, the giants turned against them and devoured mankind. And they began to sin against birds, and beasts, and reptiles, and fish, and to devour one another's flesh, and drink the blood. Then the earth laid accusation against the lawless ones. And Azazel taught men to make swords, and knives, and shields, and breastplates, and made known to them the metals of the earth and the art of working them, and bracelets, and ornaments, and the use of antimony, and the beautifying of the eyelids, and all kinds of costly stones, and all olouring tinctures. And there arose much godlessness, and they committed fornication, and they were led astray, and became corrupt in all their ways. Semjaza taught enchantments, and root-cuttings, 'Armaros the resolving of enchantments, Baraqijal (taught) astrology, Kokabel the constellations, Ezeqeel the knowledge of the clouds, Araqiel the signs of the earth, Shamsiel the signs of the sun, and Sariel the course of the moon" (7.1-8.3).

As we can recognize in both accounts of the story, the immaterial angels that take wives of earth are defiled by their material forms, which seems to be even more central than their defilement through sex. As coming conversations will further show, sex is repeatedly presented as one of the two primary pathways (along with eating) by which the soul is corrupted by matter. Ironically, it is exactly matter that Iblis sees himself above, as both stories associated with the fall of Satan are centered around an interpretation of matter as a corruptive or inferior presence to the divine. It should also be noted that, as with those of Prometheus, both stories are associated with the bringing of knowledge, even fire and metallurgy.

In the version of the angelic fall by which the giants are generated, instead of a cosmic war, the obliteration of the fallen force comes in the form of Noah's flood. When "Michael, Uriel, Raphael, and Gabriel looked down from heaven and saw much blood being shed upon the earth, and all lawlessness being wrought" they brought the case of the humans to the Most High" (Enoch 9: 1-4). In the story God responds by telling Uriel, "Go to Noah and tell him in my name "Hide thyself!" and reveal to him the end that is approaching: that the whole earth will be destroyed, and a deluge is about to come [3] upon the whole earth, and will destroy all that is on it" (10 2-4). He then said to Michael, "bind Semjaza and his associates ... for seventy generations in the valleys of the earth, till the day of their judgment and ... in those days they shall be led off to the abyss of fire: and to the torment and the prison in which they shall be confined forever" (10:11-14). This is of course similar to the Christian and Islamic stories of Satan's exile and confinement to Hell. Likewise, both stories are followed closely by the flood.

The Yezidi descendants of the Assyrians, "devil worshipers," tell an entirely different story in which Satan—a name that should probably be but is not avoided— never fell.[154] And though the fall of Iblis finds special emphasis in the Quran, there is no mention of angels following him, nor is there a description of a war in heaven. Where we find more specific writings on this war, later mirrored in *Revelations,* is in the stories of Egyptian and Ethiopian Churches before Milton picked up the thread in *Paradise Lost.*[155]

According to the "Fathers of the Egyptian and Ethiopian Churches … Satan, or Saṭnâêl, was greatly astonished at the beauty and splendor of the sun and moon, and on the Fourth Day of the week he declared to himself that he would set his throne above the stars and make himself equal to God" (Cave of Treasures, Note). They continue:

> One week after the creation of Adam, Satan declared war on the hosts of Almighty God. These were commanded by Michael and consisted of 120,000 horsemen, 600,000 shield bearers, 700,000 mail-clad horsemen in chariots of fire, 700,000 torch bearers, 800,000 angels with daggers of fire, 1,000,000 slingers, 500,000 bearers of axes of fire, 300,000 bearers of fiery crosses, and 400,000 bearers of lamps. The angels uttered their battle cries and began to fight, but Satan charged them and dispersed them; they reformed, but again Satan charged them and put them to flight. Then God gave the angels the Cross of Light, which bore the legend, "In the Name of the Father, and the Son, and the Holy Ghost." And when they attacked the hosts of darkness under this Cross, Satan became faint, and he and his forces withdraw, and Michael hurled them down into hell. (Cave of Treasures Note)

Such an epic battle is not unlike that described in *Paradise Lost*, in which the battle plain was "covered with thick embattled squadrons bright, / chariots and flaming arms, and fiery steeds" (Milton VI: 15-17).

According to the Coptic version of the legend, "When the Father saw [Satan's] overbearing attitude, He knew that Satan's wickedness and rebellion had reached their highest pitch. He ordered the celestial soldiers to take from him the written authority that was in his hand, to strip off his armor, and to hurl him down from heaven to earth" (VI: 15-17). By this telling he had been "the greatest of the angels, and God had made him the Commander-in-Chief of the celestial hosts" (VI: 15-17). In fact, as in *Paradise Lost* when Satan is stabbed in "his right side," (Milton VI. 327), in this Coptic telling God commands angels "to bring a sharp reaping-knife, and to stab him therewith on this side and on that, right through his body to the vertebrae of his shoulders, [so] he was unable to hold himself up" (*Cave of Treasures* 484). And then God "smote him, and cast him down from heaven upon the earth, because of his pride, and he broke his wings and his ribs and made him helpless, and those whom he had brought with him became devils with him" (484). And it was then that he became "the Arch-Devil and the leader of those who were cast out of heaven … who henceforth were devils" (Budge, *Coptic Martyrdoms* 484).

The war reinforces a strong vision of Satan as in a dualistic relationship with God in which they represent polar opposites of one another. According to Satan in *Paradise Lost*, "never can true reconcilement grow/ where wounds of deadly hate have pierced so deep" (Milton IV. 98-9). This irreconcilability of God and Satan is a deep feature of the Abrahamic tradition. And a distilled version of the war between light and dark is found featured in the *Dead Sea Scrolls*. Religious and mythological history has repeatedly witnessed the descriptions of simplified and perpetual battle between angels and demons in a struggle of evil, materiality, and darkness against the supra-material forces of light and good. In *Passion of the Western Mind*, Dr. Tarnas pulls together a wide array of the antecedent and eventual traditions that follow this pattern:

> The Platonic element in Christianity … encouraged a … dualism between body and spirit. The focus for the Platonic divine-human identity was the nous, the spiritual intellect; the physical body did not participate in his identity, but rather impeded it. In its more extreme forms, Platonism encouraged in Christianity a view of the body as the soul's Prison. As with the physical body, so with the physical world. … Man had once possessed a blissful divine knowledge but had fallen into dark ignorance, and only the hope of recovering that lost spiritual light motivated the Christian soul while detained in this body and this world … this later theological development had numerous antecedents: Stoicism, Neo-Pythagoreanism, Manichaeism, and other religious sects such as the Essenes all possessed marked tendencies toward religious dualism and asceticism that affected the Christian view. And Judaism itself, with its characteristic imperative against worldly and fleshly defilement of the divine and holy, lent support to such tendencies from the outset of the new religion. But it was certain streams of dualistic Gnosticism, probably originating from the penetration of mystical Judaism by Zoroastrian dualism, that were the most extreme in this regard during Christianity's first centuries, holding an absolute division between an evil material world and a good spiritual realm … such a vision amplified related tendencies in John's Gospel stressing the divisions between light and darkness, between Christ's kingdom and the

world under Satan, between the spiritual elect and the worldly unredeemed, as well as between Yahweh and Christ, Old Testament and New. (140-141).

The Cathars and Cistercians also played major roles in building and perpetuating the Christian sense of asceticism and religious dualism, especially in the context of Medieval Europe and the Grail romances. Up and down the time-line, Christians have been encouraged to recognize the world—like the Essenes and Zoroastrians before them—as the battleground for an ongoing war between God's light and the devil's evil. According to a literalist read of the New Testament, this war will eventually blossom into the epic war described in *Revelations*.

The thoughts Tarnas offers on the consistent association of matter with the fallen and dark side of this dualistic system are integral to the dissertation and will be more deeply engaged in the chapter's final section. For now we should transition to the lovers' Fall in Eden with mention that the very story of Satan's fall and war in the heavens was recounted to Adam by Gabriel as an example and warning against his own fall, which Satan is plotting (Milton V. 240).

Before paradise can be disrupted (for those versions of the story conflating the devil and serpent) Satan has to escape Hell and enter Eden. When attempting to depart, he encountered the Portress of Hell, who bore him—at the threshold of Hell—Sin. As Adam was made in the image of God, so was Sin made in the "perfect image" of Satan (II. 764). She should not open the gates for him, but—for him—she does. To the great dismay of all posterity, "she opened … [but] to shut excelled her power, the Gates wide open stood … like a Furnace mouth" (II. 883-888).[156] And what they saw was the wide expansive abyss, "the hoarie deep, a dark / illimitable ocean without bound, / without dimension, where length, breadth, and highth, / and time and place are lost; where eldest Night / and Chaos, ancestors of nature, hold / eternal anarchy" (II. 891-896).[157] The prince of darkness then flew into the great gap of directionless uncertainty to find a path, which Milton, at one point, likened to the Argo's challenge of passing through the clashing rocks, and at another to Ulysses passing between Scylla and Charybdis (II. 1017-1020). Both images express a difficult voyage between dangers that close on both sides. It is on this voyage that he sees heaven, beneath which dangles the "pendant world" of earth, like a fruit for him to pluck.

Fall & Exile

According to Milton, Satan cleared Eden's "Gate/ ... at one slight bound [with which he] high overleaped/ ... [the] highest Wall" (IV. 178-182). In the *Book of Adam and Eve* it is Eve herself who lets him in. In this version the seducer has convinced her to eat the fruit, yet she is "afraid to stretch out [her] hand and take it ... [while he is] not afraid" (Malan, 44. 18.6). For his assistance, she then opened "the gate for him and he ... entered paradise" (44. 18.6).

Several accounts associate an animal with Satan's entry. According to Ethiopian legend, an "animal called "Taman ... the front part of which was like a camel's foal," agreed to help (*Cave*, 1st 1000 Years). In the Irish *Saltair Na Rann* the serpent helps him enter. Satan says to him, "Give me a place in thy body, / with my own laws, with my own intellect, / so that we both may go from the plain / unexpectedly to Eve" (24).

In the Islamic tradition Iblis was allowed into the garden by a peacock ("Qissas al Anbia").[158] The presence of the beautiful yet grounded (flightless) bird would later be recalled in Anderson's fairytale, *The Garden of Paradise*, when he describes a near hallucinatory scene in which the prince saw "a flock of peacocks with outspread iridescent tails," before, upon touching them, "he realized that they weren't animals but plants" (88). The peacock also plays a central role in the version of the Eden narrative told by the Yezidi, who many middle-eastern Muslims see as "devil worshipers:"

> God has delegated his earthly powers to seven angels led by the Peacock Angel, who have responsibility for human and worldly affairs. In Yezidi belief, this angel is the mediator between God and the Yezidi people. He leads directly to God and is not in opposition but is an independent entity. At the same time, he is God's alter ego who became the same, a united and inseparable. He is the manifestation of the Creator, not the Creator himself. Nevertheless, Muslim and Christian neighbors of the Yezidis in the Middle East consider the Peacock Angel as the embodiment of Satan and an evil rebellious spirit. The devil was identified with the fallen angel, who was expelled from Paradise because of his disobedience to God. And as the Yezidis pray to God through his banners in the form of the peacock, they were considered to be worshipers of Satan. … Although Yezidis recognize this concept of evil, they do not have the same comprehension of Satan as the other religions do. In the Yezidi religious belief system, Satan is not a fallen angel but the only representative of God on earth. (Acikyildiz 2).

This other side—Satan's side—of "The Fall" represents the Yezidi version of the story. The Yezidi, it should be noted, are not *Abrahamic*—according to their history they do not (mythically) descend from Eve.

In some versions of the story the seduction of Eve is conflated with the entry of Satan into the Garden. For example, in the *Cave of Treasures*, Satan waited and "watched for the opportunity," until finally he "saw Eve by herself … and led her astray with his lying words" (*1st 1000 years*). "The serpent became spokesman for him," (*1st 1000 years*) and he said to Eve, 'I am distressed for you, for you are like the (dumb) animals. God was jealous of you and he has not permitted you, but I, I do not desire your ignorance" (*Book of Adam* 44. 18.1-2). He asks, "'Has God commanded you not to eat from every tree of the garden?' She said to it, "God told us that we can eat all the fruit of the trees in the garden, but God told us that we are not to eat or touch the fruit of the tree which is in the middle of the garden, for fear that we will die" (*Book of Jubilees*, 15-16). "I am afraid of dying" she said (*Book of Adam*). The serpent replied, "You will not surely die" (*Genesis 3*:4). "How should ye? By the Fruit? It gives you life" (Milton, VIII. 687-88). "What is death and how does one die? Death is life! … at the moment when you eat your eyes will be opened" (*Book of Adam* 44. 18.3-4).

"Look at the tree and see the glory around it'" (44. 18.3-4). "Here grows the cure of all, this fruit divine, / fair to the eye, inviting to the taste, / of virtue to make wise. [He asks] what hinders [you] then / to reach, and feed at once both Body and Mind" (Milton, VIII. 776-779). The "knowledge of Good and Evil" is "enclosed" in "this tree" (VIII. 722-23). "God knows that when you eat of it your eyes will be opened, and you will be like God, knowing good and evil" (*Genesis*). "Your eyes that seem so clear, / yet are but dim, shall perfectly be then/ opened and cleared, and ye shall be as Gods" (Milton, VIII. 706-8). "And when Eve had heard from him concerning that tree, straightway she ran quickly to it" (*Cave of Treasures*, "1ˢᵗ 1000 years"). And "When [she] saw that the tree was delightful and pleasant to look at" (*Book of Jubilees*; 15-16), and "that the tree was good for food, and … to be desired to make one wise, she took of its fruit" (*Genesis*), "and she ate" (*Little Genesis* 16). Because of this, Adam tells his son, "we are going to die. When it was the final hour for the guardian angels to ascend to worship God, the enemy deceived her and she ate of it" (*Book of Adam* 32. 7.1-2).

In the *Book of Adam*, before he ushers Eve to the tree, he says to her "swear to me truly that, if I make you eat it, you will not be jealous of Adam, your husband, but will make him eat of it and give of it also to him" (*Book of Adam* 44 19.2). And her husband came, believing he had sensed a beast entering paradise. Upon seeing her he said:

> 'What are you thinking for and why do you have this fig-leaf on yourself? I replied to him and I told him, 'Do you wish me to tell you something or not? Until today we were like (dumb) animals. When I understood (that of which) the Lord had said to us, 'Do not eat of this' and when I saw its splendor, I took of it and ate of it and I knew good and evil. Now, eat also of it and you will you become like God.' Adam replied to me and told me, 'I fear lest God be angry with me and tell me, "My commandment which I gave you, you did not keep it!"' But I told the father, "On me shall be this blame. If He asks you, say thus: 'This woman whom you have given me is to blame for that; (she said) See the flavor of this glory.' (44 21.3-5).

According to a rabbinic version, Adam continued to refuse until she said, "What do you think, that I will die and another Eve will be created for you? Or perhaps, that I will die and you will sit around idle?" In a third exegesis, Eve began to wail at Adam until he ate of the tree (*Gen. Rabbah*19:5)" (Kadari "Eve: Midrash and Aggadah").

When he agreed, Eve says, "I gave him of it and he ate of it and became like me, and he also took a leaf of the fig tree and covered his nakedness with it' (*Book of Adam* 44 21.3-5). In the Syrian text, "she cried out to Adam, and he came to her, and she handed to him some of the fruit of which she had eaten, and he also did eat thereof … " (*Cave of Treasures: 1ˢᵗ 1000 years*). "Thus did [he] disobey His Lord, and allow himself to be seduced" (*Sura XX Ta-Ha* 7:121). And in victory the devil declares, "Him by fraud I have seduced/ from his Creator/ … with an Apple/ … To Sin and Death a prey" (Milton IX. 485-490).

Though Genesis and the Judeo-Christian literature gives emphasis to Eve as the first to fault, the Islamic tradition—in which the earlier fall of Satan is emphasized—does not distinguish the blame between the first couple. As mentioned, the *Quran* does not even include Eve's name. In the *Quran* it is written that Satan began "to whisper suggestions to them, bringing openly before their minds All their shame that was hidden from them" (VII *A'raf*, 2:20-21). He said, "your Lord only forbade you this tree, Lest ye should become angels Or such beings as live forever. … And he swore to them both, that he was their sincere adviser" (VII *A'raf*, 2:20-21). Then he asked, "Shall I lead thee to The Tree of Eternity and to a kingdom That never decays?" (XX *Ta-Ha* 7:12). "Thus did he lead them on with guile" (*Al-Araf*, 7:22). Unlike other versions, this scene describes Adam and Eve as both present during the first seduction.

"And when they tasted of the tree their shame was manifest to them and they began to hide" (Al-Araf, 7:22).[159] "The eyes of both were opened, and they knew that they were naked" (*Genesis*). "Immediately she found herself stripped naked, and she saw the hatefulness of her shame, and she ran away naked, and hid herself in another tree. … And when he had eaten he also became naked" (*Cave of Treasures: Satan's Attack on Adam and Eve*). The "conscious dreams" in which they had been "encumbered … left them, [and] up they rose/ as from unrest, and each the other viewing, / soon found their eyes now opened, and their minds/ how darkened; innocence, that as a veil / had shadowed them from knowing ill, was gone" (Milton VIII. 1052-1058). "Love was not in their looks, either to God/ or to each other, but apparent guilt, / and shame, and perturbation, and despair, / anger, and obstinacy, and hate, and guile" (IX. 111-114).

Spurred on by their shame, "they began to sew together, for their covering, leaves from the Garden" (*XX Ta-Ha* 7:121). "After she covered her shame with fig leaves. … He took fig leaves and sewed them together, and made an apron for himself, and covered his shame" (*Little Genesis* 15-16). "He and Eve made girdles for their loins of the leaves of the fig-trees" (*Cave of Treasures: Satan's Attack on Adam and Eve*). "They sewed fig leaves together and made themselves loincloths. (Genesis). Rather consistently, and again in the Sistine Chapel, the genital shame and clothing is remembered as the fig leaf. In both *Little Genesis* and the *Cave of Treasures* they receive a second set of clothes from god, made of "skin," which, in the *Cave of Treasures*, "was stripped from the trees … [which] in Paradise had soft barks … softer than the byssus and silk wherefrom the garments worn by kings are made" (*Cave of Treasures: Satan's Attack on Adam and Eve*).[160] On the other hand, Milton wants to emphasize how "solid and stained" are "our wonted ornaments" (VIII. 1076). Virtually none of the variations leave out the detail of the first clothes.

One of the questions is why the fig leaf has so consistently been chosen as the covering. I am not going to suggest that it is an ancient big penis joke in the form of one of nature's largest leafs, but it is undeniable that the fig leaf is one of few that is actually large enough to cover much. Did I really just make a penis joke in a dissertation? Did he really just break the fourth wall? Taboos feel awkward. This was the first taboo in God's creation. It creates a break in the status quo – my style has changed and this feels completely out of place in the context of what has thus far been written. The fall created such an effect: a part of creation, for the first time, stood out as inconsistent. As discussed in the section on fruit, the fig comes with particular sexual connotations. First of all, it is comprised of flowers, which are sexual organs. Secondly, the inside is hollow, like a womb. And third, seeds are eaten with the fig, which implies fertilization. There is no differentiation of flowering and fruiting in the life cycle of the fig, much like Eve, who is born as a fully blossomed flower only just before conceiving. Consider the ravishing of Persephone—with which we have already associated Eve's seduction—and Milton's reference to the flowers surrounding Eve upon the creation of her fully blossomed form. Persephone is plucked from maidenhood at the moment she plucks the fully blossoming Narcissus flower. Returning to the fig, and its symbolic synthesis of both the fruit and flower, the covering of the genitalia with fig leaves appears as a synergetic reference to both sexual maturity and the birth it will portend.

It seems obvious that the motif of shame and first clothing, following the first sin, is a reaction to the discovery of sexuality and perhaps the first act of intercourse.[161] This is contextually reinforced by the reciprocal seduction of the woman by the masculine (phallic) snake in the context of the fruit, which has long been associated with the child— born by a mother as a tree bears fruit. But on another level, the motif of clothing is also involves that of concealment. In fact, in the Rabbinic tradition it seems as though it was believed that women wore an additional article of clothing to specifically conceal their shame. This is communicated by a conversation with *Rabbi. Joshua:*

> [He] was asked: "Why does a man go forth with uncovered head, while the woman goes forth with her head covered?" He replied: "This is like someone who committed a transgression and is embarrassed before other people, therefore the woman goes forth covered [for she sinned and is ashamed]." He was further questioned: "Why do women go to the corpse first [it was the custom in Judea that women preceded the corpse in a funeral procession, while the men followed the bier]?" He answered: "Because they caused death to come to the world, they go first with the corpse" (Gen. Rabbah 17:8). (Kadari, "Eve: Midrash and Aggadah")

We gave special attention to the motif of concealment in the context of the Pandora and ox-sacrifice scenes in the Prometheus myth, which, as in this story, were associated with the distancing of humans from Gods. To recall, the bad food was hidden in the good wrappings and all the suffering Pandora brings was hidden behind her beauty—not unlike the vessel she opened, which concealed the worst in the world. [162]

Following the transgression, God prepared the angels for the coming sentencing. "He summoned the angels and told them.' … Come to paradise and hear the sentence to which we are going to judge'" (*Book of Adam* 44. 22.2). Adam also prepares. He tells

Eve, "We have sinned, for God is going to come to judge us'" (44. 22.2). She recounts, "we were afraid, and … hid" (44. 22.2). "And God came to paradise sitting upon the Cherubs and the angels were singing hymns before him. When he had arrived at paradise, at once all (the) tree(s) cast off their (its) foliage, and thrones were set up near the tree of life. [And] God summoned Adam and told him, 'Adam, Adam, where are you? Are you hiding from me? Or how will a house hide from its builder? Or why have you hidden near the tree of paradise?'" (44. 22.3-23.1). Having "heard the sound of the Lord God walking in the garden in the cool of the day … the man and his wife hid themselves from the presence of the Lord God" (*Genesis* 3:8). Then Adam "replied and told the Lord, 'I have hidden because I am afraid: I am naked and I am ashamed.' God replied to him and told him, "Who told you that you are naked? Have you scorned the commandment which I gave you?" (*Book of Adam* 44. 23.2-4). "Who told you that you were naked? Have you eaten from the tree of which I commanded you not to eat?" (*Genesis* 3:11). "Did I not Forbid you that tree, And tell you that Satan Was an avowed Enemy unto you?" (VII *A'raf* 2:22-23).

In the *Quran*, together they say, "Our Lord! We have wronged our own souls: If Thou forgive us not and bestow not upon us thy mercy, we shall certainly be lost" (2:22-23). According to the Islamic telling, they take blame together, and immediately repent. This is far different than Iblis, who makes an argument on his own behalf, which is why the fall of Satan is more severe to Muslims. However, in the Judeo-Christian versions, Adam does defend himself, in fact he shifts the blame to Eve. The positioning of Eve as the very first to pluck the fruit—much like Pandora opening the box—is likely to have meaning beyond the sort of misogynistic interpretation one recognizes in both *Genesis* as well as *Works and Days*. We discussed this a bit in the context of Satan's fall, but it is beyond our scope to further explore the meaning behind this omission.

In *Genesis*, "The man said, 'The woman whom you gave to be with me, she gave me fruit of the tree, and I ate'" (3:12). "Then the LORD God said to the woman, "What is this that you have done?" And the woman replied, "The serpent deceived me, and I ate." (3:13). "It is the serpent who deceived me!" (*Book of Adam*). And "at mid-day they received [their] sentence of doom" (*Cave of Treasures: Satan's Attack on Adam and Eve*), bringing to justice those foreshadowing words of Milton's Eve, "Adam shall share with me in bliss or woe/ so dear I love him, that with him all deaths/ I could endure; [and] without him live no life" (VIII. 831-833).

God "was angry with the woman, because she listened to what the snake said, and ate" (*Book of Jubilees* 15-16). He turned to her and said, "Why did you hearken to the serpent and abandon my commandments with which I commanded to you?" (*Book of Adam* 44. 25.1-2). "The Rabbis were intrigued by [this] question of how the serpent succeeded in enticing Eve to transgress the word of God. They used Eve's sin, the first transgression on earth, as a model for all human sins, and by means of this initial trespass they seek to understand what motivates people to sin?" (Kadari "Eve: Midrash and Aggadah"). In one Midrash Eve answered that "the serpent aroused me, obligated me and deceived me" (*Gen. Rabbah* 19:12). And by these means the serpent seduced, compelled and concealed the truth from her in such a way that she made the choice. No matter her answer, God responded with a series of curses. "(May you) be in toils and pains; (may you) give birth to many fruits and when you give birth to them you will despair of your life" (*Book of Adam* 44. 25.1-2). He said to her, "I will greatly increase your sorrow and your pains, in sorrow you will bring out children" (*Book of Jubilees* 15-16). "Thy sorrow I will greatly multiply by thy conception" (Milton, IX. 193-4). "You will harden your heart in view of the great combat which the serpent instituted with you. (But may you) return at once to the same point, may you bear your offspring in hurt and return in pity to your husband, and he will rule over you" (*Book of Adam* 44. 25.4-25.1). (The imagery of the hardening heart will become a crucial point of later conversation). As with the narrative in which Pandora becomes the first mother and unleashes suffering into the world, Eve is punished with birth-pains themselves.

After punishing Eve, God "became very angry with the serpent" (*Book of Adam* 44. 26.1), and "cursed the snake" (*Book of Jubilees*, 15-16). He told it, "You, too, perish and be cursed among all the (dumb) animals. May be withheld from you food which you used to eat and may the soil be to you as food all the days of your life; you shall go on your breast and on your stomach; your hands and your feet will be taken from you. May you have neither ears nor nails and may not even one limb remain for you" (*Book of Adam* 44. 26.1-4). "Because you have done this … on your belly you shall go, and of dust you shall eat" (*Genesis* 3:14). "May you again be crushed and broken because of the evil of your heart. And I will set enmity between you and the offspring of the woman: she will lay in wait for your head and you will lay in wait for her heel until the Day of Judgment" (*Book of Adam* 44. 26.1-4).

Then to Adam He said, "Because you have listened to the voice of your wife, and have eaten from the tree about which I commanded you, saying, 'You shall not eat from it'; Cursed is the ground because of you; In toil you will eat of it All the days of your life. 'Both thorns and thistles it shall grow for you; And you will eat the plants of the field; By the sweat of your face You will eat bread," (*Genesis* 2:17-19).[163] And the *Book of Adam* repeats, "By the sweat of your brow you shall eat bread" (44. 24.3). (And I love the likely unintentional English-based pun), "'Till" you "return to the ground, Because from it you were taken; For you are dust, And to dust you shall return" (*Genesis* 2:17-19). "By the sweat of your brow you will make food, until you return to the earth from where you came! You are earth, and to earth will you return!" (*Book of Jubilees*, 16). "Dust thou art, and [thou] shalt to dust return" (Milton IX. 208). "Let the earth be cursed in your deeds. May you work it and it will give you no fruit ... you shall have (no) rest. You shall hunger and you shall (not) be sated. You shall be affected by bitterness and you shall (not) taste sweetness; you shall be tormented by heat and will undergo cold ... you shall *eat* and shall (not) grow fat; you shall warm yourselves with fire, and ... not be heated" (*Book of Adam* 44. 24.1-24.1). From then on "he must work the ground from which he was taken" (*Genesis* 3:23) and all He will ever "eat or drink or ... beget, is propagated curse" (Milton IX. 205 728-9). Such context provides the potency behind T.S. Eliot's statement in *The Waste Land*, "I will show you fear in a handful of dust" (1).

After the condemnation of the first couple, "he commanded both of [them] to be expelled from paradise" (*Book of Adam* 44. 27.1). The Lord God said, "'Behold, the man has become like one of us in knowing good and evil. Now, lest he reach out his hand and take also of the tree of life and eat, and live forever ... the Lord God sent him out from the garden of Eden to work the ground from which he was taken" (*Genesis* 3:23). In the Quran, Allah proclaims, "Get ye down, Both of you—all together, from the Garden, with enmity One to another: (XX *Ta-Ha* 7:123). "Get ye down, with enmity between yourselves. On earth will be your dwelling-place and your means of livelihood— for a time" (VII *A'raf* 2:24-25). And he tells Michael to, "without remorse [,] drive out the sinful pair, / from hallowed ground … and denounce/ to them and to their progeny / … perpetual banishment" (Milton X. 105-114). He tells them, on Earth "shall ye Live, and therein shall ye Die" (VII *A'raf,* 2:24-25).

In the *Book of Adam* he does not want to accept the punishment. He responds with an appeal and plea to angels:

> Wait for me to beseech the Lord; who knows, perhaps the Lord will grant me a penitence for that which I have done and I will not go out of paradise." Then the angels waited for us to ask. Adam besought the Lord and said, "I beseech you, Lord, pardon me for what I have done." Then the Lord told the angels, "Why have you been waiting (before) separating Adam from paradise? Is the blame mine … or have I not judged justly?" Then the angels fell to the ground and told him, bowing before the Lord, "You are just, Lord, and you sentence is upright." The Lord turned and told Adam, "You are not to remain in paradise." Adam replied to the Lord and told him, "I beseech you, Lord, give me of the tree of life so that I may eat before I have gone forth." Then the Lord addressed a speech to Adam and told him, "You will not take any of it anymore in your lifetime. I have posted burning Cherubs and a turning sword to keep it from you, lest you should taste it and become immortal and boast saying, 'I shall not die ever'; and you will conduct the fight which the enemy has conducted against you. If you go out of paradise and guard yourself from every evil, you will die and after death you will arise in the future resurrection. Then,

indeed, I will give you of the tree of life and you will be immortal

forever. (44. 27.3-28.4).

In *Paradise Lost* the prophecy of resurrection is explicitly given to soften the sadness of

the couple. God says to Michael, "least they faint/ at the sad sentence/ … for I behold

them softened and with tears bewailing their excess … reveal/ to Adam what shall come

in future days" (Milton X. 105-114). The *Cave of Treasures*—as in the *Book of Adam* and

Quran—also follows the condemnation of the first couple with a promise of eventual

redemption. In its case, the reference to Christ is direct: "After the fulfilment of the times

which I have allotted that you shall be in exile outside [Paradise], in the land which is

under the curse, behold, I will send my Son. And He shall go down [from heaven] for thy

redemption, and He shall sojourn in a Virgin, and shall put on a body [of flesh], and

through Him redemption and a return shall be effected for thee" (*Cave of Treasures:*

Adam's Stay in Paradise). We should note the clear allusion to the soul's entry into the

material body. Similar prophecies are given in the *First Book of Adam and Eve*, only after

the couple had suffered expulsion for some time.

The presence of the flaming sword is a consistent motif in this sequence that

should also be addressed—especially for its clear comparability with the flaming torch of

Prometheus. In *Paradise Lost* God says to Michael, "Take to thee from among the

Cherubim/ Thy choice of flaming Warriors / … And on the East side of the Garden place,

/ Where entrance up from Eden easiest climbs, / Cherubic watch, and of a Sword the

flame / … guard all passage to the Tree of Life" (X. 100-122). This is the same Michael

who squared off with Satan in the earlier fight for Heaven, when the two "waved their

fiery swords … and in the air/ made horrid circles; two broad suns their shields" (VI.

324). And this is the Satan who would become lord of Hell, whose "bounds high reaching to the horrid Roof, / And thrice threefold the Gates; three folds were Brass / Three Iron, three of Adamantine Rock, / Impenetrable, impaled with circling fire" (II. 645-648). In all cases the flame is presented as a cutting barrier—the very swords of a fight with Satan, the gates of hell, and the disaster of Eden's invasion.

Insofar as Satan and the garden are associated with the knowledge of Eden, these fiery swords are in symbolic concert with the boundaries (or edges) of knowledge. And in all three cases we get the image of enclosure—the walls of Hell, walls of Eden, and the horrid rings of fire made by Michael and Satan's duel. In fact, it is with "thoughts inflamed of highest design" that "the adversary of God and Man" speeds "towards the Gates of Hell" in "solitary flight" (II. 629-632), which not only emphasizes the association of fire with a gate, but also solitude and knowledge. Though knowledge is not presented in the form of a flame—as in the myths of Prometheus—the fire-stick is still highly associated with knowledge and its Abrahamic origin story. In fact, one might even see the fire-stick as the very boundary between the garden of innocence and knowledge of life beyond its new-born paradise. When we reflect on the events of this chapter, the gates—as a symbol of enclosure much like skin and clothing—will be of central significance, as will the symbolic location of fire in the roles of division. Of most significance will be the constellation of both notions—enclosure and separation—seen in this single image of the flaming sword at Eden's gate, which bring to consciousness the forms required for self-identity and subject-object distinction.

When God finally "made Adam go out of the Garden" (*Cave of Treasures* 1), he was led by Michael, whose "brandished Sword of God before them blazed, fierce as a comet; which with torrid heat, and vapor as the Libyan air a dust began to parch that temperate clime" (Milton X. 1523-27). "And when they came to the opening of the gate of the garden, and saw the broad earth spread before them, covered with stones large and small, and with sand, they feared and trembled, and fell on their faces, from the fear that came upon them; and they were as dead" (Malan, *First Book of Adam and Eve* 2:2). In this version, the first things they see outside, before even leaving the garden, is sand and stone; such as that from which they are made and to which they are cursed. They "beheld a field" (Milton X. 429), where they were made to "to dwell there in a cave in a rock— the Cave of Treasures below the garden" (*First Book of Adam and Eve* I. 9). "And Adam cried and wailed, and beat his chest, for being severed from the garden" (*First Book of Adam and Eve* IX: 4).

Post Exilic Reality: Exiting the Garden and Entering the Body, Senses, and Tomb

According to Milton, "God, to remove his ways from human sense, / placed Heaven from earth so far, that earthly sight, / if it presume, might ere in things too high, / and no advantage gain" (VII. 756-760). This distancing of divinity from human sensory experience will be important to us shortly, but we should first note the distancing of Heaven itself, which, like the morning star, is unattainably further than one can possibly travel. In Hans Christian Andersen's repetition of the Eden story "there was a thunderclap louder and more dreadful than had ever been heard before, and everything fell down: the lovely Fairy and the blossoming Paradise sank. It sank so deep, so deep, the prince saw it sink in the black night … it was the morning star in the sky" (93). And as the morning star rises with the sun, by the time it ripens red, the star (Venus) is also setting. This distancing of Eden mimes the distancing of the first couple from its garden, God and sometimes each other.

Once "Adam our father, and his wife, too, / were driven from Paradise to labor/ … cast out to woe and pain" (Chaucer, *Pardoner's Tale* 505-7), a number of changes in the land and their bodies began to occur. As I will show, many of these changes are consistent with the motifs of drought and wasteland. Throughout this dissertation we have engaged the tension between particles and waves, which, I would like to now suggest, is mimetic with the tension between dry and wet. Classical atoms are each individually solid, which, by definition, is not liquid. Historians of philosophy and science have noted the association of water with life—and the mythic substrata that supported this belief. They have also explained that the dominant vision of matter is as internally dead and inert. These two notions reinforce one another symbolically, as to withdraw the water (and thereby internal liquidity) is to symbolically withdraw life.

This is the foundational structure of the "wasteland" motif, made famous by T.S. Eliot, James Joyce, Jessie Weston and James Frazer. Eliot's *Wasteland* was of "dry stone" in which there was "no sound of water" (1). Campbell, who was particularly engaged by Joyce's use of the Wasteland motif, noted that, "in the pages of Ulysses, [he] depicts a world of rock-hard, separate men, moving dryly among and around each other. There is a drought in the land" (*Creative* 283). Neither plant nor animal can grow without water, which was emphasized in the mythologies of the Nile, Indus, Tigris and Euphrates river valleys, where the Egyptian, Mesopotamian, and Harappan cultures depended on floods to water their grain. With the flood cycle comes a cycle of dryness, during which time the fields wither and die. Where I live in Southern California, not far from the *dust bowl*, life depends on a cycle of rain. Cycles of dryness can also result from extreme heat or extreme cold. Antarctica is the largest desert in the world. Not only is there no water—as in hot deserts of sand—but the ground itself is frozen fluid, as internally motionless as dry particles or atoms. Where Hell is often envisioned as a pit of fire—the opposite of water—*Dis*, Dante's Satan, resides in the depths of dry cold. As we now consider the post exilic reality into which the first couple entered, we will recognize the repetitive symbolic representation of solids and dryness.

First and most centrally, because of Sin, the flow of water stopped between the Tigris and underground gulf "at the foot of Paradise" that opened into a "Fountain by the Tree of Life." (Milton, VIII. 69-73). In fact, in *The First Book of Adam and Eve* the "tree … changed … into another form, and … withered" (Malan, III. 8).

Upon leaving the Garden, what they first see, in the *Cave of Treasures*, is a landscape of sand and stone—dry, solid, and, like the fruit, picture-perfect examples of distinctly isolated subjects and objects. Shortly after their exit from paradise the first couple was "burning with thirst, and heat, and sorrow," but afraid to consume even water, lest "it comes into [their] inner parts" and "increase [their] punishments" (1st *Book of Adam and Eve* 10; XI 1-3). So they "withdrew from the water, and drank none of it at all" (XI 1-3), communicating, through this mythic framework, the severe dryness defining their state, which, for Milton and others was mirrored by the withered tree and lifeless fountain in the garden.

Continued engagement with the wasteland motif will show us that it stretches beyond drought and into famine, (in)fertility, and any massive presence of death—that of body, mind, or spirit—from war, plague, tyranny, or even ignorance. Ultimately, what I will try to show, is that dry matter is like atomic matter—both of which are lifeless—and that, as dry sand and stone are associated with the wasteland, so too should be the driest form of atomism. This would give us reason to associate the knowledge of materialism with that of the fallen world.

The distancing of the couple from divine light and into fallen earth is further expressed by their exile into the cave. When finally they "found a cave in the top of the mountain … they entered and" (*Cave of Treasures: Expulsion*) "went gently down into the Cave of Treasures" (Malan, *First book of Adam and Eve* IV. 2). In lamentation "Adam cried over himself and said to Eve …

> Look at this cave that is to be our prison in this world, and a place of punishment! What is it compared with the garden … its narrowness compared with the space of the other? What is this rock, by the side of those groves? What is the gloom of this cavern, compared with the light of the garden? ... What is the soil of this cave compared with the garden land? This earth, strewed with stones; and that, planted with delicious fruit trees? (IV. *3-7*).

Here the cave is described as the prison of this world, which resonates with the conversations in previous chapters about Classical religious, mythical and philosophical expressions of a vision in which the soul is imprisoned by its body and world. And, as can be seen in the quotation, this fallen world is filled with soil and stone.

The darkness and enclosure of the cave introduces the darkening of their own senses and the resulting enclosure of their individualities behind the organic faculties:

> Adam beat himself, and threw himself on the ground in the cave, from bitter grief, and because of the darkness, and lay there as dead. But Eve heard the noise he made in falling on the ground. And she felt about for him with her hands, and found him like a corpse. ... 'Since we came into this cave, darkness has covered us, and separated us from each other, so that I do not see her, and she does not see me' (XII. 1-10).

In reaction Adam complains that "the Word of God is hidden from us; and the light that shown over us is so changed as to disappear, and let darkness and sorrow come over us. And we are forced to enter this cave which is like a prison, in which darkness covers us, so that we are separated from each other; and you cannot see me, neither can I see you" (Malan, *First book of Adam and Eve* XXVI. 3-4). In every way we can see an allegory for the soul's entry into the material world and the loss of its original mode of being to bodily experience, which, as expressed in this story, is a far more limiting experience. Not only is there an imprisonment within the body and cave. Their imprisonment is accompanied by a loss of sensory access to the divine.

The motif of Adam and Eve's separation—first presented in her creation by separation—is consistent with the Muslim vision of the fall, in which "Eve fell upon [Mount] Arafat and Adam in Ceylon. Adam [then] sought his wife ... and finally found her upon Arafat" (Chatautauquan Vol 21, 577). What this image offers is a complete form of solitude. Adam and Eve are separated from each other's companionship, which reinforces the other images of separation in the story.[164] The plucked fruit, exile from the garden, severance from God, walls, skin, clothing, sensory darkness, etc. are complimented by the isolative image of the cave—especially when it will be later sealed in the form of an ancient Jewish tomb for Adam's burial.

In addition to losing the ability to see one another in the darkness of the cave, "the roof of the cave that covered him overhead … prevented him from seeing either heaven or God's creatures" (Malan, *First Book of Adam and Eve* V. 2). Adam cried and said, "O God, when we lived in the garden, and our hearts were lifted up, we saw the angels that sang praises in heaven, but now we can't see like we used to; no, when we entered the cave, all creation became hidden from us" (*First Book of Adam and Eve* VIII. 1). This is reminiscent of when it is said in the *Book of Jubilees*, "On that day the mouth of all beasts, cattle, birds, whatever walks, and whatever moves, was shut so that they could no longer speak, as they had all spoken with each another with one language" (*Book of Jubilees* 16). According to a Midrash, Eve actually fed the fruit "to the cattle, beasts and birds. … All the living creatures heeded her and ate of it, except for the phoenix (*Gen. Rabbah* 19:5). The sin harmed all of creation: it caused the animals, as well, to descend to a lower level and all of them were driven out of the Garden and became mortal. (Kadari "Eve: Midrash and Aggadah"). The Brothers' Grimm fairy tale, "The White Snake," offers an inversion by which, upon "eating the snake" the fairy tale hero gains the "power of understanding the language of animals" (*White Snake*).

What the First Book of Adam and Eve seems to be emphasizing is that the sensate experience of the first couple had shifted to reflect their bodies, which are to become dependent on the fallen earth. As Adam said to Eve, "Look at your eyes, and at mine. … Our eyes have become of flesh; they cannot see like they used to see before. … What is our body today, compared to what it was in former days, when we lived in the garden?" (*First Book of Adam and Eve* IV. 8-10).

The transformation of the senses into organs of flesh was mirrored by that of the digestive system (and entire body). After leaving the garden the divine couple fasted until, in the first book of Adam and Eve, God gave them each a fig. When "they sat down to eat the figs … they knew not how to eat them; for they were not accustomed to eat earthly food" (LXIV. 4), and in addition to their lack of technique "they were afraid that if they ate, their stomach would be burdened and their flesh thickened, and their hearts would take to liking earthly food" (LXIV. 4). But God sent an angel to tell them, "You do not have the strength that would be required to fast until death" and to "strengthen [your] bodies" with "food and drink" (5-6). In obedience, "Adam and Eve took the figs and began to eat them. But God had put into them a mixture as of savory bread and blood" (7). And once they had "satisfied their hunger … by the power of God, the figs became whole again," and Adam and Eve got up and prayed with a joyful heart and renewed strength" (8-9).[165] But their fears were true, and their bodies transformed.[166] According to the Yezidi, "Adam was troubled because his belly was inflated, for he had no outlet. God therefore sent a bird to him which pecked at his anus and made an outlet, and Adam was relieved" (Joseph, *Devil* 39). In a midrash he proclaims, "'Just as my teeth have been blunted, so, too, shall the teeth of all creatures be blunted' (*Avot de-Rabbi Nathan* version B, chap. 1)" (Kadari "Eve: Midrash and Aggadah").

The next day they "became sick from the food they had eaten because they were not used to it … Adam said to Eve, 'This pain did not come to us in the garden, neither did we eat such bad food there. Do you think, O Eve, that God will plague us through the food that is in us, or that our innards will come out?'" (LXV: 1-10). And when Adam besought God he "looked at them, and then fitted them for eating food at once; as to this day; so that they should not perish" (LXV: 1-10).

As a result of this metamorphosis "Adam and Eve came back into the cave sorrowful and crying because of the alteration of their bodies. And they both knew from that hour that they were altered beings, that all hope of returning to the garden was now lost; and that they could not enter it" (LXV: 1-10). They knew:

> Now their bodies had strange functions; and all flesh that requires food and drink for its existence, cannot be in the garden. Then Adam said to Eve, "Behold, our hope is now lost; and so is our trust to enter the garden. We no longer belong to the inhabitants of the garden; but from now on we are earthy and of the dust, and of the inhabitants of the earth ... That night Adam and Eve spent in the cave, where they slept heavily by reason of the food they had eaten. (LXV: 1-10)

This transformation by/for food expresses the codependence of the material body with the material world, which is ultimately a re-expression of the body as (and in cycle with) "dust" or "earth." Perhaps one of the most direct examples of the association between fruit and flesh is in the *Epic of Gilgamesh,* when, in a garden of paradise, "The tree bears carnelian as its fruit" (9.281). The word "carnelian" comes from the Latin word for flesh (carne) and refers to the flesh color and qualities of the stone. This image of flesh-stone as fruit mirrors the fruit in Eden which results in the fall into fleshy matter. To exist in a corporeal body is to exist in a corporeal world, and for living creatures this means to be in such a symbiosis with nature that all substance of which we are made first comes from that which was previously consumed. To put fruit in one's mouth and to swallow it into the stomach is to start the otherwise circuitous patterns of eating and digesting.

This direct association of eating with the fall is echoed by Chaucer, who writes, "while Adam fasted, as I read, / he was in Paradise; and when he / ate of the forbidden fruit on the tree, / he was at once cast out to woe and pain. / O gluttony, we certainly ought to complain against you!" (*Pardoner's Tale* 505-511). As Chaucer points out, the craving for food drives far more than the consumption of sustenance. He writes, "Oh, if a man knew how many maladies / follow from excess and gluttony, / he would be more temperate in his diet / when he sits at his table. / Alas! The short throat, the sensitive mouth, / make men labor east and west and north and south, / in earth, in air, and in water, to get / a glutton dainty food and drink" (514-521). Milton adds, triggered by their eating, "immediately inordinate desires / and upstart passions catch the government / from reason, and to servitude reduce / man till then free" (X. 979-82). In these quotations there is a near immediate transition from this initiatory meal and full blown gluttony. The direct association between eating and the commitment to materialisty (including the body's transformation) was described in the previous paragraphs. Milton and Chaucer, however, seem to be emphasizing the development of runaway appetities initiated by the fruit. The arising questions are then: is the negative consequence of the fruit corporeality or the domination of instinct; are these problems entangled; can they be disentangled? What this dissertation tries to argue, in various ways, is that the greatest problem is the entanglement itself—the reductive conflation of corporeality with the realm of appetites and corruption.

This tyranny of one's own appetites reads to me like what Prometheus would have disliked about the gift of Pandora—the problem was not the woman, it was the new and corresponding servitude to the stomach and womb that completely changed the mode of human life and creativity. What Milton is pointing out is that the governance of reason that comes from the consumed knowledge is of a certain form. We discussed the Pythagoreans and Socrates in the last chapter as examples of philosophers who developed this point and went out of their way to liberate their psyches from the influences of food, sex, and other carnal cravings. Milton writes, "food alike those pure / Intelligential substances require/ As doth your rational; and both contain / Within them every lower faculty / Of sense, whereby they hear, see, smell, touch, taste, / Tasting concoct, digest, assimilate, / And corporeal to incorporeal turn. / For, know, whatever was created, needs / to be sustained and fed" (V. 408:-15). What he is saying is that all of these faculties emerged from, and are dependent on, the sustenance of food. And, according to Milton, these newly illuminated/darkened faculties were charged with "high passions, anger, hate, / Mistrust, suspicion, discord, and [they] shook sore / Their inward state of mind … once / Full of peace, now tossed and turbulent / … In subjection now/ to sensual appetite, who from beneath / Usurping over sovereign reason claimed/ Superior sway" (VIII. 1122-1131). As a result of this transformation, with "stony hearts" (III. 189), "love was not in their looks, either to God / or to each other" (IX. 111-114). Instead they were filled with "apparent guilt, / and shame, and perturbation, and despair, / anger, and obstinacy, and hate, and guile" (VIII. 111-114).

The fruit and fall initiate the development of corporeal digestive and sensory organs with which a certain range of emotions and modes of reason are contingent. This is something we saw recognized by the philosophy of Pythagoras and Plato, as well as the Orphics, who were concerned with the corruption of reason by its bodily participation in the material world. What we shall turn to next are the living roles of the fallen couple, in labor, for children and food.

"Adam made love to his wife Eve, and she became pregnant and gave birth to Cain" (Genesis 4:4). During her pregnancy, "they lived on the earth, working in order to keep their bodies in good health; and they continued [to do] so until the nine months of Eve's pregnancy were over" (Malan, *First Book of Adam and Eve* LXXIV. 1). "When the time came for her to give birth, she strained a lot. Adam felt sorry, and he was very worried about her because she was close to death, and the words of God to her were being fulfilled: 'In suffering shall you bear a child, and in sorrow shall you bring forth a child'" (3). In the coupling of labor for food and childbirth is the mirroring of labor for the belly's filling and emptying. Not only does food provided by the farmer fill the belly, the very act of growing food relies on the earth's impregnation with seed. The birth of child then not only represents the emptying of a belly filled with fertilizing seed, it is the growth of that seed with the food matter consumed by the mother.

Without entering into the narrative of Cain and Abel, it should simply be stated that the "first-born son … Cain" (*First Book of Adam and Eve* LXXIV. 5-6), was also the first murderer. In Genesis this first murder (and death) immediately follows after the first birth, reinforcing the fundamental relationship between birth and death, as though one brings the other into the world. This is displayed in *Paradise Lost*, when the Portress of Hell gives birth to death. Returning to their starting point, Adam and Eve "live 'till like ripe fruit [they] drop into [their] mothers lap" (Milton X. 532-34). The overlay of the plant and human cycle, working with the wasteland motif, was essential to T.S. Eliot, who asks, "That corpse you planted last year in your garden, has it begun to sprout? Will it bloom this year?" (Eliot 3). His lines convey a theory he learned from Jessie Weston's work with James Frazier's work on fertility kings. He and those influenced by his work (Weston, Neumann, Campbell, etc.) present numerous examples of the land's health in codependence with the King's virility. When he is restored (or replaced with a younger incarnation) so too is the land and its fields.

Further association of human and nature's cycles might be seen in the ancient kurgans or burial mounds. The burial of men in grassy mounds mimes the burial of a seed in the earth and the rising belly of a pregnant mother. The 13th century *Aurea Legenda* (Golden Legend), as summated by Manly P. Hall, tells of an angel giving Seth "three seeds from the Tree of Life (some say the Tree of Knowledge). With these Seth returned to his father, who was so overjoyed that he did not desire to live longer. Three days later he died, and the three seeds were buried in his mouth, as the angel had instructed.[167] The seeds became a sapling with three trunks in one, which absorbed into itself the blood of Adam, so that the life of Adam was in the tree" (*Secret* 181; Jacobus de Vorgaine). In the *Zohar* it is explicitly phrased that "God planted man, that is, Israel, in the sacred garden of Eden" (134). This reminds us of the Tree of Life in the Aztec and Mayan tradition, which grows from the navel of the Aztec man. The image is also similar to the lotus of Vishnu's navel, which grows into the world, as well as the growth of grain from the body (and coffin) of Osiris. What all of these images reinforce is the (perhaps symbolic) transition from death into new life (perhaps through a navel or axis like center).

For the purposes of this dissertation it should be mentioned that, according to several sources, a stone was used to kill Abel. In Paradise Lost Cain "smote him into the midriff with a stone" (Milton X. 445). In *The First Book of Adam and Eve* it is written that, "in a lonely place," Cain, "the hard-hearted, and cruel murderer, took a large stone, and beat his brother's head with it" (Malan, LXXIX. 7). Again we get the association of the heart with stone-like hardness, and the stone is used as the instrument of first murder. The image of Abel's head smashed in "with stones" is repeated in the *Book of Bees* (XVIII). Likewise, in the Syrian *Cave of Treasures* Cain "killed [Abel] with a blow from a stone flint" (Budge). In The Book of Adam it is written that God "'established an end for all human beings' [When] two demons resembling Cain and Abel came. One demon reproached the other demon. He became angry with him and took a stone sword, which was of a transparent stone. He cut his throat and killed him. And when Cain saw the blood, he went quickly and took the stone in his hand(s)" (*Book of Adam* 23. 3.3c-d). This recalls Campbell's attention to Joyce's image of "rock-hard, separate men, moving dryly among and around each other" (*Creative* 283). As we will continue to discuss, the stone as an instrument of murder and post-exilic wasteland appears to be far more than an arbitrary symbol.

In *The First Book of Adam and Eve*, the couple's attempt at their own life is similarly against the rigid edge of stone. "Adam threw himself down from atop of that mountain; his face was torn and his flesh was ripped … [and Eve] threw herself after him; and was torn and ripped by the stone" (*Malan,* XXI. 4-7). In addition to the presence of the stone as the instrument of death, the scene also reinforces the association of death with a fall. The stone is then again seen as an agent of death when Satan "took a huge rock" and commanded his host to "throw [it] flat on them" (XLVII; 5-6). Later, in one of Adam's many attempts on the wellbeing of Adam and Eve, "Satan, the hater of all good ... took a sharp stone from among the sharp iron stones ... and pierced Adam on the side" (LXIX: 1-3).

As Prometheus established the first sacrifice, in an Egyptian version, so too did "Adam and Eve, [who] took stones and placed them in the shape of an altar," to enact the first sacrifice with "blood they had spilled" (*First Book of Adam and Eve* XXIII. 4-6). In response to this gesture, God promised the coming of his son and the redemption of the couple through his blood. Resonance of the sacrifice with that of Prometheus is more directly expressed in *Paradise Lost*, in which Milton writes of the first observed sacrifice as "inwards and their fat" consumed by a "propitious fire from heaven" (X. 441-2).

One of the recurring dynamics of Adam and Eve's life after the garden, as recounted in the First Book of Adam and Eve, are the repeated plots of Satan. Though they do not all demand our attention, one stands out for its congruities with Plato's *Allegory of the Cave*, which we have discussed as an expression of the dualistic experience of matter and the immaterial realm. The Ethiopian text provides a description:

> When Satan, the hater of all good, saw how they continued in prayer, and how God communed with them, and comforted them, and how He had accepted their offering—Satan made an apparition. 2 He began with transforming his hosts; in his hands was a flashing fire, and they were in a great light. 3 He then placed his throne near the mouth of the cave because he could not enter into it by reason of their prayers. And he shed light into the cave, until the cave glistened over Adam and Eve; while his hosts

began to sing praises. 4 And Satan did this, in order that when Adam saw

the light, he should think within himself that it was a heavenly light, and

that Satan's hosts were angels; and that God had sent them to watch at the

cave, and to give him light in the darkness" (Malan, *First Book of Adam*

and Eve, XXVII. 1-13)

As in Plato's allegory, illusions are being created with light at the mouth of a cave for

those who are deluded within. Like those shackled in the cave of Plato's imagination,

"When … Adam and Eve saw the light, fancying it was real, they strengthened their

hearts" XXVII. 1-13). Once Adam prayed for clarification; however, "an angel from God

appeared to him in the cave, who said to him, 'O Adam, fear not. This is Satan and his

hosts; he wishes to deceive you as he deceived you at first" (XXVII. 1-13). He explains,

"the first time he was hidden in the serpent; but this time he is come to you in the likeness

of an angel of light; in order that, when you worshipped him, he might enslave you, in the

very presence of God" (XXVII. 1-13). He then "went from Adam and seized Satan at the

opening of the cave, and stripped him of the pretense he had assumed" " (XXVII. 1-13).

Considering this was written many centuries after Plato's allegory, it is distinctly

possible that diffusion is at play, but whether or not that is the case, what is essential to

realize is the repetition of the allegory in the context of the fall. Perhaps there could be no

clearer evidence of congruity between the way Plato was talking about the world of

particulars compared with the eternal forms and the way the Abrahamic Fall represents

an entry of the mind into delusion. In both cases the fallen or secondary world is

distinctly material, and in both cases the allegory presents an illusion of light and shadow

taken as real. As we will eventually discuss more fully, this allegory seems to point towards the image of reality shared by Orphics, Buddhists and others who see the reduction of the world to its phenomenal plane as delusional.

Though Adam and Eve are perpetually assisted (or renewed) after Satan's attacks, they do, eventually, die; at which time, the first father was buried. Though it may be that death is to be seen as coming into this world by way of Cain, it is very clear that "Adam died because he had eaten of the fruit of the tree of knowledge" and that ultimately it is because of "his sin" that "all his descendants likewise die" (Polano, *Talmud* 19). In *Paradise Lost* Milton writes that there are many "ways that lead to [man's] grim cave, all dismal" (X. 468-9). The passage equates death with the entry into a cave, a form of burial that is not only mimetic with burial in the earth, but also a standard mode of burial for Jews. According to the *Book of Jubilees*, when Adam died, "all his sons buried him in the land where he was created, and he was the first to be buried in the earth" (*Book of Jubilees* 19). In the *Midrash Tanhuma* it is said that, Adam "was buried with great honors by Seth, Enoch, and Methuselah, His body was placed in a cave, which according to some authorities was the cave of Machpelah. From this time, the time of Adam's burial, it has been the custom to perform funeral obsequies over the dead" (Polano, *Talmud* 19). This cave is near Hebron, and is known as the "Cave of the Patriarchs" by the Jews.

The Christians similarly envision Adam as having been buried in a cave. In the *Cave of Treasures*, as Adam had commanded, "Adam's dead body ... [was buried] in the earth ... in the Cave of Treasures" (*Burial of Adam*). In the Second Book of Adam and Eve Seth "laid his body on the eastern side [of the "Holy Mountain"] of the inside of the cave" (67). In the Syrian text, Adam tells his sons, "when I die ... deposit my body in the Cave of Treasures. And whosoever shall be left of your generations in that day, when you're going forth from this country, which is round about Paradise, shall take place, shall carry my body with him, and shall take it and deposit it in the center of the earth, for in that place shall redemption be effected for me and for all my children" (*Death of Adam*). After the flood, Noah's son "Shem took the body of Adam" to the destined place:

> And when they arrived at Gâghûltâ (Golgotha), which is the center of the earth, the Angel of the Lord showed Shem the place. And when Shem had deposited the body of our father Adam upon that place, the four quarters [of the earth] separated themselves from each other, and the earth opened itself in the form of a cross, and Shem and Melchisedek deposited the body of Adam there (i.e. in the cavity). And as soon as they had laid it therein, the four quarters [of the earth] drew quickly together, and enclosed the body of our father Adam, and the door of the created world was shut fast. And that place was called "Karkaphtâ " (i.e. "Skull"), because the head of all the children of men was deposited there. And it was called "Gâghûltâ," because it was round [like the head], and "Resîphtâ " (i.e. a trodden-down thing), because the head of the accursed serpent, that is to say, Satan, was crushed there, and "Gefîftâ " (Gabbatha), because all the nations were to be gathered together to it. (*Cave of Treasures: Adam to Golgotha*)

This tradition of Adam's burial in Golgotha is now continued by the Catholics, Eastern Orthodox, Syrians, Coptic Christians, and all of those who jointly inhabit the Church of the Holy Sepulcher, where, beneath the crucifix, is an exposed crack in the stone beside which a placard describes Adam's burial. Even the Protestants, who do not share the church, participate in the legend by way of a different site at which a garden tomb neighbors a mountain face in the shape of a skull. In the *Aurea Legenda* it is actually the tree growing from Adam's mouth and his skull that "Noah dug up this tree by the roots … took … with him into the Ark … [And] buried … under Mount Calvary, [where he] planted the tree on the summit of Mount Lebanon" (qtd. by Hall 181, Vorgaine).

Though less is made of her burial, when Eve died, her body was placed "where they had placed Adam's body" (*Book of Adam* 51. 43.1), and with her burial the mother returned to earth. Nothing is said in Genesis or the Torah, but the "Midrash relates that she was buried in Kiriath-arba—so named because the four (*arba*) Matriarchs are buried there: Eve, Sarah, Rebekah, and Leah (*Gen. Rabbah* 58:4)" (Kadari, "Eve: Midrash and Aggadah"). By any and all accounts, Adam and Eve were buried in the earth, mostly in caves—in stone.

Post-Edenic Reflection

We have followed the story of Eden from the creation of the first couple to their burial in its various manifestations through Islamic, Christian, and Hebraic sources: *Genesis* and Jewish lore, the first Christian retellings, *Quran*, and European versions from Dante, Óengus, Milton and Chaucer. We have become familiar with the falls of Satan, Iblis and angels; the creation of Adam and Eve; garden; tree; fruit; serpent; and the fall into exile; flesh; flesh-senses; mortality; digestion; gestation; sexuality; labor; and such emotional attitudes as pride, envy, discord, blame, enmity, shame, guile, guilt, despair and sorrow as were born from the self-assertion of the first craving. Having extended our vision of the story from beginning to (death-defined) end through the voices of these core sources, we are ready to return our focus to the dissertation's thesis.

There have been some small conversations along the way concerning the relationship of key story elements with the first couple's entry into materiality in the context of first knowledge, but in an attempt to offer an honest and minimally-biased account of the content, I have withheld a full dose of applied reason and conversation until the conclusion of the survey. We are now, however, prepared to walk through the position with nothing but pre-demonstrated points.

All of the Abrahamic traditions variously associate Adam with the center of the earth. He was created, placed, and or buried there. Such an association with centrality is reinforced by the axis mundi symbolism recognized in the tree at the garden's center and the mountain on which the garden was represented in Ezekiel. We explored the amplifications and reinforcing examples of trees and mountains in the roles of *axis mundi*, which Eliade and Campbell further explored through religious mythologies of world navels, axial poles, ladders to heaven, entwined snakes, and even towers like the Tower of Babel and Ziggurat. Campbell especially focuses on the serpent and maiden as characters consistent with the context of mythic centers (and starts). Eliade is particularly interested in such centers as sacred spaces of the holy and numinous with pronounced philosophical implications. Without having reflected on the temporal element of the story's orientation, its recurring symbolic, explicit, and even ritual emphasis on centrality suggests a certain centrality to the meaning built into the story. Importance is here.

To add the temporal dimension: Eden has been frequently associated with the east—where the sun rises to start the day. Adam was the first human, father and husband, just as Eve was the first mother, the first to taste knowledge, first to be seduced and— more beautiful than Pandora—the first to seduce *Man*. Even though the narrative is likely predated by a number of texts presented later in the Torah's sequence, the situation of Adam and Eve in Eden within the first books of *Genesis*—more than anything—situates the meaning of this story within the context of beginnings. As Adam simultaneously represents centrality and beginning it is clear that this origination myth engages territory pursued by the Pre-Socratics in their search for *arche*—a word that carries Homeric overtones of temporal beginnings but essentially means the primary substance at the foundation(s) of reality. To return to the second chapter on Prometheus, it is easy to now recognize the myth's emphasis on axis mundi symbolism in the context of beginnings as indicative that the Titan's origin story of knowledge and human creation was similarly engaged with territory pursued by the Pre-Socratic (if not human) search for *arche*.

Recognizing the orientation of the Eden myth as a central narrative of beginnings and the establishment of foundations, the emphasis of this origin story of knowledge becomes unquantifiably significant to the understanding of Abrahamic traditions and the psyches that have emerged therefrom. While the dissertation has limited itself to a conversation about Western psyches, it is clear that a discussion of the Abrahamic and scientific origin stories of knowledge extend well beyond the Western world and its history. Considering the presence of the Abrahamic traditions in the history of the world, it is at this point that we should begin to more fully recognize how significant this myth's motifs could be to the history of humanity (of human psyches). That the Eden myth has been so pervasively shared and presented as a communicator of foundations draws our attention to those foundations it has invariably transferred to psyches throughout history. As influential as the story has been beyond Western psyches, we should mostly retain our focus on the origin story as it has influenced Western minds—to be compared with other Western origin stories of knowledge like Prometheus and the Pre-Socratics.

Reflecting now on the "knowledge" of the myth and fruit, we see that the reduction of that knowledge conveyed to a single dimension could be misleading (if not tyrannical). As traditionally expressed, the knowledge of the fruit has been associated with sexuality and mortality.[168] The resulting life-lessons are those of digestion and gestation—the secrets of vegetal and human fertilization cycles. With this knowledge comes that of the seasonal cycles and the congruity of human and vegetal "fruitfulness." This mimesis is acted upon in the form of the ceremonial burial—planting—of Adam in the earth (to which they were destined to return). Connecting the end of the human cycle with the beginning of the vegetal, in a variant we discussed, a tree grew up from Adam's grave—like grain from Osiris or the world lotus from Vishnu. This mirrors the ripe finale of the vegetal cycle with the beginning of human reality. On a cosmological level, these associations represent the understanding of human life as mimetic with—and situated within—cycles of the natural cosmos.

The story also describes the coming to knowledge of one's own will and its freedom to independently act; which, as existentialists often find so disparaging, can be difficult without certain knowledge. These empowered and disparaging reactions to the fall echo throughout its many reads—from those who see the birth of human will and individuality as the first step towards progress of science and civilization to those who see this as the step off the summit towards an ongoing fall. Tarnas comments, "The first paradigm, familiar to all of us from our education, describes human history and the evolution of human consciousness as an epic narrative of human progress ... the other great historical vision … [is a] tragic narrative of humantiy's gradual but radical fall and separation from an original state of oneness with nature and an encompassing spiritual dimension of being" (*Cosmos and Psyche* 13). In short he calls these, respectively, the "myth of Progress" and the "myth of the Fall" (13). What he suggests is that "both historical paradigms are at once fully valid and yet also partial aspects of a larger frame of reference, a metanarrativem in which the two opposite interpretations are precisely intertwined to form a complex, integrated whole" (13). Insofar as both are contingent with the emergence of the isolated and self-aware individual, "they are embedded in each other's truth. They underlie and inform each other, implicate each other, make each other possible" (14). What one might recognize at this point, is that the narratives of progress and the fall mime the major tones of Adam's fall and Prometheus' delivery of fire and technology. Of course, Adam receives knowledge and Prometheus is punished, but the tonal qualities of the myths resound quite clearly. Though this dissertation is focused on the inner workings of the fall, by no means does it devalue the mechanisms of progress. Before moving on from this point, it might be noted that the Yezidi read of the peacock angel is distinctly not contextualized by the narrative of the fall.[169]

It is the story of learning the knowledge on which to act—the knowledge of right and wrong, good and bad, God and the devil, Man and Woman, Paradise and Earth, beginning and end, as well as all such dualistic structures that emerge from consciousness and reason once committed to the structures of dualism. Such duality was symbolized in the two sided, snake-eyed, split-tongued serpentine seducer in the story—as well as the battle between divine good and devilish evil. The story also describes the initiation of consciousness into the dualistic experience if inner and outer, as conveyed by the walls of the garden and flaming sword, skin of the fruit, first clothes, the exile of both Satan and the first couple, the soul's entry into body and the repeated enclosure within a cave. The knowledge of inner and outer is that of me and other, us and them, chosen people and not chosen people. This conceptual structure is foundational to the recognition of subjects and objects—a framework that depends on the recognition of entities as enclosed and isolated objects.

As I will now demonstrate, this cycle-initiating entry into dualistic thought and the perception of things as isolated objects is consistent with the narrative repetition of entry into matter and materialistic thought patterns. To start with a recap of such entries: by all accounts, the first human awakes when soul enters clay (most notably breath through the nostrils), which reinforces the lived experience of the human body as material substance. This entry into the body is a simultaneous entry into the earthly domain of material existence. In those versions of the story that follow Adam and Eve after their exile, this entry of soul into the material body and world is echoed by the transformation of a holy body into flesh. It is also seen in the differentiation of Eden as a holy place from the fallen world of the wasteland like exile, which is described with repeated references to lifeless landscapes of sand, dust, and stone. This pattern is again reinforced when Adam and Eve enter a stone cave to find their divine senses replaced with fleshy organs. The children of Adam and Eve are born within a rock dome, and Adam—by all accounts—was buried in a cave. This repetitive narrative of the entry into matter presented through the imagery of the human body's creation, exile, materialization of the body, birth and death suggest the same thing as the Milesians—matter as the ground of being as we know it. In addition to the many qualities of the knowledge conveyed in and by this story, that pertaining to the materiality into which the human soul has entered must be included. To neglect the motif of entry into matter would leave a glaring hole in one's interpretation of the narrative.

The entry into matter (mater) is also represented by the sexual act of literally entering Eve, who represents the primal *mater* of human existence—the substance from which all humans were made. In the story, sexual union and mortality followed the eating of a fruit, which is the essential act of internalizing matter for the purpose of the material body. In this way the eating of fruit represents the commitment to the material reality into which their bodies—and souls—fell. In this world Adam and Eve are forced to labor for sustenance and procreation—cycles that simultaneously depend on matter while enclosing humans within their circuits. The craving for food and procreation have thus been taken to represent the foundations behind cravings for all material things (and perhaps all labors to counteract mortality).

While on one level there is a clear expression of the entry into materiality, on another level, this is presented as a terrible experience. Iblis refuses to bow to Adam because he is made of earth. Eve, as mater, is villainized as the seducer into the body's mortal sexuality and is cursed to pain during childbirth. She is also blamed, in some variants, for our need of digestive organs. The serpent was similarly demonized and forced to eat dust while Adam's labor in the earth for food was presented as a curse. Appetites for both food and sex are corruptive in the story—they draw the soul deeper into its irreversible entry into matter. Eventually even the first murder weapon, used to kill Abel, was a stone. Throughout, we recognize a take on the world as a "fallen" wasteland without divine vitality (or water) that is filled with dust, sand, stone and dark caves. While the story establishes an entry into this material world, at the same time, its various expressions of material existence are bleak. Even the death-bringing-fruit—as ultimate symbol of knowledge—is an earthly symbol that grew from the ground itself.

Combined with the entry into matter and materiality is also the experience of isolation that derives from the experience of inner-outer and apartness. The walls of Eden, for example, implicitly designate inner from outer – not unlike the skin of the fruit, skin of the body, clothing, the walls of the cave of treasures, the dome rock in which Adam and Eve lived and the cave in which Adam was buried. The story conveys tremendous separation anxiety over the isolation from God and lover in the context of estrangement in a fallen world. The impression of Adam and Eve as separated from the Garden and in isolation from the divine source reinforces the imagery of the fruit being separated from a tree by way of a fall or pluck. Eden becomes removed from human reach and there are versions of the story in which Adam and Eve are separated from one another by either great distances or disparaging sensory darkness.[170]

The motif of isolation also extends into concealment. This can be seen in the serpent's concealing of truth when he seduced Eve, in the seed hidden within fruit, first clothing, the shameful hiding of the first couple from God after sin, God's hiding of Eden, and the loss of humanity's ability to commune with animals. Milton even describes the truth of Good and Evil as explicitly concealed within the tree of knowledge. Beneath and beyond the potential emotional experience of isolation and concealment, the imagery of the story repeatedly demonstrates the boundaries of subjects and objects, of inner and outer, of Adam and Eve, of Man and God, of Earth and Paradise. Such duality is simultaneously imposed on the notions of right and wrong, good and evil, knowledge and lack of knowledge, divine purity and sinful corruption, God-given soul and fallen matter.

With the motif of isolation—and even concealment—comes that of the self-aware individual. This is the story of men and women learning the distal limits of their own bodies and the temporal limits of its lifespan. This is the story of self-asserting disobedience. As in the stories of Prometheus and the Pre-Socratics, this is a story of humans seeking truth for themselves without the permission of divine authorities. Though on one hand this is villainized decision, on the other, it realistically expresses the human trajectory towards its own search for knowledge (in and through this world). As Le Grice writes, the story conveys "movement towards the realization of autonomous egoic selfhood characteristic of the modern sense of identity" (personal correspondence). From Neumann's point of view, the story pertains to the development of the ego and reflects that of the human child. Where on the surface it appears that the primary impulse of the ego is desire, the motif of separation and the recognition of the self's boundaries is built into the experience of self-oriented desire (and the recognition of desire as self-oriented). This introduces one of the essential significances of the recurring symbolic enclosures—layer after layer, the story expresses the development of embodied self-awareness and perhaps the emergence of an ego.

In addition to the story's clear description of the world as fallen and its negative description of a materialistic cosmos, there is also a redundant expression of water's disappearance. The fountain in the garden dried up, the tree withered, the first couple became extremely thirsty, the land they entered upon leaving the garden was described as dry sand and stone, and even Adam's curse to work was detailed by the expulsion of his body's water—sweat on the brow. We read examples in which the heart is described as stone. This return of water will become especially important to our conversation to come (in later chapters) about water, blood and other elixirs associated with Christ. What is important to us at this juncture is the recognition that the entry into materiality is, in this story, combined with an entry into a wasteland defined by drought, despair, distance from the divine and inner isolation.

What I have been attempting to argue throughout the dissertation—when the opportunities emerge—is that this conflation of material entry and fluid loss holds true to a meta-form of logic that recognizes the relationship between dryness and isolation with cosmological implications. The loss of fluids within such wasteland-like situations is expressive of the loss for the potential of such union as embodied by water and its behavior. Dry matter is defined by the boundaries of its solid being. Separating grains of sand is mechanical whereas drops of water merge. Water is the ultimate solvent. Fluids also behave as waves, which do not necessitate the same hyper focus on isolation as paradigmatic particularization. With the loss of fluids and the entry into dry matter is the loss of that which fluid represents—the potential for wave behavior and solvation. Necessarily this coincides with an emergent emphasis on the patterns of dry and isolated matter if not the (reductive) transposition of material behavior onto reason and knowledge itself. From this point of view the eating of the fruit was not just a commitment to material embodiment, it was also a commitment of the mind to a cosmology defined by materialistic metaphors. The loss of water was not just about thirst, it was about the loss of such metaphors as fluids are able to convey.

Part I Reflection: Adam, Prometheus, and the Pre-Socratics

We have seen the three primary Western origin stories of knowledge conveyed various entries into matter and materialistic cosmologies. Before proceeding to the next portion of the dissertation, I would like to consider congruities between the symbolic entries of psyche into matter and the initiation of philosophical thought with the foundations of theoretical materialism. I would also like to consider the consistency of the materialistic paradigm that solidified in the form of atomism in the context of the condition into which humans entered in each origin story.

In the myths of Prometheus and Adam, the material bodies of humans are created and—then—animated by divine breath or spark. Such an entry of psyche into body and their implied dual nature would later become a philosophical interest of the Pre-Socratics, who began with conceptions of matter as animated by (but not necessarily separate from) divine mind. Contemporary Orphics, later Pythagoreans, and Platonists, however, present a vision of the individual's divine essence as imprisoned within body. In this way, it can be said that the Classical, Abrahamic and Pre-Socratic origin stories of knowledge relay the notions of psyche/soul/spirit/mind's entry into body.

The Orphic's Pythagoreans and Platonists saw the state of psyche in body as a state of imprisonment. We have also seen this perspective in Kabbalist and Gnostic texts. Returning to the myths of Prometheus and Adam, the emphasis on bondage is similarly conveyed. Stories of Adam and Eve gave special attention to the first human experience of bondage—within bodies, senses, toils, mortal needs and cycles, as well as to one another. Following their exile they are repeatedly imprisoned in caves, within which they conceive, give birth, and are buried for ages. In the myth of Prometheus, not only do the (less described) first humans suffer many of the same entries into body, world and marriage, the progenitor himself—like Adam—is also left in bondage. Infamously, he is restrained to—and sometimes within—stone. In addition to demonstrating an entry of psyche into body, the myths convey a strong sense of bondage. This bondage is matched by the Orphics and Pre-Socratic philosophers who saw body as the prison of psyche. Insofar as this perspective was well established by the Pre-Socratics and implicit within the myths of first knowledge, each of the Western knowledge narratives compliment their image of psyche's entry into body with strong descriptions of bondage.

The common denominator of body and bondage is matter: bodies, chains, caves and mothers are all material. Prometheus, who created humans from clay, is bound to or buried in stone just as Adam, created from clay, is buried in a cave. There they stay until saved. Humans, similarly, are bound in their bodies and to their work in the field for food on this earth. Bondage is not just to body; more fundamentally, it is to the earth from which its substance was taken and to which it will return. As Pandora represented Gaia in human form, marriage with Pandora for the fruits of her labor was mimed by labor in the field for fruits of the harvest. This describes the post-golden age reality for Hesiod and the fallen state that followed Eden. Together the stories depict the bondage of humanity to the mortal tasks of baring food and offspring while conveying the inseparability of these human conditions from the material matrix of reality upon which the mortality of their bodies depend and within which they are thus imprisoned.

Insofar as these myths describe the entry into and/or existence of humans within a materially defined matrix of reality, they should be seen as foreshadows of the historic engagement of philosophy and science with materialistic theory. As the Promethean and post-Edenic worlds of the first humans were anchored by their materiality, Western philosophers also worked with an image of nature as fundamentally material. According to Aristotle, this was the premise of the very first philosophers. By the time of the Scientific Revolution and for the time to follow, scientists shared the perspective of reductive materialism. Perhaps straddling the mythic and philosophical forms of materialism, Aristotle, famous for his belief that matter was before essence, claimed Gaia to be mother of all things. The Deists were famous for their vision of the clock-work universe, which is an eloquent symbol used to communicate an understanding of the universe as an exclusively material machine.

Philosophy that trends towards reductive materialism, however, comes to estrange God and soul from its paradigm or worldview. To clarifty, I am talking about philosophers who make the move to distinguish between psyche and matter as part of their reduction of the cosmos to what is material. The clockwork vision of the universe insists that, if God or soul do exist, they do not influence the material world—or, if they do, they break its laws in the form of a miracle. To Deists, God was the first cause of a universe that, afterwards, unwound without his participation. Such a perspective still reinforces the notion of an otherwise enclosed materialistic paradigm. This materialistically driven understanding of God and soul's estrangement from embodied reality is not unlike the mythic estrangement of Adam, Prometheus and the first humans from the divine. Thus not only do we see bondage within the material body and world, we see the corresponding estrangement from that which does not fit into the materialist worldview, most usually God and soul.

To clarify, theories like pantheism and animism that might be called "materialistic" for various reasons are not what I am talking about—even the "materialism" of Thales does not fit what I am calling "reductive materialism;" because, ultimately, animistic persepectives—as well as that of Thales—are inclusive of spirit, which, as articulated with intentional clarity during the Enlightenment, is not itself material. To clarifty, I am talking about philosophers who make the move to distinguish between psyche and matter as part of their reduction of the cosmos to what is material.

In addition to the estrangement of psyche and god from a materialistic reality and/or worldview, matter is also dependent on the form of divisibility. Conceptual differentiation is different than material differentiation, thus a materially differentiated thing, is, by description, divisible from other material things based on its material boundaries. A material thing, by its classical definition, is divisible from another material thing. Regardless of whatever philosophers or physicists might say, regardless of what may actually be true on a less perceptible level, "objects" are immediately experienced as having boundaries. Articulated more fully, this evolves into a theory of (Classical) atomism, which presents everything as divisible into indivisible particulates. When the early philosophical reduction of everything to material evolved into the atomistic and Cartesian reduction of all "objects" to material "things," a commitment to reductive materialism came to necessitate an image of the self as material and isolated. In the chapter on Western philosophy we saw Pascal make this exact projection of the atom on the self, which was joined with a deep sense of isolation and anxiety. We then continued with a brief look at the relationship of existential despair and isolation to find that the sense of estrangement and limitation are fundamental to the anxiety. In the myths of

Prometheus and Adam—in concert with mythic entries into matter, restraint, and estrangement—isolation is again essential and disparaging. Both progenitors cry out in woe for their state of exile.

Where most images of isolation are hard to distinguish from estrangement, we might give special notice to Prometheus' solitude on the mountain, the narratives in which Adam and Eve are separated after the fall—by senses and/or distance—and the repeated emphasis on caves, which shelter what is inside from the outside world. This matches the emphasis on inner and outer conveyed by the exile from Eden, the putting on of clothes, and, perhaps, fruit skin and human rind. Inner and outer is also the foundational structure beneath the distinction of subjects and objects established by the same philosopher—Descartes—as the European solidifier of mind-body dualism. More will be said of this distinction when we are ready to discuss its potential breakdown.

In the next chapter, we will see such divisive opposites as inner and outer, subject and object, I and other, human and divine, break away like egg-shells. Limiting, isolative and reductively materialistic modes of seeing will give way to the perspectives delivered by the mythic labors and theoretical insights of Herakles, Christ and Einstein. The prison of the psyche within materiality will be relieved, as well as the reductive vision of the body as matter; consequently, in the religious myths, human estrangement from the divine will be resolved.

Chapter 5: Heracles, Christ and Einstein – A Sip Beyond Material Limitation

The story of Prometheus does not end with his abandonment on the precipice, Adam is not condemned forever, and theoretical science has taken major turns since the Pre-Socratic developments development of atomistic materialism. What I will argue is that the later developments in the stories of the progenitors demonstrate, through narrative turns, an evolution of the conscious knowledge they represent. After working through Herakles' liberation of Prometheus from stone, Christ's liberation of Adam from stone, and Einstein's liberation of physics from reductive materialism, I will draw the stories together in an attempt to discuss their congruous responses to the materialistic knowledge incited by the origin stories of their respective traditions.

We will look at the liberation of Prometheus by Herakles, followed by the liberation of Adam by Christ. We will see that Christ's liberation of the Abrahamic progenitor is contingent with his own death and transcendence, which will lead into a consideration of Heracles' death. After reflecting on these myths of the Abrahamic and Classical Hero-Saviors, we will look more closely at the contributions of Einstein— specifically those in contrast with classical materialism. Finally, we will consider these scientific, mythological and religious narratives in the context of one another to elucidate their deeper and perhaps more meta-commonalities.

Introduction: Herakles & Christ

We begin with an introduction to Heracles—known to the Romans and posterity as Hercules. "Heracles is the greatest and most popular Greek hero" (Morford 353). And in Rome, "according to Dionysus (*Roman Antiquities* 1. 40), 'one could hardly find any place in Italy where the god Hercules is not honored" (Stafford 196). Where the Greeks traveled so did Herakles, and what the Romans conquered so did Hercules. Statues of his figure, for example, can still be found along the Roman reaches of Hadrian's Wall in northern Britain (presenting his most obvious point of entry into the English speaking tradition).[171] Even after the arrival of Jesus onto the scene of Classical religion, "The ubiquity of Herakles/Hercules in the Roman empire made it inevitable that early Christians would encounter him wherever they went … the popularity of his cult made him at first a rival to Christ" (Stafford 202). Stafford writes, "In popular religion … Hercules' worship remained important throughout the first to third centuries AD" (196). His "popularity endured in the face of the growing appeal of Christianity, and even after Christianity became the official religion of the empire in the early fourth century, Hercules continues to be ubiquitous" (197). Even today, as I complete this dissertation, there have been three Hollywood movies on the hero this year.[172] He has been and long will be, ubiquitous.

The core stories of Herakles include his conception and birth, his establishing sin, the twelve labors and his eventual death. Countless additional stories are mixed into the Labors as well as his life and death thereafter. Recurring features of the hero's cult include an "association with athletics, *ephebes* [young men] and initiation, the involvement of *nostoi* and slaves, the special form of shrine, a particular emphasis on feasting, and a sacred marriage with Hebe" (197). We will become especially interested in his sacred marriage with Hebe, feasting, and the initiative qualities of his narratives. Though the openness of Herakles' cult with slaves may be compared with the Christian receptivity of the downtrodden, we will generally leave this conversation aside, as well as the complications that arise from the fact that on one hand the cult only initiated men and on the other it glorifies his marriage with Hebe. As the Abrahamic traditions variously associate Adam and Christ with the center of the world, the Orphics describe a version of the universe's creation in which there is "'a god's face in the middle,' who is also known as Herakles; Time/Herakles in turn generated an egg, from which the gods and ultimately the whole world are descended (Orphic fragment 54)" (129). This matches the image in which Heracles holds up the cosmos while Atlas retrieves the apples, (Pausanias, *Description* 5. 11. 6).

His name was given to him by "the priestess of Apollo [at Delphi]" (358 Morford). Its obvious meaning, 'he to whom Hera gave glory'" (Kerenyi, *Heroes*127) demonstrates his close connection with the Olympian matriarch. Though he could have originally been a servant of the goddess (Stafford 139), by the time of Classical mythology she had been pitted against him for the infidelity of his father, Zeus, upon his begetting.[173] In the end however, as we will see, his marriage to Hebe mimes his reunion with Hera.

It was Herakles who founded the Olympic Games and began the tradition of garlanding the winners with twigs of olive, which he introduced to Greece from the Hyperboreans (Kerenyi *Heroes* 185). As the victor of victors and athlete of athletes Herakles was also the great monster slayer, to which his many adventures attest. Starting around the early fifth century B.C., "we can also see the development of Herakles as the *exemplum virtutis*. This traditional Latin term means something like 'model of virtue', virtus being a translation of the Greek arête, which encompasses physical and intellectual, as well as moral, qualities and is sometimes rendered more broadly as 'excellence'"

(Stafford 121). In this way he became seen as something like the high water mark for humanity, as an example.

We will soon discuss his liberation of his and humanity's benefactor, Prometheus. We should note that Herakles was also elevated to the status of humanity's benefactor. In his second set of labors he "passed from being a local hero into being the benefactor of all mankind" (Morford 358). In 1609 the Englishman, Francis Bacon—credited for having both edited the initial King James Bible and articulated the Scientific Method— echoes this interpretation of Herakles as humanity's hero. In his work, *On the Wisdom of the Ancients* he describes an image of "Hercules [crossing] the Ocean in a clay cup to save Prometheus" (26) and suggests that he "seems to represent an image of the divine word, hastening in the flesh, as it were in a fragile vessel, to the redemption of the human race" (Staffford 205). Not only does this pivotal Bible-editor and science champion here associate Heracles and Christ, he also does so in the context of the cup and the redemption of humanity.

For Pindar and a certain contingency of those interested in Herakles, like Bakchylides, he is a heroic champion of good and "punisher of evil doers" (122). Such versions emphasize "the justice of Herakles' victories by making his enemies 'lawless' monsters, men characterized by 'crooked excess'" (122). This emerges from a strong and especially Stoic interpretation of Herakles' challenges as an externalized narrative of inner and philosophical struggles against what they see as a corrupt way of life. This is made explicit by Apuleius description of Krates, a philosopher, "Just as the poets say that Hercules subdued the savage monsters amongst men and beasts by his virtue and cleansed the world, in the same way this our philosopher [Krates] was a Hercules against

quick temper, envy, avarice, lust and other monsters and crimes of the human spirit"
(Apuleius (Florida 22.3-4; Stafford 126)

This role of Herakles as champion of virtue is especially conveyed by a story in
which the personifications of virtue (*arête*) and vice (*kakia*) present themselves to him.
He is told if he chooses vice he "will always be considering what tasty food or drink [he]
can find, what sight or sound may please, what scent or touch [he] may enjoy, which
boyfriend's society will gratify most, how [he] can sleep most comfortably, and how [he]
can come by all these with the least trouble" (Xenophon *e.1.21-34;* Stafford 123). The
personification of virtue, on the other hand, tells him "if [he] expects to be admired for
virtue by the whole of Greece, [he] must strive to benefit Greece" (123). The dichotomy
of such avarice and virtue is familiar from chapter three's examination of Pre-Socratic
and Socratic philosophy, which was adopted by Alexandrian and Roman philosophers.

Following an interpretation of Herakles as an anti-hedonist, "systemic use was
made of Herakles ... by the Cynics and later by the Stoics, both of which ... regarded
him as an archetype for the struggle for arête, and in particular the virtue of endurance"
(Stafford 125). In this way there developed a "trend for casting Herakles more
specifically as a role-model for the philosopher" (Stafford 125). "In *The Cynic*, Herakles
is cited as "being 'the best of men', his virtues including steadfastness, patience and
rejection of luxury. The Cynic who appears in Lucian's *Philosophies for Iale* (8)
similarly claims Herakles as the hero he emulates ... 'campaigning against pleasures just
like him ... undertaking to cleanse life'" (Stafford 127). "Seneca himself cites the hero
alongside Odysseus as having been exemplars of Stoic wisdom ... 'because they were
unconquered by toils, despised pleasure and were victors over all terrors'" (*On firmness*

2.1; Stafford 128). The Stoic "also contrasts the hero's altruism with Alexander the Great's selfishness in *On Benefits* (I. 13.3): Hercules conquered nothing for himself; he crossed the world not desiring, but judging, what he would conquer, an enemy of evil men, champion of good, and bringer of peace to land and sea" (Stafford 128). For Herakleitos, Herakles should be seen as "a sensible man and an initiate of heavenly wisdom who brought to light philosophy" (128).

Where the emphasis of Herakles path is on one hand justice and virtue in the face of avarice and evil, this dichotomy has also been associated with a corruptive world and transcendent values. "In a story told by Antisthenes, the traditional founder of Cynicism and pupil of Sokrates, "Prometheus exhorted him to eschew worldly concerns and strive for knowledge that is higher than mankind" (fr. 27 Caizzi; Stafford 125). We should note that it is Prometheus, bound to the earth, a symbol of the human condition, who urges his freedom from worldly concerns (for the purpose of knowledge beyond human life). This is in place of the typical conversation in which Prometheus sends Herakles for the golden apples—gifts of Earth—which, as we will see, he releases with no sense of attachment. As I will continue to argue, Herakles' release of Prometheus from the mountain is mimetic with the liberation of psyche from worldly concerns that will be ultimately symbolized by his Olympic reunion.

As his life and labors were interpreted as various successes against various opportunities for worldly corruption, his decay and death were seen as the consequence of a lapse in his resistance. As if following the traditions of the Orphics, Pythagoreans or Plato, Dio Chrysostom believes that Herakles ultimately dies because "he is persuaded to abandon his lion skin for normal clothes, to sleep in comfort and eat refined food, as a result of which he becomes weak and flabby, and eventually sets fire to himself in disgust at his own self-indulgence" (Stafford 126). We will repeatedly see Herakles labor against mortality, and insofar as the western knowledge narratives have been shown to convey the tangled nature of mortality and materiality, we can understand why his mortal struggle has been conflated with challenges of the worldly flesh. A later Christian author would pick up on this vision of Hercules, which led to his focus on Antaeus, an adversary of the hero's, who drew his strength from earth. He describes his force as "a sort of lust, 'born of the earth" (Fulgentius *Mythologies* 2.4; Stafford 203), and relays the Christian belief that "lust alone is conceived of the flesh'" (203).

On the one hand this follows our conversation about the mythic and philosophical association of the worldly with the corruptive and repressive, which is the point of view shared by ascetics around the world—and Vulcan.[174] On the other hand, Hercules' story concerns freedom from all forms of tyranny and oppression. We will later discuss the narrative in which he frees Prometheus, but we should mention here that the successor of Antistthenes (who wrote about Prometheus' charge to eschew worldly concerns), Diogenes of Sinope, "is supposed to have written a tragedy entitled *Herakles* (fr. 1c TrGF), and to have declared that the characteristic mark of his life was that, like Herakles, 'he put nothing before freedom' (Diogenes Laertius, Philosophers' Lives 6.71; Stafford 126). A later story by Dio Chrysostom describes a story in which he was "taken as a young man to a mountain which had two peaks, one the seat of Royalty, the other of Tyranny" (Stafford 126). Presumably, Herakles chose royalty. Such twin peaks are reminiscent of those atop Mt. Elbruz, where the freedom fighter, Prometheus, was bound.

But the paradox of duality is otherwise resolved in the figure of Herakles, who "was unusual in the ancient world for being both a hero and a god" (197). A parallel "for Herakles' ambiguous status is provided … by the healing hero-god Asklepios … [who] seems to have been promoted to divine status in cult in the late sixth or early fifth century, and this is marked by the acquisition of several deified abstractions as daughters, such as Hygeiea (Health), just as the divine Herakles acquires Hebe (Youth) as a wife" (171-2). This dual role as man and God will become invaluable in our discussion of Herakles and Christ, who, as we will see, restore a relationship with divinity once lost by their progenitors. This dual nature of god and man and the role of restoration to the divine relate to his role in "the mystery cults [which] held out … hope for happiness in the afterlife … the story of Herakles' initiation at Eleusis shows that the overcoming-of-death theme apparent in several of his exploits was associated with this hope" (172).

Such an effort to heal the soul of death (or fear thereof) may be associated with his role as a healer, which we see in Athens (185). "In Boiotia, Pausaniuas (9. 24.3) reports a temple of Herakles, which had a crude statue 'of the ancient sort', where the sick were able to obtain cures. A similar concern may be reflected in Herakles' association with the hot springs in the pass at Thermopylae … According to Athenaios (12.512f) all hot springs were sacred to Herakles" (Stafford 185). As we will see, his association with rebirth and healing involves his relationship with elixirs and cornucopias, which relate to the rituals and feasts we will eventually explore in the context of Christian communion and potentially related rituals.

Before moving into an introduction of Christ, we should consider some of the characters most commonly compared with Herakles', the most common of which is perhaps Melqart, a Phoenician figure:

> Herodotus believed that Herakles the god … was one of the twelve ancient gods of Egypt. Herodotus himself even traveled to the Phoenician city of Tyre, whose chief god, Melkart, was identified with Heracles, to find support for his theory. Since, however, the mythology of Melkart is virtually unknown, we cannot bare certain what exactly were the similarities between him and Heracles. Nor can we establish the exact relationship between Heracles and other Oriental figures with whom he shares many similarities—the Jewish hero Samson, the Mesopotamian Gilgamesh, and the Cicilian god Sandas. All that can be said is that these figures may have contributed elements toward the Greek hero's legend. (Morford 372)

Stafford writes, "The 'Tyrian Herakles' … is usually identified by modern scholars as the Phoenician god Melqart … whose name means 'Lord of the city' … founder and protector of Tyre, and by extension as patron of Phoenician foundations overseas" (191). She says, "From at least the fifth century BC, there was frequent conflation of the two in the minds of Greek writers," and adds that, "in some locations, the complete assimilation of the two gods can be seen in cult practice" (Stafford 191).

At a Phoenician colony "from at least the eighth century, [a] sanctuary of Melqart is identified by Greek writers as a Herakleion" (192). Silius Italicus gives a description of what the cult there looked like towards the end of the first century AD. According to

Silius, the wooden doors were carved with images of Herakles labors, and inside "there was no image of the god, but a perpetual fire was kept alight on the altar; the priests, who were vowed to chastity, went barefoot, with shaven heads and wearing plain linen garments; no women or pigs were allowed to enter" (*Punica* 3.21-44; Stafford 192). Stafford comments, "the prohibition of women [is] elsewhere in Herakles' cult, and even the barefoot priests have a Greek parallel in the priests of Zeus at Dodona, but other elements (the absence of an image, the ban on pigs) are characteristically Semitic and clearly belong to Melqart" (192). In the context of our discussion of Melqart, it should be noted that far nearer to Tyre than Greece were the ancient Jews, the neighbors of Tyre to the south with whom, unlike the Greeks, they shared the Semitic language.

The scene of Herakles' "resurrection, may be indicated [by] Melqart's ancient sanctuary at Tyre, where, according to Josephus (*Antiquities*8.146), king Hiram, a contemporary of Solomon, 'built a temple of Herakles and Astarte, and was the first to perform the awakening (*egersis*) of Herakles, in the month of Perdition'" (Stafford 192).[175] "Whatever other traits the two deities shared, a major point of contact, which suggested their identity to the Greeks, seems to have been the belief that they had been burnt on a pyre and subsequently resurrected" (192). The same comparison is made to the Hittite Santan. "Both burning and subsequent ascension to the heavens are found in the ritual of the Hittite god Santan at Tartassos in Cilicia, who again was identified by the Greeks with Herakles" (192). Other potentially influential myths of resurrection include those of the Phoenician Adonis and the Egyptian Osiris.

A set of additional associations were made in antiquity and are made today. Lucian describes a villa in the Rhone valley whose "inhabitants identified Herakles with a Celtic hero called Ogmios" (192). "The Greeks in Bactria and in India identified Krishna with Heracles" (Campbell, *Occidental* 240). As a super-strong giant killer with a blunted weapon, he has been associated with Thor (477). And as a Greek hero, we might also consider the likelihood of mimetic motifs in the stories of Jason, with whom he was an Argonaut, Theseus, who he freed from stone in the underworld, and his great-grandfather Perseus.

As we transition into an introduction of Christ, we should consider some of the typically acknowledged overlaps of the two characters. "Both gods born of mortal woman, who suffer, rid the earth of evil and overcome death" (Stafford 202). By at least the second century AD, analogies were being drawn by theologians like Justin Martyr who wrote, "When it is said that Herakles was strong, that he traveled the whole world, that he was born of Zeus and Alkemene, that after his death he was taken up to heaven, do I not understand that this is an imitation of the Scripture ... about Christ?" (*Dialogue With Trypho*69.3; Stafford 202). The hero also appears alongside images of the Old Testament and Gospels in "the Christian catacombs of Via Latina at Rome" (Stafford 203). In 1555, Pierre de Ronsard's hymn, "the Christian Hercules", "identifies eighteen parallels between Hercules and Christ, [including] their half-mortal half-divine parentage to their triumph over death ... Hercules' marriage to Youth is matched by Christ's to Eternity, and as for their opponents (II. 173-82: Stafford 205). Not unlike the Cynics and Stoics, he wrote that the monsters Herakles faced were the "Vice and the enormous Sins which Jesus Christ, by the celestial effort of his great Cross, put to death at a single blow" (205). Echoing this interpretation, "in 1648 the Scottish polymath Alexander Ross provide[d] a fairly systematic list of analogies between the labors and the Christian's duties" (*Mystagogus Poeticus, s.v.* 'Hercules'), which led to his summative statement that "By Hercules may be meant every good Christian" (Stafford 205).

More recently James Hillman commented on the fact that "in the early centuries of Christianity Christ had various pagan identifications, principally Hercules, and was in competition, so to speak, with both that hero and Mithra. Christ was imagined as well, against the backgrounds of Perseus, Asclepius, Orpheus, and Dionysus, and then later as Eros, Apollo, and also Jupiter" (Hillman *Revisioning* 97). To transition into an introduction of Christ, we will continue into his comparison with other deities and heroes. Perhaps the most monumental work on Christ and his relationship with resurrection deities (and Kings) is George Frazer's *Golden Bough*, who describes congruities with the figures of Herakles, Christ, Melqart, Sandan, Attis, Adonis, Osiris and a number of other kings and deities.

One of the essential deities to discuss in the context of Christ is the Persian Mithras. "The immense popularity of his worship is attested by the monuments illustrative of it, which have been found scattered in profusion all over the Roman Empire. In respect both of doctrines and of rites the cult of Mithra appears to have presented many points of resemblance ... to Christianity. The similarity struck the Christian doctors themselves" (Frazer 1.303). Frazer continues, "there can be no doubt that the Mithraic religion proved a formidable rival to Christianity, combining as it did a solemn ritual with aspirations after moral purity and a hope of immortality" (1.304). Hillman adds, "the early image of Christ ... compounded with the military Mithra and the muscular Hercules ... turned the tide against classical polytheism" (*Revisioning* 28).

Perhaps the most discussed similarity of Mithras and Christ is their December twenty-fifth birthday. "In the Julian calendar the twenty-fifth of December was reckoned the winter solstice, and it was regarded as the Nativity of the Sun, because the day begins to lengthen and the power of the sun to increase from that turning-point of the year" (Frazer 1.303). It is attested that the "ritual of the nativity, as it appears to have been celebrated in Syria and Egypt, was remarkable. The celebrants retired into certain inner shrines, from which at midnight they issued with a loud cry, 'The Virgin has brought forth! The light is waxing!' The Egyptians even represented the new-born sun by the image of an infant which on his birthday, the winter solstice, they brought forth and exhibited to his worshippers"(1.303). With this in mind, Frazer adds that "Mithra was regularly identified by his worshippers with the Sun, the Unconquered Sun, as they called him; hence his nativity also fell on the twenty-fifth of December"(1.303).

Considering the fact that "The Gospels say nothing as to the day of Christ's birth, and accordingly [that] the early Church did not celebrate it" (1.303) Frazer questions why the date was chosen. It was not until the "end of the third or the beginning of the fourth century [that] the Western Church ... adopted the twenty-fifth of December as the true date, and in time its decision was accepted also by the Eastern Church" (Frazer 1.303-304). Continuing to pull on the thread he refers to a Syrian Christian who wrote:

> The reason why the fathers transferred the celebration of the sixth of January to the twenty-fifth of December was this. It was a custom of the heathen to celebrate on the same twenty-fifth of December the birthday of the Sun, at which they kindled lights in token of festivity. In these solemnities and festivities the Christians also took part. Accordingly when

the doctors of the Church perceived that the Christians had a leaning to

this festival, they took counsel and resolved that the true Nativity should

be solemnized on that day (1.305).

What this shows us is that the rebirth of Christ was associated with the renewal of the annual cycle and rebirth of nature in the context of human fertility—as represented by the child's birth. We have seen and will continue to witness the association of birth with sunrise, which is to the day what the winter solstice is to a year.

The world knows Christ, the Nazarene, as the founding and foundational figure of Christianity, which emerged from the Semitic tradition of the Jews into Classical Rome before replacing Mithras as the primary deity of the Roman military and Constantine's Roman Empire. The conversion predated the schism of the Eastern and Western Empire, and thus Eastern Christianity endured, inhabiting Israel, long after Rome had fallen. When the state fell the religion continued, and through a partnership of Charlemagne with the western pope, Europe was reborn. First were the Christian crusades of Spain, and then those centered on Jerusalem. Shortly thereafter the Grail Romances became popular. Over the course of this period, Europe re-galvanized as a Christian culture.

It seems less needs to be said about Christ for the purposes of familiarization—he is presented as an example (both human and man), as the son of a virgin, and as a healer of sight and soul. As we will see, he repeatedly called for his followers to leave their worldly possessions behind (Luke 12:33) and was presented as the champion of the good and savior of humanity. As mentioned, he is a representative of resurrection, which we will soon discuss further. Lastly, as with Herakles, his deliverance has been associated with a divinizing drink.

Introduction: Einstein

It would be a stretch to call Einstein an ascetic or to align him with philosophies that call for a less material lifestyle, but his tendencies to withdraw from and/or neglect worldly and personal affairs in order to focus on physics was a defining feature of his way (Isaacson 41, 211, 214). It might be said that this is a common way of being for many academics, who exhibit an ascetic ability to disengage from the worldly to pursue deeper thoughts. It might also be said that Einstein shared more than this behavior with the extended community of academics—the humanities and sciences. As we have seen, the study of physics has tended to maintain an important relationship with the whole of an intellectual paradigm. As if his life was itself an elegant display of the universe, Einstein did not just usher in a new scientific theory and groundwork for intellectual thought, he also personified a new type of academic.

The earlier scientists who rebelled to distinguish science from religion should certainly be seen as defiant, but as much as the winning of scientific independence from religion can be seen as rebellious, it also gave birth rise to the tradition as a new authority on truth. The image of the good student has long been as a follower, one who takes good notes, one who obeys, and one who learns what he is taught. Einstein experienced many of the schools he attended as demanding of this kind of student. However, as we will see, Einstein was anything but an obedient follower who relied on teachers for knowledge. Einstein did not give epistemological authority to the institutions or teachers from which he learned, instead, he absolutely insisted on understanding truth for himself. Where he hit walls, he fell them with breakthrough theory.

Our last conversation about the historical trajectory of philosophy and science left off with the atomistic paradigm of the Enlightenment. As was stated by a number of scholars, the Enlightenment paradigm and the atomistic worldview continue to live on. Perhaps this is what has really driven this dissertation: a sense that a new set of foundations has been established and a recognition that they have not flowered far enough afield (from physics). We have certainly witnessed the extension of atomic theory beyond the realm of science: Ethics, politics, economics and a number of fields have used the atomistic framework to consider their own challenges. That having been said, the attempts to extend the new foundations of physics beyond the realm of technology has had limited success.

Perhaps we are centuries from a full extension of the post-atomic foundations into popularly acknowledged and embraced social theories, but my sense is that more than slow progression is required. My aim is to make essential metaphysical and epistemological moves that will enable the (less-than-new) scientific foundations to emerge with their full force into the social sciences and humanities. Very specifically, my intention is to observe the scientific breakthroughs that enabled the revolutionary transcendence of reductive atomism so that I can abstract them into their essential metaphorical breakthroughs. In the same way that atomistic metaphors permeated their way into the social sciences and humanities—not the atom itself—it will be the essential set of foundational metaphors—not the photon itself—that transpose their way into greater worldviews.

By the end of this chapter we will be comparing the metaphors I will have extracted from the salvation of Classical and Christian progenitors with the breakthrough metaphors at the foundation of modern physics that finally transcended the reductively materialistic paradigm established by the progenitors of theoretical science. Up until this chapter the entirety of the dissertation has been dedicated to the demonstration of how the stories of Adam, Prometheus and the pre-Socratic philosophy adopted by science has conveyed an entry into a material world and/or a materialistic way of interpreting existence. With Heracles, Christ and Einstein we will not only see a transcendence of the reductively materialistic foundations presented by the origin stories of knowledge, we will also see the presentation of a new foundation, which, through image or scientific theory, presents a synthesis of the traditional material/atomic paradigm with a recognition that waves share in the foundation of reality.

Ultimately the dissertation does not call for an ascetic-like abandonment of one's considerations for the body and material world. Rather, as I will show, the form of departure from reductive materiality presented by the Classical, Christian and scientific traditions all present a retained value for the worldly and atomic. I cannot overstate how important it is to clarify that the liberation from a reductively materialistic worldview is not being presented as a complete departure there-from: I am presenting my findings that there is an integration of that which had been subtle enough to elude common recognition through everyday experience or an empirical science that has primarily operated at the macro level.

Returning to an introduction of this chapter's work with modern physics, the great breakthrough we will be discussing is the integration of wave dynamics and particle physics into the scientific understanding of light, atoms and all matter. While it was Einstein who synthesized the particle and wave into a single particle-wave foundation, it was Maxwell who popularly undermined the reductively atomistic or corpuscularean worldview with a major emphasis on wave dynamics. His contributions to the study of electricity, magnetism, and, ultimately, electromagnetism, led to a popular embrace of light—by the scientific community—as the effect of ripples in ether. From this point of view, light was immaterial. At most light's medium was material. Meanwhile, the ether itself was still essentially conceptualized as substantive (like water or air), while the belief that all matter is atomic was retained. Though most would agree that Einstein's contributions have triggered the most revolutionary new paradigm since the Newtonian Enlightenment, I want to recognize Maxwell as he who opened the mind of the scientific community to the significance of non-atomic behavior—that of waves.[176]

As Newton was born the day Galileo died (December 25th), Einstein was born the day Maxwell died (Isaacson 91-2). The paradigm Galileo and Newton combined to establish, which presented a mechanistic universe that possessed absolute space and time, was majorly refined by the combined work of Maxwell and Einstein, who, together, integrated the behavior of waves into the evolving worldview of theoretical physicists.

In telling the story this dissertation follows, we should consider a focus on Maxwell as opposed to Einstein. With the supporting contributions of Faraday and Huygens, it was he who popularly integrated wave (field) theories into contemporary science. For a number of reasons, we will instead focus on Einstein. The first is that, as Einstein showed, the wave theory of light is ultimately limited (and thereby incorrect). Einstein's theory of the photon is what stands. In that this dissertation's work with physics serves to challenge the truth-value of the work it does with religious mythology, it is better to use accepted scientific theory than that which has since evolved. This brings us to the second reason we focus on Einstein over Maxwell – while Maxwell's work was revolutionary and posed many challenges to the Newtonian paradigm, it was Einstein's physics that solidified into a paradigm capable of supplanting the Newtonian worldview. Even the theories of Quantum Mechanics that would follow and develop alongside Einstein's relativistic theories were based on his new image of the photon as both wave and particle. It was Einstein who truly synthesized the two forms of behavior in a single entity. He did so first with the photon before his friend and colleague, De Broglie, did so with electrons (matter). This line of work eventually led to the recognition of all matter as fundamentally field and particle. In this way it was Einstein who rolled away the stone of reductive materialism to assert energy as a more essential cosmic foundation, and it was his synthesis of particles and waves in the image of the photon that resulted in the now dominant scientific paradigm, which recognizes all light and matter as particle and wave.

Having settled on Einstein as our focus on the third of this chapter dedicated to physics, we should say more about the man and "rock star" (S. James Gates Jr. *Elegant* 1), "Newton's true successor" (Greene 1). He resides in the "pantheon inhabited by Aristotle, Galileo, and Newton" (Isaacson 5)."The exotic ideas of relativity and the gentle, unpretentious persona of its creator excited the imagination of the press and public, and Einstein became the most famous scientist who ever lived" (12 Taylor et. al.). At the outset of his thorough biography on the near-mythic figure, Isaacson writes:

> Looking back at a century that will be remembered for its willingness to break classical bonds, and looking ahead to an era that seeks to nurture the creativity needed for scientific innovation, one person stands out as a paramount icon of our age: the kindly refugee from oppression whose wild

> halo of hair, twinkling eyes, engaging humanity, and extraordinary
> brilliance made his face a symbol and his name a synonym for genius.
> Albert Einstein was a locksmith blessed with imagination and guided by a
> faith in the harmony of nature's handiwork. His fascinating story, a
> testament to the connection between creativity and freedom, reflects the
> triumphs and tumults of the modern era. (Isaacson 2).

As Prometheus, Adam, Heracles and Christ have all been presented as representatives and examples of a people and/or period, so, here, is Einstein. Over and again we will see him as an example, benefactor, and even a father figure. He is the father of modern physics – more specifically, he is the father of relativity theory as well as the photon, and in this way, quantum theory. He was not only a father of physics (and his children) – he was also asked to serve as the Israeli presidential patriarch after his friend, Chaim Weizmann, the first president of Israel, died. More will be said of his relationship with Judaism and religion.[177] I introduce this point now to suggest that the paternal image of Einstein had the opportunity to extend beyond science and into the (religious and secular) Jewish population.

Einstein should be seen as a benefactor and knowledge bringer. We will speak more to his performance as a benefactor when we discuss his rebellious streak, but to bring knowledge is certainly to be a benefactor—asserts this academically minded writer. "A century after his great triumphs, we are still living in Einstein's universe, one defined on the macro scale by his theory of relativity and on the micro scale by … quantum mechanics" (Isaacson 4-5). His theoretical contributions have translated into "nuclear power and fiber optics, space travel, and even semiconductors" (Isaacson 5). Such are his Promethean (and or Pandoran) gifts of knowledge and technology.

Even more specifically, as a light bringer, it is he we give credit for atomic energy and the atom bomb—the greatest fire made by man. Further, as the theoretician who revealed the essential nature of matter to be energetic, as far as energy has been compared with fire, he might again be seen as a fire bringer.[178] He even made the classical association between fire and consciousness himself when he "eulogized the physicist Rudolf Ladenberg ... [with the words] 'Brief is this existence, as a fleeting visit in a strange house. ... The path to be pursued is poorly lit by a flickering consciousness'" (536). For story sake, I should also mention that his father's lighting company "provided the first electrical lights for Munich's Oktoberfest" (22-3). I might also remind the reader that he has hardly been envisaged without a pipe. And for good measure (or fun), we should also remember the fire-bringer's "explosion in Pernet's lab" he caused as a boy (35)—an event mimed in countless stories since (when a precociously brilliant character blows up a lab experiment, often giving them Einstein hair).

Eventually institutions of knowledge requested his advice. "Near the end of his life, Einstein was asked by the New York State Education Department what schools should emphasize. 'In teaching history,' he replied, 'there should be extensive discussion of personalities who benefited mankind through independence of character and judgment'" (6). He added, "Critical comments by students should be taken in a friendly spirit. ... Accumulation of material should not stifle the student's independence" (6-7). "A society's competitive advantage will come not from how well its schools teach the multiplication and periodic tables, but from how well they stimulate imagination and creativity" (6-7).

Before addressing his support for the individual, I want to acknowledge his emphasis on creativity. Unlike many of the scientists and mathematicians of his time, "his success came not from the brute strength of his mental processing power but from his imagination and creativity" (7). Like the youthful sunrise, "throughout his life, Albert Einstein would retain the intuition and the awe of a child" (14). He is believed to have said, "Imagination is more important than knowledge" (7), though the quote may be more related to the myth of Einstein than his historic statements. He surely said, however, that "if you want your children to be intelligent, read them fairy tales. If you want them to be more intelligent, read them more fairy tales" ("Fairy Tale Quotations"). [179] One of the essential qualities of his mode of thought is that he "generally preferred to think in pictures, most notably in famous thought experiments. ... 'I very rarely think in words at all,'" he said (9).[180] These "visualized thought experiments— Gedankenexperiment — became a hallmark of Einstein's career" (26-27).

His own emphasis on visual learning and respect for the individual mind was nurtured and furthered by the philosophy of Heinrich Pestalozzi, whose philosophy defined a school he attended in Aarau. According to the Swiss philosopher, it is,

> ... important to nurture the "inner dignity" and individuality of each child. Students should be allowed to reach their own conclusions, Pestalozzi preached, by using a series of steps that began with hands-on observations and then proceeded to intuitions, conceptual thinking, and visual imagery. ... Rote drills, memorization, and force-fed facts were avoided. Einstein

loved Aarau. "Pupils were treated individually," his sister recalled, "more emphasis was placed on independent thought than on punditry, and young people saw the teacher not as a figure of authority, but, alongside the student, a man of distinct personality." (26)

It was here he "first engaged in the visualized thought experiment that would help make him the greatest scientific genius of his time: he tried to picture what it would be like to ride alongside a light beam" (26). Later he recalled "In Aarau I made my first rather childish experiments in thinking that had a direct bearing on the Special Theory. … If a person could run after a light wave with the same speed as light, you would have a wave arrangement which could be completely independent of time. Of course, such a thing is impossible" (26). We will come back to this famous thought experiment when we reach the stories of his theoretical reformations.

Contingent with his freethinking spirit was a deeper non-conformist and even rebellious way of being. Before he had come to wield his own energies, he was prone to tantrums. "At such moments his face would turn completely yellow, the tip of his nose snow-white, and he was no longer in control of himself," Maja remembers. Once, at age 5, he grabbed a chair and threw it at a tutor, who fled and never returned" (12). I cannot help but include this detail because it mimes a scene from Heracles childhood in which, in a tantrum, he threw his lyre at a tutor. In the myth of Herakles, the tutor died. Einstein's did not return.

Perhaps the tutor was undeserving, we will never know, but this clear demonstration of his perpetual refusal of authority as an epistemological ground remained essential to his development. "Skepticism and a resistance to received wisdom became a hallmark of his life. As he proclaimed in a letter to a fatherly friend in 1901, 'a foolish faith in authority is the worst enemy of truth'" (22). His belief was that one should "embrace nonconformity. "Long live impudence!" he exulted to the lover who would later become his wife. 'It is my guardian angel in this world" (7). "His cocky contempt for authority led him to question received wisdom in ways that well-trained acolytes in the academy never contemplated" (9).

This fierce sense of individuality remained strong through the Prussian preparation for WWI, when he witnessed "the military tone of [his] school, the systematic training in the worship of authority that was supposed to accustom pupils at an early age to military discipline" (21). "When troops would come by, accompanied by fifes and drums, kids would pour into the streets to join the parade and march in lockstep. But not Einstein. Watching such a display once, he began to cry. "When I grow up, I don't want to be one of those poor people," he told his parents" (21). This does not mean, however, that he was unwilling to gather courage for the purpose of confrontation. In 1901, for example, after having struggled with authorities over his dissertation, "the unemployed enthusiast engaged in a series of tangles with academic authorities. The squabbles show that Einstein had no qualms about challenging those in power. In fact, it seemed to infuse him with glee. As he proclaimed … 'Blind respect for authority is the greatest enemy of truth'" (67).

In his lifetime, this struggle was far more than for academic freedom. "Einstein's contempt for Germany's authoritarian schools and militarist atmosphere made him want to renounce his citizenship in that country" (29). He was "allergic to nationalism, militarism, and anything that smacked of a herd mentality. And until Hitler caused him to revise his geopolitical equations, he was an instinctive pacifist who celebrated resistance to war" (4). Before WWI he had "generally shunned public activism" (205). However, he then stepped into the role of an active pacifist with a conviction that "scientists in fact had a special duty to engage in public affairs. 'We scientists in particular must foster internationalism'" (205). He even created a "Manifesto to Europeans" which "appealed for a culture that transcended nationalism" (207).

Where in WWI he felt compelled to call for pacifism, WWII and Hitler's Germany seemed to be a force he believed in more directly opposing. Where WWI brought forth Einstein's anti-militaristic and anti-conformist streaks, his relationship with religious authority became relevant during WWII. And though he went into exile as a Jew—not unlike Adam or Prometheus—and even though he was offered the presidency of Israel, he was not particularly religious. Not unlike the tradition of science itself, "Einstein's exposure to science produced a sudden reaction against religion at age 12" (20). He would later write, "through the reading of popular scientific books, I soon reached the conviction that much in the stories of the Bible could not be true" (20). As any good scientist, his criticism of the text was the discontinuity of its literal interpretation with scientific theory. "'Suspicion against every kind of authority grew out of this experience, an attitude which has never again left me,' he later said" (Isaacson 21). Reflecting on this his biographer writes:

> His success came from questioning conventional wisdom, challenging authority, and marveling at mysteries that struck others as mundane. This led him to embrace a morality and politics based on respect for free minds, free spirits, and free individuals. Tyranny repulsed him, and he saw

tolerance not simply as a sweet virtue but as a necessary condition for a creative society. "It is important to foster individuality," he said, "for only the individual can produce the new ideas" (7).

In his anti-authoritarian and disobedient response to religious authority we recognize his willingness to steal the fruit of knowledge and/or fire of consciousness against the will of his would-be authorities. As we will see Jesus challenge the religious authorities of his day, Einstein challenged the authorities of science and refused the epistemological authority of religious or state dogma.[181] And in his rebelliousness against a militaristic state on behalf of humanistic morals and creative freedom—as a refugee—we recognize a deeply Promethean pattern.

But as we will see with Prometheus, he was not only a rebel, in the end, he came back into resonance with the positive side of Zeus. He became a supporter of a strong and centralized government and developed a profound relationship with his spirituality. The reason he believed that a strong central government was necessary was to avoid war, "a theme he would pick up … when he engaged in a public exchange of letters with Sigmund Freud on both male psychology and the need for world government" (209). Before this he had become a member of the New Fatherland League, which "published a pamphlet titled 'The Creation of the United States of Europe,'" (207-8).

His relationship with religion was defined by "a profound reverence for the harmony and beauty of what he called the mind of God as it was expressed in the creation of the universe and its laws" (20). "Later in life, beginning with his exposure to virulent anti-Semitism in the 1920s, Einstein would begin to reconnect with his Jewish identity. 'There is nothing in me that can be described as a 'Jewish faith,'" he said, "however I am happy to be a member of the Jewish people'" (30). Famously, when asked if he was religious, the great physicist said, "Yes, you can call it that" (384). He continued, "try and penetrate with our limited means the secrets of nature and you will find that, behind all the discernible laws and connections, there remains something subtle, intangible and inexplicable. Veneration for this force beyond anything that we can comprehend is my religion. To that extent I am, in fact, religious.' (384-5).

I wonder if this response was at the end of an evolving perspective first triggered by the invisible force of magnetism. "When he was sick in bed one day … his father brought him a compass. He later recalled being so excited as he examined its mysterious powers that he trembled and grew cold" (13). The radical quality of the experience was that "the magnetic needle behaved as if influenced by some hidden force field, rather than through the more familiar mechanical method involving touch or contact" (13). He later reflected that this experience "produced a sense of wonder that motivated him throughout his life. "I can still remember— or at least I believe I can remember— that this experience made a deep and lasting impression on me. … Something deeply hidden had to be behind things" (13). "After being mesmerized by the compass needle's fealty to an unseen field, Einstein would develop a lifelong devotion to field theories as a way to describe nature" (13).

Whether or not this early experience of invisible waves inspired his later comments on the invisible divine, his organic religious attitude was complimented by a deep sense of compassion matched only by those in the pantheon of great spiritual gurus. It is true that he "could be detached and aloof from those close to him, but toward mankind in general he exuded a true kindness and gentle compassion" (Isaacson 5).

"Max Born later said. 'Einstein [is] a citizen of the whole world, little attached to the people around him, independent of the emotional background of the society in which he lived" (95). And thus when he died, at the age of 76, "at his bedside lay the draft of his undelivered speech for Israel Independence Day. [It opened,] 'I speak to you today not as an American citizen and not as a Jew, but as a human being," (543).

As with Heracles, he did not fear death. And, like Herakles, his body was cremated "the afternoon he died" (544).[182] What he left behind was "one of history's most imaginative and dramatic revisions of our concepts about the universe … .a whole new way of regarding reality" (223). "Another of the great giants of twentieth-century physics, Max Born, called it 'the greatest feat of human thinking about nature, the most amazing combination of philosophical penetration, physical intuition and mathematical skill'" (223-224).

Heracles and Christ – Hero Saviors of the Classical and Abrahamic Progenitors

We now turn to the stories of our heroes and saviors essential to our conversation—starting with the liberation of their progenitors. To focus on the story of Heracles' in which he frees Prometheus requires the discussion of a number of interconnected stories. To summarize before we engage a few: Heracles reaches Prometheus on the sun's golden cup-boat. He defeated the Eagle defending the Titan with Hydra-blood tipped arrows (which will lead to his own death). When Zeus agrees to free Prometheus, Chiron is only available to take his place because Heracles had previously wounded the centaur with the same hydra-blood-arrows. In new concordance with Zeus, Prometheus warns him that a son with Thetis would be his end, which results in the substitutive birth of Achilles. Prometheus agrees to wear a wreath and ring to remember his restraint. He then tells Heracles to ride the golden cup boat West towards his brother, Atlas, for his help retrieving the apples. Until the titan returns with apples of gold, the hero holds earth (and/or the cosmos) on his back. Upon his return with the apples, he faces a final labor and numerous adventures before his death and divine union—the topic of a later section. First we will expand on the sequence described above.

The blood of the hydra wounds Chiron, frees Prometheus, and kills Heracles. For this reason, before proceeding to the events surrounding the unbinding of Prometheus, we should consider the myth of Hercules' confrontation with the hydra. As Karl Kerenyi tells the story:

> The hero came with Iolus … and found the infernal serpent in her lair by the spring. … He shot fire arrows into the lair and so forced her to crawl out. … The Hydra coiled around one of the hero's feet. On old pictures we see Heracles attacking the serpent, not with his club but with a sickle shaped sword. But every time he struck off a head, two living ones grew in its place. (*Heroes* 144)

As a sickle is used for the harvest, Heracles "took all that trouble to liberate some little snaky brook like Lerna, by cutting down the self-growing first-fruits of the lurking serpent, as that plentiful crop of snakeheads grew spiking up" (Nonnus 25. 196). Here the heads of the hydra are described as fruits on a tree, harvested by Heracles. And where one branch is cut—as occurs with trees—multiple grow back. Of course, part of the reason to consider the hydra in the context of the tree is that the serpent frequently occurs next to a tree, as we saw in Eden and will see again in the Hesperides.[183] We should also note the harvesting imagery and its consistency with our conversations about the mortal cycles against which Herakles' labors.

Before we consider the weapon with which he successfully dispensed of the serpent, we should frame it by recognizing that it was with the blood of the hydra that he dispensed of virtually all of his future enemies. "Against a thing so difficult to manage as this Herakles devised an ingenious scheme and commanded Iolaos to sear with a burning brand the part which had been severed, in order to check the flow of the blood" (Diodorus Siculus 4. 11. 5). Iolus destroyed "the heads as they grew afresh, by lifting a burning torch" (Nonnus 25. 196). "The young hero used up almost a whole forest to cauterize the wounds of the snake with burning brands, so that she could not grow new heads" (Kerenyi, *Heroes* 145). And thus, with the firebrand, the hydra was subdued.

As mentioned, the blood will later prove instrumental to the liberation of Prometheus, whose gift and emblem is the burning torch. Further connecting the fire of Prometheus with that used to defeat the Hydra, Boethius writes, "when one doubt has been cut away, innumerable others grow up, like the hydra's heads ... there can be no end unless a man controls them by the most lively fire of the mind (4.6.3)" (Stafford 204). Plato's Socrates also compares the Hydra fight with a philosophical challenge (Euthydemos 297b9-d2).[184] The hero "dipped the heads of his arrows in the venom, in order that when the missile should be shot the wound which the point made might be incurable" (Diodorus Siculus 4. 11. 5). And thus, "whatever later he hit with his arrows did not escape death" (Pseudo-Hyginus, 30). In the context of the Caucasian eagle and the liberation of Prometheus, what we realize is that it was precisely his fire-brand gift that enabled the defeat of the hydra and his own liberation. A close read of this myth might even lead one to consider the starting weapon (a burning-(red)-fire-tipped torch) and the resulting weapon (a sharp-(red)-blood-tipped arrow) as mimetic to some degree. If we were to accept a symbolic relationship between these, then we would be forced to consider the possibility that the blood-tipped arrows somewhat symbolize the fire brand. What holds here is that Heracles' arrows are the specific technological advantage he has against a majority of his assailants.

Before we can get to the scene in which Heracles shot down the eagle of Zeus with his hydra-blood-arrows, we should first consider the wounding of the centaur who will eventually take Prometheus' place. During his labor to retrieve the Calydonian boar, Heracles "was hospitably received by the Centaur Pholos" (Kerenyi, *Heroes149*). "When Herakles called for wine, he said he feared to open the jar which belonged to the Kentauroi (Centaurs) in common" (Pseudo-Apollodorus 2. 83 - 87). "It is even said that this wine was a gift of Dionysos intended by the god for the hero himself; a dangerous gift, for evidently the Centaurs did not yet know its nature" (149). "Herakles, bidding him be of good courage, opened it" (Pseudo-Apollodorus 2. 83-7). Shortly thereafter "the Kentauroi arrived at the cave of Pholos, armed with rocks. ... The first who dared to enter ... were repelled by Herakles with a shower of brands, and the rest of them he shot and pursued (2. 83-7).

The centaurs then "took refuge with Kheiron (Chiron). ... As the Kentauroi cowered about Kheiron, Herakles shot an arrow at them, which, passing through the arm of Elatos , stuck in the knee of Kheiron [Pholos in Peloponnesian account]" (Pseudo-Apollodorus 2. 83-87). This was to the great distress of the hero, who "ran up to him, drew out the shaft, and applied a medicine which Kheiron gave him" (2. 83-87).

Unfortunately, however, "the poison of the hydra was too strong" (Kerenyi, *Heroes* 150). In agony, "Kheiron retired to the cave and there he wished to die, but he could not, for he was immortal" (Pseudo-Apollodorus 2. 83 - 87). It is there and in this state that he would wait until "he could be offered to Zeus in place of the tormented Prometheus. Then at last Chiron died and Prometheus was freed" (Kerenyi, *Heroes* 150).

The wounding of Chiron was not the first event to prophecy Prometheus' freedom. In Aeschylus' *Prometheus Bound*, after consorting with Zeus, the maiden Io visited the protector of humanity. After he foretold Zeus' downfall, she asked, "Has he no means to avert this doom?" and he replied, "'No, none--except me, if I were released from bondage'/ 'who then is to release you against the will of Zeus?'/ 'It is to be one of your own grandchildren [i.e. Herakles]'" (Aeschylus, *Prometheus Bound* 753-57). He later repeated, "Of her [Io's] seed ... shall be born a man of daring [Herakles], renowned with the bow, who shall deliver me [Prometheus] from these toils. Such is the oracle recounted to me by my mother, Titan Themis, born long ago'" (869).

As recounted by Hesiod, Prometheus and innumerable others, the prophecy of Prometheus' mother came true, and, using a weapon won with fire-brands, a grandchild of Io's freed the bringer of fire. In *Prometheus Unbound*, as noted by Herington in his introduction to the text, "Prometheus was released in the end ... by Herakles, the descendant of Io" (Aeschylus and Herington 16-17). As we will explore, the "half son of Zeus ... shoots the liver eating eagle/vulture in return for information Prometheus has on the location of certain apples" (Smith 26). According to Valarius Flaccus and Apollonius Rhodius (2. 1238), the Argonauts witnessed Prometheus in Colchis, where the Golden Fleece, like the Titan, was associated with the sunrise. "The cruel resting-place of

Prometheus comes into view [of the Argonauts as they approach Kolkhis (Colchis)], where Caucasus rises in the cold northern air. That day by chance had brought Alcides [Herakles] also thither, to change the Titan's fate ... in their ignorance ... his comrades proceed upon their way" (Zissos and Flaccus; 5. 155 ff). We should recall that Heracles, by most accounts, was one of the original Argonauts. Here, on the eastern edge of the world, Prometheus and the Golden Fleece will be freed at virtually the same time. And, as we will soon discuss, both Jason and Prometheus will make for the Western garden of the Hesperides, where their narratives will re-inwine.

Hercules, "when sent by Eurystheus for the apples of the Hesperides, out of ignorance of the way came to Prometheus, who was bound on Mount Caucasus" (Pseudo-Hyginus, *Astronomica* 2. 15). And "when Herakles saw him suffering such punishment because of the benefit which he had conferred upon men ... with an arrow," (Diodorus Siculus, *Library* 4. 15. 2), "one morning, when the eagle was coming," (173), "that bird Herakles, the valiant son of shapely-ankled Alkmene, slew" (Hesiod, *Theogony* 511).[185] In one of the few surviving fragments of Aeschylus' Prometheus Unbound, the hero prays before the shot, "may hunter Apollon speed my arrow straight!" (qtd. by Plutarch, *On Love* 14. 757E; Fragment 113)

Recalling his second labor, these were no ordinary arrows. Pseudo-Apollodorus describes the interconnected events in which Heracles "cut up the Hydra's body and dipped his arrows in its venom" (2. 80) before "kill[ing] with an arrow the Eagle on the Kaukasos" (2. 120). The defeat of Prometheus' defender at the eastern sunrise was also mirrored by the defeat of the snake beneath the golden apples of the western sunset, who, like the Eagle, (by one account) was "poisoned by arrows steeped in the gall of the Hydra Lernaia" (Apollonius Rhodius, 4. 1390).

Having been "fastened and bound for many years" (Pseudo-Apollodorus 1. 45), he addresses Heracles as his awaited savior. "Of his sire, mine enemy, this dearest son" (qtd. by Plutarch, *Life of Pompey* 1; Aeschylus, *Prometheus Unbound* Fr. 114). After slaying the eagle Herakles set to work, "rending Prometheus' chains, and hurling them this way and that with fragments of the rock where into they were riveted" (Quintus Smyrnaeus, *Fall of Troy* 6. 269). With all his might he labored:

> Wrenching sturdily at the rough fetters on every side, 'mid wreckage of the long-gathered ice, with gripping hands he had torn them from the bed-rock, towering high and with left foot bearing the weight; huge Caucasus echoes from the sound, as tree-trunks following the mountain-summit fall, and rivers are turned back from the sea. There is a crash, as though Jupiter has risen in might and overthrown the citadels of heaven . . . The vast length of Pontus [Black Sea] trembled, and all the Iberian land ... and as the ocean shook to its utmost depths the Minyae [Argonauts] feared the Cyanean Rocks they had left behind. Then as the noise grew nearer the sound of the iron and the rending of the crags and the manifold travail of the mountain is heard, and the loud clamour of Prometheus while his rock-bound limbs are torn. (Zissos and Flaccus 5. 155)

And thus "Heracles ... delivered the son of Iapetos from the cruel plague, and released him from his affliction (Hesiod, *Theogony* 511).

"Some say that he [had been] bound in a cave, which as a matter of fact is shown in a foot-hill of the mountain; and Damis [companion of Philostratus C1st A.D.] says that his chains still hung from the rocks … others say that they bound him on the peak of the mountain … [with] two summits" (Philostratus, 2. 3). In the chapter on Prometheus we introduced the tale of Amirani in which the Promethean figure was trapped within a cave. This will be an important parallel when we look at Adam's liberation. The twin-peaked mountain is a clear reference to Elbruz, the tallest mountain in Europe, which possesses these two peaks. If we consider the cavernous enclosure of the fire bringer in the context of the volcanic Elbruz, we might imagine Prometheus as the fire in the cavern within the great mountain. This would suggest that the liberation of Prometheus is mimetic with the eruption of a volcano. Such a liberation of a fiery being from a cave was re-enacted in the Roman legend in which Hercules defeats the fire breathing Cacus by bursting through the dome of his cave and squeezing his neck until the face of the giant burst through his eyes. We will later compare this story with Odysseus' in Polyphemus' cave and the liberation of Adam and Christ from caves.

As Christ's father supported his death and liberation of Adam, so did "the will of Olympian Zeus" support his son" (Hesiod, *Theogony* 511). Previously, "From the crags and amidst the very ravening of the dreadful Vulture, Prometheus too [had beset] Jove [Zeus] with groans and piteous pleas, uplifting eyes that the cruel frosts have seared" (Zissos and Flaccus 4. 60). Finally the supreme deity was "moved by the goddesses' [Leto's & Artemis'] tears" (4. 60). And so he sent the rainbow, Iris, as a symbol of his relent and to beacon the great hero.

After the Eagle was defeated, "Herakles offered Zeus Chiron in Prometheus stead" (Kerenyi, *Heroes* 126). As we recall, "Kheiron [had] moved into his cave, where he yearned for death, but could not die because he was immortal" and thus Heracles proposed to Zeus that Prometheus "become immortal in place of Kheiron: and so Kheiron died" (Pseudo-Apollodorus 2. 83) "and Prometheus was freed" (Kerenyi *Heroes* 150).

But Zeus "didn't go so far as to free him from all binding, since he had sworn to that, but for commemoration bade him bind his finger with the two things, namely, with stone and with iron. Following this practice men have rings fashioned of stone and iron, that they may seem to be appeasing Prometheus" (Pseudo-Hyginus 2. 15). As Kerenyi writes, "In the Kabeirian sanctuary of Samothrace there was probably a primitive smelting furnace, use for the manufacture of the iron rings which the initiates … wore in imitation of Prometheus" (Kerenyi 73).[186] "Texts relating to the wearing of rings in antiquity make it clear that iron rings were a sign of membership in the Samothracian cult" (Kerenyi. *Heroes* 124).[187]

In addition to the ring, "Some also have said that he wore a wreath, as if to claim that he as victor had sinned without punishment. And so men began the practice of wearing wreaths at times of great rejoicing and victory. You may observe this in sports and banquets" (Pseudo-Hyginus 2. 15). When "Herakles offered Zeus Chiron in Prometheus stead, we read that he took an olive branch 'as a fetter' for himself, for he too, after his act of violence against the order of Zeus, was in need of atonement … expressed in the form and in the wearing of the wreath. In Attica … it was only natural to wear olive wreaths in memory of the beneficent Titan" (Kerenyi, *Heroes* 126). These rings and wreaths they wore "in honor of Prometheus and in exchange for his fetters"

(126). It was a "sign and token of release and redemption, of repentance and reconciliation with Zeus" (127). Athenaeus himself (15. 16. 674D) states that Aeschylus, in the *Prometheus Unbound*, distinctly says: "In honour of Prometheus we place garlands on our heads as an atonement for his bonds." (qtd. by Athenaeus, 15. 16. 674D, Aeschylus, Fr. 128).

Before transitioning through Prometheus' directions to Heracles into his search for the golden apples, I want to pause to consider two parallels to this story in which Prometheus saves men from their stone restraints. When Heracles journeys through the cavernous underworld, he comes across Askalaphus and Theseus on separate occasions. "Under a stone, as it were in a tomb in the very underworld, lay Askalaphos" (Kerenyi, *Heroes* 180). Upon encountering the restrained man, "Heracles lifted the stone and set the daimon free" (181). Later, "near the gate [Heracles] saw two captives, Theseus and Peirithoos, who were under punishment. … Both heroes were sitting on a stone, condemned to sit there forever. … Herakles was able at least to free Theseus from his rigidity; he took him by the hand and aroused him to life again" (181). Such examples of Heracles as a liberator from stone and *rigidity*—especially within caverns of the dead—will become our primary focus once we work through the stories.

"Aeschylus … in his tragedy 'The Freeing of Prometheus,' provided Heracles with a counselor and prophet in the person of the suffering Titan, the benefactor of mankind" (173). "In his search for the golden apples of the Hesperides, Heracles … receives from [Prometheus] directions concerning his course" (qtd. by Weir Smyth, Aeschylus, *Prometheus Unbound*).[188] "So Prometheus sent the hero to Atlas, the neighbor of the Hesperides, and advised him not to force a way into the Garden himself but to ask

Atlas for the golden apples" (Kerenyi, *Heroes* 173). And thus the progenitor again played his role as the benefactor of man.[189] On this journey, as Askalaphus bears the weight of a great stone in death, Herakles will hold up the earth while he waits for apples of life.

Though we will proceed into the story of the golden apples because they are contingent with the freedom of Prometheus, in other versions of the story, it is Nereus who tells Heracles where to find the apples. "In that cave in which this divine stream breaks forth from beyond the world … The Moirai … daughters of Zeus and Themis, [like] the Hesperides … advised him to seek out Nereus and use force on him until the Old Man of the Sea showed him the way" (172). And so "Herakles took hold of him as he lay sleeping, and bound him fast as Nereus changed himself into all sorts of shapes; he did not let him loose until Nereus told him where the apples and the Hesperides were" (Pseudo-Apollodorus 2. 114). It was said in these versions of the story that "Heracles got the gold cup in which to sail to Erytheia from Nereus, even that he started the journey to the Hesperides from Tartessos, and finally, that he used the Sun's cup on this journey, too" (Kerenyi, *Heroes* 172). Erytheia is the red island where Heracles defeated Geryon and procured the cattle of the sunset, with which the island was even more specifically associated than its neighbor the Hesperides. Both journeys to these sunset islands are enabled by the golden cup boat of the sun, which, in another variant, was won with the threat of his mighty arrows.

Following the advice of Prometheus, instead of going directly to the garden, he first met Atlas. "Prometheus advised Herakles not to go after the apples himself, but rather to relieve Atlas of the celestial sphere and dispatch him. So when Herakles reached Atlas he remembered Prometheus' advice and took over the sphere" (Pseudo-Apollodorus

2. 119 – 120).[190] "At Olympia [in the temple of Zeus around his statue] there are screens … [that]show pictures … among them is Atlas, supporting heaven and earth, by whose side stands Herakles ready to receive the load. . . [elsewhere in the painting] two Hesperides are carrying the apples, the keeping of which, legend says, had been entrusted to them" (Pausanias, *Description* 5. 11. 6). Kerenyi tells the fan-favorite:

> Nothing is told us of the ruse by which [Atlas] got the apples, but something of the trick he played on Heracles. He brought the golden fruit, but not to give it to the hero, who was to continue to hold up the sky in his stead. There was a comical old tale according to which Heracles made a show of agreeing, but asked just one favor of Atlas, that the Titan should take the sky on his shoulders again while Heracles prepared a cushion for his head. And now the cunning Titan proved a stupid Titan, for he laid the apples on the ground and took over the weight of the sky; while Heracles for his part hurried away with his booty. (*Heroes* 175)

During the time that Heracles holds the heavens and earth, like Atlas, he is the axis-mundi. At this moment a Man can be seen as the foundation (though it should be mentioned that, A, Atlas is still an anthropomorphized foundation of the cosmos, and B, that Ovid describes Oceanids beneath the mountain into which his Atlas turns). Here we see mythic reinforcement of the Greek tendency to see man as the foundation (and measure) of all things. Simultaneously, we see the reciprocal binding of Prometheus to stone and the boulder atop of Askalaphus. We see the great hero laboring beneath the great weight of the world. It is exactly his cleverness that frees him from the burden.

In another form of the story Heracles "forces his way to the Hesperides, attacked the guardian serpent and finally killed it. On vase paintings we see him also peacefully in the Hesperides' company; according to this version, he accomplished his task with the agreement and help of the goddesses" (176). "For many, the Garden of the Hesperides lay where the voyage through the red waters by Atlas in the west ends. Zeus had a palace there and Hera her marriage-bed, by immortal fountains, where the fruitfulness of the soil beatified even the gods" (148). This was "the apple-bearing Hesperian coast, of which the minstrels sing" (Euripides, *Hippolytus* 742). This is the place "where the Lord of Okeanos denies the voyager further sailing and fixes the solemn limit of Ouranos (Heaven), which Giant Atlas upholds. [Where] the streams flow with ambrosia by Zeus's bed of love and holy Gaia … giver of life, yields to the god's rich blessedness" (742). Gaia "produced the golden apples of Hesperia to celebrate the bridal of the heavenly gods Zeus and Hera. These were entrusted to the care of the Hesperides, handmaidens and daughters of the goddess Nyx (Night), who heralded the onset of night and bridal of these two gods with the golden glow of sunset" (Nonnus 38. 135). He adds, "Apples, in Greek tradition, were a symbol of love" (38. 135).

In addition to the Hesperides, "an immortal serpent guarded" the apples (Pseudo-Apollodorus 2. 113- 114). "Posted there by Hera … Ladon [was] a being which never closes its eyes" (Kerenyi, *Heroes* 174). "Ladon was the name both of the river and of the serpent that watched over the tree of the golden apples" (148). "The Hesperides, gave dainties to the dragon and guarded the sacred bows on the tree, sprinkling dewy honey and slumberous poppies" (Virgil, *Aeneid* 4. 480). As beautiful as one might imagine the defenders of the Golden Apples to be, we should remember their monstrous side. "The three Hesperides … [were] equated with the death-goddesses who carried off their prey, the Sirens. … Anyone who came to … the Island of the Blessed [did not find] the road thither … and if also he dared lay hands on the property of the Queen of the Gods, the golden fruit, that would have been double death for him" (Kerenyi, *Heroes* 175).

It is actually the rarer story in which Heracles kills the serpent. Further entwining the myths of Prometheus and Jason, "the Attic master painter Meidias … makes the sorceress Medeia with her box of magic herbs take part in the journey" (176). There are also scenes in which Omphale appears, Queen of the island of the navel of the earth. "Assteas of Paestum … puts Kalypso there … she is offering the drink to the dragon in a cup, and he merely laps it up, without noticing that on the other side a Hesperid is plucking the fruit, nor that Heracles has already got one apple, and two Hesperides are actually eating others" (176). According to yet another master, "again of Attica, who also painted the Omphalos, the navel of the earth, on the vase, the magic drink was wine" (176). In this scene "a great mixing bowl stands there, the serpent is quite tame, the three Hesperids have become maenads, Panes are looking at them from the backgrounds, Iolaos is present also, and Heracles in the middle of the picture is garlanded by a flying Nike, for victory is his." (176).

In yet another "vase painting … the hind stands beneath the tree of the golden apples, guarded by two women, the Hesperides … According to another [story], his booty was the golden antlers" (148). As the voyage to retrieve the cattle of the sun has been associated with the retrieval of the golden apples, so too has the search for the golden hart, whose antlers, like fruit, fall seasonally each winter. Morford offers the common interpretation of the Hesperian apples as symbols of immortality and "the Hesperides

Labor [as] a conquest of death" (360). "The story of the Cerynean stag," he says, "is another version of the same theme" (360).

Pliny the Elder claims that the gardens of the Hesperides were off the Atlantic coast of Africa. According to him, "On the island there also rises an altar of Hercules, but of the famous grove in the story that bore the golden fruit nothing else except some wild olive trees" [N.B. The Lixos is probably the Moroccan river Draa.]. Not only did the hero "carry a great club of olive-wood" (Apollonius Rhodius 4. 1390), one of his most distinguishing symbols, he is also said to have introduced the Olive to Greece by some accounts, "with the garland of olive twigs that Heracles had brought with him from the land of the Hyperboreans" (Kerenyi, *Heroes* 185). As the olive gave oil for fire, "there was another sacred tree which Heracles had transplanted from Acheron to Olympia, the white poplar; only from its wood might the altar fire of Zeus at Olympia be lit" (185). As the bringer of the holy olive and poplar, Heracles, like Prometheus, was a bringer of (divine) fire. Where there are many other versions of the golden apple, we should at least consider the golden fruit as the fire fruit. One of the most interesting symmetries this would establish is the connection between the fire flower and spark stolen from Hephaestus and the ripened fruit of the olive, whose fruit will produce new fire and seed will give rise to the next fire-flower. My imagination is even tempted to draw a connection between holy flame—which was rarely allowed to die out—and the dragon, "set to watch over the precious fruit, [with] his ever-waking eyes" (Seneca 526ff).

Perhaps, however, it was not the olives of the grove that were to be associated with the golden fruit at all. "Others assert that the Hesperides possessed flocks of sheep which excelled in beauty and were therefore called for their beauty, as the poets might do, 'golden mela' [meaning apples and sheep] ... and the Drakon was the name of the shepherd" (Diodorus Siculus 4. 26. 2). According to this account, "In the country known as Hesperitis there were two brothers whose fame was known abroad, Hesperos and Atlas. These brothers possessed flocks of sheep which excelled in beauty and were in colour of a golden yellow, this being the reason why the poets, in speaking of these sheep as mela, called them golden mela" (4. 26. 2). We have already discussed the conflation between the fruit and the sheep. One of the crucial connections is to the golden fleece of the Argonauts, another is that the ram was associated with Ra, sun-god of the Egyptians, who are more relevant in the less fantastic version of the story in which Heracles rescues the princesses in place of apples.[191] Whatever the apples were, "We are told merely that he simply showed the [them] to Eurystheus ... it was stated that the king of Mycenae would not take possession of the booty at all ... for the apples of the Hesperides constituted the property of the gods, even more sacred than their temple-treasures" (Kerenyi, *Heroes* 177).[192]

Before leaving the Hesperides, I want to look at the finale described by Apollonius of Rhodes in the *Argonautica*, partially to see another variant of the myth—in which Heracles is vilified by the Hesperides—but also to witness the juxtaposition of a thirsty desert with its vivifying fountain. Having ported their ship across the Libyan desert, "They set her [the ship Argo] down from their sturdy shoulders in the Tritonian lagoon. Once there, it was their first concern to slake the burning thirst that was added to their aches and pains. They dashed off, like mad dogs, in search of fresh water" (4. 1390). What they found was Heracles' aftermath, for which "they were fortunate" (4. 1390). Upon wrriving "they found the sacred plot where, till the day before, the serpent Ladon, a son of the Libyan soil, had kept watch over the golden apples in the Garden of Atlas, while close at hand and busy at their tasks the Hesperides sang their lovely song. But now the snake, struck down by Herakles, lay by the trunk of the apple-tree" (4. 1390). Avvording to Apolonius, "only the tip of his tail was still twitching; from the head down, his dark spine showed not a sign of life: His blood had been poisoned by arrows steeped in the gall of the Hydra Lernaia, and flies perished in the festering wounds" (4. 1390).

What this scene reveals are the ripples of Herakles' Eleventh Labor. Near the place where the serpent lie dead, 'with their white arms flung over their golden heads, the Hesperides were wailing as the Argonauts approached. The whole company came on them suddenly, and in a trice the Nymphai turned to dust and earth on the spot where they had stood" (4. 1390). Thus, not only is the wasteland motif displayed by the party's thirsty arrival from the desert, it can also be found in the bodies of the Hesperides', who turn to dust after the fruit has been plucked. This is not unlike the emphasis on the human body as that which will return to dust following the Edenic fruit theft. In this scene, however, Orpheus is there to interpret "the hand of Heaven," and to pray on behalf of his comrades "Beautiful and beatific Powers, Queens indeed, be kind to us … make yourselves manifest to our expectant eyes and lead us to a place where we can quench this burning, never-ending thirst with fresh water springing from a rock or gushing from the ground" (4. 1390). He then promises that they will later respond to their generosity with "innumberable gifts of wine and offerings at the festal board" (4. 1390), which further emphasizes the elixir symboloism at play.

The Nymphai then responded with a miracle characteristic of wasteland redemption, "First, grass sprung up from the ground, then long shoots appeared above the grass" (4. 1390), and, not unlike the story of Adam's tree, "Hespere became a poplar; Erytheis an elm; Aigle a sacred willow. Yet they were still themselves; the trees could not conceal their former shapes--that was the greatest wonder of all" (4. 1390). Aigle spoke:

> You have indeed been fortunate. … There was a man here yesterday, an evil man, who killed the watching Snake, stole our golden apples, and is gone. To us he brought unspeakable sorrow; to you release from suffering. He was a savage brute, hideous to look at; a cruel man, with glaring eyes and scowling face. He wore the skin of an enormous lion and carried a great club of olive-wood and the bow and arrows with which he shot our monster here. It appeared that he, like you, had come on foot and was parched with thirst. For he rushed about the place in search of water; but with no success, till he found the rock that you see over there near to the Tritonian lagoon. Then it occurred to him, or he was prompted by a god, to tap the base of the rock. He struck it with his foot, water gushed out, and he fell on his hands and chest and drank greedily from the cleft till, with his head down like a beast in the fields, he had filled his mighty paunch. (4. 1390)

According to this description, not only did Heracles retrieve the Golden Apples, he also drank from the spring at the Western limit of the Classical cosmos. When the Argonauts heard this, "they ran off in happy haste towards the place where Aigle had pointed out the spring" (4. 1390).

In this exquisite finale sequence we recognize the slaking of thirst and the redemption of what had become a wasteland-like zone of death. In this story we see the pinnacle of the disaster communicated as the transformation of the Hesperides into dust, the reversal of which takes the form of a fountain, growing grass, and the rebirth of Hesperides as trees. It should also be noted that, like the story of Moses in the desert, the thirst quenching water is freed from within a *stein*.

Considering the potential relationship of both Heracles and Christ with the figure of Mithras, we should take this chance to consider the impeccable resonance of his imagery with that from this scene. Campbell engages the overlap of these figures:

> Mithra, like Gayomart, of whom he is in a certain sense the antithetic counterpart, was born beside a sacred stream beneath a sacred tree. In works of art he is shown emerging as a naked child from the 'Generative Rock', wearing his Phrygian cap, bearing a torch, and armed with a knife. His birth is said to have been brought about solo aestu libidinis, 'by the sole heat of the libido (creative heat),' and, as C. G. Jung has pointed out in one of his numerous discussions on this subject, here all the elemental mother symbols of mythology are united, earth (the rock), wood (the tree), and water (the stream). The earth has given birth—a virgin birth—to the archetypal Man. And so that we may know the birth to be symbolic (not prehistoric, as the claim would be for, say, in Adam or a Gayomart) nearby are shepherds witnessing the birth coming with their flocks to pay the savior worship, as in Chirstmas nativity scenes. Christ, the Second Adam, was the renewer of the image of man. In the Persian savior Mithra the two Adams are united; for there was no sin, no Fall, involved in his enactment of the deeds of temporal life. With his knife the child culled the

fruit of the tree and fashioned clothing of its leaves: once again like

Adam—but without sin. And there is another scene, which shows him

shooting arrows at a rock, from which water pours to refresh a kneeling

suppliant. We do not possess the myth, but the episode has been compared

to that of Moses producing water from the rock in the desert with his rod

(exodus 17: 6). However, Moses sinned, for he struck twice, and

consequently, was denied entry into the Promised Land—as Adam sinned

and was denied paradise. But the savior Mithra both ate the fruit of the

mother tree and drew the water of life from his mother rock—without sin.

(*Occidental* 261)

We get a set of parallels concerning the birth of water and life from stone, Abrahamic,

and Mithraic, as seen in the Hesperides spring brought forth by Heracles. Not only does

the use of arrows to release the spring resonate with the image of Heracles—the image of

the kneeler is particularly direct. The constellation of Hercules is also known as the

"Kneeler ... [Who] others say ... is Prometheus, bound on Mt. Caucasus" (Pseudo-

Hyginus 2. 6). We will come back to some of these details when considering Christ and

Heracles in the context of one another.

Christ Frees Adam, Dies, and Is Resurrected from the Cave

In what follows, the Classical stories of Prometheus' liberation and Herakles'

death are interrupted by the liberation of Adam and death of Christ because, in the

Christian narrative, the Progenitor's liberation is contingent with the savior's sacrifice.

As we will see, the sequences of Herakles' death and Prometheus' liberation are only

symbolically connected; for example, through the dual role of hydra-blood in

Prometheus' liberation and Herakles' death. Once we have worked through the entangled stories of Christ's death and Adam's liberation, we will return to the death of Herakles. What meta-pattern we extract from the progenitor and savior stories will then be compared with the historical narrative of science's development.

To summarize the series of events this section will engage, we will start with the prophecies of Christ in the context of Adam and Eve—before and after the Fall—we will then look at Christ's own prophetic comments about his impending death. The story includes the Last Supper and the foundation of Christian communion, Christ's capture at the garden of Gethsemane, his torture and trial, and the extended sequence of the crucifixion. As we will see, at the crucifixion, Christ's side was pierced and his heart fountained blood and water. These fluids trickled down and baptized Adam, liberating him from the stone cave below. According to Arthurian Legend, Joseph of Arimathea caught the savior's blood in a vessel—some say Christ's chalice from the last supper. Upon his final passing the veil separating the holy of holies from the common worshiper was ripped. Between life and death, Christ harrowed hell, freeing Adam and Eve as well as countless others. This was followed by his own resurrection from the dead, which is especially symbolized by the rolling away of the stone covering his garden cave, the emptying of his sepulcher, and, eventually, encounters with the resurrected Christ and his empty palms.

The section, *In Paradise,* in the Syrian *Cave of Treasures* includes a description of the first couple "going forth sorrowfully" from Paradise, "God spake unto Adam, and heartened him, and said unto him,

Be not sorrowful, O Adam, for I will restore unto thee thine inheritance. Behold, see how greatly I have loved thee, for though I have cursed the earth for thy sake, yet have I withdrawn thee from the operation of the curse. … Inasmuch as thou hast transgressed my commandments get thee forth, but be not sad. After the fulfilment of the times which I have allotted that you shall be in exile outside [Paradise], in the land which is under the curse, behold, I will send my Son. And He shall go down [from heaven] for thy redemption, and He shall sojourn in a Virgin, and shall put on a body [of flesh], and through Him redemption and a return shall be effected for thee. But command thy sons, and order them to embalm thy body after thy death with myrrh, cassia, and stakte. And they shall place thee in this cave, wherein I am making you to dwell this day, until the time when your expulsion shall take place from the regions of Paradise to that earth which is outside it. And whosoever shall be left in those days shall take thy body with him, and [Fol. 7b, col. 2] shall deposit it on the spot which I shall show him, in the centre of the earth; for in that place shall redemption be effected for thee and for all thy children." And God revealed unto Adam everything which the Son would suffer on behalf of him. (*Cave of Treasures: In Paradise*)

This description of the scene offers the full interconnected vision of Christ as the redeemer of Adam who waits within the cursed earth. Christ is God himself come down to redeem Adam and his race. He is God in Adam's flesh. Born through a virgin, he will suffer for humanity.

The same prophecy is echoed in the *First Book of Adam and Eve*, which may have shared an original and lost source with *The Cave of Treasures*. It should also be noted that it was not until modern scholarship that the pre-Christ date was definitively challenged and it was revealed that the texts were not themselves pre-dating prophecies of Christ. Keeping this in mind, we return to the foretelling. When the two were forced from the garden, "God said to Adam,

> All this misery that you have been made to take on yourself because of your transgression, will not free you from the hand of Satan, and will not save you. 4 But I will. When I shall come down from heaven, and shall become flesh of your descendants, and take on Myself the infirmity from which you suffer, then the darkness that covered you in this cave shall cover Me in the grave, when I am in the flesh of your descendants. 5 And I, who am without years, shall be subject to the reckoning of years, of times, of months, and of days, and I shall be reckoned as one of the sons of men, in order to save you." (Malan, *First Book of Adam and Eve* XIV. 3-5).

Again, prophecy demonstrates symmetry between Adam's liberation and Christ's death.

Naturally, for humans like Adam and Eve, such a prophecy was not fully satisfying when they were painfully present with their loss. In this version of the story, the first couple pleads for the nourishment of the garden, to which God responds: "O Adam, as to the fruit on the Tree of Life that you have asked for, I will not give it to you now, but only when the 5500 years are fulfilled. At that time I will give you fruit from the Tree of Life, and you will eat, and live forever, you, and Eve, and your righteous descendants" (*First Book of Adam and Eve* XXXVIII: 2). In response, God foretells the harrowing of hell, which we will soon discuss: "And if you said, 'Give me of the Water of Life that I may drink and live'—it cannot be this day, but on the day that I shall descend into hell, and break the gates of brass, and bruise in pieces the kingdoms of iron. 6 Then will I in mercy save your soul and the souls of the righteous, to give them rest in My garden" (XXXVIII: 5-6).

The water of life is then associated with the blood of Christ as God continues, "in regards to the Water of Life you seek, it will not be granted you this day; but on the day that I shall shed My blood on your head in the land of Golgotha. 8 For My blood shall be the Water of Life to you at that time, and not to just you alone, but to all your descendants who shall believe in Me; that it be to them for rest forever" (7-8). These are the events we will soon encounter when we discuss the narrative of Christ's death.

To further accentuate the parallel between Adam and Christ in the context of the fallen world, the first couple made the first altar and gave the first sacrifice, which, as will be seen in detail, is distinctly mimetic with the death of Christ:

> 4 Adam and Eve took stones and placed them in the shape of an altar; and they took leaves from the trees outside the garden, with which they wiped, from the face of the rock, the blood [of theirs] they had spilled. 5 But that which had dropped on the sand, they took together with the dust with which it was mingled and offered it on the altar as an offering to God. 6 Then Adam and Eve stood under the Altar and cried, thus praying to God, "Forgive us our trespass and our sin, and look at us with Thine eye of mercy. For when we were in the garden our praises and our hymns went

up before you without ceasing. 7 But when we came into this strange land, pure praise was not longer ours, nor righteous prayer, nor understanding hearts, nor sweet thoughts, nor just counsels, nor long discernment, nor upright feelings, neither is our bright nature left us. But our body is changed from the likeness in which it was at first, when we were created. 8 Yet now look at our blood which is offered on these stones, and accept it at our hands, like the praise we used to sing to you at first, when in the garden. (**Malan,** *First Book of Adam and Eve* XXIII. 4-8)

Here we see the mixing of blood with the dust as the offering given on a stone altar. This will later be mirrored by the blood of Christ trickling into the earth and baptizing Adam in the stone below. In the *First Book of Adam and Eve*, God accepts his offering and says to Adam, "As you have shed your blood, so will I shed My own blood when I become flesh of your descendants; and as you died, O Adam, so also will I die. And as you built an altar, so also will I make for you an altar of the earth; and as you offered your blood on it, so also will I offer My blood on an altar on the earth" (XXIC:4-6). God says he "will I make My blood forgiveness of sins, and erase transgressions in it … then will I bring you back into the garden" (XXIC:4-6).

To finally articulate the image of Christ's death, when Adam and Eve are in the place known as the dome of the rock, God tells Adam he has not "placed this dome of rock over you to plague [him] with it. 6 It came from Satan, who had promised you the Godhead and majesty. It is he who threw down this rock to kill you under it" (Malan, *First Book of Adam and Eve* KXIX: 5-6;). The emptying of this rock into a dome (so that it would not crush the first couple) is then compared with the future emptying of Christ's cave. God tells Adam that "just as that rock was falling down on you, I commanded it to form a dome … [this] will happen to Me at My coming on earth: Satan will raise the people of the Jews to put Me to death; and they will lay Me in a rock, and seal a large stone over Me, and I shall remain within that rock three days and three nights. But … I shall rise again" (Malan, *First Book of Adam and Eve* KXIX: 7-9). As Christ emptied his cave after three days and three nights, "after three days and three nights, God created an opening in the dome of rock and allowed them to get out from under it. Their flesh was dried up, and their eyes and hearts were troubled from crying and sorrow" (*First Book of Adam and Eve* KXIX: 10-12)

The Cave of Treasures delivers more of the prophecy in the context of Adam's death and through the descriptions of the narrator as opposed to the words of God. "At the same hour in which the Son of Man delivered up his soul to His Father on the Cross, did our father Adam deliver up his soul to Him that fashioned him; and he departed from this world" (*Cave of Treasures: Death of Adam*). Milton gives the prophecy when Satan falls. He follows his description with a comment on the future: "Jesus son of Mary second Eve/ Saw Satan fall like Lightning down from Heav'n … / Whom he shall tread at last under our feet (IX. 183-189). According to Milton's description:

> hee, who comes thy Saviour, shall recure,
>
> Not by destroying SATAN, but his works
>
> In thee and in thy Seed …
>
> The Law of God exact he shall fulfill
>
> Both by obedience and by love, though love
>
> Alone fulfill the Law; thy punishment

<blockquote>
He shall endure by coming in the Flesh

To a reproachful life and a cursed death,

Proclaiming Life to all who shall believe

in his redemption (X. 1284-1299)
</blockquote>

Here Milton, like the authors of the books of Adam, gives myth to the symmetry between the first fall and Christ's sacrifice.

Leading up to these events, Christ similarly prophesies the events of his death. For example, in Matthew it is written that, "As they were gathering in Galilee, Jesus said to them, 'The Son of Man is about to be delivered into the hands of men, and they will kill him, and he will be raised on the third day.' And they were greatly distressed" (17: 22-23). In Mark he says, 'The Son of Man is going to be delivered into the hands of men, and they will kill him. And when he is killed, after three days he will rise.' But they did not understand the saying" (9:32-33). He says "they will mock him and spit on him, and flog him and kill him. And after three days he will rise" (Mark 11: 34). Similarly in Luke, he prophesies, "The Son of Man must suffer many things and be rejected by the elders and chief priests and scribes, and be killed, and on the third day be raised" (9:21). "And he strictly charged and commanded them to tell this to no one, saying, "The Son of Man must suffer many things and be rejected by the elders and chief priests and scribes, and be killed, and on the third day be raised" (Luke 9:21-22). In another tale he was asked by the Pharisees for a miracle to prove his divinity, and "he answered them, 'An evil and adulterous generation seeks for a sign, but no sign will be given to it except the sign of the prophet Jonah.[40] For just as Jonah was three days and three nights in the belly of the great fish, so will the Son of Man be three days and three nights in the heart of the earth" (Matthew 12: 40).[193]

The other (and perhaps more familiar) scene in which Christ prophesies his death is during the last supper. "The Feast of Unleavened Bread, which is called the Passover, was approaching.2 The chief priests and the experts in the law were trying to find some way to execute Jesus, for they were afraid of the people. 3Then Satan entered Judas" (Luke 22:1-3). And the apostle sold out Jesus for "thirty silver coins" (Matthew 26:15).[194]

When "the day for the feast of Unleavened Bread came, on which the Passover lamb had to be sacrificed" (Luke 22:7), Jesus sent Peter and John to prepare the Passover. They asked, "Where do you want us to prepare it?" 10 He said to them, 'Listen, when you have entered the city, a man carrying a jar of water will meet you. Follow him into the house that he enters'" (Luke 22:9-10). This cup-bearer and guide to the last supper of Jesus Christ knew him as "The Teacher" (Matthew 26:18; Luke 22:11). "When the hour came, Jesus took his place at the table and the apostles joined him. 15And he said to them, "I have earnestly desired to eat this Passover with you before I suffer.16 For I tell you, I will not eat it again until it is fulfilled in the kingdom of God" (Luke 22:14-16).[195]

Before the scene transfers into a precursor of the communion, Jesus tells his apostles, "'I tell you the truth, one of you will betray me.' 22 They became greatly distressed and each one began to say to him, 'Surely not I, Lord?'" (Matthew 26:21-22). To which he answered "'The one who has dipped his hand into the bowl with me will betray me. 24 The Son of Man will go as it is written about him, but woe to that man by whom the Son of Man is betrayed! It would be better for him if he had never been born"

(26: 23-24). Judas, the one who would betray him said, "'Surely not I, Rabbi?' Jesus replied, 'You have said it yourself.'" (26: 21-25).[196]

It is after his moment that the Passover meal became associated with his impending sacrifice. "While they were eating, Jesus took bread, and after giving thanks he broke it, gave it to his disciples, and said, 'Take, eat, this is my body.' 27 And after taking the cup and giving thanks, he gave it to them, saying, 'Drink from it, all of you, 28 for this is my blood, the blood of the covenant, that is poured out for many for the forgiveness of sins'" (Matthew 26: 26-28). In Mark it is similarly recounted that, "as they were eating, he took bread, and after blessing it broke it and gave it to them, and said, "Take; this is my body." 23And he took a cup, and when he had given thanks he gave it to them, and they all drank of it. 24And he said to them, "This is my blood of the covenant, which is poured out for many" (*Mark* 14: 22-24). In Luke, also:

> He took a cup, and after giving thanks he said, 'Take this and divide it among yourselves … Then he took bread, and after giving thanks he broke it and gave it to them, saying, "This is my body which is given for you. Do this in remembrance of me." And in the same way he took the cup after they had eaten, saying, "This cup that is poured out for you is the new covenant in my blood. (Luke 22:17-20).

This alignment of body and blood with bread and wine, respectively, was also followed, in each version, with a statement that he "will not drink" of the "fruit of the vine until" he drinks it in the kingdom of God after death (Luke 22:18; Matthew 26:29; Mark 14:25). The ritual is echoed in First Corinthians, "Every time you eat this bread and drink from this cup you are telling of the Lord's death until He comes again" (11:26). This sharing of

God's blood is associated with the statement in Leviticus 17:11, when God says, "For the life of every living thing is in the blood. So I myself have assigned it to you on the altar to make atonement for your lives, for the blood makes atonement by means of the life." The wine thus, in the form of Hebraic atonement by blood sacrifice, becomes (a representation of) Christ's blood. .

Following the meal, "after singing a hymn, they went out to the Mount of Olives" (Matthew 26:30). The Mount of Olives is also known as the Garden of Gethesemane, where ancient olives continue to thrive and tour guides continue to point out the more than two thousand year age of some trees. One of the things I learned here is that the word Gethsemane actually translates as "oil press." The oil press, of course, was used to juice olives. Though the story at hand most relevantly mimes the juicing of the grape, our study of the Classical stories have often centered around the olive—the trees of the Garden of the Hesperides, for example, have been associated with olives, which Herakles brought to Greece. Clearly the death of Christ mimes the pressing of grapes, as blood-wine fountains from his crucified body; but in this detail of Gethsemane's translation, we also see the olive press.

What follows is known as the "Via Dolorosa", the "Way of Grief," which consists of fourteen stations that begin with Christ's condemnation and end with his entombment. There exists today a set of fourteen locations associated with these points. I and many other pilgrims have walked the path we should now contemplate.[197]

The first station is where Jesus was condemned to death. At the second station, as was foretold, Jesus was tortured. It was then that Roman "soldiers twisted together a crown of thorns and put it on his head and arrayed him in a purple robe … saying, "Hail,

King of the Jews!" (John 19:2-3). [198] He is then given the cross from which he began his path "into a place called the place of a skull, which is called in the Hebrew Golgotha" (John 19:17). At the third station, Jesus falls for the first time under the weight of the cross. At the fourth station Jesus "saw his mother, and the disciple standing by, whom he loved, [and he said] unto his mother, 'Woman, behold thy son!'" (John 19:26). At the fifth station he was helped by "Simon, a Cyrenian, coming out of the country, and on him they laid the cross, that he might bear it after Jesus" (Luke 23:26). Station six is where he wiped his face with a linen cloth, upon which was "miraculously impressed" the features of Christ" (*New International Encyclopedia* 86).[199] As the story is told, the cloth was given to him by "Veronica," "from a medieval corruption of the Latin *vera icon*, true image." At the seventh station Jesus falls for the second time under the weight of the cross after walking through the "Gate of Judgment." At station eight Jesus said "Daughters of Jerusalem, weep not for me, but weep for yourselves, and for your children" (Luke 23:27). At station nine Jesus falls for the third time, this time nearer to Golgotha. At station ten he is stripped of his garments, which were given away based on the casting of lots (Mark 15:24). At the eleventh station, Christ was nailed to the cross.

Legend has it that a woman named veronica gave her veil to Christ on his way to Golgotha. When Christ handed it back after wiping his perspiring face, his image was imprinted on the veil. In the seventeenth century,

As we have discussed, the cross was located at Golgotha, also known as Calvary. Here we should re-familiarize ourselves with its essential details. "Golgotha (goal-goth-uh) was the hill outside the walls of Jerusalem where Jesus was crucified. Its exact location is not precisely known, but the Church of the Holy Sepulcher is believed to have been constructed on this hill" (Malan, *First Book of Adam and Eve* XLII. 13). As we discussed in the chapter on Adam, both Jewish and Christian stories convey the creation of the first human at the center of the world, which, according to the Christians, is Golgotha" (Eliade, *Eternal Return* 16-17).[200] It is also the place Christians believed Adam to have been buried. This can be seen, in the "symbolism of the Middle Ages (for example, as in the Tree-of-Jesse window of Chartres Cathedral), whence the Second Adam, Jesus, was derived; or the cross itself on which Jesus hung, placed on the hill of Golgotha, 'Hill of the Skull,' so called because it was there that the skull was buried of Adam" (Campbell, *Primitive* 107). According to the *Cave of Treasures* the location also relates to the halted sacrifice of Isaac:

> Now Mount Yâbhôs is the mountain of the Amôrâyê (Amorites), and in that place the Cross of Christ was set up, and on it grew the tree which held the ram that saved Isaac. And that same place is the centre of the earth, and the grave of Adam, and the altar of Melchisedek, and Golgotha, and Karkaftâ, and Gefîftâ (Gabbatha). And there David saw the angel bearing the sword of fire. There, too, Abraham took up Isaac his son for a burnt offering, and he saw the Cross, and Christ, and the redemption of our father Adam. The tree (i.e. thicket) was a symbol of the Cross of Christ our Lord, and the ram [caught] in its branches was the mystery of the manhood of the Word, the Only One. And, because of this, Paul cried out and said, "If they had only known [it] they were not crucifying the Lord of glory." Let the mouths of the heretics be stopped who in their madness impute passibility to the Eternal God. Child according to the

Law, and he circumcised Him according to the custom that was the Law. In like manner Abraham took up his son as an offering, but he at the same time [fore]saw in this [act] the crucifixion of Christ. And this ... did Christ openly proclaim before the multitudes of the Jews, saying, "Abraham, your father, wanted to see My days, and he saw and was glad" (John viii. 56). Abraham saw the day of the redemption [Fol. 26a, col. 2] of Adam, and he saw and rejoiced, and it was revealed unto him that Christ would suffer on behalf of Adam. (*4th Thousand Years*)

This association of Christ with Isaac is pervasive, and the Paschal Lamb of the last supper recalls the ram sacrificed in Isaac's place, which, according to this legend, also took place on Golgotha.

While Christ was on the cross, "one of the soldiers pierced his side with a spear, and at once there came out blood and water" (John 19:34). And here we have the image of Christ and the tree as a fountain. "Thus the blood of the Savior falls upon Adam's skull, buried precisely at the foot of the Cross, and redeems him" (Eliade, *Eternal Return* 14). And God's prophecy to Adam came true, "When the Cross of Christ, the Redeemer of Adam and his sons, was set up upon it, the door of that place was opened in the face of Adam. And when the Wood (i.e. the Cross) was fixed upon it, and Christ was smitten with the spear, and blood and water flowed down from His side, they ran down into the mouth of Adam, and they became a baptism to him" (*Cave of Treasures: Crucifixion of Christ*). This is not unlike a more usual Christian baptism, through which, "Tertulian affirms, 'man recovers the likeness of God" (De Bapt., V). For Cyril, 'baptism is not only purification from sins and the grace of adoption, but also antitype of the Passion of Christ'" (Eliade, *Sacred* 134).

Before he died, Christ was offered "wine to drink, mixed with gall, but when he tasted it, he would not drink it" (Matthew 27:34). "He did not take" the "wine mixed with myrrh" (Mark 15:23). And "When Jesus had received the sour wine, he said, 'It is finished,' and he bowed his head and gave up his spirit (John 19: 30). "At the same hour in which the Son of Man delivered up his soul to His Father on the Cross, did our father Adam deliver up his soul to Him that fashioned him; and he departed from this world" (*Cave of Treasures: Death of Adam*).[201]

When Christ died (at the twelfth station), "there was darkness over the whole land until the ninth hour, while the sun's light failed. And the curtain of the temple was torn in two" (Luke 23:44-45), "cleft in twain" (*Cave of Treasures: Crucifixion*). Similarly in Matthew, "the curtain of the temple was torn in two, from top to bottom. And the earth shook, and the rocks were split. The tombs also were opened. And many bodies of the saints who had fallen asleep were raised, and coming out of the tombs after his resurrection they went into the holy city and appeared to many" (27: 51-52). And "when the centurion and those who were … keeping watch over Jesus, saw the earthquake and what took place, they were filled with awe" (27:54).[202] The overlap of the ripping of the veil and resurrection of the dead is amplified through the "Harrowing of Hell," when Christ helps Adam and others to overcome the veiled barrier between death and new life.

Christians are most familiar with the Harrowing of Hell through the Apostle's Creed, "he descended into hell; the third day he rose again from the dead." This is repeated in the Athanasian Creed, "He suffered death for our salvation. /He descended into hell and rose again from the dead." Additional support for the story is found in 1 Peter 4:6 where it is said that the gospel was "proclaimed even to the dead." Another cited reference can be found Zachariah 9:11 God says that "by the blood of [the Jew's covenant with God] I have sent forth thy prisoners out of the pit wherein is no water." The Harrowing of Hell is also described in the *Cave of Treasures*, "at the ninth hour Adam went down into the lowest depth of the earth from the height of Paradise, and at the ninth hour Christ went down to the lowest depths of the earth, to those who lay … in the dust, (*Cave of Treasures: Crucifixion of Christ*). It is also said in the text:

> The descent of Sheol was not in vain, for it was the cause of manifold benefits to our race. He dismissed Death from his domination. He preached the resurrection to those who were lying in the dust, and He pardoned those who had sinned against the Law. He laid waste to Sheol, and slew sin. He put Satan to shame, and made the devils sad, and He abrogated sacrifices and offerings and made an apology for Adam, and abolished the festivals of the Jews. (*Crucifixion of Christ*)

In all of the variants of the harrowing, Adam is the central figure saved by Christ, and as is consistently the case, this gesture represented a radical shift for the human race.

The most detail is given to the story in the *Gospel of Nicodemus* when "The Lord of majesty appeared in the form of a man and lightened the eternal darkness and broke the bonds that could not be loosed: and the succor of his everlasting might visited [the dead] that sat in the deep darkness of our transgressions and in the shadow of death of our sins" (Beer, VI(XXII)- IX (XXV)). As the text recounts, "Thou that didst lie dead in the sepulchre hast come down unto us living and at thy death all creation quaked and all the stars were shaken and thou hast become free among the dead and dost rout our legions" (VI(XXII)- IX (XXV)). Upon his arrival "the legions of devils were stricken with like fear and cried out all together in the terror of their confusion. … Who then art thou that so fearlessly enterest our borders … to bear away all men out of our bonds? Peradventure thou art that Jesus, of whom Satan our prince said that by thy death of the cross thou shouldest receive the dominion of the whole world" (VI(XXII)- IX (XXV)). The "King of glory" then "laid hold on Satan the prince and delivered him unto the power of Hell," before destroying the "strong depths of the prisons" and drawing "Adam to him unto his own brightness" (VI(XXII)- IX (XXV)). Finally he "let out the prisoners and loosed them that were bound … the Lord stretching forth his hand, said: Come unto me, all ye my saints which bear mine image and my likeness. Ye that by the tree and the devil and death were condemned, behold now the devil and death condemned by the tree" (VI(XXII)- IX (XXV)). Adam then addressed his savior:

> I will magnify thee, O Lord, for thou hast set me up and not made my foes to triumph over me. … I cried unto thee and thou hast healed me … thou hast brought my soul out of hell, thou hast delivered me from them that go down to the pit. Sing praises unto the Lord all ye saints of his, and give thanks unto him for the remembrance of his holiness. For there is wrath in his indignation and life is in his good pleasure (VI(XXII)- IX (XXV))

It was then acknowledge by the saints that that which God "didst foretell by the law and by thy prophets" has been "accomplished in deed. Thou hast redeemed the living by thy cross, and by the death of the cross thou hast come down unto us, that thou mightest save us out of hell and death through thy majesty" (VI(XXII)- IX (XXV)). At last Christ "stretched forth his hand and made the sign of the cross over Adam and over all his saints, and he took the right hand of Adam and went up out of hell, and all the saints followed … the Lord holding the hand of Adam delivered him unto Michael the archangel, and all the saints followed Michael the archangel, and he brought them all into the glory and beauty (grace) of paradise" (VI(XXII)- IX (XXV)).

I give the entire story because it is the ultimate description of this dissertation's primary thesis in that it is the description of the ultimate emptying of and redemption from the earth for humanity. Distilling this story to its essence, Peter writes, "He himself bore our sins in his body on the tree, that we may cease from sinning and live for righteousness. By his wounds you [we/ the many] were healed" (2:24).[203]

Meanwhile Jesus has been taken down from the cross (13th station of the Via Dolorosa). "Joseph of Arimathea, who was a disciple of Jesus, secretly for fear of the Jews, [had] asked Pilate that he might take away the body of Jesus, and Pilate gave him permission" (John 19:38 ESV). "This man went to Pilate and asked for the body of Jesus" (Luke 23: 52). "And when [Pilate] learned from the centurion that he was dead, he granted the corpse to Joseph" (Mark 15: 45 ESV), who came to take "away his body … Nicodemus also, who earlier had come to Jesus by night, came bringing a mixture of myrrh and aloes, about seventy-five pounds in weight. So they took the body of Jesus and bound it in linen cloths with the spices, as is the burial custom of the Jews" (John 19: 38-40). *The Cave of Treasures* also describes Nicodemos' presence, "And Nicodemos also embalmed the body of our Lord [and swathed it] in clean, new linen swathings" (*Christ's Body is Embalmed*). Luke 23:53, Matthew 27:59, and Mark 15:46 similarly describe the "linen shroud" in which he was "wrapped." The four gospels then describe how he was laid in a new grave "cut out of the rock" (Mark 15:56), "cut in the rock" (Matthew 27:59), "cut in stone" (Luke 23:53), "in the place where he was crucified … in the garden" (John 19:41).[204]

It is said that "Joseph … [then] rolled a … stone [to/against] the entrance of the tomb" (Mark 15:46; Matthew 27:59). In the *Cave of Treasures* this stone was specific, "because he saw with the eye of the Spirit and the way of the Dispensation of Christ had appeared to him, he took the stone which had travelled about with the children of Israel in the desert and … when Joseph, and Nicodemus, and Cleophas … buried Christ, they laid that stone before the door of the building of the tomb" (*Christ's Embalmed*).[205] In addition to the boulder's weight, Christ was further secured in his tomb by Roman soldiers, "Pilate said to them, 'You have a guard of soldiers. Go, make it as secure as you can." So they went and made the tomb secure by sealing the stone and setting a guard" (Matthew 27:65-66). "The high priests, and men of the house of Pilate, went out and set seals on the grave and on the stone" (*Cave of Treasures: Christ Embalmed*).

It is during the days and nights that Christ is buried in the tomb that the harrowing of hell occurs. His resurrection is synchronized with those he frees from Hades. But before we discuss his rebirth from the cave, we should recall that, according to the Eastern Orthodox tradition, Christ was conceived, born, nursed, and trained as a carpenter in caves. The detail of Christ's birth in a cave can also be found in the *Cave of Treasures* (*Birth of Christ*).

As the Virgin Mary witnessed the birth of Christ in the cave, "on the first day of the week Mary Magdalene came to the tomb early, while it was still dark, and saw that the stone had been taken away from the tomb" (John 20). In the other versions she is joined by the "other Mary" "mother of James", who is also the mother of Jesus. As the Western church was founded by Peter, the Eastern Church was founded by James, who they remember as the brother of Christ. "Mary Magdalene, Mary the mother of James, and Salome bought spices, so that they might go and anoint him. And very early on the first day of the week, when the sun had risen, they went to the tomb. And they were saying to one another, 'Who will roll away the stone for us from the entrance of the tomb?' And looking up, they saw that the stone had been rolled back— it was very large" (Mark 16:1-4). In Matthew it is written that when "Mary Magdalene and the other Mary went to see the tomb … there was a great earthquake, for an angel of the Lord descended from heaven and came and rolled back the stone and sat on it" (Matthew 28). In Luke they similarly went to the tomb at dawn with spices to find "the stone rolled away from the tomb" (Luke 24:2-3). And when "they went in they did not find the body of the Lord Jesus" (24:2-3).

"While they were perplexed about this, behold, two men stood by them in dazzling apparel. And as they were frightened and bowed their faces to the ground, the men said to them, "Why do you seek the living among the dead? He is not here, but has risen" (Luke 24:4-6). "Do not be afraid, for I know that you seek Jesus who was crucified. He is not here, for he has risen, as he said. Come, see the place where he lay" (Matthew 28:5). "Remember how he told you, while he was still in Galilee, 7 that the Son of Man must be delivered into the hands of sinful men and be crucified and on the third day rise?" (Luke 24:4-7). "'He has risen; he is not here … But go, tell his disciples and Peter that he is going before you to Galilee. There you will see him, just as he told you.' 8And they went out and fled from the tomb" (Mark 16:5-8).

Jesus then appeared to his disciples. "On the evening of that day, the first day of the week, the doors being locked where the disciples were for fear of the Jews, Jesus came and stood among them" (John 20:19-20). At first "they were startled and frightened and thought they saw a spirit. And he said to them, 'Why are you troubled, and why do doubts arise in your hearts? See my hands and my feet, that it is I myself. Touch me, and see. For a spirit does not have flesh and bones as you see that I have.' And when he had said this, he showed them his hands and his feet. And while they still disbelieved for joy" (Luke 24:37). "When he … showed them his hands and his side … the disciples were glad when they saw the Lord" (John 20:19-20). But when he "appeared to the eleven themselves as they were reclining at table … he rebuked them for their unbelief and hardness of heart, because they had not believed those who saw him after he had risen" (Mark 16:14). However, with forgiveness in his heart, "Jesus said to them again, 'Peace be with you. As the Father has sent me, even so I am sending you.' And when he had said this, he breathed on them and said to them, 'Receive the Holy Spirit. If you forgive the sins of any, they are forgiven them'" (John 20:21-23). "And he said to them, "Go into all the world and proclaim the gospel to the whole creation" (Mark 16:15).

Jesus again revealed himself to the "disciples by the Sea of Tiberias" (John 21:1-2). Simon Peter, the sons of Zebedee, and two others of his disciples were together when Simon Peter decided to go fishing. They came with him and they caught nothing. But, "Just as day was breaking, Jesus stood on the shore; yet the disciples did not know that it was Jesus" (John 21:4). He asked if they had any fish and they answered no, to which he responded, "'Cast the net on the right side of the boat, and you will find some.' So they cast it, and now they were not able to haul it in, because of the quantity of fish. That disciple whom Jesus loved therefore said to Peter, "It is the Lord!" John 21:6-7 ESV).

Many see this as related to Matthew 4:19 in which Christ said, "Follow me, and I will

make you fishers of men." This reference would later become crucial to the Christian

version of the Fisher King of the Arthurian Grail romances.

As Eliade recounts, the English memory of the story continues into the growth of

herbage from the place of Christ's crucifixion and burial. "Two formulas of incantation,

used in England in the sixteenth century at the gathering of simples, state the origin of

their therapeutic virtue" (*Eternal Return* 30-31):

> 'Haile be thou, holie hearbe, growing on the ground;
>
> all in the mount Calvarie first wert thou found.
>
> Thou art good for manie a sore, and healest manie a wound;
>
> in the name of sweet Jesus, I take thee from the ground [1584].
>
> Hallowed be thou, Vervein [verbana], as thou growest on the ground,
>
> for in the Mount Calvary, there thou wast first found.
>
> Thou healedst our Saviour Jesus Christ, and staunchiest his bleeding
>
> > wound;
>
> in the name of [the Trinity], I take thee from the ground.'

Their efficacy is due to their growth, "for the first time, on the sacred hill of Cavalry at

the 'center' of the Earth. ... Their prototypes were discovered at a decisive cosmic

moment on Mount Calvary, they received their consecration for having healed the

Redeemer's wounds" (30-31).

When Christ ultimately transcended to Heaven he led his disciples "as far as

Bethany, and lifting up his hands he blessed them. While he blessed them, he parted from them and was carried up into heaven. And they worshiped him and returned to Jerusalem with great joy" (Luke 24: 50-52).

The Apostles then proceeded to spread the news of Christ. And as there came to be more followers, the ritual associated with Christ's mastery over death was shared and adopted—over time—throughout the Mediterranean. These rituals include the Roman Catholic Mass as well as a number of lesser known and far more taboo rituals. It may be that all of the above eventually influenced the Arthurian Grail romances, which revolved around an elixir often recognized as Christ's blood, and helped to spread/assimilate Christianity into (non-Roman) European culture. Campbell was especially interested in the confluence between the Last Supper, Mass, and Christian, Classical, and Arthurian rituals involving holy foods, drinks, rebirth and often sexuality. To begin with the Mass, Campbell describes the standard interpretation as it constellates with the last supper and the fall of Adam and Eve:

> In the Roman Catholic mass … when the priest, quoting the words of Christ at the Last Supper, pronounces the formula of consecration—with utmost solemnity—first over the wafer of the host … ("for this is My Body"), then over the chalice of the wine … ("For this is the Chalice of my Blood, of the new and eternal testament: the mystery of faith: which shall be shed for you and for many unto the remission of sins") … the bread and wine become the body and blood of Christ … every fragment of the host and every drop of the wine is the actual living Savior of the world. The sacrament, that is to say, is not conceived to be a reference, a mere sign or symbol to arouse in us a trail of thought, but is God himself, the

Creator, Judge, and Savior of the Universe, here come to work upon us

directly, to free our souls (created in His image) from the effects of the

Fall of Adam and Eve in the Garden of Eden. (*Primitive* 24)

The mass is known to Protestants as "Communion", but there is less emphasis on the

literal transmutation of the bread into the body of Christ or the wine into his blood. If we

recall Kerenyi's association of Prometheus' first sacrifice and the Mass from chapter two,

we recall its association with a new foundation of human reality. He wrote, "Christ's

action at the Last Supper took on the significance of a prototypical ritual act, it became a

foundational sacrifice, the great sacrifice by which the world of salvation was

established" (Kerenyi, *Prometheus 43-44*). In the same way Prometheus' fire sacrifice

was designed to create a bridge between humanity and the divine, so too was the blood

sacrifice of Christ.

Campbell recounts a set of more colorful interpretations of the Christian ritual; for

example, he describes an account given by Saint Epiphanius, who, in his youth, had

become involved with a "Syrian Gnostic congregation known as the Phibionites"

(Campbell, *Creative* 159). According to the saint's captivating account, they share their

women "in common" (Epiphanius 159-161). The ritual begins with a feast in which they

"a lavish bounty of meats and wines, even though they may be poor" (Epiphanius 159-

161). Following the banquet, at which they "fill their veins" they "proceed to the work of

mutual incitement. Husbands separate from their wives, and a man will say to his own

spouse: 'Arise and celebrate the 'love feast' (agape) with thy brother.' And the wretches

mingle with each other" (159-161). Epiphanius continues:

> After they have consorted together in a passionate debauch. ... The woman
> and the man take the man's ejaculation into their hands, stand up, throw
> back their heads in self-denial toward Heaven—and even with that
> impurity on their palms, pretend to pray as so-called Soldiers of God and
> Gnostics, offering, to the Father, the Primal Being of All Nature, what is
> on their hands, with the words: 'We bring to Thee this oblation, which is
> the very Body of Christ,' Whereupon, without further ado, they consume
> it, take housel of their own shame and say: 'This is the Body of Christ, the
> Paschal Sacrifice through which our bodies suffer and are forced to
> confess to the sufferings of Christ.' And when the woman is in her period,
> they do likewise with her menstruation. The unclean flow of blood, which
> they garner, they take up in the same way and eat together. And that they
> say, is Christ's Blood. For when they read in Revelation, "I saw the tree of
> life with its twelve kinds of fruit, yielding its fruit each month' (Rev.
> 22:2), they interpret this as an allusion to the monthly incidence of the
> female period.

This fascinating description offers an interesting variation to Communion and the grail banquets that center around Christ's blood. As in the Grail romances, mortality is a central theme that relates to the Grail. Beyond wine and even menstrual blood, however, the community described by St. Epiphanius follows a literal interpretation of the symbolic canabalism in the Christ story:

> In their intercourse with each other they nevertheless prohibit conception.
> For the goal of their corruption is not the begetting of children but the

mere gratification of lust … They gratify their lust to the limit, but

appropriate the seed of their impurity to themselves, not letting it pour in

for the procreation of a child, but themselves eating of the fruit of their

shame. And if it should occur in the case of any one of them that the

implanting of the natural effusion should take effect and the woman

become pregnant … they tear out the embryo as soon as it can be reached,

take the misborn unborn fruit of the body and pound it in a mortar with a

pestle, after which they mix with it pepper, honey, and certain other balms

and herbs so that it should not nauseate them: and then … each dips up

with his finger a morsel of the immolated child. And when they have thus

consummated their cannibal act, they pray, as follows to God: 'We have

not let ourselves be tricked by the Archon of Desire but have harvested

our brother's error.' And they believe this to be the perfect Mass.

(Epiphanius 159-161)

These descriptions provide a fully literal and cannibalistic—if not also vampiric—

interpretation of Christ's mysteries—especially those pertaining to his blood and

immortality.

Epiphanius (judgmentally) compares this ritual with that of a Christian

community discovered in Orleans France in 1022 A.D. According to their methods, the

"'Food from Heaven', as they call it, is produced … on certain nights of the year [when]

they come together in a designated house, each bearing in hand a lantern …

They chant the names of the demons in the manner of a litany, until

suddenly they see that the Devil has arrived among them in the likeness of some beast. And he having been seen somehow by them all, they put out the lanterns and immediately every man grabs whatever woman comes to hand, even though she may be his own mother, his sister, or a nun, without thought of sin; for such tumbling is regarded by them as holiness and religion. And when a child is begotten in this utterly filthy way, they reassemble on the eighth day and, kindling a large fire in their midst, pass it, like the old heathens, through that fire, and thus cremate it. The ashes then are collected and kept with as much reverence as Christians reserve for the blessed Body of Christ; and to those on the point of death they administer a portion of these ashes as a viaticum. Moreover, there is such power in those ashes, infused by the Devil's deceit, that when anyone tainted by that heresy happens to have tasted even the smallest quantity, his mind can hardly thereafter be turned from … to the way of truth. (qtd. by Campbell, *Creative* 167-68; Leisgang,).

Reflecting on these rituals, Campbell explains that "there was … an extremely archaic biological theory … that is in fact largely held to this day … namely, that the miracle of reproduction is effected in the womb through a conjunction of semen and menstrual blood" (*Creative* 161). This is believed because "the interruption of the woman's periods during pregnancy conduces the assumption that the blood withheld was being formed into the body of the child by virtue of the influence upon it of the sperm" (161). For this reason "menstrual blood and … semen were at once feared and revered … as the very vehicles of life" (161). With this premise, they believed that through their striking (abortive) practices they were "increasing in themselves the force of this life without allowing it to produce new bodies of bondage ... [which] they believed [was the] divine work of redemption" (161).

To avoid a thorough survey of the rituals as they occur throughout the Grail romances, much to the dismay of this author, we turn to a summation in the recent *Arthurian Encyclopedia*:

> In the many works in which this precious vessel appears, the Grail or Holy Grail assumes many forms and functions, although in all cases it retains its basic power as a food-provider or as associated with food consumption at table. In Chrétien, it seems clearly a platter that sustains the old king in the second chamber. In Robert, it is a cup used at table that assumed later characteristics of the Mass chalice and whose service broke the famine. In Wolfram von Eschenbach's *Parzival*, it is a *thing* called a Grail, a stone or *lapsit exillis* that produces an abundance of the most savory foods. In the First Continuation of the *Perceval*, the Rich Grail, floating about the hall, provides good and drink to all in attendance ... Manessier, in his Continuation, depicts the Grail carried by a maiden as in Chrétien. The Welsh *Peredur* presents the gruesome spectacle of a great salver carried by two maidens in which a man's head is found swimming in blood. In the *Perlesvause,* the Grail is, as in Robert's poem, the vessel used by Joseph to collect the blood of Christ, but it causes rejuvenation and is carried in a ceremony before Gauvain, who perceives in it visions of a chalice, then the form of a child (signifying the real body of Christ), and finally the Crucifixion. In the Prose *Lancelot,* the Grail assumes the shape of a

> chalice. In the *Quest del Saint Graal*, as in Malory, it becomes
> synonymous with the beatific vision and is an object of quest by Bors,
> Perceval, and the pure knight, Galahad. (213)

In each story, a ritual is associated with the grail (or head) and with the blood. It was De Boron who made the connection between the Grail and Christ explicit. For him "the Grail is nothing other than the bowl from which Jesus ate the lamb at the Last Supper, and in which, according to the supposedly apocryphal Gospel of Nicodemus, Joseph of Arimathea gathered the blood of the Crucified" (Strauss 223). Similarly, by his telling, "The bleeding lance was the one used by Longinus to deal the fatal blow to the Savior. [And] supposedly, Joseph brought the Grail to England, where his descendants … guarded it. The Fisher King is the latest descendant … Perceval's grandfather" (223).

In the Medieval period, especially in the context of the Grail romances, it was believed that "Christ's blood contained both the 'soul', and possibly even the Divinity of the Savior … unlimited powers of healing, and it was [seen as] a means of transmitting a direct apprehension of God" (Mathews 11). Additional "iconographical sources represent Christ in the wine press, recalling His statement 'l am the True Vine' … depicting the blood spurting forth to feed the … Christian believers" (11). Matthews suggests, "when one realizes that behind the word 'sangreal', used by the later romancers, lie the words 'Saint Grail' (Holy Grail) and 'Sang Real' (Royal Blood), one can see how easily the life giving properties of the blood could be extended to include the cup in which it had been carried (11).

Though the first remembered Grail author, Chrétien, did not explicitly connect the dish with Christ, he articulated the essential narrative of his sacrifice with an emphasis on the blood:

> He became man for the sins of the entire world … for the entire world was corrupt. It is true that He was God and man, and was conceived by the Holy Spirit and born of the Virgin' In Him God took on flesh and blood, and His divinity was clothed in the flesh of man. This is a certainty, and he who will not believe it will never look on His face. He was born of the Virgin Lady and took on both the form and the soul of man with His holy divinity. Truly on such a day as this was He put on the cross. He then delivered all His friends from hell. Most holy was that death which saved the living and the dead, bringing them from death to life. (415).

This is what all of the rituals express—that the blood (and body) of Christ's sacrifice is the way through which participants may be saved from death.

Before we continue into a consideration of the Grail in the context of these narratives, we should continue into the story of Herakles' death, after which we will finally compare the stories of these two great Classical and Abrahamic heroes.

Heracles Dies and Becomes Immortal

Perhaps it is for the very reason that Herakles' death is not synchronized with Prometheus' liberation that the imagination has found it more difficult to consider Christ's liberation of Adam in the context of Herakles' liberation of his progenitor. This is despite the fact that the deaths of Christ and Herakles have been repeatedly compared, as these pages will show. It is the overlap of the death of Jesus and liberation of Adam in the story of Christ that has encouraged this chapter's—and dissertation's—dual focus on the liberation of progenitors and resurrections of hero-saviors. In the Christian narrative the two events are on top of one another in one climactic sequence. The complication with exclusively comparing the sequence of Christ's transcendence of mortal limitation with the series of events associated with Heracles' death is that, as we have seen, many if not most of Heracles' stories have been taken as confrontations and triumphs against death. In fact some have even said that the successful completion of all the labors is what earned the hero his immortality. Most importantly for us, the Golden Apples in the Garden of Hesperides, with which the story of Prometheus' liberation is distinctly entwined, is one of the stories that many authors have recognized as a clear confrontation with death and conquest for immortality—essentially symbolized by the apple itself. But we have already entertained the Hesperian tale. What is left is to consider the hero's penultimate confrontation with death—not his underworld journey and return in pursuit of the Hell Hound, which has been compared with Christ's harrowing of hell—his murder, cremation, and resurrection.

To summarize before expanding: Heracles is mortally wounded by putting on a cloak given to him by Deianira, his wife, who he won with a cornucopia from Achelous. This was after Meleager, whose life had been entangled with a fire-brand, asked him to marry her during his descent through Hades. This cloak his wife later gave him was coated in the blood of the centaur, Nessus, which was poisoned by the Hydra-blood on an arrow shot by Heracles. As the story goes, when Heracles and Deianira had come to an unfordable river, the centaur offered to carry the maiden across, but for molesting his wife on the other side, Heracles, loosed his arrows. The dying centaur deceived Deianira by telling her that his blood would act as a sort of love potion. When she was insecure that Heracles was interested in another woman, she gave him the blood-coated cloak as the centaur had suggested. Later, when he put it on, he could not take it off. Feeling the bloody coat burning his skin like fire, he knew he would soon die. Taking the authority of his own death, he had a funeral pyre built. A traveler lit the pyre for him, and he gave his bow as a gift—the bow required to win the war at Troy. All that was mortal burned away and his divine-self ascended to heaven, where he married the cupbearer of the gods, Hebe, daughter of Zeus and Hera. When he drank the divine nectar he became the first and only (classical) hero to achieve immortality.

In the scene leading to Heracles' death, after the centaur had begun molesting his wife on the other side of the river, "[Herakles] pierced Nessus with his arrows" (Pseudo-Hyginus 34). "Out from his breast the barbed point stuck. / He wrenched the shaft away, / and blood from both wounds spurted, blood that / bore Lernaei's [Hydra's] poison" (Ovid, *Metamorphoses* 9. 152-155). "While dying he still had time to deceive Heracles' wife. He wished, said the liar, to do her a last favor" (Kerenyi *Heroes* 200). "'I'll not die unavenged' (Ovid, *Metamorphoses* 9. 156). "Nessus, knowing how poisonous the arrows were ... drew out some of his blood and gave it to Deianeira, telling her it was a love-charm. If she wanted her husband not to desert her, she should have his garments smeared with this blood. Deianeira, believing him, kept it carefully" (Pseudo-Hyginus, 34), "in her house, hidden in a bronze cauldron" (Kerenyi, *Heroes* 201).

Eventually an occasion arose in which Deianira became insecure and fearfully jealous of another woman. Thus, "In fear lest Herakles desire Iole more than herself [Deianira], and in her belief that the blood of Nessos was truly a love-potion, she doused the robe with it" (Pseudo-Apollodorus 2. 157). "She chose to send the shirt … to fortify her husband's failing love. Not knowing what she gave, she entrusted her sorrow to Lichas (ignorant no less) and charged him with soft words to take it to her lord" (Ovid, *Metamorphoses* 9. 129 & 158). "Without suspicion, he accepted the splendid poisoned robe which Deianira, also without suspicion, had sent him to wear when he made his thank-offering to Zeus" (Kerenyi, *Heroes* 202). "And Hercules receiving the gift and on his shoulders wore, in ignorance, Echidna Lernaea's [Hydra's] poisoned gore. The flame was lit; he offered words of prayer and incense, pouring on the marble altar wine from the bowl. That deadly force grew warm. Freed by the flame, it seeped and stole along, spreading through all the limbs of Hercules" (Ovid, *Metamorphoses* 9. 129 & 158). "For the arrow's barb had carried the poison of the adder [Hydra], and when the shirt became heated, [it] attacked the flesh of the body" (Diodorus Siculus 4. 38. 1). "He could not tear away the poisoned material" (Kerenyi, *Heroes* 202).[206] "He ripped off his flesh along with it"(Pseudo-Apollodorus 2. 157). Ovid offers his account:

> While he still could, that hero's heart of his stifled his groans, but when the agony triumphed beyond endurance, he threw down the altar, and his cries of anguish filled the glades of Oeta. Desperately he tried to tear the fatal shirt away; each tear tore his skin too, and, loathsome to relate, either it stuck, defeating his attempts to free it from his flesh, or else laid bare his lacerated muscles and huge bones. Why, as the poison burned, his very blood bubbled and hissed as when a white-hot blade is quenched in icy water. Never an end! The flames licked inwards, greedy for his guts; dark

perspiration streamed from every pore; his scorching sinews crackled; the

blind rot melted his marrow. (Ovid, *Metamorphoses* 9. 129 & 158)

And so the great hero "recognized the sign [of his death]" (Kerenyi, *Heroes* 202), "He

had himself taken to Mount Oeta in Trachis where he built a great pyre" (Mayerson 315).

The grass on mount Oita "was never mown. As Milton recounts, "Alcides/ … felt

the envenomed robe, and tore / Through pain up by the roots Thessalian pines" (Milton

II. 541-43). Once it was built, "Heracles sat on the great pile of wood and awaited some

friend, some traveler on the road leading over Mount Oita to Delphi. Philoktetes, the son

of Pois, came by, he who was one day to cry out the same words in the like pains, 'Light

the fire, good man, light the fire!'" (Kerenyi, *Heroes* 203). According to comparable

variants, "it was Poias himself, searching for his strayed sheep on the mountain, who lit

the pyre" (203). "As the funeral pyre blazed up, there was a flash of lightning, and amid

peals of thunder, a cloud passed under his body and bore him to Mount Olympus … the

pyre … burned away his mortal nature" (Mayerson 315).[207] Peregrinos presents his

ultimate suicide as a demonstration of "philosophical courage" (Stafford 127) that one

might compare with the death of Socrates—whose death was also contingent with a cup.

The river itself "sprang forth from the mountain" (Kerenyi, *Heroes* 202) to aid

Herakles against the fire that consumed him" (Herodotus, Histories 7. 198. 1). But it was

"in vain, for to burn was Heracles' own will" (Kerenyi, *Heroes* 202). "The reward for

[lighting the pyre] was great, nothing less than the bow of Heracles. … Only by means of

this bow could Troy one day be taken" (203). "Before he died, he left his bow and arrows

to Poeas, or to his son Philoctetes" (Mayerson 315). It is said that "from the pyre of

Herakles a swarm of locusts flew out which ravaged the countryside like a plague before they were destroyed." (summary from Photius, 190; Ptolemy). "Deianeira … had already taken her life" (Kerenyi, *Heroes* 202).

According to Kerenyi, this spot is still venerated. "Ever since the pyre of Heracles blazed for the first time and, surrounded by a stone curb which has preserved the ashes to our own day, was lit again at his festivals, the spot bore the name Phrygia, 'the burned place'" (Kerenyi, *Heroes* 202). "A master painter of vases, and probably before him the author of a satyr-play, immortalized the search or Heracles' bones; they represented it as made by satyrs, who leaped back in fright when they found the hero's armor empty on the pyre, which was not completely burned out" (203). Perhaps the empty pyre and armor reminds us of the empty tomb and/or sepulcher of Christ, which we will consider in the following sections.

The ascent of Heracles to Olympus had been foretold. After Heracles strangled two serpents in his crib, the seer Teiresias told his father "what chance of fortunes Herakles should encounter … [and that] He [Herakles] in peace for all time shall enjoy, in the home of the blessed, leisure unbroken, a recompense most choice for his great deeds of toil" (Pindar 1. 61 ff). He was also told he will "win" "the lovely Hebe for his bride, and [share] his marriage feast beside Zeus, son of Kronos, [where he] shall live to grace his august law" (Pindar 1. 61 ff). According to Philostratus the Elder, before he died, he was told he would "live with them in the sky, drinking, and embracing the beautiful Hebe (Youth); for you are to marry the youngest of the gods and the one most revered by them, since it is through her that they also are young" (2. 20).

As Mayerson writes, "His end was tragic, and yet, by the agency of fire, it spelled the beginning of a new life among the immortals" (315). "Heracles, became young again, almost a child, [and] went with Pallas Athene over the summit of Oita in a four horse chariot. Astrologers knew that he passed through the gate of heaven which is in Scorpios, close to the archer, the centaur that was transported to the skies" (Kerenyi, *Heroes* 203). And "so the mortal part of Heracles was burned away and he gained immortality, ascending to Olympus, there to be reconciled with Hera and to marry her daughter Hebe" (Morford 371). In a Roman variant, the burning symbolized a direct craving for Hebe, "The passion of Hercules [Herakles], all afire for divine Hebe, tasted [her] first raptures after he had burned on an Oetean pyre" (Propertius, 1. 13).

Meanwhile, not unlike Christ after his death, "the phantom of the earthly Heracles—for there was no forgetting even of the wanderer on earth with his toils—his eidolon, went to the underworld" (Kerenyi *Heroes* 204). As Homer recounts, when he stared into the cavernous underworld, Odysseus met "the mighty Herakles (Heracles)— his phantom; for he himself among the immortal gods takes his joy in the feast, and has to wife Hebe, of the fair ankles, daughter of great Zeus and of Hera, of the golden sandals" (*Odyssey* 11. 601).

Having now introduced the story of Herakles' death, we should consider key parallels with the story from within Herakles' extended narrative. Perhaps a majority of Herakles' adventures relate to the struggle of immortality, "As a hunter, Heracles did not exterminate ordinary beasts of the earth, like Orion, nor appear in the role of lord of the underworld as a hunter-god; what he hunted was apparently death" (Kerenyi, *Heroes* 141). In the story of the Nemean Lion he awakes from unconsciousness "on the thirtieth day, [and] crowned himself with wild celery, like one come from the grave, for graves were garlanded with this plant. Later, the victors at the Nemean Games … wore the same garland" (142). As discussed in the chapter on Prometheus, celery grew over the grave of the sacrificed third brother of the Kabeiroi, with whom we have recently found congruities in the form of Christ's purple cloak and wreathed head. In one of the footnotes of the last section, I also noted the potential that the thirty silver pieces for which Jesus was sold out to the Romans may relate to the lunar cycle, which has long been associated with resurrection. Here in this story of Christ, he sleeps for thirty days and afterwards adorns himself with a living symbol of death.

In a story we have discussed in association with the Golden Apples, he offered himself as sacrificial tribute to put an end to human sacrifice. Kerenyi describes the story in which "the tellers of the tale have transformed Osiris, god of the dead, into the tyrant, Busiris. This king was in the habit of sacrificing strangers to Zeus, and devoured human flesh himself … it was alleged that Egypt had been visited by nine years of drought. … When Heracles arrived in Memphis, he was made captive; he let it happen" (*Heroes* 167). Then that he defeated the King of death.

In another story he took Death head on. Kerenyi writes, "Thanatos, Death … [had] come to fetch queen Aklestis" who had sacrificed her life for her husband's just before Herakles arrived. When Death arrived behind the sepulcher, to drag the dead queen away with him. … The hero learn[ed] what has happened. [And ran] after the funeral procession and … tears Death's prey from him" (*Heroes* 156).

As in the Harrowing of Hell, sometimes referred to as "Hades," Herakles descends to and returns from the underworld. "The final test of the divinity of the hero, the last attempt to send him to his death, was the task to capture the hound of Hades from the underworld" (177). Before he could partake in the journey, he first had to be initiated into the Eleusinian mysteries, which were long associated with the dissolution of one's mortal fears. "Long after this story arose," Herakles continued to be associated with death and the mysteries. For example, he was represented on a "sarcophagus and a marble urn found in the neighborhood of Rome. There Heracles is sitting, with his head veiled, on a throne and having performed over him the sacred ceremonies that would give him back purity in the eyes of gods and men" (*Heroes* 178). "On the closed basket, which contained the secret objects used by the cult" Demeter "the foundress and patroness of the Mysteries, [is] sitting" (178).[208]

The last story of Herakles' I want to bring into consideration is the Roman narrative in which he faces Cacus. Kerenyi recounts, "In those days a son of Volcanus … had his dwelling on the Aventine; this was Cacus whose shape was only half human. He was a fire-breathing murderer, well worthy of his father, whose power was felt not far from the Aventine in the pyres where corpses were burned" (*Heroes* 169). When Heracles was passing through with the cattle of Geryoneus, the fire-breathing giant desired his cows. The "imprisoned beasts bellowed when the herd … was moving [and] Heracles turned angrily back and ran to the Aventine, following the lowing of the cattle. Cacus was terrified and lowered a block of stone on chains before the entrance to the cave" (169). Heracles then "tore a great rock from the hill, so that the cave was suddenly unroofed" (169). And what he found was like the underworld, "the realm of the departed" (170). The Hero "laid hands on the ogre, who vainly was vomiting flame through the mirk, got a quick hold, knotted him double, and throttled him" (Virgil, *Aeneid*, 8.195). Then he squeezed his throat; he writhed his neck around, / and in a knot his cripple members bound; Then from their sockets tore his burning eyes" (8.195). And "once the doors were torn open and the dark den exposed, [he brought] to light the cattle which Cacus had stolen" (8.195).

With the bursting roof of the cave, the vomiting fire and the bursting eyes of Vulcan's son we recognize an allusion to the volcano, which we discussed in the context of Prometheus unbound from Mt. Elbruz. If we recall that the liberator of Prometheus was a descendent of Io, a cow, we recognize the liberation of cattle—like that of Prometheus—as a reference to the liberation of humanity. This is just one of the many examples through which Herakles and Christ are presented as liberators of others in addition to themselves.

The motif of prison/cave-escape has recurred consistently throughout the dissertation. We have seen it by now in versions of Prometheus' liberation, Herakles' return from the underworld, Plato's Allegory of the Cave, the rescue of Adam, Harrowing of Hell, and Christ's own resurrection from the tomb. Another story remains that, I believe, draws close parallels with both the resurrection of Christ and Herakles' defeat of Cacus: the escape of Odysseus from Polyphemus' cave in Book IX of *The Odyssey*. My sense is that a consideration of this story will help us transition into a more direct reflection on Heracles, Christ, and the motifs they share.

To start with the framework for the story of Polyphemus' cave, we should recognize that it is in the same book (IX) that the story of Troy's fall was told. The challenge at Troy was the penetration of its great "cyclopean walls" (Byrne 2).[209] The reason they are called "cyclopean walls" is because the stones seem too big to have been moved by men, and similarly, in Book IX, only the Cyclops can move the doorway of stone. According to legend the walls of Troy had been built by Poseidon, father of

Polyphemus.[210] To win the Trojan War, it was Odysseus who crafted a way through the walls. In his encounter with Polyphemus, he again conceived of a plan to penetrate the cyclopean boundaries of stone—this time to escape.[211] As Atlas retrieved the Golden Apples for Herakles, the walls of Troy and the cavern of Polyphemus were opened by their own guards. Similarly, it was not Christ who rolled away the stone of his cave.

As we will see, the beginning of Book IX and the scene in Polyphemus' cave carry the essential elements of the Christian, Grail, and Classical rituals. Odysseus opens it with a toast:

> Alkinoos, king and admiration of men,
>
> how beautiful this is, to hear a minstrel
>
> gifted as yours: a god he might be, singing!
>
> There is no boon in life more sweet, I say,
>
> than when a summer joy holds all the realm,
>
> and banqueters sit listening to a harper
>
> in a great hall, by rows of tables heaped
>
> with bread and roast meat,
>
> while steward goes to dip up wine and brim your cups again/
>
> Here is the flower of life, it seems to me!" (Homer IX. 2-11).[212]

Not only does the great adventurer refer directly to the cup of wine as the "flower of life" and sweetest "boon," the scene also displays bread, meat, wine-steward, and music. Later, when he describes his defeat of Polyphemus, he uses "an ivy bowl of … dark drink" (IX. 375), "wine" (IX. 377), "pure and fiery" (219), "honey smooth" (223),[213] given to him in a "solid silver wine bowl" (217). Upon giving it to Polyphemus, he called the drink "nectar and ambrosia" (IX. 390).

As in the story of Christ, cannibalism is an essential theme. Where Christ is eaten, so too are Odysseus' men. And as Christ traveled with his twelve apostles, Odysseus had entered the cave with his "twelve best" (IX. 210). As the story of Christ's resurrection transpires over three nights, so too does this scene in the cave. Though Odysseus is most frequently depicted as a captain like Jason or warrior like Achilles, to escape the cave, not unlike Christ, he is a carpenter.[214] In the cave he saw a "club, or staff/ … An olive tree, felled green and left to season/ for Kyklops' hand. And it was like a mast/ … I chopped out a six foot section of this pole/ and set it down before my men, who scraped it; / and when they had it smooth, I hewed again/ to make a stake with pointed end" (IX 356-352). Once it was crafted he "held this/ in the fire's heart and turned it, toughening it" (IX. 346-356). This reminds us of other narratives in which gods placed children in fires to increase their resistance to death. The olive club that will become his weapon also reminds us of Herakles.

It might be noted that he almost stabbed Polyphemus where the midriff "holds the liver" (IX. 317), but he realized they would never be able to "move his ponderous doorway slab aside" (IX. 320). Here the liver reminds us again of Prometheus, whose liver was no longer sacrificed once Herakles set him free. Once the one-eyed giant is asleep, they proceed to heat the olive-spike in embers and "bore that great eye socket … eyelid and lash … [and] pierced ball" (9.420).[215] We should recognize the fire-brand again, another symbol of Prometheus. Where the olive club is ablaze in this story, Herakles' club is dormant and the face of Cacus spews fire. The bored fire-brand and the fire coming from the giant's face seem to offer complimentary details that describe something like the production of flames with the fire-drill of Prometheus.

In addition to the Heraclean olive club and Promethean fire-brand, the eye-destruction of Polyphemus and Cacus is found in the story of Orion and Oenopion. Oenopion's name is an allusion to wine, and when Orion came to his house he greeted him with hospitality. The hunter became drunk and tried to sleep with his daughter, for which Oenopion punctured the eyes of Orion. The hunter is then given a Kabeiroi-like helper, Kedalion, who leads him to the sunrise where his eyes are healed. The story this draws into immediate consideration is that of Horus, whose eye was destroyed by Seth and restored at the sunrise.[216] With Busiris, we have seen substantial overlap between the Egyptian myths and those of Herakles. What the stories of Horus and Orion especially add is the step in the story where the wounded eye returns, which suggest that the narrative is in fact not about the acquisition of sight—not its loss. From this angle the puncturing of the eyelid might also be compared with the ripping of the veil in the story of Christ, the removal of the splinter in front of one's eye (or in Buddhist terms "dust").

As the stories of popping eyes clearly relate to seeing, so too does the ripping of the veil represent the expansion of seeable horizons. My suspicion is that these stories emanate the common religious belief that fleshly senses limit perception to the corporeal world. Consistent with this theory, both Cacus and the Cyclopes are distinctly brutish. Odysseus anticipates the Cyclopes as "all outward power, a wild man, ignorant" (IX. 229-231). Such an outward description of the giant's (whose flesh eyes would be destroyed) as limited to the life of flesh suggests that an attack on their eye is simultaneously an attack on their outwardly and embodied emphasis on life. My read is that the mythic destruction of the fleshly eyes reflects the religious attempt to transcend the cyclopean tunnel vision effect that our fleshly senses were believed to have had on perception. Where on one hand the stories are about destroying the eyes, they are also about liberation from imprisoning caves.

On one hand the stories convey a liberation from matter by way of the exit of cavernous prisons, but, in the case of Christ and Odysseus (and the Buddha if allowed into the conversation), such a liberation is contingent with a transcendence of a self-referential point of view. Little needs to be said of Christ's urges to abandon selfish and worldly ways. In the story of the Buddha's enlightenment, his penultimate insight was the triune recognition of *Sunyatta, Paticca Samupadda,* and *Anatta*—the three gems. The first typically translates as "emptiness," the second as "dependent co-arising," and the third as emptiness of self, often translated as "no-self." As mentioned, the path towards enlightenment is often associated with the loss of dust from one's eye. Famously, in the story of Polyphemus, Odysseus escapes because he tells the giant called "death" his name is "Nohbdy" (IX. 397). And it is because the Cyclopes call him "nobody" (446), and "no man" (440) that he is able to escape.

The Micro-Narratives of Hero-Saviors and their Macro-Narratives with the Progenitors

Our goal is now not to compare and contrast Heracles and Christ. We have already engaged the consistency of their associations among Roman and later European Christians: both were born of virgin mothers, both died and were resurrected; both were champions of humanity before reuniting with the divine. And for those seeking similarities the labors have appeared similar to the inner challenges of Christ—the cynic and Stoic Heracles is especially interpretable this way. What we should now turn to address is the way stories of the hero-saviors align—not just connect or overlap—with the stories of their progenitors. What I mean to show is that the stories of the two saviors individually mime the meta-narrative of the stories our hero-saviors and progenitors combine to create. This is to say, the stories of Christ and Heracles depict entry into mortal materiality in a way that sets up their eventual transcendence there from.

Before his respective transcendence of the worldly, Christ was buried in a cave sealed by stone (Mark 15:56 Matthew 27:59; Luke 23:53. John 19:41). This burial was associated with that of Adam's (Malan, *First Book of Adam and Eve* XLII). Similarly, as I interpret the burial of Adam and Christ as the imprisonment of psyche in matter, Dio Chrysostom interpreted the exchange of Herakles divine lion-skin with irremovable bloody clothes as his corruption into inescapable flesh. Following Heracles blunder of the blood-cloak, his soul is carried to Olympus where he will receive the drink of immortality. Following Christ's burial he is resurrected before his undying form ascends to heaven.

As these symbolic entries into flesh/matter immediately precede the transcendence achieved by Christ and Heracles, I would like to suggest that their immaculate conceptions and births similarly represent an entry into mortal materiality to which they will ultimately respond.

The Son of God, Christ, was conceived in a stone cave. Heracles, also the Son of God, was similarly conceived without a father of mere flesh. Conception, in these immaculate examples, is the entry of divine seed into mortal flesh. Stepping back, one might see that all births will appear as an entry of soul into matter to an individual following the Classical, Abrahamic and philosophical traditions that saw body as animated by the energy of psyche. Conceivably, the moment of animation (conception or birth) would have been seen as the moment of entry. From the point of view of such Classical traditions as imagined psyche as imprisoned in the body it animates, the birth of Heracles might similarly be seen as an entry into the prison of mortal-material-flesh. As if to accentuate this interpretation, according to the Eastern Orthodox tradition, Christ was both born and conceived within caves (as well as breast-fed by his mother and trained in carpentry by his father).

In suggesting that the birth and death of Christ and Heracles establishes the mortal and material limitations they later transcend I am suggesting that the births of these liberators should be seen as mimetic with the creation of first humans and the bondage of mythic progenitors. The birth sequences of Heracles and Christ—like the creation and bondage of Adam and Prometheus—convey the entry and imprisonment of divine essence into material flesh. As these hero-saviors liberate their progenitors from material restraints, they also liberate themselves from the limitations of the mortal bodies into which they were born. In this way the self-liberation of the hero-saviors as well as the liberation of their progenitors can be seen as synchronized micro and macro-narratives. The micro-narrative would be the story of Christ (or Heracles) coming into the bondage of life and death followed by his eventual liberation. The macro narrative would be the story of Adam (or Prometheus) initiating the bondage of life and death for all humanity followed by the eventual liberation of these progenitors and humanity from said bondage with the guidance of Heracles and Christ.

We can now consider the hero-saviors in the context of this dissertation's two essential motifs: liberation from or beyond matter and the roles of associated elixirs.

Review of the Evidence: Liberation of Progenitors from Material Restraint

As has been stated and shown many times, the hero-saviors liberated their progenitors from material restraint: Prometheus was shackled to stone and Adam was buried in stone. As Christ was Adam's savior and Prometheus addressed Heracles as such, (Aeschylus, Fragment 114 *Prometheus Unbound* from Plutarch, Life of Pompey 1). Herakles broke the bedrock and snapped the fetters of Prometheus (Zissos and Flaccus 5. 155 ff), finally setting the great man free (Hesiod, *Theogony* 511). Christ's rescue of Adam is presented in two forms – his baptism by way of Christ's blood, which freed him from the stone (*Cave of Treasures: Crucifixion*), and the Harrowing of Hell, which emphasizes the rescue of Adam (*Gospel of Nicodemus* VI. XXII- IX. XXV. As the liberation of Adam was God's will, the liberation of Prometheus was permitted by Olympian Zeus (Hesiod, *Theogony* 511 ff).

The freeing of the progenitors from stone restrictions reverberates in the liberation of the hero-saviors themselves. Heracles' mortal part is burned away (Morford 371; Mayerson 315) and his pyre is found empty of bones (Kerenyi, *Heroes* 203). Christ's sepulcher was similarly emptied, and in his case, the stone was rolled away and the cave emptied (Luke 24:2-3).[217] This followed his death in which the temple veil ripped, the earth shook, and stones split (Matthew 27: 51-52). This kind of liberation from stone in the context of death is seen in Heracles' rescue of Askalaphus and Theseus from the stones that kept them imprisoned in the underworld (Kerenyi 180-181). The motif in Christ and Adam's departure from a cave can be seen in Heracles' own escape from the underworld (with the hell hound), the rescue of Chiron from his wounded state in a cave (Pseudo-Apollodorus 2.83-87), and the breaking out of Cacus from his cavern of the dead

(Kerenyi, *Heroes* 169). We have also discussed versions of Prometheus' restraint in which his prison was a cave.

The liberation from stone, cave, and flesh is contingent on their transcendence of corporeal concerns. The Stoics and Cynics interpreted Heracles as an ideal philosopher who maintained control over his emotions and appetites in favor of a more altruistic mode of being (qtd. by Stafford 123, Xenophon *Memorabilia e.1.21-34*; qtd. by Stafford 126, Apuleius 22.3-4). In fact, in one story, it was even Prometheus who told him to give up his worldly concerns (qtd. by Stafford 125, Caizzi fr. 27). The early Christian Pierre de Ronsard even made the explicit connection between Heracles' confrontation of monsters representing vice and sin, which Christ also confronted (qtd. by Stafford 205, II. 173-82). Heracles defeat of Antaeus has perhaps been most associated with his confrontation with earthen-flesh-inspired lust (qtd. by Stafford 203, Fulgentius 2.4). Christ's call to leave behind worldly possessions (Luke 12:33) is one of his better-known urges, which corresponds with the Christian tendency towards virgin purity and the extreme focus on such purity shared by Christian groups like the Cistercians, Cathars, Quakers and Puritans.

Review of the Evidence: Role of Elixirs

Looking more closely at the liberation of heroes and progenitors we recognize that the stories have been consistently colored if not actuated by symbolic elixirs. Starting with the Progenitors, most directly, Adam is said to have been freed from his burial place in stone—at Golgotha—by Christ's blood (and water), which poured from his body like a fountain that baptized him (*Cave of Treasures: Crucifixion*). As Christ freed Adam, Heracles, who slayed the Caucasian eagle, freed Prometheus. His ability to slay the eagle was dependent on his hydra-blood tipped arrows (Pseudo-Apollodorus 2.80). In this way, the hydra-blood was the breakthrough actuator that enabled Heracles to free Prometheus.

By one line of reasoning I should stop this section here and say "done," as, by my read, these gestures are definitive. In the great climax of the great macro-narratives made up by the restraint and liberation of the progenitors, the actuating agent is fluid. By another line of reasoning, this interpretation would be more powerful with validation from extended ripples and qualities of these stories (and their associated religions). In the mind of the author, the crucial summation was just delivered – the liberation of Adam and Prometheus has been shown as a liberation from material constraint by the powerful blood carried by their saviors. With this in mind, we will pursue further details. I pause for these statements to be sure that the additional details to follow are seen as supportive evidence and not experienced as dilutive addendums.

Starting with Heracles, the hydra-blood was also responsible for Chiron's agreement to replace Prometheus, which was requisite for his freedom. As the hydra-blood was responsible for the wounding, death and liberation of Chiron and Prometheus, it was also responsible for the wounding and death of Heracles, which liberated him from the mortal world. His eventual apotheosis, however, was dependent on the drink of Hebe, the nectar of the gods (Philostratus the Elder 2. 20), which symbolized the restoration of his relationship with the divine company.

To follow the image of the imbibed elixir, we return to the scene in which Chiron was wounded, when Heracles drank the divine wine of Dionysos—his half brother and partner in war against the giants. He also gained divine energy by drinking Hera's milk, with whom he would later reconcile (to many, Hebe is to Hera what young Persephone was to Demeter). As we can see, directly and indirectly, these elixirs led towards liberation from material limitation and a return of Heracles to the divine graces of Hera, Zeus and the Olympians.

Another example of divine elixir that appears in the story is that of Prometheus' blood, which dripped on the earth when he was restrained and caused flowers to grow forth. Medea then used these flowers to create a balm that enabled Jason to steal the Golden Fleece and his father (Aeson) to be restored to youth (Apollonius 3. 844).

We should also consider the quest for the golden apples, understood as a quest for immortality, in which Prometheus took part. Not only did Herakles cross the western waters in a cup-boat, he also cracked a stone in the garden from which water sprung (Apollonius 4. 1390). How could this not remind us of the spring in Eden that went dry with the Fall? The dehydrated Argonauts drank from this spring, after giving their gifts of wine (4. 1390). In some versions, the snake defending the apples was sprinkled with honey (Virgil, *Aeneid* 4. 480) and subdued with wine (Kerenyi, *Heroes* 176) or killed with hydra-blood (arrows) (Apollonius 4. 1390). The name of the serpent, Ladon, was even shared with the garden's river (Kerenyi, *Heroes* 148). This is not unlike the hydra herself, the serpentine monster responsible for the blood whose name that essentially means water, *hydra* (*hydro*).[218] I consider these details strong evidence that we should be recognizing these fluids, or more generally, fluid, as actuators of freedom, divinization, and the restoration of communion with the divine. Most immediately, Heracles' conjunction, his marriage—his union—is with Hebe, the goddess of nectar herself. His marriage to her represents his union with the divine company.

The story of Christ similarly accentuates the roles of elixirs and fluids. We have reflected on the baptism of Adam with his blood, and though Christ is not himself liberated from his cave by way of blood, it was this blood that became seen as a vehicle of liberation for all Christians in the form of mass or communion (*Arthurian Encyclopedia* 213; Campbell *Primitive* 24). His blood has been called the water of life (Malan, *First Book of Adam and Eve* XXXVIII. 5-6), it was written in Leviticus that life is in blood (17:11), and in Matthew that it is Christ's blood which forgives sin (26:26-28). Before his death, a man distinguished by his jar of water led his disciples to the location of "the last supper" (Luke 22:9-10). There Christ drank his last cup of wine, which he declared he would also drink in heaven—not unlike Heracles drinking nectar (Luke 22:18; Matthew 26:29; Mark 14:25).

The name of the place Christ was captured by the Romans translates as an olive press, which refers to the creation of oil from a stone fruit.[219] On his path towards death, his "true image" was conveyed by blood and sweat, which was wiped from his wet face. His crucifixion was a display of blood (and water), which, as mentioned, trickled down to free Adam. After his death, according to the Grail Romances, Joseph of Arimathea captured his blood for posterity (Strauss 223; *Arthurian Encyclopedia* 213). It was believed that this blood carried the soul and divinity of the savior and sometimes even that it offered access through which god could be directly apprehended (Matthew 11). Perhaps the most famous qualities of this blood, in the Grail Romances, include the ability to heal, sustain life, and/or rejuvenate (Arthurian Encyclopedia 213; Matthews 11). In a truly immaterial way, the grail is even depicted, in many versions, as magically floating through the air (Arthurian Encyclopedia 213).[220]

To step beyond imbibed elixirs, we see the Christian emphasis on baptism—of Adam and initiates (Eliade *Sacred* 134)—mirrored by the role of Heracles as the god of healing hot springs (qtd. by Stafford 185, Pausanias 12.512f). Frazer even associates Christ with Adonis and Tammuz, whose name meant "true son of the deep water (1.007-008). Perhaps reflecting this quality, it is at the Dionysian mouth of hell, where the Jordan pours forth from Mount Hermon, where Jesus states, "upon this rock I will build my church" (Matthew 16:18). Though the words would suggest anemphasis on the stone, the context of this specific rock is that from which water pours. Because this is also a place that was recognized as an entry to the underworld, for which reason animals were sacrificed to Pan here, it has also been common to interpret his statement in the context of the religion Christianity will react against. The specific "rock" ("petra") in this statement has sometimes been interpreted as a pun on the name "Peter," "Petros," whose name sounds like "petra" and became the first Pope. The "rock" has also been interpreted as Peter's preceding recognition of Jesus as Christ, which has been interpreted as the foundation of Christian faith. It has also been recognized that the stone of Mount Hermon is that down which the knowledge bringing angels descended to mate with women. All of these interpretations add display a depth to the scene that, I believe, is further enhanced by the lucid recognition that the stone upon which he claims his entire church will be built is that from which water pours forth.

Christ's miracles relating to water should now be dutifully introduced. Jesus "walked on the water" (Mathew 14:22-23), turned water to wine (John 2:1-11), and healed a blind man through a sequence in which mud was washed from his eyes (John 9:1-12). Again, these details are meant as amplifications of this dissertation's primary interest in the role of fluid in the liberation of Adam and the followers of Christ—including knights of the Grail.

Having looked at the stories of Christ and Heracles in the context of material transcendence and liberation by way of elixir, we should turn now to the work of Einstein. Our final summation of the meta-narrative will then be delivered in the dissertation's conclusion.

Einstein: Steins of Energy

There are two essential contributions of Einstein's on which we will now focus, and they are entwined: one is the recognition of matter as reducible to energy; the other is a synthesis of particle and wave physics into a coherent interpretation of light and matter. The following section will track the story of these transformational insights—where they came from and where they have gone. For any reader familiar with the history and contributions of modern physics, the following section offers few and relatively inconsequential new insights. I am only retelling what is told in every presentation of the history of modern physics—from my undergraduate course in modern physics for engineers to Brian Greene's popular *Elegant Universe* books and TV series.

We should begin with a review of the Newtonian atmosphere in which Einstein was educated. Isaacson writes:

> The foundations of Classical physics had been laid by Isaac Newton in the late seventeenth century. Building on the discoveries of Galileo and others, he developed laws that described a very comprehensible mechanical universe: a falling apple and an orbiting moon were governed by the same rules of gravity, mass, force, and motion. Causes produced

effects, forces acted upon objects, and in theory everything could be
explained, determined, and predicted. As the mathematician and
astronomer Laplace exulted about Newton's universe, "An intelligence
knowing all the forces acting in nature at a given instant, as well as the
momentary positions of all things in the universe, would be able to
comprehend in one single formula the motions of the largest bodies as
well as the lightest atoms in the world; to him nothing would be uncertain,
the future as well as the past would be present to his eyes. (90-91)
Newton had bequeathed to Einstein a universe in which time had an
absolute existence that tick-tocked along independent of objects and
observers, and in which space likewise had an absolute existence. Gravity
was thought to be a force that masses exerted on one another rather
mysteriously across empty space. Within this framework, objects obeyed
mechanical laws that had proved remarkably accurate— almost perfect—
in explaining everything from the orbits of the planets, to the diffusion of
gases, to the jiggling of molecules, to the propagation of sound (though
not light) waves. (223)

Beyond Newton this worldview was shared by Deists and defined the Enlightenment.
Echoing the common sentiment of his peers, "'there is nothing new to be discovered in
physics now,' the revered Lord Kelvin reportedly told the British Association for the
Advancement of Science in 1900. 'All that remains is more and more precise
measurement.' He was wrong" (90).

Meanwhile a number of additional shifts took hold. "Theoretical physics was just coming into its own as an academic discipline in the 1890s, with professorships in the field sprouting up across Europe. Its pioneer practitioners … Max Planck … Hendrik Lorentz … and Ludwig Boltzmann … combined physics with math to suggest paths where experimentalists had yet to tread" (33). The combination of new positions of academic authority combined with the accrued dogmatism towards the Newtonian paradigm to present Einstein with a strong wall of professional and intellectual resistance in the context of both his career and the reception of his theories. However, he was not alone in his non-conformist reactions. "Einstein's life and work reflected the disruption of societal certainties and moral absolutes in the modernist atmosphere of the early twentieth century. Imaginative nonconformity was in the air: Picasso, Joyce, Freud, Stravinsky, Schoenberg, and others were breaking conventional bonds" (3).

Leading up to the revolution beyond the limitations of Newtonian physics and into the theory of Einstein, the Newtonian paradigm began to crack and stretch. As Brian Greene points out, "while his laws described the strength of gravity with great accuracy, Newton was harboring an embarrassing secret: he had no idea how gravity actually works. For nearly 250 years, scientists were content to look the other way when confronted with this mystery" (Greene 1). One solution was to see God through gaps in an otherwise materialistic cosmology. Others, like Einstein, fixated on the problem as a gaping hole in the materialistic worldview. While on one hand, the Newtonian system of thought is defined by mechanical causation, on the other, gravity exerts force without collision. Much to Newton's dismay, it was "action at a distance." As a parent eventually responds to the thousandth question with "just because," to call gravity a "force" was to describe it with a "just because" answer. This made Newton uncomfortable and drove

Einstein towards his brilliant explanation of gravity without "action at a distance."

The complication of Gravity as an unexplained force was compounded by the

theoretical developments of Faraday and Maxwell related to magnetism and electricity.

"In the mid-1800s, Newtonian mechanics was joined by another great advance. The

English experimenter Michael Faraday (1791– 1867), the self-taught son of a

blacksmith,[221] discovered the properties of electrical and magnetic fields" (Isaacson 91).

What he showed is that "an electric current produced magnetism, and … that a changing

magnetic field [can] produce an electric current" (91). This discovery would lead to the

invention of the telegraph by Samuel Morse, even though, "the fundamental science

driving it remained something of a mystery" (Greene 1).

However, "to a Scottish scientist named James Clark Maxwell, the relationship

between electricity and magnetism was so obvious in nature that it demanded unification"

(Greene 1). "Obsessed with this relationship, the Scot was determined to explain the

connection between electricity and magnetism in the language of mathematics" (1). The

culmination of his effort was the discovery of "four elegant mathematical equations that

unified electricity and magnetism in a single force called 'electromagnetism.' And like

Isaac Newton's before him, Maxwell's unification took science a step closer to cracking

the code of the universe" (1).

Though "at first, the electromagnetic field theory developed by Maxwell seemed

compatible with the mechanics of Newton. … By the end of the nineteenth century …

fissures had begun to develop in the foundations of classical physics" (Isaacson 92).

Maxwell's belief had been that "electromagnetic waves, which include visible light, could be explained by classical mechanics— if we assume that the universe is suffused with some unseen, gossamer 'light-bearing ether' that serves as the physical substance that undulates and oscillates to propagate the electromagnetic waves" (Isaacson 92). This theory was furthered by Christiaan Huygens, who argued "light should be seen as a wave" (110). From such perspectives, the role of ether was believed to be like that which "water plays for ocean waves and air plays for sound waves" (92). The problem was, however, that "as hard as [scientists] tried, [they] could not find any evidence of our motion through this supposed light-propagating ether" (92). The most famous evidence that disproved the ether theory came in the form of the Michelson-Morely experiment, which will soon be addressed.

The other essential problem with the Newtonian model that emerged with the study of electromagnetism had to do with the conflict of particles and waves, specifically "the study of radiation— how light and other electromagnetic waves emanate from physical bodies. ... Strange things were happening at the borderline where Newtonian theories, which described the mechanics of discrete particles, interacted with field theory, which described all electromagnetic phenomena" (92). As all objects were reduced to particles within the Newtonian paradigm "Newton had conceived of light as primarily a stream of emitted particles. But by Einstein's day, most scientists accepted the rival theory, propounded by Newton's contemporary Christiaan Huygens, that light should be considered a wave" (110). "James Clerk Maxwell helped to enshrine this wave theory when he successfully conjectured a connection between light, electricity, and magnetism ... [He] found that ... electromagnetic waves had to travel at a certain speed: approximately 186,000 miles per second" (110-111).

From these developments it "became clear that light was the visible manifestation of a whole spectrum of electromagnetic waves" (111). This "includes what we now call AM radio signals ... FM radio signals ... [Wi-Fi] and microwaves ... As the wavelengths get shorter ... they produce the spectrum of visible light, ranging from red ... to violet ... shorter wavelengths produce ultraviolet rays, X-rays, and gamma rays"(111). By the late nineteenth century, "a wide variety of experiments had confirmed the wave theory. ... For example, Thomas Young did a famous experiment, now replicated by high school students, showing how light passing through two slits produces an interference pattern that resembles that of water waves" (110).

Introducing his character, we mentioned that Einstein had been mesmerized by the invisible forces behind the movement of a compass needle. Maxwell had also been inspired by the compass (Greene 1). And as described, Just as "Newton was born in the year that Galileo died" (Whitehead 46) "so Einstein was born the year that Maxwell died" (Isaacson 110). More than this, Einstein "saw it as part of his mission to extend the work of the Scotsman ... a theorist who had shed prevailing biases, let mathematical melodies lead him into unknown territories, and found[ed] a harmony that was based on the beauty and simplicity of a field theory" (110). Einstein's biographer notes, "all of his life, [he] was fascinated by field theories, and he described the development of the concept in a textbook he wrote with a colleague: 'A new concept appeared in physics, the most important invention since Newton's time: the field" (92).

As has been repeated many times, this dissertation, too, is fascinated by field theories, their potential symbolic representation in myths of knowledge, and the philosophical solutions offered by their form/formlessness. For this reason we should follow the 19th century contributions of field theory with a consideration of its pervasiveness in the mind of Einstein. We mentioned that his first encounter with a compass and its relationship with a greater field was one of his most inspirational experiences—scientific and perhaps religious. This fascination with waves and fields continued into his first published essay, which "deals with the theory of liquids" (qtd. by Isaacson 58, Marić). Following the same pattern, his first essay on theoretical physics was entitled, "On the Investigation of the State of the Ether in a Magnetic Field" (24); his PhD dissertation relied "on classical hydrodynamics" (101);[222] and "the first paragraph of his great 1905 paper on special relativity begins with a consideration of the effects of electrical and magnetic fields; his theory of general relativity is based on equations that describe a gravitational field; and at the very end of his life he was doggedly scribbling further field equations" (13-14). His field theory reshaped the human understanding of gravity and for his synthesis of particles and waves in the form of the photon he won the Nobel Prize. Even his description of Brownian Motion, which many take as the first definitive evidence of fundamental particles, was based on their movement across water. From deep beyond his intellect, he "clung to his belief that physics should be based, as he told his old friend Besso, 'on the field concept'" (538).

Complimenting his scientific relationship with waves and fields, he had a deep personal relationship with music, which, on more than one occasion, bled into his work with theory. "His classmate Byland recalled Einstein playing a Mozart sonata ... 'what fire there was in his playing!'" (29). He once said, "Mozart's music is so pure and beautiful that I see it as a reflection of the inner beauty of the universe itself" (14). He even produced a number of his many great insights while playing the violin. A friend recalled that he used to play "late at night, improvising melodies while he pondered complicated problems. … Then, suddenly, in the middle of playing, he would announce excitedly, 'I've got it!' As if by inspiration, the answer to the problem would have come to him in the midst of music" (14). As the secrets of Orpheus flowed from his lyre, the insights of Einstein often flowed from his strings. "Alexander Moszkowski, who wrote a biography of Einstein in 1920 based on conversations with him, noted, 'Music, Nature, and God became intermingled in him in a complex of feeling, a moral unity, the trace of which never vanished'" (14). Once asked if he counted beats he replied, "Heavens no, it's in my blood" (29). "He was awed, both in music and in physics, by the beauty of harmonies" (37). What this dissertation is attempting to show is that the relationship Einstein comprehended between wave/field behavior and beauty—scientific and musical—is also communicated by the symbolic function of elixirs in mythic knowledge narratives.

To return now to the story of Einstein's work, he was especially engaged by Maxwell's discovery of the speed of light. What he was wrestling with was the notion that, if one was traveling towards a moving object, then said object appears to be moving at the combined speed of the observer moving toward the object and the object moving towards the observer. Translated into the 19th century theory of light, it was theorized that light should be experienced as faster when one moves towards it and slower when one moves away. During "the great ether hunt of the late nineteenth century" (111), "scientists devised all sorts of ingenious devices and experiments to detect such differences" (112). But regardless of such experiments, on a theoretical level, Einstein "sensed a conflict between Newton's laws of mechanics and the constancy of the speed of light in Maxwell's equations, [which] instilled in him 'a state of psychic tension' that he found deeply unnerving. … He later recalled. "When young, I used to go away for weeks in a state of confusion" (114-15). He "felt that the situation 'was very depressing.' Scientists found themselves unable to explain electromagnetism using the Newtonian 'mechanical view of nature,' he said, and this 'led to a fundamental dualism which in the long run was insupportable'" (113).

For more empirically minded physicists, the gaping crack in the theory has been remembered in the form of Michelson and Morley's long-repressed findings. What their experiment was designed to witness differences in the speeds of light based on a belief in "the existence of a unique ether frame" (Taylor et. al. 8). If one made this assumption:

> It seemed clear that as the earth orbits around the sun, it must be moving relative to the ether frame, [and that] in principle, this motion relative to the either frame should be easy to detect. One would simply have to measure the speed (relative to the earth) of light traveling in various directions. If one found different speeds in different directions, one would conclude that the earth is moving relative to the either frame, and a simple calculation would give the speed of this motion. (8)

In this quest for ether they devised a contraption that "split a light beam and sent one part back and forth to a mirror at the end of an arm facing in the direction of the earth's movement and the other part back and forth along an arm at a 90-degree angle to it" (Isaacson 112). "The two beams traveled along perpendicular paths and were then reunited to form on interference pattern; this pattern was sensitive to differences in the speed of light in the two perpendicular directions and so could be used to detect any such differences" (Taylor et. al. 9). "To their surprise and chagrin, they could detect absolutely no difference at all" (9). "No matter who looked, or how they looked, or what suppositions they made about the behavior of the ether, no one was able to detect the elusive substance. No matter which way anything was moving, the speed of light was observed to be exactly the same" (Isaacson 112). "In other words, light travels at the same speed see in all directions in many different in our photo frames, and the notion of a unique either frame with this property must be abandoned" (Taylor et. al. 9). Before Einstein's breakthrough solution, he had wanted his research thesis to be on similar work in which he would "measure how fast the earth was moving through the ether" (Isaacson 47). The proposal was rejected and Einstein was alerted to such experiments like that of Michelson and Moreley.

The theoretical tensions we have been describing led to what many have come to call the *Annus Miribilis*, Einstein's "Miracle Year." "In 1905 the 26-year-old Einstein, having failed to prepare an academic position, was supporting himself and his young family by working in a Swiss patent office … working in his spare time, [he] wrote six history-making papers – a creative outburst rivaled only by the work of the young Isaac Newton, (Taylor et. al. 105) who, "holed up at his mother's home … to escape the plague … developed calculus, an analysis of the light spectrum, and the laws of gravity" (Isaacson 93). In 1905, Einstein "laid the foundations for the two great advances of twentieth-century physics: relativity and quantum theory" (3).

"'I promise you four papers,' the young patent examiner wrote his friend. The letter would turn out to bear some of the most significant tidings in the history of science" (1). "At the heart of Einstein's paper were questions that were bedeviling physics … and in fact have done so from the time of the ancient Greeks until today: Is the universe made up of particles, such as atoms? ... Or is it an unbroken continuum . .... If both methods of describing things are valid … what happens when they intersect?" (94). He wrote:

> The first [letter] deals with radiation and the energy properties of light and is very revolutionary. … The second paper is a determination of the true sizes of atoms. … The third proves that bodies on the order of magnitude 1/ 1000 mm, suspended in liquids, must already perform an observable random motion that is produced by thermal motion. Such movement of suspended bodies has actually been observed by physiologists who call it Brownian molecular motion. The fourth paper is only a rough draft at this point, and is an electrodynamics of moving bodies, which employs a modification of the theory of space and time. (93)

"What he did not tell his friend, because it had not yet occurred to him, was that he would produce a fifth paper that year, a short addendum to the fourth, which posited a relationship between energy and mass. Out of it would arise the best-known equation in all of physics: $E = mc^2$" (2). "Icy silence followed the publication" (140),[223] but this was not to last. In these papers was seeded the great breakthroughs in physics.

As one of this dissertation's threads is the story of the atom, we should start with his third paper, which "explained the jittery motion of microscopic particles in liquid by using a statistical analysis of random collisions. In the process, it established that atoms and molecules actually exist" (2). "In 1828 a Scottish botanist, Robert Brown, discovered that tiny pollen grains, when suspended in water and viewed under a microscope, exhibited on a regular jiggling motion, which was later dubbed Brownian motion"

(Taylor et. al. 104). [224] "In the decades that followed, Brownian motion was carefully studied and a variety of explanations were suggested" (104). An explanation for this phenomenon had proven enigmatic until "Einstein showed that even though one collision could not budge a particle, the effect of millions of random collisions per second could explain the jig observed by Brown" (104).

By devising a mathematical model to explain Brownian motion with particle physics, Einstein became that scientist who finally received credit for proving the existence of atoms. Ironically, it was Einstein who discovered the most fundamental particle (the photon), which was precisely responsible for undermining the image of the simple particulate. To return to the first paper of his miracle year, it was here that he called for a dual interpretation of light as both particle and wave. His biographer suggests that it is this first of his 1905 papers "not the famous final one expounding a theory of relativity, that deserved the designation 'revolutionary.' Indeed, it may contain the most revolutionary development in the history of physics. …that light comes not just in waves but in tiny packets—quanta of light that were later dubbed 'photons'" (94). By the time he had concluded his fourth paper he realized that he had "found in a most simple way the relation between the size of elementary quanta of matter and the wavelengths of radiation" (qtd. by Isaacson 96, Einstein).

He followed these 1905 essays with an essay on light quanta in which he interpreted light as "point-like particles. … rather than being a continuous wave" (97). But "Before he made his case for a particle theory of light, he emphasized that this would not make it necessary to scrap the wave theory, which would continue to be useful as well" (97-8). He wrote, "The wave theory of light, which operates with continuous spatial functions, has worked well in the representation of purely optical phenomena and will probably never be replaced by another theory" (97-8).

> "Then came what may be the most revolutionary sentence that Einstein ever wrote: According to the assumption to be considered here, when a light ray is propagated from a point, the energy is not continuously distributed over an increasing space but consists of a finite number of energy quanta which are localized at points in space and which can be produced and absorbed only as complete units. (98)

This led to his belief that "the next phase of theoretical physics will bring us a theory of light that can be interpreted as a kind of fusion of the wave and of the emission theories of light" (Einstein; Isaacson 156). And thus a new foundation within the field of physics was established: "light exhibits wave properties and particle properties" (Taylor et. al. 140). With this synthesis he established the bedrock and throne for the entire paradigm of physics-grounded-science that has followed. The difference between this foundation and the Atoms of Democritus or Newton is that the photon is much more than stone-like.[225]

To explain how these theoretical breakthroughs led to an explanation of what's been called, "the photoelectric effect," for which Einstein won the Nobel Prize, could become overly technical for readers from the humanities and unnecessary for physicists. I will, however, attempt an essential introduction of the concepts. "In this effect, discovered by Heinrich Hertz in 1887, a metal exposed to light is found to eject electrons from its surface" (Taylor et. al. 127). To say it simply, there were problems with the wave theory of Maxwell and Huygens when it came to explaining this phenomenon.[226] The contribution science had been waiting for was that, in this scenario, a single "light quantum transfers its entire energy to a single electron" (qtd. by Isaacson 98, Einstein).

"Einstein proposed that as a natural extension of Plank's ideas, one should assume that

'the energy in a beam of light is not distributed continuously through space, but consists

of a finite number of energy quanta, which are localized at points, which cannot be

subdivided, and which are absorbed and emitted only as whole unites" (Taylor et. al.

128).[227] From here "it follows that light of a higher frequency would cause the electrons

to emit with more energy. On the other hand, increasing the intensity of the light (but not

the frequency) would simply mean that more electrons would be emitted, but the energy

of each would be the same" (Isaacson 98-99). What is important for this this trans-

disciplinary meditation on the metaphors upon which knowledge traditions have built is

that his synthesis of particle and wave behavior in the form of the photon has been

recognized as one of the most monumental breakthroughs in the history of intelligent (if

not intuitive) thought. "It was specifically for discovering the law of the photoelectric

effect that Einstein would win his only Nobel Prize" (Isaacson 101). The reason he was

rewarded this prize is because

Physicists following the work of Maxwell differentiated between light and matter,

and thus, this synthesis of the wave and particle in the form of light did not translate into

a synthesis of the wave into a theory of matter—for this, we turn to Einstein's friend, De

Broglie. He "reasoned that if light has both wave-like and particle-like properties,

material objects such as electrons might also exhibit this dual character" (Taylor et. al.

168). Later it was shown that, in fact, like photons, "electrons and neutrons are also wave

phenomena" (172). However, unlike photons, electrons have mass and are considered

matter, for which reason De Broglie used the seemingly paradoxical term, "matter waves" (168). As my modern physics professor explained to me, this is the nature of all matter—not just miniscule particles—even macroscopic things.

While it would be fulfilling to continue into a conversation of all Einstein's breakthroughs and the developments of quantum mechanics around his theory of the quanta/photon, a majority of such explorations would be unnecessary to our thesis. What remains for us is a close look at his equation, $E = mc^2$ and its re-foundation of physics on the ground of energy as opposed to matter. Special Relativity's attack on absolute space and objective time are often cited reformations of classical physics and the Newtonian paradigm, but these are less central to our conversation, as are the attacks on traditional causality levied by the quantum mechanics.[228] Our discipline instead demands a limited focus on Einstein's revolutions against reductive materialism and the synthesis of particles with waves.

Again, it is not in our interest to fully examine what Einstein meant when he revisioned gravity, previously seen as an enigmatic force, as curvature in space-time. It should, however, be noted that his understanding of matter was contingent with his understanding of space-time. One might say, "Objects curve space-time and … in turn, this curvature affects the motion of objects. As the physicist John Wheeler has put it, 'Matter tells space-time how to curve, and curved space tells matter how to move.' Thus is staged a cosmic tango, as captured by another physicist, Brian Greene" (Isaacson 220). In this way, "General relativity provides the choreography for an entwined cosmic dance of space, time, matter, and energy" (qtd. by Isaacson 220, Greene).

To take a step back and consider his equation of matter and energy outside the context of space-time curvature, we turn to one of his thought experiments:

> Coupling Maxwell's theory with the relativity theory, he … calculated the
> properties of two light pulses emitted in opposite directions by a body at
> rest. He then calculated the properties of these light pulses when observed
> from a moving frame of reference. From this he came up with equations
> regarding the relationship between speed and mass. The result was an
> elegant conclusion: mass and energy are different manifestations of the
> same thing. There is a fundamental interchangeability between the two. As
> he put it in his paper, "The mass of a body is a measure of its energy
> content. (Isaacson 138)

The formula through which he described this relationship was the iconic $E = mc^2$
(though presented with different letters in its earliest form). The equation states that
"energy equals mass times the square of the speed of light. The speed of light, of course,
is huge. Squared it is almost inconceivably bigger. That is why a tiny amount of matter, if
converted completely into energy, has an enormous punch … the energy in the mass of
one raisin could supply most of New York City's energy needs for a day" (139).

Einstein's breakthrough understanding of matter and energy's transmutability
"require[s] the classical law of conservation of mass [and thus matter] to be violated"
(Taylor et. al. 59).[229] "In classical physics it was believed that mass was always
conserved" (53). However, in that the "rest energy of the mass m … can be converted
into other forms, such as the kinetic energy of other bodies" (53), "the classical law of
conservation of mass turns out to be wrong" (53). With this destruction of previous
theory, Einstein rolled away the stone that had imprisoned scientists within a closed
system of mass to match its recurrent drift towards reductive materialism.

Immediately reflecting on the contributions of his we have discussed—Einstein transcended the paradigm of reductive atomistic materialism by recognizing the reality that all matter is made of energy that behaves like both waves and particles. Before now moving to a consideration of everything we have discussed throughout this chapter (and dissertation), I want to take advantage of one more obsession of Einstein's to help frame our next moves.

Though the humanities have come to shun any claims for capitalized Truth, no scientist has shame over the fact that this is exactly what they are doing. Einstein's theory of relative frames may seem to de-capitalize truth, but the tradition pursues laws that are far more universal and objective than even time or space. Brian Greene explains, "Newton had unified the heavens and the earth in a theory of gravity. Maxwell had unified electricity and magnetism. Einstein reasoned all that remained to build a 'Theory of Everything'—a single theory that could encompass all the laws of the universe" (Greene 1). His biographer, Isaacson, claims that "his life was a constant quest for unifying theories." (148). "'The mind striving after unification cannot be satisfied that two fields should exist which, by their nature, are quite independent,' Einstein explained in his Nobel lecture" (339).[230] In "his last two decades … Einstein relentlessly sought a single theory so powerful it would describe all the workings of the universe. Even as he neared the end of his life Einstein kept a notepad close at hand, furiously trying to come up with the equations for what would come to be known as the 'Theory of Everything'" (Greene 1). This continued up until the "equations [he] scribbled while on his deathbed in 1955" (Isaacson 4). Now, this work has been continued by string theorists, who seek "to unify our understanding of everything from the birth of the universe to the majestic swirl of galaxies in just one set of principles, one master equation" (Greene 1).

As mentioned in one of the footnotes, Einstein's approach was "heuristic" and his contributions are called "theories," because both Einstein and physicist recognize them as working progresses. As we can see, there is an easily resolvable paradox between the pursuit of cosmic truth and the recognition that every breakthrough participates in a theoretical framework that is incomplete. This heuristic recognition, in my mind, should become a framework for humanities scholars seeking to move beyond postmodern deconstructionism. The remainder of this dissertation will work through my understanding of how the three knowledge narratives we have discussed present a meta-narrative, but in no way will I claim a belief that my interpretation is complete, flawless, or transcendent of the frame I have defined by Classical, Abrahamic and scientific knowledge traditions.

Though I admit a somewhat clunky structure to this chapter, its form enabled us to contemplate the resonance of Herakles and Christ before comparing their labors with the contributions of Einstein. By now we have summated the ways Einstein and these two hero-saviors acted as liberators from matter and integrators of waves. Where the myths of religious hero-saviors described the rescue of progenitors—and themselves—from material limitations, the theories of Einstein carried physics beyond the limitations of reductive materialism. Complimentarily, as said mythic liberations were actuated by symbolic elixirs, the paradigmatic shift of physics away from reductive materialism coincided with the entire field's recognition that what had been seen as particles should also be seen as waves. In the next and final chapter, we will elucidate the metanarrative anchored by material entry and wave integration in the Classical, Abrahamic, and scientific origin stories of knowledge in a more consolidated way before reflecting on the potency of its presence.

Chapter 6: Conclusion

Our survey of Western knowledge narratives has now been completed. They have been discussed in relation to one another throughout our conversation—especially in the reflection on part one and in the previous chapter. We will now draw them all into a focused discussion of the metanarrative and key motifs they have been shown to share. From here we will consider the existential implications of our study, after which we will contemplate its contemporary value. Finally we will reflect on the epistemological position of the dissertation's conclusions (from the angles of Foundationalism and Coherentism). As I will argue, the metanarrative and motifs of interest to this dissertation are coherent within the overlapping "Western" frames of the Classical, Abrahamic, and Western philosophical/scientific traditions. This will lead into a consideration of the directions in which the study might expand its frames in the future, for example, into a concerted analysis of Semitic and Indo-European myths beyond their Abrahamic and Classical forms. Finally we will conclude.

Core Conclusion

Each of the three narratives of knowledge studied throughout this dissertation present a metanarrative that begins with an entry of the psyche into an engagement with matter, to which Prometheus, Adam, and the first Greek philosophers were limited and into which the hero-saviors were born. This narrative arc is then defined by material transcendence: Prometheus is freed from his stone, Adam from his cave, and, in the context of divine union and escape from mortal isolation, the material remains of Christ and Herakles cannot be found in the pyre or tomb (as would be dictated by the matrix of mortal materiality). Miming this sequence, as philosophy and science were triggered by the materialistic and atomistic foundations of Thales and Democritus, Western intellectual thought has since been re-founded by Einstein's theory of mass's convertibility to energy and his grail-stone-like particle, the photon, which synthesized particles and waves into a single microcosmic image. Einstein's influence on the departiculization of matter and dematerialization of particles depended on the integration of waves into a theory of matter. Congruently, the transcendence from matter enacted by Herakles and Christ was triggered by the symbolic integration or addition of fluids: hydra blood was responsible for the liberation of Prometheus from stone and Herakles from his body—he then drank divine nectar to affect his divinization. Blood also liberated Adam from stone and flowed at Christ's death, which he drank in the form of wine at the Last Supper and in the afterlife before it became an essential symbol of divine immortality in the forms of Catholic Mass and European Grail Romances.

The following sections expand on these core parallels that Classical and Abrahmic knowledge narratives share with the canonical history of scientific knowledge, anchored by what appears to be a fundamental theme in the history of Western consciousness—an entry into a materialistic cosmology followed by the transcendence of a reductively materialistic worldview. As I have shown, and will now recapitulate, this sequence is apparently core to the core knowledge narratives of historical Western thought. As far apart as the categories of science and religious mythology may be, the congruities of discussed substructures draw them into dialogue.

Entry into Matter

The entry into and imprisonment within matter—and/or a materialistic mode of reason—ripples across these mythical and scientific knowledge stories as well as the religious and philosophical texts that interpret them. For example, contingent with the myth of Prometheus, as the remainder of his clay hardens into stone (Pausanius, *Description* 10. 4. 4), his offspring, specifically Deucalion, and his wife Pyrrha, repopulated the earth with humans born from boulders. Pausanias added that from then on humans were called *laoi*, stones. In another parallel myth concerning human creation, Dionysus was eaten by titans, who were reduced to ash by Zeus' thunderbolt and moistened into clay with which humans were made—the story has been especially associated with the imprisonment of psyche in body. The story of Adam's creation from clay was later repeated in the form of the Jewish Golem, who was also made of matter and animated by the divine. This is not unlike the story of Pygmalion, in which a sculpture of the Hephaestian craftsman was brought to life.

Complementing the images of humans crafted from matter are those of infants born from mothers. We have repeatedly discussed the conflation of mother and matter, especially through the word *mater*. From the starting point of this conflation, we see the first sexual act and marriage in the origin myths as entries into mater and its commitments. As the double entendres of *labor* and *bear* suggest, labor to bear children is matched by labor to bear food; and as Pandora has been seen as a personification of Gaia, both of whom were depicted as emerging from the Earth, we can see that labor in Gaia's mater for food mimes labor in Pandora's mater for children.[231] Integral to the knowledge of these myths is the mimetic process of planting human and vegetal seeds in mater. As Gaia and Pandora were earthen, the cycles of mortality are thus presented as grounded by materiality. In this way we can see the paradigmatic falls into mortality as contingent with entries into a world grounded by matter. This has been especially symbolized by the wasteland imagery of Adam and Eve's exile, which, in the Books of Adam, is characterized by sand, stone and caves. Their experience during this time is defined by the entry of their divine souls into increasingly material bodies—their eyes turn to flesh and their digestive as well as sexual organs come into use. This returns us to the essential act associated with the entry into materiality, the eating of the fruit, the taking in of matter upon which the body will come to rely. As mater, Eve and Pandora are vilified; similarly, Satan has been demonized for his associations with materiality—partially as a result of his conflation with the seducer and fallen world. Ironically, before this, he refused to bow to Adam because he was made of clay, which he saw as inferior. The serpent was cursed to eat dust, and the murder of Able was with a stone. The first altar and sacrificial knife were also made of stone, as was the cave in which the first couple conceived and had children. Christ's conception and birth has been similarly associated with the cave, which we have already discussed in the context of Adam's and Christ's burials and resurrections. These are only some of the many details of/related to the myths we have discussed that demonstrate an entry into or demonization of mat(t)er.

The history of philosophy and science is also filled with various angles of emphasis on matter and materialism. In addition to the Aristotelean (and thus common) narrative of philosophy in which it begins with the premise of materialism, atomism has also been fundamental to the development of science and Western reason. We have seen that it emerged from the same Edenic origin point as materialism—Miletus—and from within the same "Pre-Socratic" origin-period. It can be argued that, theoretically, causation and the study thereof has been as or more foundational to Western science than the premise of materialism. Whether or not this is the case, what atomism represents is the synthesis of materialistic and causal theories that immediately became a talking point for Plato, a teaching point for Aristotle, and a foundation for Epicurean philosophy in Alexandrian Greece, Rome, Newtonian physics and Enlightenment philosophy. From within this paradigm of atomism and causality, thinkers like Locke, Hobbes, Marx, Franklin, and Jefferson, to name a few, established the political ideologies through which the contemporary world operates. In my own field, academics like Lévi-Strauss have exported atomism into a way of interpreting myth, which is not unlike Russell and Wittgenstein exporting atomism into their logic systems. As Blow described, atomism has permeated thought to extend itself into countless theories and interpretations well beyond the range of physics.

Material Prisons and Atomic Isolation: Existential Estrangement and Moral Egoism

One might see that Classical and Newtonian atomism is materialism within a philosophical framework of subjects and objects, or that a philosophy of subjects and objects is necessitated by a foundation of atomistic materialism. Classical and Newtonian atoms are, by definition, isolated material objects. If one sees reality as made up of objects, Classical and Newtonian atoms are then, by their own definition, the smallest of all objects. With Descartes, a philosophy defined by subjects and objects paralleled the notion of mind-body dualism. His understanding of mind as within the material body presented a world of minds as isolated from one another by the objectified bodies they possess. This notion of mind in matter was foreshadowed by the Orphics, Pythagoreans, and Platonists, who saw psyche as imprisoned within body—a view shared by Manicheans, Essenes, Gnostics, and Kabbalists, and other ascetic groups. We have also found religious/philosophical interpretations of the Herakles and Christ myths that follow this form. Similarly, Jewish mystical texts explicitly interpret the Eden myth as a description of psyche's fall into flesh. And, despite secrecy of the Kabeiroi cult, the religious and philosophical environment in which they were surrounded offers support for a symbolic interpretation of the myth as expressive of psyche's entry into and imprisonment within mater.

Beyond the imprisonment of psyche in body, what many of these ascetic traditions emphasize is the way life in a body within the material world can corrupt one's philosophical clarity by limiting understanding to the realm of sensory experience. Reflecting on the exile from Eden, Tillich described it as a "cognitive fall." To recognize the parallel between the imprisonment within matter and the imprisonment of thought within materialism is to actually shift an understanding of the problem away from matter and into the misunderstanding generated by a limitation of one's understanding to material processes. From this point of view, matter is not the problem (and mater should not be demonized). But before we discuss the transcendence of this limitation, we should stick with the imagery of imprisonment in the context of existential estrangement and egoism.

Following our look at atomism as a paradigmatic foundation, in our conversation about existentialism, we saw that philosophers like Kierkegaard, Pascal and Tillich were highly concerned with the entanglement of finitude, isolation, and estrangement in the context of human anxieties concerning choice. To act and to believe one must choose, but the finitude of human existence implies an inescapably subjective foundation to any understanding that might motivate actions or belief. These existential philosophers were deeply concerned with solitude and aloneness. Through his estrangement, Pascal even compared himself with an atom surrounded by infinities. On the level of choice, such a sense of confinement makes it logically impossible to use information beyond the prison of one's own frame to enter into an accord with the world beyond self, where exist others, god, nature, and universe. Again, the senses are as inescapably subjective as the atomized body is isolated. The recognition is that we cannot situate our lives in the context of the universal or transcendent – we are confined to a framework of understanding that ends at our own being. Pascal used the atom as an image because it is a perfectly confined entity, which is why I believe it fits as a poetic description of encompassing isolation.

Though many suffer pain and angst from the inability to choose that emerges from this sense of isolation, on another level, a sense of immediate discomfort seems to come from the feeling of estrangement itself. Believing in or suspectinga larger cosmos, god, field of souls or parallel universe while—right or wrong—envisioning the self as isolated from nature, universe, god and/or other souls—even one's spouse and family members—can, for some, produce a strong sense of loneliness if not despair. This is where we started the dissertation. This is why all this work matters. The first focus of the dissertation was an effort to learn and comprehend the details and form of the cognitive fall. Metaphysical and spiritual implications of the fall have been of interest, but the shift in perspective associated with the fall has been primary. The secondary effort has been to examine the mythic and theoretical inversions of the fall to elucidate a path through which conscious intelligence might resolve the fallen state and be free of the existential anxiety that follows from this inciting misstep.

What we found was that, in the Classical and Abrahamic origin stories of knowledge, there are numerous expressions of the human entry into matter—from the divine soul/flame entering material (literally clay) bodies to exile into a material world to material bondage and burial. Comparable beliefs in the psyche's imprisonment within body, entry into a materialistic mode of seeing, and the (theoretical) limitation of all things to matter were also characteristic developments of Pre-Socratic philosophy. In demonstrating the necessary relationship of material atomism and existential isolation, I believe that by displaying the consistent association of matter with isolation and despair in these origin myths I have been able to show that the entry into matter and the entry into isolation are presented as inseparable. Greek and later philosophers similarly recognized the isolative implications of materialism and atomism, which, as we have seen, led many towards a state of spiritual and/or existential despair. What I have tried to show again and again is that such isolation and estrangement can emerge from the form(s) of materiality, or rather, that belief in one's own isolation and estrangement is contingent with a belief in the material prison. In contrast, I have also described paths and theories of Heracles, Christ and Einstein that undermine the interpretation of incarnate life as a state of inescapable imprisonment.

The Holy Grail and a Theory of Unified Fields

What Herakles, Christ and Einstein have all shown are ways to transcend material limitation, and/or a belief in reductive materialism. All of them offer paths away from the despair of an isolated self-image in a world of materially divisible objects. While many philosophers—from Pythagoras to the Buddha—have called for a transcendence of materiality, what I believe I have found is the actual (meta-)form for such transcendence, the wave. We have seen fluids actuate the symbolic liberation of both progenitors and hero saviors from their material enclosures and limitations, and we have seen theoretical waves and fields free physics from a fundamentally particulated perspective of the universe, which, thanks to Einstein's contributions, is no longer reduced to matter. Most essentially, what an analysis of these stories has inspired is the recognition that the form of a wave—knowable by the mind—offers a path towards its transcendence beyond a cosmology founded upon and limited by the perceptible patterns of isolated material objects. I do not mean to stipulate the archetypal or ontological status of the wave in this work, the prison I am concerned with is one made in the human mind.

In addition to liberating the progenitors from matter, upon their liberation, both progenitors and heroes were reunited with the divine company—all estrangement was resolved. Even the rift between Hera and Herakles was resolved when he drank from Hebe's cup. Considering the fluid form, the narrative positioning of the fluid in a place that symbolizes liberation from material limitation and transcendent union makes sense geometrically: As was explained in the dissertation's introduction—and additionally throughout—waves and fields, unlike classical atoms and matter, are capable of union. Classical atoms can fit like puzzle pieces and synchronize like gears, but the boundaries of the smallest objects remain. The foundations of reality, from this point of view, are discontinuous with one another. Waves and fields are continuous and capable of union. The simultaneous notes of an entire symphony orchestra can be recorded as a single wave, recreated by a single coned speaker, and heard through a single ear drum. If the cognitive fall is a commitment to particularization, the solution is wave dynamics.

When the fruit of the fall was eaten, the water beneath the tree dried up and the land became a waste. As Joyce's wasteland was one of stone-like isolated people, my interpretation of post-Edenic drought symbolism is as an expression of paradigmatic isolation. It is not just that the human is isolated within a fallen world—a dry world is a world in which all things are in isolation. A world of sand like a world of atoms is dry and particulated. Everything is isolated from everything. To compliment a theory of particularized matter with a theory of wave-particle duality is to transform the image of self and cosmos from the bottom up. It is to moisten the atoms and water the desert—to see nature as a lush field as opposed to as an arid wasteland. From this perspective, the body is not only comprehended as building blocks: Insofar as we are our body's particles, we are isolated. Insofar as we are waves, we are one with the continuums of our body, local environment, and the cosmos. Though a wave-particle in Miletus may have zero measurable effect on a wave-particle in Los Angeles, there is no hard barrier between the fields of the distant wave-particles—they exist in a continuum. To share Einstein's interest in invisible fields he first saw in a compass is to see the invisible water of a moist cosmos that might otherwise be experienced as an atomic wasteland. To drink from the Holy Grail or cup of Hebe is to become capable of union, a capacity conveyed by fluid.

Together, Einstein, Herakles and Christ bruised to pieces the foundations of paradigmatic isolation—from the isolation of material particles to the isolation of living humans. Not only do they undermine materialistic foundations, which I have shown to be one of the primary perpetuators of an isolated self-image, they also offer new foundations that demonstrate union as opposed to estrangement. Not only does this provide respite and resolution to the existential experience of fundamental estrangement, but by transforming the self-image into one that is as continuous as it is islanded, the purely self-motivated foundations of moral egoism are undermined. Percy Shelley wrote of a world of empty thrones in his *Prometheus Unbound*. I am talking about a world empty of thrones: a throne-less inner-world in which the ego is forced to see through its perceived wall of isolation.

But it is important to note that individuality does not dissolve from field theories. During my first AAR conference, at the very first panel I sat in on, a group of scholars were reflecting on Cornell West, isolation and togetherness, and music. Dr. West was present. In fact, it was the identifiable back of his head that lured me in. He had spoken to my class at Sewanee before my upper level education even began, and I had admired the Wachowski's for casting him in *The Matrix* sequels. After some time, I found the courage to raise my hand and direct my thoughts directly to Dr. West. In brief I shared my perspective that the transpiring conversations about musical harmony and community were mimetic—I gave the example of the single microphone. Dr. West immediately understood what I was saying about harmonic unity, but he challenged my thought and insisted that, with emersion, individuality should not be lost. I would like to say I was too shy to respond to his response, but instead I explained how, even though all the music synthesizes in the form of a single wave, the mind has no problem identifying the guitar or drums. This is to say, the wave solution to the problem of isolation we have engaged does not compromise individuality, it shatters the interpretation of one and manyness as a paradox at all. Despite the resolution of "I" and "other," the "I" does not dissolve.

Epistemological Positions

Having laid out to my position, I would like to reflect on its epistemological structures. As I will show, the simplest seed of the argument is *a priori* and self-evident.

The fuller form of the position is supported by each of the three traditions we have discussed and the three of them combined. As I will explain, the dissertation has been designed to superimpose four epistemological frameworks—the first takes Classical religion as a foundation, the second takes any of the Abrahamic versions of Eden as foundational, the third takes the scientific epistemological system as foundational, and the fourth finds epistemic value in the coherence of the three traditions. The three traditions have been considered together because they are the only three to have extended in a dominant way throughout the entirety of whatever has been called and remembered as the "West"—this is the relative frame within which I have attempted to find coherence. Following a closer look at the four epistemological positions of this discourse, we will look at what directions we might extend its frame.

The theoretical structures of classical atoms and waves can be discovered a priori and/or a posteriori. A priori, the monadic structure of a conceptually isolated entity provides the theoretical form of an atom, which, as we remember, was never empirically proven during the Classical or Enlightenment periods. As the same time, the structure of an atom—insofar as it is an isolated material object with rigid boundaries—is immediate to the experience of any and all things. Similarly, in the same way a billiard ball atom can be described mathematically, so too can a sinewave. The structure and behavior of waves can be imagined (in mathematical detail) without the experience of their form. Yet again, waves are regularly experienced atop fluids—from soup to sea. The point is, before considering whether or not the basic position I am about to describe is *a priori*, the forms of the particulate and wave are themselves available to both *a priori* reason and *a posteriori* observation. By reason and experience particulates are isolated and waves/fields are continuous and capable of (mathematically expressible) harmonies. A system built on a meta-logic of waves allows for union while a worldview built on a meta-logic of particles does not. Therefore, any cosmology that excludes wave/field behavior in favor of purely particulated perspective of reality will, upon integrating the behavior of waves/fields, no longer be limited to isolative structures. *A priori*, a theory of particle-wave duality steps beyond the inescapable isolation of things within hard boundaries to ground a cosmological metaphysic in which distinctiveness and union are the norm. Regardless of how such paradigms relate to reality, worldviews that emerge from their distinct meta-structures suggest completely different interpretations of reality. My demonstrations of reductively materialistic perspectives as inconsistent with reality extends into *a posteriori* territory.

What I have tried to show is that each of the three starting places of Western knowledge was a worldview or paradigm grounded by matter and isolation. The overall argument is designed to respect those who give foundational epistemic value to any, all or none of the Classical, Abrahamic, or scientific presentations of knowledge. The discussions of each progenitor and the history of Pre-Socratic philosophy have been designed to stand on their own. Separately, all of their origin stories of knowledge convey—as previously argued—a material ground to human existence and the reality in which they live. Also separately, we find fluids and waves in the fulcrum position from which materiality and isolation were transcended and a new union was achieved. As far as each demonstration holds, the Classical, Abrahamic ad scientific stories of Prometheus and Herakles, Adam and Christ, the pre-Socratics and Einstein all present matter and its domain or reductive theory as based on and inspiring of isolation. And not only do each of the stories present fluids or waves as continuous or capable of actuating union, separately, the stories all present the same sequence. Each of the stories demonstrates an entry into the materialistic mode of thinking or state of being, and each of the stories see an exit or transcendence from the limitations of matter and/or materialism.

Having shown the patterns in each separate tradition, we can also discuss their coherence. Instead of giving foundational value to Christian, scientific or Classical representations of knowledge, a Coherentist's approach finds epistemic value in the consistency of the traditions with one another. This is not to say that coherence can imply objective truth. By definition, coherence is only comprehended within a frame. The frame of reference we have used as our anchor is defined by the three knowledge traditions of Western history, which we have reflected upon with the support of complimentary philosophical commentary. Further work may expand the frame, but my belief is that recognizing the coherence of the meta-narrative we have discussed within the triune frame we have chosen carries meaning: this epistemological angle passes on the direct pursuit of objective truth in favor of insights concerning the selected relative frame and its form of developmental conditioning for anyone enclosed therein or influenced thereby.

Before continuing into a consideration of how we might extend the study's frames, I would like to compare what I have found through this comparative study with Karen Armstrong's work to show a foundation of compassion as coherent with all the world's religions. She writes, in her "Compassion Charter:"

> The principle of compassion lies at the heart of all religious, ethical and
>
> spiritual traditions, calling us to always treat others as we wish to be
>
> treated ourselves. Compassion impels us to work tirelessly to alleviate the
>
> suffering of our fellow creatures, to dethrone ourselves from the center of

our world and put another there, and to honor the inviolable sanctity of every single human being, treating everyone, without exception, with absolute justice, equity and respect … to incite hatred by denigrating others—even our enemies—is a denial of our common humanity. We acknowledge that we have failed to live compassionately and that some have even increased the sum of human misery in the name of religion. … We therefore call upon all men and women to restore compassion to the center of morality and religion; to return to the ancient principle that any interpretation of scripture that breeds violence, hatred or disdain is illegitimate; to ensure that youth are given accurate and respectful information about other traditions, religions and cultures; to encourage a positive appreciation of cultural and religious diversity; to cultivate an informed empathy with the suffering of all human beings—even those regarded as enemies (ctd. by Mahaffey 30, 6-8).

I have not had the chance to test my thesis beyond the western psyche, but I can say that the foundations I have found supports entirely the foundation of compassion. In fact, in my mind, this dissertation presents a meta-logic, if not a cosmological metaphysic, that gives ground to such a position on compassion. This position is not unlike Plato's conflation of *Love/Good/*and *Harmony.* What this dissertation has shown is that features of love like union and non-isolated egos are inconsistent with a system of logic grounded by reductive materialism; whereas, the logic of waves and fields gives ground to the intention to be in harmony as opposed to isolation. A wave-particle worldview is not inconsistent with a non-selfish decision; in fact, it might be seen as supportive of an altruistic appreciation for other as participatory in a shared continuum that allows for union. My hypothesis is that, the more we look the more we will find fluids as actuators of union and expressions of love in the traditions throughout the world. My suspicion is that a clear comprehension of the metaphysical ground expressed by Einstein, Christ, and Herakles will unlock the hearts whose keys are defended by brainy thoughts.

Extended Frame: Further Study

Before going into the ways I would like to expand the study outward, I would like to describe the more inward directions of growth that could make the study more thorough. I would have very much liked to have gone deeper into the Enlightenment and the pervasiveness of atomism as a paradigm. With this I would have also liked to have gone deeper into the egoistic developments and existential reactions to this paradigm; for example, I did not discuss Camus' mountain and stone because it would have opened into a complex and derailing conversation.

The study also became Christian-heavy for my Abrahamic conversation, which was partially because I was working with a two-part narrative, and partially because of limited space. I have a number of ideas about what direction I would take a conversation that included more Islamic details, but I was also wary about speaking for Muslims about their mythology. The identification of Western Christians—secular and practicing—with the Old Testament is a long standing tradition I am comfortable engaging. A new level of complexities would have emerged were I to continue much further into Islamic myth— that having been said, I want to remember once more the water of knowledge that Gabriel poured into Mohammad breast on the night he visited the Holy City and Heaven.

I would also like to spend more time working with the feminine characters in the stories, which would have not just doubled the length, it would have exponentially increased any potential for confusion. The reason for this is because I am not so sure that the narrative I have described applies to feminine dimensions of psyche, which might be reflexively seen as moving in the opposite direction (towards individuality from a state of union as opposed to union from a state of individuality). To start talking about the differences of masculine and feminine characters I would have had to negotiate the sometimes tricky position of describing the human as possessing both masculine and femanine qualities. The roles of Eve and Pandora—not to mention Eve and Hebe—were far too underdeveloped in our conversation. If we were to extend our analysis in this direction, I believe we would find that the synthesis of particle and wave would start to mime a conjunction of masculine and feminine in numerous mythologems—as hinted in the wedding of Herakles and Hebe. The text also leaves out any mention of Einstein's consort, which is a result of my hesitation to describe the myth of Einstein as opposed to discussing the mythic qualities of his history. If I were able to spend paragraphs situating what I mean, I would have spoken more about his marriage to a physicist. I would have also talked more about his sister, Maia, who shares a name with Mercury's mother, Mejia, and the mother of Buddha, Mahamaya. To say any more would be to leave open wounds, but I certainly would like to better understand how the male and female roles fit into this conversation. Again, part of the reason I did not further engage these topics and directions is because I wanted to maintain our central simple focuses.

In addition to a deeper look at the masculine/femanine dimensions at play in the myths we discussed, I would also like to look at the solar and lunar symbols and qualities.

They are extremely present and were sparsely discussed. Similarly, an extension of the conversation into the psychological language of consciousness and unconsciousness would be distinctly valuable. It seems fluids are juxtaposed with fire as an opposite. As the gift of fire represents the birth of conscious reason—defined by its distinctive clarity—elixirs have served as the less conscious and more elusive agents of transformation—characterized by their actuation of union and wholeness. One of my professors and mentors, Walter Odajynk, was especially interested in the moment within the Egyptian *Book of the Dead* when the solar and lunar eyes become aligned and equally sized (Eleventh Hour-Upper Register, Warburton 330). He worked with something like an interpretation of the solar eye as representative of waking consciousness and the lunar eye as representative of our unconscious psyches. This is not unlike Nietzsche's description of Apollo and Dionysus in *Twilight of the Idols*. In this light the balanced eyes are seen as expressive of a centroverted state of psyche that synthesizes solar awakeness with lunar unconscious in a focus of individuated wholeness.

Had we spent more time on the moon, I would have spent more time demonstrating its conflations with grails and fluids. Had we spent more time on the sun, I would have demonstrated its conflations with such waking, causal and mechanical reality as has been based on atoms. In his final work, *Inner Reaches of Outer Space*, Campbell discussed the yogic tradition of solar and lunar breath, he writes, "sun and moon, in the practiced disciplines of the yoga of expanding consciousness, are associated psychophysiologically with two subtle nerves, or channels, of 'vital energy' … which are related to the breathing and breaths of the right, respectively, and left nostrils" (43). The sun, in this tradition, is "'masculine,' fiery, poisonous, and deadly … a blaze of sheer spirit" (43). Lunar energy, conversely, is "associated with moisture, [is] 'feminine,' cooling and refreshing" (43). To break such duals, "so runs the argument of yoga … [is for] the mind [to] regain possession of Original Knowledge: the salt doll walks into the ocean" (44).

Together the dichotomoes of moist and dry, female and male, moon and sun offer opportunities to expand the cosmological conversation we have engaged. In addition to discussing the particulated and wave-patterned meta-forms at the foundation of our worldviews filled with scientific and social theories, these natural pillars of our corporeal experience also anchor the human experience of world and cosmos. The cycles of sun and moon have long served to situate human experience, as have the seasonal battles like dry and wet. Not only do the qualities constellated around these dichotomies offer opportunities to enrich and enhance a human's cosmology, they also mime, in many ways, the meta-formal dichotomy upon which this work has been fixated. To comment on how they do so would open a box of Pandora's that could threaten, by distraction and complication, the simple conclusions I hope to land. As mentioned in the first chapter, I look forward to potentially growing a more inclusive project in these directions.

One of the major next steps of this study would be to extend this essentially mythological dissertation into religious studies and anthropological directions. For example, to take the conversation to the next level of depth, I would like to spend more time with the religious interpretations, rituals, and hymns associated with the myths we engaged. I would also like to entertain more of the historical narratives and influences on the myths. A deeper look at the history involved would not only further develop the work's conversation about the narratives, it would help expand the discussion of the influential presence of these myths in history.

Perhaps the most obvious direction to extend the study is into a more worldly set of mythologies. I would like to start in the Semitic and Indo-European language groups—this would include myths of near eastern civilizations like the Assyrians, Babylonians and Akkadians; as well as the Indo-European mythologies of the Norse, Narts and Vedas. Expanding from a consideration of the *Vedas*, I would like to do a survey of ascetic and meditative traditions around the world, as my suspicion is that many of them are also consistent with the study's work.

It would also be valuable to extend into a consideration of the Grail Seeker and Fisher King in roles that parallel those of the Classical/Abrahamic progenitors and hero-saviors. This would take us into a direct look at the Holy Grail, which, I have come to believe, carries many meanings; one of which, I would like to argue more fully elsewhere, is that all it offers is delivered in the form of a fluid. Maybe the true secret of the Grail is historical, but my interpretation of the emphasis on elixir has very much to do with the fact that elixirs and fluids are the only substances literally capable of conveying the (wave) behavior of reality through which isolation could be escaped for the achievement of union, with which the vessel is associated.

Perhaps one of the most likely next steps I will take this study is into playful essays about individual fairy stories, like *White Snake*, by the Brothers Grimm, and contemporary fiction from Middle Earth to a "galaxy far, far away." Where many of the motifs can be found in the world of literature, the full meta-narrative seems to me present in *The Hobbit* and *Lord of the Rings*. The ultimate delivery of the ring to the liquid magma that will destroy its powerful evil and material enclosure follows the meta-narrative anchoring this dissertation, but further discussion of this will have to wait for a later essay, as will a conversation about Mary Shelley's brilliant synthesis of Adam and Promethean mythologies in *Frankenstein: a Modern Day Prometheus.*

The last direction I would like to expand this study, which I would like to actually address a bit here, is the historic narrative of technological progress personified by Prometheus, or, in its darker days, Frankenstein. In the last century or so, we have experienced extreme dematerialization and the distinct addition of wave technology. For example, money went from gold to credit numbers that do not even require a plastic card. The musical instrument and performer were recorded onto vinyl. Then, when the analogue recordings became digital, the material on which the music was delivered was discarded all together thanks to Napster and iTunes-like services. First automobiles got lighter and now people call into their work places on video-phones. As paper has been replaced by screens, consumerism has become decreasingly driven by goods with material value, that is, if it is driven by material goods at all. The iPhone, for example, offers no material value to its owner. Further, it floats on a sea of Wi-Fi, cell phone and satellite waves. An exploration of technological dematerialization and inundation by fields is worthy of an extended study. We will instead end with this example of apple's iPhone, which, as an apple, completely inverts the apples of Newton and Eve. The iPhone, while perhaps one of the greatest achievements of human technology and light, is barely a material good. It is a material vessel—like the grail—that connects individuals, through fields, with their worlds and other people. Whether or not the iPhone is a stein or Frankenstein will only be known to posterity.

Reflection on Comparative Myth – Diffusion and Collective Unconscious

We have seen diffusion by way of conquest and subjugation as well as trade and industry. We have also recognized the enhanced ability of stories to propagate between peoples of the same language groups. Without a doubt, all the religious narratives and symbols we have discussed have had bountiful and repeated opportunities to diffuse between the Classical, Abrahamic and scientific traditions. For this reason the Jungian theory of the Collective Unconscious or something like it is unnecessary to explain the similarities and congruities displayed by the stories engaged in this dissertation. That having been said, my sense is that diffusion is a mechanism for propagation, not a motivation. Sure, conquest, subjugation, trade and business relationships may motivate the sharing and uptake of religious beliefs, symbols and narratives, but none of these motivations are intrinsic to religion or myth. To reduce the coherence of these knowledge traditions to the agendas of conquest and industry is to not look for the religious and philosophical motivations of both individuals and communities who adopted and shared the religious and philosophical insights conveyed by others. My sense is that, to some degree, the coherence addressed by this dissertation is a result of the value provided by the metanarrative to individuals and communities. That value, by my understanding, is the ability to see oneself as beyond isolation—consciously or less than consciously. My sense is that this is the deepest existential anxiety of any and all humans, and that all religions and healing mythologies are as tonic to this psychological and philosophical condition. That tonic must be consistent with a meta-logic that is actually capable of providing a way around the self-image of isolation.

Are the myths we have discussed consistent because they emerge from a shared Collective Unconscious? I do not know. But what I do seem rather sure of is that the consistency of these stories, as the foundations of Western psyche, has generated a collective unconscious. Whether or not there is a Collective Unsconscious proper, the commonality of our unconscious minds may result from our collective experiences. This is why pervasive stories are so important.

Definitely there is a background of conditioning by way of these three knowledge traditions that generates a paradigm beneath aware consciousness that became common to the collective. The paradigm defined by the first step – entry into matter – became very conscious to philosophers and enlightenment thinkers. Stories should unconsciously condition us towards conscious insights about the paradigm called for by the hero-saviors of Western Religion and Scientific Materialism. Consciously we now recognize the dual metaphorical foundations of particulates and waves so that the narrative of intelligent development expresses an entry into matter and the materialistic paradigm before a transcendence from limitations of the paradigm by way of elixirs/waves: over and over the ego in self-isolation is taught and shown to transcend its isolation like a seed sprouting towards water and sunlight.

Conclusory

The estrangement(s) of self from lover, God, Nature and Cosmos are conceptual consequencesof a commitment to a materially grounded cosmology, which has been presented as the foundation of human existence by the three primary origin stories of knowledge told throughout Western history: Prometheus, Pandora and the fire theft; Adam, Eve and the Forbidden Fruit; and the story of Greek philosophy that leads into science. However, each of these stories continue until their narratives eventually convey the entry into a cosmology in which it becomes conceivable to experience union with lover, God, Nature and Cosmos. Though Adam was buried under stone and Prometheus was chained to rock, they were set free by Christ and Heracles. And though most of scientific history was anchored by atomism, and even more so materialism, physics was freed from the limitations of matter by the contributions of Albert Einstein. The primary effort of this dissertation has been to explore these three Western origin stories of knowledge, and their continuations, with special emphasis on their demonstration of materialistically grounded cosmologies. Complimenting this effort, the dissertation has also followed these narratives into their eventual description of human transcendence from the reductively materialistic cosmologies established by their respective forbares.

The secondary emphasis of the dissertation has concerned a consistency shared by the stories of liberation from cosmologies grounded by matter. Upon entering into this research it has become clear that actuators of a shift beyond the limited ground of matter appear, consistently, in the form of waves. The revolution Einstein started was contingent with the integration of the waveform into atomic theory; and for this reason, as the waveform is visually apparent in fluids, it has been meaningful to find the symbolic involvement of waves in narratives of material transcendence. The liberation from material limitation, for each of the four progenitors and saviors, is contingent with the use of an elixir capable of actuating the process: Adam is freed from the stone when the blood of Christ baptizes him. Prometheus is freed from the stone when hydra blood kills the eagle. Heracles marries the cupbearer of the gods and drinks the divine nectar. Christ makes wine, drinks wine, and gives blood, then—after the stone is rolled away and his cave is emptied—returns to union with God. His cup of elixir would later become the central symbol of divine union in the Grail Romances of Medieval Europe. Together, the three essential Western knowledge narratives provide a path beyond the estrangement of self from lover, God, Nature, and cosmos through the integration of elixir-waves.